GERMAN KNIGHTHOOD
1050–1300

GERMAN
KNIGHTHOOD
1050–1300

BENJAMIN ARNOLD

CLARENDON PRESS · OXFORD
1985

Oxford University Press, Walton Street, Oxford OX2 6DP

Oxford New York Toronto
Delhi Bombay Calcutta Madras Karachi
Kuala Lumpur Singapore Hong Kong Tokyo
Nairobi Dar es Salaam Cape Town
Melbourne Auckland

and associated companies in
Beirut Berlin Ibadan Mexico City Nicosia

Oxford is a trade mark of Oxford University Press

Published in the United States
by Oxford University Press, New York

British Library Cataloguing in Publication Data

Arnold, Benjamin
German knighthood. 1050–1300.
1. Knights and knighthood——Germany——History
I. Title
929.7'43 CR5100
ISBN 0-19-821960-1

Set by Butler & Tanner Ltd
Printed in Great Britain
at the University Press, Oxford
by David Stanford
Printer to the University

For

EMMA JOYNES-JONKER

Acknowledgements

I AM truly indebted to Professor Karl Leyser, who for many years has generously given scholarly encouragement and constructive criticism to my work. He read this book in typescript, to my great advantage. I am also indebted to Professor Alan Harding and Miss Patricia McNulty, who read early versions of the text and made innumerable valuable suggestions, most of which I adopted. For financial assistance towards research and writing, I am grateful to the Wolfson Foundation, the German Academic Exchange Service (D A A D), and Reading University Research Fund.

B.A.

Contents

Abbreviations

A D	*Archiv für Diplomatik.*
A Q	Ausgewählte Quellen zur deutschen Geschichte des Mittelalters. Freiherr vom Stein-Gedächtnisausgabe.
A U	*Archiv für Urkundenforschung.*
Bosl, *R M*	K. Bosl, *Die Reichsministerialität der Salier und Staufer* (1950-1).
Burchard of Ursberg	O. Holder-Egger and B. von Simson, *Die Chronik des Probstes Burchard von Ursberg.*
C D Nassau	K. Menzel and W. Sauer, *Codex Diplomaticus Nassoicus.*
C D Salem	F. von Weech, *Codex Diplomaticus Salemitanus.*
C D Saxony	O. Posse and E. Ermisch, *Codex Diplomaticus Saxoniae Regiae*, part 1.
C D Westphalia	H. A. Erhard, *Codex Diplomaticus Historiae Westfaliae.*
D A	*Deutsches Archiv.*
Ekkehard of Aura	F-J. Schmale and I. Schmale-Ott, *Frutolfs und Ekkehards Chroniken und die Anonyme Kaiser-chronik*, pp. 124-208, 268-376.
Frutolf of Michelsberg	ibid., pp. 48-120.
Gislebert of Mons	L. Vanderkindere, *La Chronique de Gislebert de Mons.*
Helmold of Bosau	H. Stoob, *Helmold von Bosau. Slawenchronik.*
H J	*Historisches Jahrbuch.*
H Z	*Historische Zeitschrift.*
Jaffé, *M B*	P. Jaffé, *Monumenta Bambergensia.*
Kluckhohn	P. Kluckhohn, *Die Ministerialität in Südostdeutschland.*
Lampert of Hersfeld	O. Holder-Egger, *Lamperti Monachi Hersfeldensis Opera.*

Metz, *SG*	W. Metz, *Staufische Güterverzeichnisse.*
MG	Monumenta Germaniae historica.
MGC	MG Constitutiones et Acta Publica.
MGD	MG Diplomata Regum et Imperatorum Germaniae.
MGS	MG Scriptores.
MG schol.	MG Scriptores Rerum Germanicarum in usum scholarum.
MIöG	*Mitteilungen des Instituts für österreichische Geschichtsforschung.*
Mon. Boica	*Monumenta Boica.*
Mon. Carinthia	A. von Jaksch, *Monumenta Historica Ducatus Carinthiae.*
Otto of Freising	A. Hofmeister, *Ottonis Episcopi Frisingensis Chronica sive Historia.*
Otto and Rahewin, *Gesta Friderici*	G. Waitz and B. von Simson, *Ottonis et Rahewini Gesta Friderici I. Imperatoris.*
QE	Quellen und Erörterungen zur bayerischen Geschichte.
Reg. Eichstätt	F. Heidingsfelder, *Die Regesten der Bischöfe von Eichstätt.*
Reg. Straßburg	(i) P. Wentzcke, (ii) A. Hessel and M. Krebs, *Regesten der Bischöfe von Straßburg.*
Reimann	J. Reimann, 'Die Ministerialen des Hochstifts Würzburg in sozial-, rechts-, und verfassungsgeschichtlicher Sicht', *Mainfränkisches Jahrbuch für Geschichte und Kunst* xvi (1964), 1–266.
Thietmar of Merseburg	W. Trillmich, *Thietmar von Merseburg. Chronik.*
Tr. Passau	M. Heuwieser, *Die Traditionen des Hochstifts Passau.*
Tr. Regensburg	J. Widemann, *Die Traditionen des Hochstifts Regensburg und des Klosters S. Emmeram.*
Tr. Tegernsee	P. Acht, *Die Traditionen des Klosters Tegernsee 1003–1242.*
UB Asseburg	J. Graf von Bocholtz-Asseburg, *Asseburger Urkundenbuch.*

U B Halberstadt	G. Schmidt, *Urkundenbuch des Hochstifts Halberstadt und seiner Bischöfe.*
U B Hanau	H. Reimer, *Hessisches Urkundenbuch ii. Urkundenbuch zur Geschichte der Herren von Hanau.*
U B Hildesheim	(i) K. Janicke, (ii–iii) H. Hoogeweg, *Urkundenbuch des Hochstifts Hildesheim und seiner Bischöfe.*
U B Krain	F. Schumi, *Urkunden- und Regestenbuch des Herzogtums Krain.*
U B Land ob der Enns	*Urkundenbuch des Landes ob der Enns.*
U B Mainz	(i) M. Stimming, (ii) P. Acht, *Mainzer Urkundenbuch.*
U B Mittelrhein	H. Beyer, L. Eltester, and A. Goerz, *Urkundenbuch zur Geschichte der mittelrheinischen Territorien.*
U B Münster	R. Wilmans, *Die Urkunden des Bisthums Münster 1201–1300.*
U B Niederrhein	T. J. Lacomblet, *Urkundenbuch für die Geschichte des Niederrheins.*
U B Nürnberg	*Nürnberger Urkundenbuch.*
U B Osnabrück	F. Philippi and M. Bär, *Osnabrücker Urkundenbuch.*
U B Salzburg	W. Hauthaler and F. Martin, *Salzburger Urkundenbuch.*
U B St. Stephan	F. J. Bendel, F. Heidingsfelder, and M. Kaufmann, *Urkundenbuch der Benediktiner-Abtei St. Stephan in Würzburg.*
U B Steiermark	J. Zahn, *Urkundenbuch des Herzogthums Steiermark.*
U B Weida	B. Schmidt, *Urkundenbuch der Vögte von Weida, Gera und Plauen.*
U B Wirtemberg	*Wirtembergisches Urkundenbuch.*
V F	Vorträge und Forschungen.
V S W G	*Vierteljahrschrift für Sozial- und Wirtschaftsgeschichte.*
Weinrich	L. Weinrich, *Quellen zur deutschen Verfassungs-, Wirtschafts-, und Sozialgeschichte bis 1250.*
W F	Wege der Forschung.

Wipo, *Gesta* *Chuonradi*	H. Bresslau, *Die Werke Wipos*, pp. 3-62.
ZBLG	*Zeitschrift für bayerische Landesgeschichte.*
ZRGGA	*Zeitschrift der Savigny-Stiftung für Rechtsgeschichte. Germanistische Abteilung.*

Monarchy, Lordship, and Violence in the Medieval German Empire

The new empire founded by Otto the Great, 936–973

The medieval German empire established in the tenth century by Otto the Great's martial prowess was a huge conglomeration of diverse provinces almost entirely lacking the characteristics of a state governable in the Roman or the modern manner. It was thought to be the restored Roman empire, whose authority had been conveniently translated in 800 to the Frankish people under Charlemagne, and then, in 962, claimed by Otto for himself and the East Franks.[1] In practice the new empire was a jumble of German and Italian secular lordships and ecclesiastical immunities which actually predated the Saxon monarchy of Otto and his father Henry I (919–36). One of the principal results of Charlemagne's conquest of the Lombard kingdom in 774, and of the regions east of the Rhine completed in 804, had been to reinforce a pattern of local power exercised by prominent secular landowers, Frankish or native, and by the prelates of the Church. When Carolingian imperial predominance passed away in the ninth century, these persons and their heirs retained an authority based upon foundations not undermined until modern times.

They enjoyed first of all the prestige and functions of the military offices of count, duke, and margrave, which had originally been bestowed by the Carolingians, or of the higher ecclesiastical functions, bishop, archbishop, and abbot. Secondly, they inherited great patrimonies composed of lands, peasants, villages, towns, and fortifications, and all the jurisdictions, juridical immunities, and manorial rights, services, and revenues which went with them. The

---

[1] W. Goez, *Translatio Imperii. Ein Beitrag zur Geschichte des Geschichtsdenkens und der politischen Theorien im Mittelalter und in der frühen Neuzeit* (Tübingen, 1958), chs. 4 and 5.

secular patrimonies were liable to erosion, since the principle of
primogeniture did not recommend itself to the medieval German
aristocracy; but the ecclesiastical patrimonies were supposed to be
the indivisible property of the patron saints to whom the great
churches were dedicated. Thirdly, the magnates maintained retinues
of armed men to defend the patrimonies and to prosecute the feuds
which were characteristic of political life in medieval Germany. The
Saxon monarchs were themselves late-Carolingian magnates of this
kind, and necessarily continued their conflicts with their former
compeers after Henry I's election to the East Frankish throne in
919.[2]

Certainly the magnates owed homage to the king as vassals rendering a variety of political, military, and economic services, and
one mark of Otto the Great's success was his regulation not only
of all the important ecclesiastical appointments, but also of the
succession to the East Frankish duchies. Nevertheless, the political
ambitions of the Saxon monarchs, and of the imperial dynasties
which succeeded them in the eleventh and twelfth centuries, did not
include a fundamental reversal of the older framework of autonomous local power. They had little reason to attempt this, since they
had nothing to put in its place, a 'centralized' empire not being a
practical possibility. The new empire was a loose military hegemony created by Otto the Great's victories over the Slavs, the
Magyars, the Italians, and his own East Frankish rivals.[3] The lustre
of conquest, the Roman imperial title, and the sacral or theocratic
style of monarchy,[4] supported though they were by an extensive
imperial fisc, the homages of the great, and the services of the
Church, were not themselves convertible into effective central

---

[2] K.J. Leyser, *Rule and Conflict in an Early Medieval Society. Ottonian Saxony*
(London, 1979), pp. 1-47.

[3] On Otto and his victories, see A. Bauer and R. Rau, *Quellen zur Geschichte der
sächsischen Kaiserzeit*, A Q, VIII (Darmstadt, 1977), K.J. Leyser, 'The Battle of the
Lech, 955. A Study in Tenth-century Warfare', *History* 1 (1965), 1-25, and H.
Zimmermann (ed.), *Otto der Große*, W F, CCCCL (Darmstadt, 1976).

[4] On the theory behind German imperial monarchy, see Leyser, *Rule and Conflict*,
pp. 75-112, T.E. Mommsen and K.F. Morrison, *Imperial Lives and Letters of the
Eleventh Century*, Records of Civilization, Sources and Studies, LXVII (New York
and London, 1962), pp. 3-51, R. Folz, *The Concept of Empire in Western Europe
from the Fifth to the Fourteenth Century* (London, 1969), pp. 44-52, 61-74, E.
Hlawitschka (ed.), *Königswahl und Thronfolge in ottonisch-frühdeutscher Zeit*, W F,
CLXXVIII (Darmstadt 1971), and Weinrich, pp. 34-46.

authority over the social orders and far-flung provinces of medieval Germany.

Since Otto the Great and his successors were formidable rulers, why did they not seek to break up the antecedent configurations of regional power? The history of medieval Germany is, after all, punctuated by dangerous and long-lasting conflicts between individual emperors and their aggressive vassals, who drew their active strength from those configurations. Combinations of these vassals could pose a serious threat to the security, stability, and survival of the imperial dynasty, as the reigns of Henry IV (1056-1106), Philip of Swabia (1198-1208), or Conrad IV (1250-4) only too clearly revealed. The short answer must be that the ancient and autogenous structure of local authority was itself too powerful for any monarch to contemplate more than piecemeal measures of change. The revolutionary notion of overthrowing such a pattern is an anachronism which might occur in modern historiography, not in the thought-world of medieval German politics, principally because emperors were themselves products of a limited definition of lordship which respected local powers and did not include the concept of centralization.

Competition or collision with the entrenched rights of the magnates was not what the imperial office was thought to be for. Otto the Great, technically lord over his ducal vassals since 936,[5] had elevated his monarchy into a restoration of Charlemagne's empire by a series of successful military and diplomatic strokes inside and beyond the confines of East Francia. The imperial title acquired in 962 conferred the final mark of distinction upon his achievement, the prescriptive right to dictate to the Church within his frontiers, and a legacy of continued diplomatic, military, and missionary effort beyond them. Military exertion outside the East Frankish realm was the main task of the Roman emperor, and it was primarily for this purpose that the ecclesiastical and secular magnates were prepared to give their support. The contemporary histories are full of expeditions against the Slavs east of the Elbe, to Hungary, Bohemia, and Poland, over which the emperors claimed some sort of hegemony, and to Italy and Burgundy, whose royal titles the emperors bore since 961 and 1033 respectively. The chief burden of the imperial office continued to be an annual or nearly

[5] P. Hirsch and H.-E. Lohmann, *Die Sachsengeschichte des Widukind von Korvei*, MG schol., LX (5th edn., Hanover 1935), pp. 63-7.

annual military effort against the principal external, or if necessary, internal foe of the time.

Emperors and the regional powers

Medieval German emperors accepted that they stood within, not above, the regional organization of power because they were themselves, as landowners, part of it. In origin the Ottonians were dukes of Saxony, and so was Lothar III (1125-37); Henry II (1002-24) was duke of Bavaria; the Salian dynasty (1024-1125) had always exercised ducal and comital authority in the Rhineland; and the Hohenstaufen (1138-1254) had risen to prominence as dukes of Swabia since 1079.[6] By virtue of adding their own patrimonies to the imperial fisc, the royal dynasties themselves became the most significant elements in the regional anatomy of authority. They were in a strong position to dominate their neighbours in one or more duchies,[7] and sought to outface malcontents everywhere by means of their feudal supremacy, their subventions from the Church, and well-timed armed force.

If emperors were able to interfere with the local structures, this did not necessarily mean tearing them apart. In 939, when Otto I suppressed the ducal title to Franconia, he did not thereby destroy its principal families, the Conradines and the Babenbergs. In 976, when Otto II (973-83) set up Austria as a new march and Carinthia as a new duchy, he reduced without eradicating the prestige of his contentious cousin, Duke Henry of Bavaria, to whose sphere of influence those regions had hitherto belonged. Conrad II (1024-39) also altered the internal balances by uniting the Saxon and Salian patrimonies in 1024, by promoting the Rhineland as the political centre of the empire, and by acquiring Burgundy in the 1030s. However, when his grandson Henry IV attempted to resume crown rights alienated during his minority, 1056 to 1066, he met

---

[6] On this duchy, H. Maurer, *Der Herzog von Schwaben. Grundlagen, Wirkungen und Wesen seiner Herrschaft in ottonischer, salischer und staufischer Zeit* (Sigmaringen 1978).

[7] On the earlier duchies, W. Kienast, *Der Herzogstitel in Frankreich und Deutschland* (Munich and Vienna, 1968), pp. 313-451, H. Kämpf (ed.), *Die Entstehung des deutschen Reiches*, WF, I (3rd edn., Darmstadt, 1971), and H. Stingl, *Die Entstehung der deutschen Stammesherzogtümer am Anfang des 10. Jahrhunderts*, Untersuchungen zur deutschen Staats- und Rechtsgeschichte, n.s. XIX (Aalen, 1974). By the 12th c., ducal titles had entirely changed their character, see p. 12, n. 30.

with strong and successful resistance from the Saxon and Thuringian nobles. So did Henry V (1106-25) and Conrad III (1138-52)
when they proposed to evict formidable rivals from the dukedoms
of Bavaria and Saxony, although Frederick I Barbarossa (1152-90)
did manage to achieve this by banishing Duke Henry the Lion in
1180.

As dukes of Swabia, the Hohenstaufen dynasty inherited a
three-cornered struggle for supremacy there with the Welf and
Zähringen families, who also enjoyed ducal titles and were rich in
Swabian estates. After long and destructive feuds going back three
generations, Frederick Barbarossa finally secured the reversion of
Duke Welf VI's patrimony in the 1170s, ensuring Hohenstaufen
predominance as dukes of Swabia. But none of these regional manœuvres added up to an effective substitution of imperial authority
for the *de facto* independence of the magnates in their own localities.

The resources for imperial power

The German emperors could not have attempted to create a detailed juridical and fiscal administration because there were no techniques, personnel, or traditions carrying knowledge of them, or
motivation for them. In Germany the emperors had their manorial
incomes, their silver mines, their tributes from the Slavs, and their
renders or *servitia* from the Church. In Italy they had their
forage-taxes or *fodrum*, based upon Lombard and Frankish antecedents, and other valuable rights.[8] In the juridical sphere, most
of the population upon the land was subject to the seigneurial
and advocatial jurisdiction of the magnates.[9] Dukes, counts, and

[8] On the imperial resources, K.J. Leyser, 'Ottonian Government', *English Historical Review* xcvi (1981), 721-53, M. Stimming, *Das deutsche Königsgut im 11. und 12.
Jahrhundert*, Historische Studien, CXLIX (Berlin, 1922), B. Heusinger, 'Servitium
regis in der deutschen Kaiserzeit', *A U* viii (1923), 26-159, C. Brühl, *Fodrum, Gistum,
Servitium Regis. Studien zu den wirtschaftlichen Grundlagen des Königtums im Frankenreich und in den fränkischen Nachfolgestaaten*, Kölner historische Abhandlungen,
XIV (Cologne and Graz, 1968), W. Metz, *Das Servitium Regis. Zur Erforschung der
wirtschaftlichen Grundlagen des hochmittelalterlichen deutschen Königtums*, Erträge der
Forschung, LXXXIX (Darmstadt, 1978), and *id.* 'Quellenstudien zum Servitium
regis (900-1250)', *A D* xxii (1976), 187-271 and xxiv (1978), 203-91, and J.P. Niederkorn, 'Die Datierung des Tafelgüterverzeichnisses. Bemerkungen zu einer Neuerscheinung', *M I ö G* lxxxvii (1979), 471-87.

[9] On the criminal jurisdictions of the magnates, H. Hirsch, *Die Hohe Gerichtsbarkeit im deutschen Mittelalter* (2nd edn., Graz and Cologne, 1958).

margraves retained some of their original military functions, and appear to have exercised jurisdiction over small groups of free men on the emperor's behalf. All magnates were the juridical superiors of their military vassals, and the emperor's court was the court of appeal for magnates, free men, and vassals.[10] The emperor did not lack fiscal and juridical rights and resources of his own, but they were not technically of an advanced or 'state-building' character. From the start the empire lacked the essential formal institutions such as imperial assizes or a general levy of taxation upon which centralization might have been based, and which did prove useful in creating more centralized styles of regal authority in France, England, Castile, Sicily, and Hungary in the twelfth and thirteenth centuries.

In summary, emperors carried enough weight to intervene in the regional structure of power and to change its contours, for its human representatives and beneficiaries were their vassals or subjects against whom it was possible to act. They might break individuals who were their enemies and prevail against kindreds, churches, and localities which had offended them. But they had neither grounds nor strength for overturning a political edifice in which they enjoyed the principal share. The arrangements of regional authority might change over the generations, notably in the process which modern German historiography calls 'the rise of territorial lordship', but its fundamental basis in regional diversity and autonomy did not. This was solid geographical, psychological, and political reality which no emperor, however enterprising, could possibly have subverted in favour of a new form, the centralized state, for which, in any case, the institutional resources and ideological impetus did not exist.

Warrior-emperors and support from the Church

If medieval Germany did not possess a central government to pitch against the effective authority of the magnates in the regions, this does not mean that emperors were weak rulers. It means that their aims were limited. Military command was their original business, and this did not change throughout the middle ages. Imperial biographers such as the Saxon monk Widukind of Corvey on Otto I,

---

[10] K.-F. Krieger, 'Die königliche Lehngerichtsbarkeit im Zeitalter der Staufer', *DA* xxvi (1970), 400-33.

Henry III's chaplain Wipo on Conrad II, and Bishop Otto of Freising on Frederick Barbarossa, emphasize that military competence was the secret of their credibility as rulers.[11] War demanded armed men, and Henry I had trained the Saxons and Thuringians as the most formidable of the East Frankish peoples for this purpose.[12] Otto the Great was able to call upon forces from all quarters of the East Frankish realm in order to crush the Magyars, as Widukind relates, and it is clear that he and his successors adopted Carolingian precedents in levying recruits to carry German arms far beyond the nucleus of duchies which had originally recognized Henry I and Otto I as their kings.[13] As a result, men such as Otto I and Conrad II were explicitly likened to that pattern of war-commanders, Charlemagne.[14] Even the anonymous biographer of Henry IV, who was facing quite different problems in his struggle with the Saxons, the papacy, and his own sons, returns again and again to the monarch's military exertions in defending his empire and people from the repeated treasons of his unfaithful magnates.[15]

Apart from their own armed retinue, emperors relied upon dukes, margraves, and counts for support, and even more upon the prelates of the Church. Otto the Great's adoption of the Roman imperial title endowed him, amongst other things, with theoretical dominion over Christian society in partnership with the pope. More significantly, it endorsed far-reaching imperial control over the Church in Germany, an authority shaken but not destroyed by the War of Investitures (1076-1122) and subsequent manœuvres of the Reformed Papacy. As the emperor's servants, the German bishops and abbots, with their literate skills, their commitment to the theocratic imperial ideal, their huge resources in lands, armed men, fortresses, and communications, and their diocesan organization

[11] Hirsch and von Lohmann, *Sachsengeschichte Widukinds*, pp. 61-154, Wipo, *Gesta Chuonradi*, pp. 1-62, in translation in Mommsen and Morrison, pp. 52-100, and Otto and Rahewin, *Gesta Friderici*, in translation in C.C. Mierow and R. Emery, *The Deeds of Frederick Barbarossa by Otto of Freising and his Continuator Rahewin*, Records of Civilization. Sources and Studies, XLIX (New York, 1953).
[12] K.J. Leyser, 'Henry I and the beginnings of the Saxon empire', *English Historical Review* lxxxiii (1968), 1-32.
[13] K.-F. Werner, 'Heeresorganisation und Kriegführung im deutschen Königreich des 10. und 11. Jahrhunderts' in *Ordinamenti militari in Occidente nell'alto Medioevo*, Settimane di studio del Centro italiano di studi sull'alto Medioevo, XV (Spoleto, 1968), pp. 791-843.
[14] Thietmar of Merseburg, pp. 32, 82, and Wipo, *Gesta Chuonradi*, pp. 28 f.
[15] W. Eberhard, *Vita Heinrici IV. Imperatoris*, MG schol., LVIII (3rd edn., Hanover and Leipzig, 1899), in translation in Mommsen and Morrison, pp. 101-37.

with its concomitant jurisdictions and immunities, furnished him with a source of influence over the German regions which he would not have been able to exercise from his household alone. The prelates of the Church thus provided an extension of imperial power into the provinces, but even more important to the political processes of the empire were their military and economic contributions to the imperial court and campaigns, usually on an annual basis.[16]

Archbishops, bishops, and abbots were the emperor's men and were appointed or confirmed in office by him, but ecclesiastical administration did not of itself supply a substitute for detailed methods of government technically beyond the competence of the imperial household. This peripatetic institution was, in part, staffed by clerics who ran the imperial chapel and writing-office under bishops acting as chancellors.[17] The chief reason for its mobility did not lie in a programme of imperial administration, but in military, economic, and political needs. The purpose was to reach far-flung theatres of war, in reasonable weather if possible, to draw sustenance from royal manors and host-churches throughout Germany, Burgundy, and Italy in annual or longer cycles, and to exhibit the power and the glory of the emperor to the nobility and their retainers.[18]

The symbiotic relationship of the Church with the imperial court explains why, apart from pious motives, the Ottonian and Salian dynasties endowed abbeys and bishoprics on a magnificent scale, and founded new sees, Magdeburg with its suffragans in 968 and Bamberg in 1007. An imperial grant to Fulda Abbey illustrates the secular motive for imperial generosity: 'It is fitting that riches

[16] F. Prinz, *Klerus und Krieg im früheren Mittelalter. Untersuchungen zur Rolle der Kirche beim Aufbau der Königsherrschaft*, Monographien zur Geschichte des Mittelalters, II (Stuttgart, 1971), L. Auer, 'Der Kriegsdienst des Klerus unter den sächsischen Kaisern', *MIöG* lxxix (1971), 316-407 and lxxx (1972), 48-70, M. Weikmann, 'Königsdienst und Königsgastung in der Stauferzeit', *ZBLG* xxx (1967), 314-32, and E.N. Johnson, *The Secular Activities of the German Episcopate, 919-1024*, University of Nebraska Studies XXX. 1 (Lincoln, Neb., 1932).

[17] J. Fleckenstein, *Die Hofkapelle der deutschen Könige*, Schriften der MG, XVI (2 parts, Stuttgart, 1959-66), and H.-W. Klewitz, 'Königtum, Hofkapelle und Domkapitel im 10. und 11. Jahrhundert', *AU* xvi (1939), 102-56.

[18] H.-J. Rieckenberg, 'Königsstraße und Königsgut in liudolfingischer und frühsalischer Zeit', *AU* xvii (1942), 32-154, W. Metz, 'Tafelgut, Königsstraße und Servitium Regis in Deutschland', *HJ* xci (1971), 257-91, R. Schmidt, *Königsumritt und Huldigung in ottonisch-salischer Zeit*, *VF*, VI (Constance and Stuttgart, 1961), pp. 97-233, and J.O. Plassmann, *Princeps und Populus. Die Gefolgschaft im ottonischen Staatsaufbau*, Schriften der Forschungshilfe (Göttingen, 1954).

should be given to churches and especially Fulda, "For unto whomsoever much is given, of him shall be much required" [Luke 12;48]. Much service shall therefore be owed to the Roman [i.e. imperial] and royal court, for it is written, "Render to Caesar the things that are Caesar's, and to God the things that are God's" (Mark 12;17)'.[19]

Emperors and magnates as lords in Germany

As well as receiving active support from the Church, imperial might rested upon exploitation of the imperial fisc, but there is little detailed evidence about how this was done until Hohenstaufen times.[20] On this vast domain, the emperor as the landowner was the recognized lord and magistrate of the people dependent upon the manors, towns, and fortifications, and of the vassal-knights with their fiefs. But the bishops, counts, untitled dynasts, margraves, abbots, and dukes were also landowers, and were the recognized lords of their own people, with similar powers. This seigneurial attitude to lordship, in which every lord had autonomous rights within the hierarchy of lords, really antedates manorialism in Germany, and goes back to the pre-Carolingian past.[21] The emperor was lord of the empire, but every nobleman was the lord of his own household and fortified dwelling with its armed retinue, and of all other persons, such as the serfs, dependent upon him. This belief provided some theoretical foundation for regional independence in Germany, and inspiration for defending it.

Ideologically, the empire was the terrestial manifestation of a

[19] MGD Henry II, 509, pp. 651 f., probably 1024, the passage quoted being a 12th c. interpolation.

[20] Metz, SG, passim.

[21] See principally W. Schlesinger, Die Entstehung der Landesherrschaft (new edn., Darmstadt, 1973), O. von Dungern, Adelsherrschaft im Mittelalter, Libelli, CXCVIII (2nd edn., Darmstadt, 1972), A. Waas, Herrschaft und Staat im deutschen Frühmittelalter (2nd edn., Darmstadt, 1965), H.K. Schulze, Adelsherrschaft und Landesherrschaft, Mitteldeutsche Forschungen, XXIX (Cologne and Graz, 1963), H. Kämpf (ed.), Herrschaft und Staat im Mittelalter, WF, II (Darmstadt, 1972), and W. Störmer, Früher Adel. Studien zur politischen Führungsschicht im fränkisch-deutschen Reich, Monographien zur Geschichte des Mittelalters, VI (Stuttgart, 1973). The subject is controversial; see H. Kühn, 'Die Grenzen der germanischen Gefolgschaft', ZRGGA lxxiii (1956), 1–83, K. Kroeschell, Haus und Herrschaft im frühen deutschen Recht, Göttinger rechtswissenschaftliche Studien, LXX (Göttingen, 1968), and H. Vollrath, 'Herrschaft und Genossenschaft im Kontext frühmittelalterlicher Rechtsbeziehungen', HJ cii (1982), 33–71.

lordly hierarchy encompassing heaven and earth, from the Holy Trinity which was its protector, and in whose name the imperial letters were therefore issued from the chancery, through the saints who were the patrons and legal owners of the cathedral and monastic churches and their lands, to the emperor and pope as temporal and spiritual heads of the Christian Church and the Roman Empire, to the imperial vassals, whether dukes, archbishops, counts, or lesser men. In this cosmic scheme, the rights of lordship were considered to vary greatly in scope, objects, and limits. But all lords partook of the holy and inviolable nature of the hierarchy which, in the interests of earthly order, it was the duty of the senior sublunar lord, the emperor, to watch over.[22] Had the imperial monarchy been in a position to choose the path of administrative centralization in opposition to the institutions of local lordship, then it would have had to subvert these convictions about autogenous lordly rights lying behind aristocratic independence. The emperor would have had to betray his own position as overlord of German lords. The monarch's lordship over these men was made manifest by receiving their homage. Widukind of Corvey says that the dukes and other magnates did homage together at Otto I's coronation at Aachen in 936, while Bishop Thietmar of Merseburg tells us how Henry II had to make a rapid tour of the duchies in 1002 to secure the fidelity of each regional nobility. On the occasion of Conrad II's consecration in 1024, Wipo mentions this practice as a matter of course: 'I think it rather unnecessary to speak of the fealty rendered to the king, because of the evidence borne by frequent practice that all bishops, dukes, and the other princes, vassals of primary rank, indeed, all free-born men if they be of any moment, render fealty to kings. At any rate, all submitted themselves to him quite sincerely and willingly by oath.'[23]

These practices tied the great men to the emperor, yet their own power was strengthened by the quasi-religious ideal of lordship

[22] He did so as supreme magistrate like the four sovereigns depicted in enamels upon his imperial diadem, Christ, David, Solomon, and Hezekiah; P.E. Schramm and F. Mütherich, *Denkmale der deutschen Könige und Kaiser*, Veröffentlichungen des Zentralinstituts für Kunstgeschichte, II (Munich, 1962), pp. 141, 278-81. On the monarch as *Gerichtsherr*, Hirsch, pp. 150-7, 221-38, and Otto and Rahewin, *Gesta Friderici*, pp. 183 f.; 'iam non regni rector, sed unius domus, unius rei publicae paterfamilias et gubernator haberetur'.

[23] Thietmar of Merseburg, pp. 204-16, Mommsen and Morrison, p. 68, and p. 3, n. 5 above.

which conceded independent rights to every lord. It was therefore difficult for an emperor to deal with contumacious lords except by confiscating their fiefs in his capacity as feudal overlord. One reason for Saxon bitterness against Henry IV in the 1070s was the suspicion that he did harbour intentions of overthrowing the sacred hierarchy of lords, by abolishing its economic basis as well as by assassinating any lord who stood in his way. The contemporary Saxon author Bruno seems to have understood that a diminution of the regional forms of power in favour of an imperial autocracy of some kind must involve killing off the lords who would oppose it. And so, in his *Book of the Saxon War*, he accused Henry IV of harbouring these intentions, starting with Duke Rudolf of Swabia, Duke Berthold of Carinthia, Archbishop Anno of Cologne, and a collection of other bishops and great men. Absurd though the accusation is in itself, Bruno's words do reveal the essentially parallel and autonomous position of all German lordships; 'So that he [Henry IV] might be the sole lord of everyone, he wanted no other lord to survive in his kingdom.'[24]

Conflict and balances between emperors and lords

The martial supremacy pursued by the imperial dynasties with support from the Church was not necessarily in conflict with the fabric of local authority based upon seigneurial rights and the ideology of lordship. For long periods the two spheres, the imperial régime and the autogenous rights of lords, could exist, geographically and politically, side by side. Yet it cannot be denied that time and again the substantial edifices of regional authority, the spirit of aristocratic independence, and the juridical right of feud permitted combinations of magnates to threaten monarchs even to the point of deposition. As a result, the German monarchy has, in modern historiography, sometimes been credited with a cumulative series of political misjudgements; the lure of Italy and controversies with the Reformed Papacy, compounded by misfortunes such as royal minorities and the extinction of the Saxon and Salian dynasties which perpetuated hard-fought royal elections, distracting the crown from the 'real' task of breaking the magnates.[25]

[24] H.-E. Lohmann, *Brunos Buch vom Sachsenkrieg*, M G Deutsches Mittelalter II (Leipzig, 1937), pp. 54-6, and Schlesinger in H. Kämpf (ed.), *Herrschaft und Staat* p. 167.
[25] This unconvincing argument is examined by J.B. Gillingham, *The Kingdom of*

The monarchy did face prolonged crises and conflicts, and was not perhaps very successful in fulfilling its aims, which were to add military renown to the imperial title, to govern the Church as delegate of Christ the King, to command obedience from the secular vassals, and to 'provide judgement and justice and peace in the empire.'[26] Yet it was bound to accept autogenous lordship not only as an ideological but also as a geopolitical reality. If the enormous size of the medieval empire contributed to the monarch's prestige, it also limited his effectiveness. Ottonian illuminated manuscripts illustrate personifications of Gaul, Germany, Italy, and the Slav East offering tributes to the later Ottos,[27] but their armed might was calamitously cast down on fronts hundreds of kilometres from each other, the Calabrian coast and the Saxon marches, in 982 and 983.

The empire was large, and the German kingdom itself was much more extensive than the areas effectively administered from Paris, Westminster, or Palermo in the twelfth and thirteenth centuries; geography alone would have defeated any embryonic attempt at centralization in Germany. The Hohenstaufen recognized this when they committed portions of their fisc to the care of imperial *ministeriales* on a strictly regional basis.[28] Otto of Freising mentioned 'the immense extent of the transalpine kingdom [i.e. Germany]' and Lampert of Hersfeld the huge forests which separated Saxony and Thuringia from Franconia.[29] Geography reinforced the social and legal traditions which divided the medieval Germans into distinct peoples or *gentes*, Saxons and Thuringians, Lotharingians and Frisians, Franconians, Swabians, or Bavarians, with their own laws, dialects, and customs, compounded by numerous regional subdivisions.[30]

Germany in the High Middle Ages, Historical Association Pamphlets, LXXVII (London, 1971).

[26] These goals were advertised in theory and practice in Wipo, *Gesta Chuonradi*, pp. 20-4, 26-30.

[27] Schramm and Mütherich, pp. 147 f., 155 f., 297, 322 f.

[28] See Ch. 8 below.

[29] Otto and Rahewin, *Gesta Friderici*, p. 103, 1152, and Lampert of Hersfeld, p. 156, 1073.

[30] For subdivision and the consequences, T. Mayer, 'Analekten zum Problem der Entstehung der Landeshoheit, vornehmlich in Süddeutschland', *Blätter für deutsche Landesgeschichte* lxxxix (1952), 87-111, K.S. Bader, 'Volk, Stamm, Territorium', *HZ* clxxvi (1953), 449-77, and E. Klebel, 'Vom Herzogtum zum Territorium' in

The autogenous authority of the lords therefore had firm foundations in the legal and social geography of medieval Germany, as well as in the aristocratic mentality of the time. As Karl Leyser has pointed out: '... from the start the nobles possessed lordship and powers in their own right, outside the king's reach, and ... the *Reich* therefore was born particularistic and did not merely drift in that direction because of mishaps and catastrophes like the extinction of dynasties, royal minorities and the collision with the papacy.' The emperors shared the same thought-world as these nobles; in it centralization had no place. There was little room until the end of the Middle Ages for 'the idea of a "central authority" which, in the guise of kingship, might or should have prevailed.'[31]

The new empire, a Carolingian inheritance, was salvaged by a successful military leader during a period of intense inner conflicts in East Francia, and these well-grounded local rivalries were projected into the distant future. As feudal lord and supreme magistrate the emperor, through his court, offered arbitration in local conflicts when he was not himself involved in trying to solve them by his own arms.[32] But for the German monarchy this jurisdictional and feudal overlordship, underlined by theocratic ideals, war-leadership, and a wide fisc, did not create a royal dynamism which might have dissolved the institutional rights of the secular and ecclesiastical magnates.

Aus Verfassungs- und Landesgeschichte. Festschrift für Theodor Mayer, (Lindau and Constance 1954), vol. i, pp. 205-22. The main result was the new form of the duchy in the 12th c.: T. Mayer, K. Heilig, and C. Erdmann, *Kaisertum und Herzogsgewalt im Zeitalter Friedrichs I.*, M G Schriften des Reichsinstituts, IX, (new edn., Stuttgart, 1952), Hirsch, pp. 204-11, H. Fichtenau, *Von der Mark zum Herzogtum. Grundlagen und Sinn des 'Privilegium Minus' für Österreich*, Österreich-Archiv (2nd edn., Munich, 1965), R. Hildebrand, *Der sächsische 'Staat' Heinrichs des Löwen*, Historische Studien, CCCII (Berlin, 1937), K. Jordan, *Heinrich der Löwe, Eine Biographie* (Munich, 1979), pp. 103-64, W.-D. Mohrmann (ed.), *Heinrich der Löwe*, Veröffentlichungen der Niedersächsischen Archivverwaltung, XXXIX (Göttingen, 1980), pp. 9-304, and E. Schrader, 'Vom Werden und Wesen des würzburgischen Herzogtums Franken', *Z R G G A* lxxx (1963), 27-81.
[31] K.J. Leyser, 'The German Aristocracy from the Ninth to the Early Twelfth Century. A Historical and Cultural Sketch', *Past and Present* xli (1968), 32. *Reichsreform* came too late; see F. Hartung and K.S. Bader in translation in G. Strauss (ed.), *Pre-Reformation Germany* (London, 1972), pp. 73-161.
[32] Out of innumerable examples see Thietmar of Merseburg, pp. 206-8, 212-16, 226-34, 272-4, 280-2, 300-4, 356-60, 384, 406-8 from Books V-VII on Henry II, Wipo, *Gesta Chuonradi*, pp. 32, 38-40, 43 f., 45-7 on Conrad II, and Helmold of Bosau, pp. 164-6 on Henry V, and 252-4 on Conrad III.

The reality of violence and hopes of peace

The German aristocratic mentality took for granted violence on a considerable scale. The imperial scheme of campaigns within and beyond the frontiers of the empire, and the local rivalries which were soluble, or insoluble, only in feuds, obliged all magnates to retain substantial retinues of armed men. This political necessity itself contributed to the momentum of violence. In his account of Henry V's reign, Abbot Ekkehard of Aura touched upon the problem, complaining that though the Christian Church and all the neighbouring nations were at peace, 'only, alas! German fury, not knowing how to put aside its obstinacy, and ignorant that "Great peace have they which love thy law" [Ps. 119;165]', perversely persisted in perjury, double-dealing, and bloodshed.[33]

The ideal of the monarch as guardian of order and peace did, however, find strong echoes, just because the land was so disorderly. Wipo tells us that in 1025, in a rapid progress through the five duchies of the German kingdom, Conrad II 'bound the duchies very firmly in a bond of peace and in royal guardianship,' a state of affairs at once disrupted by the Swabians, Lotharingians, and Italians. More realistically, when he dedicated the biography to Conrad's son Henry III (1039–56), he proclaimed him as effective in war as in peace, which in truth he needed to be.[34] For within the structures of regional authority, the hierarchy of lords traditionally resorted to armed confrontations. Medieval Germans simply accepted that the nobility was justified in launching feuds in defence of rights or claims which could not be settled by agreement, blackmail, arbitration, or some other peaceable method.[35] In these innumerable conflicts, emperors themselves frequently featured as protagonists, and feuds grounded in the provincial and dynastic rivalries of the ninth and tenth centuries acquired fresh impetus over the generations. Disputed inheritances, the lack of clear principles of primogeniture except in the royal house, appoint-

---

[33] Ekkehard of Aura, p. 334.

[34] Wipo, *Gesta Chuonradi*, pp. 3, 29.

[35] Outline in O. Brunner, *Land und Herrschaft. Grundfragen der territorialen Verfassungsgeschichte Österreichs im Mittelalter* (new edn., Darmstadt, 1973), pp. 1–110, and indications in R. His, *Geschichte des deutschen Strafrechts bis zur Karolina* (new edn., Darmstadt, 1967), pp. 61 f. The early *Landfrieden* show the material extent of feuds; MGC i, 74, pp. 125 f., 1103, 140, pp. 194–8, 1152, 277, pp. 381–3, 1179, 318, pp. 449–52, 1186, and 419–32, pp. 596–617, from the 11th and 12th cc.

ments to and dismissals from dukedoms and margraviates, confiscations and reassignments of fiefs and allods, endless competitions between ecclesiastical immunity and secular advocacy for authority over Church lands, political ambitions aroused during royal minorities and upon the demise of imperial dynasties, the vindictive nature of papal propaganda after 1076; all gave depth and dynamism to these regional struggles.

The churchmen who composed chronicles, biographies, and circular letters lamented the cruel consequences of disorder, but it proved to be beyond the powers of Christian teaching, of imperial and ecclesiastical admonition, or of aristocratic prudence, to erode the ingrained traditions of armed feud until early modern times. The chroniclers were aware of the discrepancy between the Roman Empire of antiquity, admired as the model of peace and security, and the inadequacies of the present incarnation of West Rome under the German emperors. This did not surprise Bishop Otto of Freising, himself the grandson of an emperor, who believed, not in progress, but in the necessary degeneration of the empire down the ages, so that God's purpose in human history would be fulfilled in the ultimate collapse of all political order. For him, decline and fall were natural goals of the empire, and he relates its miseries as inevitable; the empire 'not only became decrepit and senile through lapse of time, but also, like a once smooth pebble that has been rolled this way and that by the waters, contracted many a stain and developed many a defect.'[36] It was the emperor's known duty to provide peace, order, and justice, but since this was for the most part beyond him, the chroniclers and biographers relied upon an explanatory convention praising rulers for their personal toughness in trying to impose order by force, while correctly perceiving that they could achieve nothing of permanence. For this they blamed the magnates who could, individually or collectively, match the emperor's forces in the field, and had no intention of surrendering their hereditary right and tradition of feud at the emperor's behest.[37]

The German ruling élite was, nevertheless, aware of some of the

[36] Otto of Freising, p. 7, the translation from C.C. Mierow, *The Two Cities. A Chronicle of Universal History by Otto Bishop of Freising*, Records of Civilization. Sources and Studies, IX (new edn., New York, 1966), p. 94.
[37] Ekkehard of Aura, pp. 306–16, 348–50, and Otto and Rahewin, *Gesta Friderici*, pp. 153 f., 183 f., 1155 and 1158.

cumulative inconveniences of disorder, and did try to erect against it the peace-keeping association or *Landfriede*, adapted from the French model of sacred truces, the 'Peace of God' or the 'Truce of God.' It appears that Henry III issued the earliest such legislation at Constance in 1043,[38] and it was repeated by his successors. The Hohenstaufen set store by it as the road to political order in Germany,[39] and Frederick II's (1212-50) edict issued at Mainz in 1235 was a step forward in its elaboration.[40] These *Landfrieden* were the imperial answer to the French royal *sauvegarde* and the English 'King's Peace', imposed for good in the thirteenth century. The German version proved useless, for the aristocratic psychology of conflict was powerful enough to prevail over counsels of peace to which, it is true, 'the princes of the entire kingdom, dukes, margraves, counts, and many others' might swear,[41] but with insincere or confused intentions. Since *Landfrieden* were voluntary associations which envisaged the imposition of order by force of arms, they did little more than provide a new mechanism for aristocratic violence under the pretext of pursuing peace-breakers. Provost Burchard of Ursberg had the last word when he commented upon Frederick Barbarossa's peace-legislation issued from Nuremberg in 1186: 'He arranged peace over the land and ordered it to be recorded in letters which the Germans up to the present time call *fridebrief*, that is, letters of peace, nor do they use any other laws. But they do not carry them out properly, being such a savage and ungovernable people.'[42]

[38] *Herimanni Augiensis Chronicon*, MGS, V, p. 124 and Frutolf of Michelsberg, p. 62.

[39] H. Hoffmann, *Gottesfriede und Treuga Dei*, Schriften der MG, XX (Stuttgart, 1964), J. Gernhuber, *Die Landfriedensbewegung in Deutschland bis zum Mainzer Reichslandfrieden von 1235*, Bonner rechtswissenschaftliche Abhandlungen, XLIV (Bonn, 1952), E. Wadle, 'Heinrich IV. und die deutsche Friedensbewegung' in J. Fleckenstein (ed.), *Investiturstreit und Reichsverfassung*, VF, XVII (Sigmaringen, 1973), pp. 141-73, and O. Engels, 'Vorstufen der Staatwerdung im Hochmittelalter. Zum Kontext der Gottesfriedensbewegung', *HJ* xcvii-viii (1978), 71-86.

[40] MGC ii, 196, pp. 241-63, 1235, E. Klingelhöfer, *Die Reichsgesetze von 1220, 1231-32 und 1235. Ihr Werden und ihre Wirkung im deutschen Staat Friedrichs II.*, Quellen und Studien zur Verfassungsgeschichte des Deutschen Reiches, VIII.2 (Weimar, 1955), and H. Angermeier, 'Landfriedenspolitik und Landfriedensgesetzgebung unter den Staufern' in J. Fleckenstein (ed.), *Probleme um Friedrich II.*, VF, XVI (Sigmaringen, 1974), pp. 167-86.

[41] MGC i, 74, pp. 125 f., 1103.

[42] Burchard of Ursberg, p. 65, and the edict itself in MGC i, 318, pp. 449-52, 1186.

The magnates' armed retinues

The imperial monarchy's commitment to martial glory abroad, and the magnates' inevitable involvement in feuds at home, made it imperative to maintain large, effective, and disciplined retinues of knights proficient in cavalry combat, competent to garrison fortifications, and ready to carry out juridical or other official tasks for their lords. Armed retinues, whether enfeoffed with lands for their support or sustained directly in the household, were essential to the political standing and survival of all magnates, even of the most saintly clerics, in the perilous world of German internal conflict. We see such men, about 2,000 *loricati* or armoured warriors, sent in 981 as reinforcements to Otto II in Italy by some fifty ecclesiastical and secular magnates in four of the German duchies.[43] But this is merely a glimpse. Very little is known about retinues before the twelfth century, yet it is clear that the type of German knight regularly called *ministerialis* in the Latin sources was being enfeoffed on a large scale in the eleventh century. No doubt the War of Investitures and its ramifications demanded an accelerated rate of enfeoffment, and the sources reveal larger war-retinues produced in those troubled times.[44] It is likely that, at the same time, more fiefs were being made available as the effort of internal colonization, made possible by population increases amongst the peasantry, placed additional productive land at the disposal of the magnates.[45] It must, however, be said that firm answers about the origins of the cohorts of *ministeriales* who, in the twelfth century, fought out the murderous feuds between the greatest families for predominance in Germany, or for their monarchs in Italy and upon the Second and Third Crusades, can hardly be found in the inconclusive eleventh-century evidence.

The rules by which German lords controlled their retinues of knightly *ministeriales* resemble those relating to the vassalage of

[43] M G C i, 436, pp. 632 f., 981.
[44] Leyser, 'The German Aristocracy' pp. 47 f. and n. 52, and Ekkehard of Aura, p. 184, 1104.
[45] G. Duby, *The Early Growth of the European Economy. Warriors and Peasants from the Seventh to the Twelfth Century* (London, 1974), pp. 157-210, A. Mayhew, *Rural Settlement and Farming in Germany* (London, 1973), pp. 37-90, and R. Kötzschke, 'Staat und Bauerntum im thüringisch-obersächsischen Raum' in T. Mayer (ed.), *Adel und Bauern im deutschen Staat des Mittelalters* (new edn., Darmstadt, 1976), pp. 267-311.

knights in France. But they differed from the French type in one important respect. Whereas French knights were free men constrained by the contractual nature of vassalage, German *ministeriales* were not free men, and their service was an ineluctable hereditary duty to the lord upon whose patrimony and into whose ownership they had been born. Both these versions of knightly service were undoubtedly descended from late-Carolingian prototypes, but the direct evidence is lost.

It is likely that in France the absence of regal authority after the Viking invasions, and the extreme fragmentation of lordship in nearly every province, permitted the vassal-knights, in practice independent in their own castles, to assume free status and to underline it by adopting the predicates *nobilis* or nobleman and *dominus* or lord in the eleventh century.[46] In the German empire, conditions were similar in that regal authority was also absent as a political or jurisdictional reality in the regions, except on the imperial demesne. It also appears that, like their French counterparts, the German magnates had difficulty in disciplining their vassals, whose unruliness was one of the social problems of the age. In the 1020s Bishop Burchard of Worms turned his legal talents to the question, and issued a code in thirty-two chapters designed to regulate and discipline his retinue, in which homicides were commonplace.[47] The emperor also stepped in to restrain quarrels between ecclesiastical retinues, such as Lorsch against Worms and Fulda against Hersfeld.[48]

Yet in building up their retinues in the eleventh century the German lords, in contrast to the French magnates, were able to insist upon the version of vassalage which included unfree status for most of their knights. This was not likely to have been a matter of conscious choice or decision, but a social consequence of precedents about vassalage going back as far as Carolingian times. The German lords also maintained a number of free vassal-knights. It is probable that these men were already in possession of hereditary patrimonies, and were substantial enough to confirm their free status when they did homage, in contrast to the *ministeriales*

---

[46] G. Duby, *Hommes et structures du moyen âge*, Le savoir historique, I (Paris, 1973), pp. 145-66, 213-25, 267-85, 395-422 and especially 'Les origines de la chevalerie', pp. 325-41. See also p. 111, n. 53 below.

[47] MGC i, 438, pp. 639-44, 1023-5, *Lex familie Wormatiensis ecclesie*.

[48] MGD Henry II, 501, pp. 639-41, 1023 and 507, pp. 648-50, 1024.

who were unfree. Actually, as the predominant pattern of knightly vassalage was that of unfree *ministeriales*, quite a number of free men opted for the status of *ministerialis* when they did homage.[49] But the vassal-knight of free status survived in small numbers throughout the Hohenstaufen period, and we hear, for example, of Duke Henry the Lion followed in Germany, in Italy, and on crusade by his free knights as well as his *ministeriales*.[50]

Comparing European retinues of knights

The size and purpose of German retinues were unlike anything known in France and England. The rapid extension of public order by the thirteenth century convinced the chief vassals of those crowns that large retinues were an expensive nuisance. In the twelfth century some of the powerful French magnates such as the bishops of Bayeux or the counts of Ponthieu still had more than a hundred enfeoffed knights,[51] comparable in military potential with a German magnate's retinue. If the numbers of knights summoned in 1272 by Philip III from his bishops and *baillis* can be taken as a guide, then such retinues must have contracted drastically in the thirteenth century.[52] The richest churches in Angevin England owed the crown the service of forty to sixty knights each,[53] but it is unlikely that they actually took the trouble to enfeoff their full quotas, preferring to compound for cash-payments to the king, or to hire knights when necessary. In the thirteenth century the English monarchy made some effort to improve the military showing of its secular tenants,[54] but the social need for retaining large retinues of active knights, which had undoubtedly secured the

[49] See p. 42 nn. 101-3.
[50] Helmold of Bosau, p. 252, 1151, K. Jordan, *Die Urkunden Heinrichs des Löwen Herzogs von Sachsen und Bayern*, M G Die deutschen Geschichtsquellen des Mittelalters, I (Stuttgart, 1957), 31, pp. 45 f., 1155, and *Arnoldi Chronica Slavorum*, M G S, XXI p. 116, 1171.
[51] I.J. Sanders, *Feudal Military Service in England* (London, 1956), pp. 32-5.
[52] M M de Wailly, Delisle and Jourdain, *Recueil des Historiens des Gaules et de la France*, vol. xxiii (Paris 1894), 'Hominum ad exercitum Fuxensem vocatorum, index secundus', pp. 752-66, and the related indices, pp. 734-52, 767-83; but the figures recorded may possibly have been fractions of the real numbers of knights retained. Dr M.C. Barber kindly drew my attention to this source.
[53] H.M. Chew, *The English Ecclesiastical Tenants-in-Chief and Knight Service* (London, 1932), pp. 4 f.
[54] Sanders, pp. 50-90.

Conquest after 1066, had quite evaporated. For a projected expedition to Brittany in 1229, Henry III considered it reasonable to demand twenty knights each from his five most prominent earls, and five to fifteen each from seven other earldoms.[55] These numbers were tiny compared with those available to German counts and bishops, who thought nothing of retaining a hundred knights or more, and the greatest magnates much larger forces.

Clearly, active military retinues on the German scale would have fulfilled no social requirement or defensive purpose or political advantage once the French and English crowns had imposed their own profitable and orderly methods of arbitration upon their nobilities. In the fourteenth and fifteenth centuries, when public order guaranteed by the king broke down in France for long periods, great men once more recruited larger armed retinues to pursue their political ambitions and to defend themselves from their rivals.

Origins and functions of ministeriales, *and the evidence from the eleventh to thirteenth centuries*

The establishment of more extensive retinues of unfree knights in the eleventh and twelfth centuries in Germany invites a number of questions which, given the infrequent nature of the source-materials, cannot always supply convincing answers. If the nine chapters which follow endeavour to answer these questions, they are limited by the uneven and sometimes contradictory evidence. Since churchmen produced and preserved the written word, information is more abundant, before 1300 at least, about *ministeriales* belonging to ecclesiastical retinues, although some remarkable secular sources have survived, notably the custumals issued by the counts of Ahr, Tecklenburg, and Sternberg-Maltein.[56] It turns out that the Latin word *ministerialis* was a scribal experiment of the eleventh century which prevailed early in the twelfth as the label for 'unfree knight' everywhere in Germany. But the exact pursuit of the institutional and genealogical origins of the *ministeriales* as a social order or class or group has not led to satisfactory historiographical conclusions, because the necessary eleventh-century and earlier evidence is so thin.[57]

[55] Sanders, pp. 115-29.
[56] See pp. 84f., nn. 28, 31, p. 87, n. 35.
[57] See pp. 37-44 below.

From the twelfth century the evidence is relatively more abundant, and so there are more fruitful grounds for investigating the legal servitude of *ministeriales*, their knightly functions in peace and war, and the practical consequences of their vassalage, for which a number of custumals exist in authentic or fragmentary forms. Here, so to speak, is to be found the professional impact of unfree knighthood in German society. It is possible to show what is meant by *ministeriales'* being in the legal possession of their lords, to unravel the apparent contradiction of their noble status coupled with servitude, to examine their legal rights and obligations, and to demonstrate from this in what degree their vassalage differed from international patterns in Christendom.[58]

Knights by profession, they were rewarded for their services with fiefs which sustained them as a hereditary landowning order, and quite substantial source-material about *ministeriales* as possessors of fiefs, proprietors of allods, and benefactors of the Church has survived. It is also possible to establish the legal history of their marriages, the important restrictions which their lords imposed upon them in this respect, and the devolution of inheritances over the generations, which had to fit their lords' rules applying to fiefs and allods.[59]

The more talented or powerful *ministeriales* were entrusted with a variety of juridical and administrative tasks by their lords. They were officials providing some sort of coherence to the magnates' ambitions of extending and defending their territories and rights. The role of the Hohenstaufen *ministeriales* as an imperial officialdom has attracted much attention in modern German historiography, and attempts have been made to identify in them the new professional class which might have converted Germany into a centralized realm upon Capetian, Hauteville, or Angevin lines. The principal modern work in this vein is Karl Bosl's *Die Reichsministerialität der Salier und Staufer*, published early in the 1950s. It is, however, unlikely that the imperial *ministeriales* entertained administrative notions at variance with the military and international traditions of empire descended from the Ottonians and refurbished by their Hohenstaufen masters.[60]

[58] See Chs. 2–4 below.
[59] See Chs. 5 6 below.
[60] See below, Ch. 8 on the imperial retinue of *ministeriales*, and Ch. 7 on office-holding.

Committed to military valour and living in fortified houses and castles, the *ministeriales* were themselves a noble landowning class with interests to defend, and were, for the purpose, imbued with the German political mentality of conflict. They took it for granted, like their masters, and it made them dangerous. Not only were they required to perpetrate violence in the service of their lords, but were also habituated to using force for their own purposes. At times they turned it against the lords they were born to serve, even to the point of assassination. More often they used it to further their own claims, whether justified or illegal, and to defend their local standing by feuds against the Church, the towns, the magnates, and their own kind.[61] The practice of redress by violence was amplified in the perilous era of economic hardship after 1300, when the *ministeriales* as a class were threatened by rapid decline, and responded with the degenerate strain of unprincipled brutality foreshadowed by such discerning spirits as Wernher der Gartenaere in his *Meier Helmbrecht*.

[61] See Ch. 9 below.

CHAPTER I

Knights and *Ministeriales* in the Eleventh and Twelfth Centuries: The Emergence of a New Knighthood in Germany

Knights called ministeriales *in Germany*

Towards the end of his reign, Emperor Frederick I Barbarossa recalled the faithful military service he had received during his attempts to restore German imperial authority over the Lombard Communes of northern Italy. At the siege of Crema in 1159, he reflected, 'we lost there our vassal noblemen, *ministeriales*, and active *servientes*, a loss which it is difficult to replace'.[1] During the twelfth century, the great majority of German knights are called *ministeriales* in the surviving sources; *serviens*, a widely-used alternative description, was already in decline after 1100. On these famous campaigns, the princes were accompanied by hundreds of *ministeriales*.[2] In 1161 Archbishop Rainald of Cologne was said to have brought more than 500, and the emperor's immediate relations, Count-Palatine Conrad of the Rhine, Duke Frederick of Rothenburg, and Landgrave Louis of Thuringia, more than 600 between them as reinforcements to the siege of Milan, which ended several months later with the Germans razing the city to the ground.[3] We know, moreover, how these knights, attended by their servants, were equipped for the long march over the Alps, with war-horses, mail-coats, and arms, besides pack-horses with saddle-bags full of necessaries such as cash, provisions, extra horse-shoes with the nails, and goatskin coats against the cold.[4]

---

[1] MGC i, 302, pp. 426-8, 1185. Rahewin recorded this siege as very bloody; Otto and Rahewin, *Gesta Friderici*, pp. 287-97, 312-18.

[2] A. Hofmeister, *Ottonis de Sancto Blasio Chronica*, MG schol., XLVII (Hanover and Leipzig, 1912), p. 26, 1167 for the composition of these armies.

[3] F. Güterbock, *Das Geschichtswerk des Otto Morena und seiner Fortsetzer über die Taten Friedrichs I. in der Lombardei*, MGS, n.s., VII (Berlin, 1930), p. 135.

[4] MGD Conrad II, 140, pp. 188-91, early 12th-c. source dated 1029, MGC i, 447, pp. 661-3, c.1160, and Weinrich, pp. 266-78, c.1165.

The Italian expeditions were expensive, and *ministeriales* were not expected to bear their entire costs out of the incomes from their fiefs. Their lords helped out with grants of clothing, money, and horses. The Cologne knights were, in addition to a handsome fitting-out allowance of ten marks, paid at the rate of one mark a month once the Alps were reached on the way south. Within a short time the ageing emperor called once more upon the *ministeriales*, this time for the Third Crusade. 'Who', exclaimed an historian of this abortive enterprise, 'is capable of counting separately the dreaded and orderly array of *ministeriales* and other chosen knights?'[5] Everywhere the knights made their arrangements and prepared to leave for the East, such as 'a certain powerful and active knight called Siegfried, one of Count Albert of Dagsburg's *ministeriales*',[6] who was the first in Alsace to take the cross, from the hands of the bishop of Strasburg.

In the Latin sources of the Hohenstaufen age, *ministerialis* is the prevalent term for knight in Germany. The word referred not to his most characteristic function, that of fighting on horseback, but to his hereditary status, and was therefore applicable to his womenfolk, children, and relatives in holy orders.[7] In other words, *ministeriales* look like a social class, with the hereditary profession or function of knightly cavalrymen.[8] The use of the word *ministerialis* increased greatly in eleventh-century sources, and with the hindsight provided by better twelfth-century evidence, we can see that it reflects the rising importance of the knight in German society, and the expansion of their military retinues by the great landowners, that is, the Salian emperors, the bishops and abbots, and the secular dynasties whose senior members were dukes, margraves, and counts.

The material available does not lend itself to a clear or conclusive account of the emergence of knighthood in Salian Germany. Much can be said about the knightly functions of *ministeriales* in the twelfth century. But there is no convincing way of arranging the

[5] A. Chroust, *Quellen zur Geschichte des Kreuzzuges Kaiser Friedrichs I*, MGS, n.s., V (2nd edn., Berlin, 1964), p. 22.

[6] H. Bloch, *Annales Marbacenses qui dicuntur*, MG schol., IX (Hanover and Leipzig, 1907), p. 58, 1187.

[7] *Annales Rodenses*, MGS XVI, p. 694, 1108, H.-J. Busley, *Die Traditionen, Urkunden und Urbare des Klosters Neustift bei Freising*, QE, XIX (Munich, 1961), 6, pp. 10 f., 1152, and Jordan, *Urkunden Heinrichs des Löwen*, 31, p. 45, 1155.

[8] CD Salem 122, p. 160, 1221 for 'et officio miles et ecclesie nostre ministerialis'.

fragmentary evidence, stretching back in some regions to Carolingian times, to account for the antecedents of this post-1100 knighthood. All that can be done is to review the early sources relating to retinues, military service, lordship over men, obligations implied by vassalage, dependence and servitude, and the changes which they appear to have undergone.

Early in the twelfth century, the scribal preference for *ministerialis* overwhelmed other words for knight, and held its own for a century. This victory testifies to one way in which the German lords had been able to take advantage of their economic opportunities in the eleventh century. These men were worth little without formidable military retinues, and much of Germany's regional history in medieval times is concerned with their tenacity in establishing, expanding, maintaining, and disciplining these followings. In the eleventh century they were able to enfeoff new retinues of knights, sometimes in very large numbers. The term *ministerialis* for such men implies that they lived under a form of legal unfreedom, in this respect unlike the vassalage which constrained French or Anglo-Norman knights in the same period. But nearly all the legal and social restraints and restrictions upon *ministeriales* were, in their functioning, reminiscent of vassalage, and had little in common with the yoke of serfdom. Nevertheless, in Germany the strong ties of personal and hereditary dependence which bound *ministeriales* to their lords were held to constitute a type of proprietary right, or *ius proprietatis*,[9] under which lords were owners of their *ministeriales*, who therefore had servile legal status.

The name *ministerialis* also implied the performance of a *ministerium* or service,[10] more especially military service, to a lord. In 1095, when certain free men agreed to become *ministeriales* of the abbot of St Mary at Trier, 'they were entered into the *ministerium* or service of the Holy Mother of God, to be counted amongst the first *ministeriales* of that church'.[11] Service was similar to what was expected of knights in Capetian France and post-Conquest England; expertise in mounted combat, obligations to garrison castles, administration of lands and jurisdictions, or a combination of these tasks. Frequently therefore, German *ministeriales* were also called

[9] CD Westphalia i, 192, p. 150, 1123.
[10] J.F. Niermeyer, *Mediae Latinitatis Lexicon Minus* (Leiden, 1954-64), pp. 687-90.
[11] UB Mittelrhein i, 389, p. 446, 1095.

milites, since both words conveyed the same range of meaning about knightly duties owed to lords. In the archbishop of Cologne's list of rules about these duties, the knights are called *milites de familia sua*, 'knights of his retinue', as well as *ministeriales*.[12]

If *ministeriales* were essentially *milites* or knights, why was the longer word adopted to describe them, and why did it prevail in the legal Latin of twelfth-century Germany? The explanation must be that *miles* was already in use for the much smaller group of free knights, sometimes distinguished as *milites liberi*,[13] and as a synonym for vassal, even for the greatest men in the empire such as dukes and margraves.[14] The awkward but necessary distinction between knights who were *ministeriales* and knights who were *liberi* continued to be made well into the thirteenth century, when the free knights, always a small minority, were rapidly dying out. At this point it became possible to make *ministerialis* and *miles* into interchangeable terms, since *ministeriales* had always been *milites* in function, and like them, were sustained as a group by their hereditary fiefs.[15] Socially, the last remnant of the free knighthood was absorbed by intermarriage with *ministeriales* in the fourteenth century.[16]

A description of the German *ministeriales* of 1100 as knightly in function and unfree in status needs further clarification, since the social realities of knighthood and unfreedom were themselves in flux. By the end of the twelfth century, a much clearer picture of their military functions, administrative capacity, social position, economic basis, and political impact has emerged. Everywhere in Germany the *ministeriales* enjoyed similar hereditary relationships *vis-à-vis* their lords, and performed similar professional functions, even though their economic standing varied widely. It is not wholly inaccurate to describe them as a class; and to search the eleventh-century evidence for the institutions, genealogies, and economic forces which conditioned its emergence.

[12] Weinrich, p. 276, *c.*1165.
[13] UB Mittelrhein ii, 54, p. 94, 1182, and Conrad of Scheyern's *Annales*, MGS, XVII, p. 630, 1184.
[14] Examples in MGC i, 441, pp. 649f., 1071, and J.M. Lappenberg, *Hamburgisches Urkundenbuch*, vol. i (2nd edn., Hamburg, 1907), 118, p. 112, 1091.
[15] UB Wirtemberg ii, 404, p. 177, 1174, Mon. Boica iii, 117, p. 303, *c.*1215, UB Osnabrück ii, 153f., pp. 113–15, 1223–4, and UB Hildesheim ii, 450, p. 212, 1236.
[16] H. Lieberich, *Landherren und Landleute. Zur politischen Führungsschicht Baierns im Spätmittelalter*, Schriftenreihe zur bayerischen Landesgeschichte, LXIII (Munich, 1964).

This approach is a difficult one because the sources are fragmentary and contradictory. Sometimes we are offered glimpses into the retinues and households, or *familiae*, to which *ministeriales* belonged. The bishopric of Bamberg provides the most illuminating example. A charter from Bishop Gunther's reign, its date about 1060, includes a brief report about the military duties and obligations of his *ministeriales*, about their hereditary fiefs, and what their legal rights were. By the mid-eleventh century, the bishops of Bamberg therefore had an unfree knightly following whose functions and status were defined, hereditary, and guaranteed.[17] But we know virtually nothing more about such rules anywhere until the twelfth century.[18]

It is in the context of retinues such as this that the norms of German knighthood must have been fashioned by the end of the eleventh century. The conditions included the military needs of the magnates, the changing techniques of open warfare and of fortification, the economic reward of fiefs, and what *ministeriales* could demand for themselves. The economic and political geography of the region in which they lived, and the relative standing of their lords, must have played their part. After 1100 the lavishly enfeoffed *ministeriales* of the imperial dynasty, or of a great prelate such as the bishop of Bamberg, were sharing a name, a type of service, and a hereditary unfree rank with the impoverished military servants of provincial magnates in the backwoods of Swabia, Bavaria, or Saxony. If these similarities permit the word 'class' to be used, contemporaries such as Abbot Ekkehard of Aura and Bishop Otto of Freising also employed the theological term *ordo* or order in a similar sense, to convey the fact that the social status of *ministeriales* was recognizable above the rules laid down for individual retinues.[19] We are warned not to confuse the language of medieval theology with social realities,[20] but the matter-of-fact use of *ordo*

[17] Jaffé, *MB*, pp. 51 f. It may have been revised by 1125 before its inclusion in the *Codex Udalrici*. On the Bamberg *ministeriales*, F. Joetze, 'Die Ministerialität im Hochstifte Bamberg', *HJ* xxxvi (1915), 516-97, 748-98, and E. von Guttenberg, *Die Territorienbildung am Obermain*, Berichte des Historischen Vereins zu Bamberg, LXXIX (Bamberg, 1927), pp. 299-358, 395-456.

[18] See Ch. 3 below.

[19] Ekkehard of Aura, pp. 184-6, 1104, and Otto and Rahewin, *Gesta Friderici*, p. 152, 1155.

[20] Brunner, *Land und Herrschaft*, pp. 398-404, L. Manz, *Der Ordo-Gedanke. Ein Beitrag zur Frage des mittelalterlichen Ständegedankens*, Beihefte zur *VSWG*, XXXIII (Stuttgart and Berlin, 1937), and G. Duby, *Les Trois Ordres ou l'imaginaire du*

ministerialium, or 'order of *ministeriales*', as a class-label became widespread in charters.[21] However, the Saxon legist Eike von Repgow still reminded his readers in the 1220s that the rules had, in theory, been dictated by each lord to his own retinue, so that 'under every bishop and abbot and abbess the *ministeriales* have different rights',[22] a manifest error.

Before turning to the intractable eleventh-century evidence, we may ask where the new *ordo* fitted into the wider structure of the German empire. In the tenth century, the East Frankish magnates maintained military retinues in the Carolingian style, nourishing their vassal *milites* in their households or upon fiefs, but very little is known of the economic or legal status of such persons. The trend towards large retinues of *ministeriales* evident by the mid eleventh century was inspired by new or newly significant events. Agrarian expansion and internal colonization were improving the position of the great lords, who could offer more fiefs in return for military services. Their administrative needs expanded with their holdings, and in the turbulent circumstances of the age, administration was inseparable from military defence. The construction of large stone castles increased the demand for competent garrisons, and violent feuds were an inescapable feature of regional and imperial politics. Expanding military retinues of enfeoffed *ministeriales* were thus promoted by economic forces at work in the German rural landscape, and by the belligerent tone of aristocratic politics. The earlier Salian age was not devoid of strife on a great scale,[23] even if the disorders in the reigns of Henry IV and Henry V, the Saxon War and the War of Investitures, seem much more imposing to us.

Parallel with all this, modern German historians have detected changes in the exercise of lordship in the eleventh and twelfth

---

féodalisme, Paris 1978, tr. by A. Goldhammer as *The Three Orders. Feudal Society Imagined* (Chicago and London, 1980).

[21] Mon. Boica xxxvii, 78, p. 40, 1131, Tr. Passau 628, p. 231, 1149-64, UB Nürnberg 70, pp. 47-9, 1163, Mon. Boica liii, 44, p. 16, 1192, and Reg. Straßburg ii, 770, 774, and 776, pp. 7f., 1209. In C. Erdmann and N. Fickermann, *Briefsammlungen der Zeit Heinrichs IV.*, MG Die Briefe der Deutschen Kaiserzeit, V (Weimar, 1950), 18, p. 211, 1063, the Bamberg *vicedominus* called Bishop Gunther's knights *ministerialis ordinis viri*, and in MGD Lothar III, 55f., pp. 87-9, 1133-4, the *de equestri ordine maiores et minores* referred to real knights.

[22] K.A. Eckhardt, *Sachsenspiegel Lehnrecht*, MG Fontes iuris Germanici antiqui, n.s. I. 2 (Göttingen, 1956), p. 82.

[23] Wipo, *Gesta Chuonradi*, pp. 32, 38-40, 43-7, 49-51.

centuries, pointing to the dynastic principalities and ecclesiastical territories of the thirteenth. This diverse process, characterized as 'the rise of territorial lordship', defies generalizations. But one could say that the magnates who wielded such power in these centuries did rely upon broadly similar methods to consolidate the future of their regional authority. Above all, they required knights in sufficient number to prosecute their feuds, to garrison their castles, and to serve the household with its widespread estates. This type of knight was the *ministerialis*, and his origins are thus connected in chronology and function to the rise of territorial lordship and the achievements of economic expansion.

In brief, the circumstances of the eleventh century both promoted the need for and provided the wherewithal to establish retinues of *ministeriales*. Obviously the impetus behind this new knighthood or *milicia*, for so the Bamberg *ministeriales* referred to themselves in 1063,[24] was the imperative pressure upon the princes to appear militarily effective. Economic expansion in their vast domains, their struggle for influence in the Salian polity, the consolidation of their regional jurisdictions, their enfeoffments of *ministeriales*, the construction of new castles, and the endowment of monasteries of which they were the secular advocates, worked together to strengthen lordship in eleventh-century Germany. Powerful as they were, the magnates may not positively have created a new armed order, like Cadmus, who sowed the soil of Thebes with dragons' teeth. But by their enfeoffments they did encourage the rise of knighthood as a social phenomenon. Otto of Freising reported of his half-brother, Duke Frederick of Swabia, that he made himself formidable in the upper Rhineland by building fortifications and by rewarding the knights who flocked into his service.[25] We must inquire further into the social matrix from which such men emerged.

Ministerialis: *the name and the man*

Since the clues to the origins of a social group such as the *ministeriales* lie in Latin charters, letters, and chronicles, the obvious approach is to follow the word back through the eleventh-century

---

[24] Erdmann and Fickermann, *Briefsammlungen*, 35, pp. 233 f., 1063.
[25] Otto and Rahewin, *Gesta Friderici*, p. 28, 1114.

and earlier sources, to ask its meaning in each case, and to weigh the evidence provided by the contexts in which it is found. Unfortunately this is a misleading exercise, for two reasons. Firstly, the label *ministerialis* only prevailed as the scribal norm over several other descriptions for the same kind of person quite late in the day, at the beginning of the twelfth century. And so we are left in the twilight as to whom precisely we should be pursuing through the eleventh-century evidence. Secondly, the word *ministerialis* already had a long history,[26] and certainly did not originate as a description for knight. It is found in late Latin as a term for an official of Roman emperors, and was used in a parallel sense by Carolingian and Ottonian scribes. In that age it referred not to legal status or military function, but simply to office, service, or *ministerium*[27] of all kinds. Bishops and counts were called *ministeriales* for this reason,[28] and though the usage was not very widespread, it persisted late, as for Emperor Otto III's faithful Count Sigibert in the 990s.[29]

Before the eleventh century, then, *ministerialis* does not refer to a knight of unfree birth, but to anyone, often of high rank, who performed an office for a monarch or prelate.[30] Louis the Pious (814-40) could therefore address a letter 'to all bishops, abbots, counts, vicars, judges, or others of our *ministeriales*'.[31] In the tenth-century Salzburg codices recording land-transfers, the scribes sometimes took the trouble to call the archbishops' *ministeriales* free men or noblemen. The chamberlain Deganbert was, for example, called *ministerialis* in 928 and free vassal in 930.[32] A late use of *ministerialis* for exalted officials of this kind occurs in the biography of Bishop Wernher of Merseburg (1063-93), whose bro-

---

[26] K. Bosl, 'Vorstufen der deutschen Königsdienstmannschaft' (1952) in *id.*, *Frühformen der Gesellschaft im mittelalterlichen Europa* (Munich and Vienna, 1964), pp. 228-76, and Niermeyer, *Lexicon*, pp. 684-7.

[27] C.E. Odegaard, *Vassi and Fideles in the Carolingian Empire*, Harvard Historical Monographs, XIX (2nd edn., Cambridge, Mass., 1972), p. 56.

[28] E.g. MGD Arnolf, 76, pp. 114f., 890 and 84, pp. 125f., 891.

[29] MGD Otto III, 180, p. 590, 995 and 248, pp. 664f., 997.

[30] For *ministeriales* serving monarchs, MGD Otto I, 26, p. 113, 940, MGD Otto II, 152, p. 172, 977 and MGD Henry II and Kunigunde, 4, p. 697, 1025-33. For *ministeriales* serving prelates, MGD Otto I, 30, p. 116, 940, MGD Otto II, 274, p. 318, 982, and MGD Conrad II, 4, p. 5, 1024.

[31] K. Zeumer, *Formulae Merowingici et Karolini Aevi*, MG Legum sectio, V (Hanover, 1886), 52, p. 325.

[32] UB Salzburg i, 35, 37f., pp. 97-100, 927-30, and see 82, p. 143, 931 for Rafolt, *ministerialis noster*, who was *quidam nobilis vir*.

ther Moricho was Henry I V's seneschal. Their parents were high-born nobility, *illustrissimi*.[33]

This broad and ancient use of *ministerialis* was dying out in the eleventh century because scribes in the German empire were using it more and more to designate knights of unfree status. The word *miles* was not proving satisfactory for this purpose because it was being used of free-born knights, that is, *liberi* or *ingenui*. In 1058, for example, Bishop Gundechar of Eichstätt visited the canons at Herrieden with a following of *milites*, all of whom were 'men of free-born condition'.[34] *Miles* was also being used of members of the great comital and princely houses, usually as a synonym for vassal.[35] Duke Magnus Billung of Saxony was called *miles* of Archbishop Adalbert of Bremen in 1066, Margrave Ernest of Austria of King Henry I V in 1074, Count Henry of Laach of Archbishop Sigewin of Cologne,[36] and so on.

How did it come about that *ministerialis* was accepted as the word for unfree knight, when previously it had been applied to counts and bishops? This can, in part, be explained because it was never the exclusive property of the exalted. Of old it referred to service-relationships and to the exercise of offices, not to any particular legal status. So the early sources also used it to depict lowly servants, as in Charlemagne's capitulary *De villis*, or in Archbishop Hincmar of Rheims' celebrated *De ordine palatii*.[37] A royal gift of lands to the archbishops of Salzburg in the tenth century included this sort of *ministerialis* amongst the appurtenances,[38] and in

[33] *Vita Wernheri Episcopi Merseburgensis*, MGS, XII, p. 245. In MGD Henry II, 440, p. 562, 1021, the county given to the bishop of Paderborn was to be administered by a *ministerialis*, probably an official in the older, wide sense. But H. Bannasch, *Das Bistum Paderborn unter den Bischöfen Rethar und Meinwerk 983-1036*, Studien und Quellen zur westfälischen Geschichte, XII (Paderborn, 1972), pp. 301-5, 309 f., 312 f., does not exclude the possibility that he might have been an unfree *ministerialis*, as in later usage.

[34] Reg. Eichstätt 221, p. 78, 1058, and see *nobilis vir* Haward, who was *miles* in Tr. Regensburg 475, p. 278, c.1043-4.

[35] For discussion of *miles* in 11th-c. Germany, J. Johrendt, 'Milites und Militia im 11. Jahrhundert in Deutschland' in A. Borst (ed.), *Das Rittertum im Mittelalter*, WF, CCCXLIX (Darmstadt, 1976), pp. 419-36.

[36] B. Schmeidler, *Adam von Bremen. Hamburgische Kirchengeschichte*, MG schol., II (3rd edn., Hanover and Leipzig, 1917), p. 192, 1066, MGD Henry IV, 271, pp. 347 f., 1074, and UB Niederrhein i, 236, p. 153, 1085.

[37] A. Boretius and V. Krause, *Capitularia Regum Francorum*, MG Legum sectio, II (2 vols, Hanover, 1883-97), i, pp. 82-91 and ii, pp. 517-30.

[38] MGD Louis the Child, 64, pp. 193-5, 908, confirmed in MGD Otto I, 32, p. 118, 940.

founding the new house of St Mary at Trier in 973, Archbishop Dietrich mentioned the menial daily services of *ministeriales* in the monastery.[39] This usage for manorial and household servants persisted into the eleventh century, and even into the twelfth.[40] In the 1020s Bishop Burchard of Worms used it in his household ordinances for prominent officials and lower servants alike.[41] In the same era, the chapter at Passau owned 'serfs in proprietary right' who served, at best, 'like *ministeriales* or bailiffs'.[42] So the word with its connotation of rendering service already reached down the social spectrum.

If the word *ministerialis* narrowed towards meaning unfree knight, a more difficult problem is that though it prevailed after 1100, it was by no means the only term employed in the eleventh and twelfth centuries. The Salian chancery was using *serviens*, *cliens*, and *minister* as well as *miles*, *servus*, and *ministerialis*.[43] If the scribes were seeking an acceptable alternative for *miles*, *ministerialis* itself was not unambiguous. All this has created great difficulties for students of the eleventh century, who have tended to conflate *milites*, *ministri*, *clientes*, and *servientes*, especially those serving the imperial dynasty, with *ministeriales*.[44]

When these labels are read in their context, usually it is fair to see *ministeriales* in the later sense behind them. Imperial *servientes* such as Nanno, presented with his lands to Archbishop Adalbert of Bremen, or Frederick, transferred into the following of Bishop Meginward of Freising, or Margrave Ernest of Austria's *serviens* Azzo, recipient of lands from Henry IV, undoubtedly fall into the right category.[45] But there are pitfalls. The *serviens* Siegfried who

[39] UB Mittelrhein i, 244, p. 299, 973.

[40] F. Tenckhoff, *Vita Meinwerci Episcopi Patherbrunnensis*, MG schol., LIX (Hanover, 1921), pp. 41 f., written in the 12th-c., UB Mainz i, 566, pp. 481 f., 1130, UB Mittelrhein i, 483, pp. 538-40, 1135, J.D. Schoepflin, *Alsatia Diplomatica*, vol. i (Mannheim, 1772), 275, pp. 225-30, c.1144. See F. von Glocke, 'Untersuchungen zur Rechts- und Sozialgeschichte der Ministerialitäten in Westfalen' in *Westfälische Forschungen*, vol. ii (Münster, 1939), pp. 214-32.

[41] MGC i, 438, pp. 639-44: preamble, ch. 29, and end of ch. 30.

[42] Tr. Passau 100, p. 86, 1013-45.

[43] For *cliens*, MGD Henry III, 92, p. 118, 1042, for *minister*, ibid. 113, p. 142, 1043, for *miles*, ibid. 210, p. 279, 1048, for *serviens*, ibid. 247 f., pp. 330-2, 1050 and for *servus*, ibid. 289, p. 392, 1052. For *ministerialis*, MGD Henry IV, 88, pp. 114 f., 1062 and 407, pp. 537 f., 1089.

[44] Bosl, *RM*, pp. 32-112.

[45] MGD Henry IV, 3, pp. 4 f., 1056, 120, p. 159, 1064 and 329, p. 432, probably 1081.

died fighting for Henry IV in the Saxon War turns out to be a count.[46] *Minister* can also be misleading, since bishops still described themselves an *ministri* in the twelfth century.[47] Nevertheless, Provost Gerhoh of Reichersberg wrote of *ministeriales* as 'knights who are called *ministri*',[48] a usage born out in contemporary charters and land-gifts.[49] *Servus* is confusing because it was simply a word for servant, and needed qualification. The Lotharingian *miles* Gislebert of Assche was called Duke Godfrey's *servus* in 1099,[50] and its occasional use for an unfree knight never died out.[51]

As we have seen, *miles* was again appropriated by the *ministerialis* of the thirteenth century,[52] but in the eleventh and twelfth it created too much confusion with free-born knights unless properly qualified. If Henry IV's seneschal, the *miles* Moricho,[53] belonged

[46] Ibid. 313 and 315, pp. 412–16, 1079.

[47] E.g. Mon. Boica xxxvii, 109–16, pp. 88–100, 1169–71 denote Bishop Herold of Würzburg *minister*.

[48] E. Sackur, *Gerhohi Praepositi Reichersbergensis Libelli Selecti*, MG Libelli de lite, III (Hanover, 1897), p. 157.

[49] UB Halberstadt i, 167, p. 138, 1133, Tr. Tegernsee 257, p. 194, 1147, O. Redlich, *Die Traditionsbücher des Hochstifts Brixen*, Acta Tirolensia, I (Innsbruck, 1886), 432, p. 151, c.1115-25 and 455, 457, pp. 160 f., 1140–7, and J. Mayerhofer, 'Codex Augiensium' in Petz, Grauert, and Mayerhofer (eds.), *Drei bayerische Traditionsbücher aus dem XII. Jahrhundert* (Munich, 1880), 35, p. 94 and 60, p. 99.

[50] *Chronicon Affligemense*, MGS, IX, p. 415.

[51] MGD Lothar III, 21, pp. 30-2, 1129, Tr. Tegernsee 360, p. 276, 1186–7, F.L. Ganshof, *Étude sur les ministériales en Flandre et en Lotharingie*, Mémoires de la Classe des Lettres de l'Académie Royale de Belgique, XX. 1, Brussels, 1926, p. 205, 1196 (Ubald of Louvignes), O. Holder-Egger, *Monumenta Erphesfurtensia saec. XII. XIII. XIV.*, MG schol., XLII (Hanover and Leipzig, 1899), pp. 286 f., 1281, Reg. Eichstätt 943, p. 292, 1282, and P. Wittmann, *Monumenta Castellana* (Munich, 1890), 244, p. 97, 1298.

[52] Further examples in UB Salzburg iii, 727, p. 245, 1218 and UB Nürnberg 839, p. 500, 1293. O. von Zallinger, *Ministeriales und Milites* (Innsbruck, 1878), claimed that, at least in the archdiocese of Salzburg, *miles* was an exclusive description for knights belonging to free lords or to *ministeriales* themselves, whereas *ministerialis* was the term for unfree knights belonging to princes and counts (p. 5). Knights belonging to *ministeriales* might indeed be called *milites*, as in UB Salzburg iii, 672, p. 177, c.1214-31 (or *ritter* as in MGC ii, 440, ch. 17, p. 607, 1256-61), but this cannot have been systematically employed in Zallinger's sense to distinguish them from *ministeriales*, because the latter were very often called *milites*, as were free knights, in the 11th-13th cc. For this reason *miles* was often avoided for knights belonging to *ministeriales* in that archdiocese, and some other circumlocution was used instead; see UB Salzburg iv, 33, pp. 30 f., 1255 for *personae de genere militari*, *Annales Sancti Rudberti Salisburgenses*, MGS, IX, p. 796, 1262 for *militares minores*, and MGC III, 289 f., pp. 293 f., 1273-81 for *condicio et gener militaris* beneath *de puro ministerialium genere*.

[53] MGD Henry IV, 213, pp. 271 f., probably 1068.

to a distinguished aristocratic house, Conrad III's *miles* Baldwin, benefactor of Weissenohe monastery in 1140, was a *ministerialis*,[54] and so, for example, was Margrave Berthold of Istria's *miles* Hartung of Nordhof, mentioned in the 1170s.[55] Some twelfth-century scribes avoided ambiguity by such devices as *proprius miles* or *miles ministerialis*.[56]

Other trial words had less luck than *serviens* or *minister*. *Cliens* had quite a long run,[57] but was in principle a synonym for vassal, who might be high-born.[58] Though *servitor* occurred from time to time, as for the abbot of Tegernsee's distinguished *ministerialis* Richer of Schaftlach,[59] its sense was too menial. The abbot of Echternach's *servitores*, for example, worked by the day in the monastic kitchen, bakery, mill, and laundry, and guarded the doors.[60] Nevertheless, in the 1120s Arnold of Dünzling was called *servitor* of St Emmeram Abbey at Regensburg, and the head of his kindred, Gebolf, was 'amongst the first *ministeriales* of this church'.[61]

Perhaps the strongest scribal contender with *ministerialis* was *serviens*, but there exist cases where successive charters, mentioning the same persons or families over the decades, show how *serviens* was ousted. Notable men serving Henry III and Henry IV, such as Rafold of Schönberg in Bavaria, Otnand of Eschenau in Franconia, and Cuno of Arnsburg in the Rhineland, were called *ser-*

[54] MGD Conrad III, 50, p. 84, 1140.

[55] Tr. Tegernsee 332, pp. 252 f., 1173-80. Another Bavarian knight, Adalbert of Eitting, was also called *miles* and *ministerialis*; Tr. Regensburg 827, pp. 395 f., c.1147 and 979, p. 497, c.1185.

[56] UB Salzburg ii, 202, pp. 294-6, 1141, F.H. Graf Hundt, *Das Cartular des Klosters Ebersberg*, Abhandlungen der historischen Classe der Akademie der Wissenschaften, XIV. 3 (Munich, 1879), 75B, p. 176, c.1165, E. Noichl, *Codex Falkensteinensis. Die Rechtsaufzeichnungen der Grafen von Falkenstein*, QE, XXIX (Munich, 1978), 4, pp. 9 f., 79, pp. 49 f., 1166, and the twelfth-century *Miracula Sancti Bernwardi*, MGS, IV, pp. 783 f.

[57] It was used in the Würzburg chancery, Mon. Boica xlv, 1, p. 4, 1099 and xxxvii, 79, p. 42, 1131, and see Duke Henry the Lion's *cliens proprius* Dietwin of Seemannshausen in O. Haendle, *Die Dienstmannen Heinrichs des Löwen*, Arbeiten zur deutschen Rechts- und Verfassungsgeschichte, VIII (Stuttgart, 1930), p. 55.

[58] Tr. Tegernsee 44, pp. 35 f., 1042-6, 68, p. 54, 1048-68, and 143, p. 110, 1092-1113.

[59] Ibid. 114 f., pp. 89 ff., 1091, 120, pp. 93 f., 1092-1113, 170, p. 135, 1121-6, and 188, pp. 150 f., 1126-7.

[60] Weinrich, p. 162, 1095.

[61] Tr. Regensburg 766, p. 356, c.1120-6, and 774, p. 362, c.1126-9. Much later, in Mon. Boica xlix, 326, p. 502, 1303, the bishop of Eichstätt's *ministeriales* were still called *servitores*.

vientes,[62] but in the twelfth century their descendants were called *ministeriales* of the kingdom.[63]

Individual cases are borne out by general examples in which *ministerialis* can be shown to lie behind other terms. A dorsal note upon Henry I Vs 1064 grant to Einsiedeln, added before 1100, reads 'Precept of Emperor Henry about the *ministeriales*', who, in the text itself, are called the abbot of Einsiedeln's *ministri* and the abbot of St Gallen's *servientes*.[64] When the Gregorian archbishop Gebhard of Salzburg was restored to his see in 1086 with the military assistance of his knights, the twelfth-century historians of the event variously call them *milites*, *servitores*, and *ministeriales*.[65] When Count Sigehard of Burghausen was assassinated in 1104 at Regensburg by *ministeriales*, the sources describe them as *clientes*, *ministri*, and *milites regis*, as well as *ministeriales*.[66] Early in the twelfth century the imperial *ministeriales* at Weissenburg in Franconia were called *clientes* and *servitores*,[67] and the codex from Oberalteich in Bavaria recording gifts to the monastery spoke of 'worthy knights, all of them *servientes*'.[68] In writing about the household of his monastery in the 1130s, Ortlieb of Zwiefalten employed the expression, 'the men whom we call *clientes* or *ministeriales*'.[69] Other twelfth-century monks, busy preparing forged imperial privileges for their houses, provided the same kind of comparative information: at Reichenau 'sons of the church or *domestici* [household knights] that is *ministeriales*', at Ottobeuren, '*militares*

[62] MGD Henry III, 261, pp. 347f., 1051, and MGD Henry IV, 21, p. 26, 1057, 198, pp. 255f., 1067, and 318, pp. 418f., 1079.
[63] MGD Conrad III, 49, pp. 82f., 1140, 53, pp. 89f., 1140, and 202, pp. 365-7, 1149. The Hagen-Arnsburg family is traced through MGD Henry IV, 137, p. 179, 1064 and UB Mainz i, 386, pp. 293f., 1093, and see Bosl, *RM*, pp. 64-70, W.-A. Kropat, *Reich, Adel und Kirche in der Wetterau von der Karolinger bis zur Stauferzeit*, Schriften des Hessischen Landesamts für geschichtliche Landeskunde, XXVIII (Marburg, 1965), pp. 76-80, and M. Schalles-Fischer, *Pfalz und Fiskus Frankfurt*, Veröffentlichungen des Max-Planck-Instituts für Geschichte, XX (Göttingen, 1969), pp. 360-73.
[64] MGD Henry IV, 125, pp. 163f., 1064, and Tr. Passau 181, p. 115, 1090-1120 uses for knights of the same lord, *ministerialis comitis*, *miles comitis*, and *servientes comitis*.
[65] *Gesta Archiepiscoporum Salisburgensium*, MGS, XI, p. 26, *Vita Gebehardi et Successorum eius*, MGS, XI, p. 39, and *Annales Admuntenses*, MGS, IX, p. 576.
[66] G. Meyer von Knonau, *Jahrbücher des Deutschen Reiches unter Heinrich IV. und Heinrich V.* (7 vols., Leipzig, 1890-1909) vol. v, pp. 195-8 and n. 3.
[67] MGD Conrad II, 140, pp. 188-91, early 12th-c. source dated to 1029.
[68] Mon. Boica xii, p. 16, 1104.
[69] *Ortliebi Zwifaltensis Chronicon*, MGS, X, p. 78.

otherwise called *ministeriales'*, and at Rott, *'viri militares* who are called *ministeriales'*.[70] *Vir militaris* or 'military vassal' was another expression which proved too imprecise, because it also applied to the high-born free nobility,[71] yet, in the thirteenth century, *ministeriales* were again quite often called *homines militares*.[72]

If scribal alternatives to *ministerialis* were on the wane after 1100, some writers were conservative in their terminology.[73] In his late-twelfth century chronicle of the county of Hainault, Gislebert of Mons frequently used the expressions *servientes* and *clientes*.[74] A variable terminology survived much longer in Saxony than in the Rhineland or the south of Germany. In the thirteenth century, the knights of the bishops of Hildesheim and Halberstadt, for example, were called *servientes*, *servi*, *famuli*, or *servi militares*, as well as *milites* and *ministeriales*.[75] The bishops of Osnabrück's knights of Warendorp were also called *ministeriales*, *milites*, *servi*, and *famuli* or servants, indiscriminately.[76] Even the mighty lineage of Wolfenbüttel-Asseburg, who served the empire and the duchy of Brunswick as seneschals and marshals, were quite often called *famuli*.[77]

---

[70] MGC i, 447, p. 662 and MGD Charlemagne, 219, pp. 292-4, dated 769, but both mid 12th c., and MGD Henry IV, 263, pp. 336-8, dated 1073, but really 1179-1226. See also C. Mohr, *Die Traditionen des Klosters Oberaltteich*, QE, XXX (Munich, 1979), 68, pp. 138-40, 1147 for *militaris vir* Gozpert of Harthof, Count Frederick's *ministerialis*.

[71] Ekkehard of Aura, p. 146, 1099, and G. Waitz, *Chronica Regia Coloniensis. Annales Maximi Colonienses*, MG schol., XVIII (Hanover, 1880), p. 50, 1111.

[72] Mon. Boica xxxvii, 221, pp. 235-7, 1230, CD Salem 187, pp. 217f., 1237, and UB Krain ii, 205f., pp. 163-6, 1254.

[73] E.g. *serviens* in MGC i, 302, pp. 426-8, 1185 and in P. Acht, 'Unbekannte Fragmente Prüfeninger Traditionen des 12. Jahrhunderts. Eine Traditionsnotiz Kaiser Friedrichs I.', *MIöG* lxxviii (1970), 236-49.

[74] Gislebert of Mons, especially p. 103, n. 5. Informative on terminology is G. Waitz, *Deutsche Verfassungsgeschichte*, V, ed. K. Zeumer, 2nd edn. (Berlin, 1893), pp. 486-508, and for discussions on how the words were used in the poetic literature, J. Bumke, *Studien zum Ritterbegriff im 12. und 13. Jahrhundert*, Beihefte zum Euphorion, I (Heidelberg, 1964), now in translation by W.T.H. and Erika Jackson, *The Concept of Knighthood in the Middle Ages*, AMS Studies in the Middle Ages, II (New York, 1982), and H.G. Reuter, *Die Lehre vom Ritterstand*, Neue Wirtschaftsgeschichte, IV (Cologne and Vienna, 1971).

[75] UB Hildesheim i, 691, p. 660, 1216-17 and 767, p. 719, 1221, and ii, 416, pp. 195-7, 1235, 452, pp. 213f., 1236, 579, p. 288, 1240, and 947, pp. 474f., 1254, and UB Halberstadt ii, 708, p. 33, 1242, 997, p. 224, 1259, and 1028, pp. 247f., 1261.

[76] UB Osnabrück ii, 218, p. 167, 1227, iii, 486, p. 337, 1273 and 615, p. 434, 1278, and iv, 326, p. 211, 1291.

[77] UB Asseburg i, 378, p. 250, 1275, 446f., pp. 287f., 1289, and 493, p. 313, 1297.

In spite of the uncertainties and contradictions of the early sources and their wording, they do bear witness to the incipient knighthood which is more fully documented in the Hohenstaufen era. After all, the various terms often occur in military contexts, or are applied to men receiving substantial rewards of land, both fief and allod, in exchange for their fidelity and service. Henry III's charter of 1050 granting lands at Rohrbach to his *serviens* and chamberlain Obbert flourished the ethos of knighthood: 'Whoever of our knights and *servientes* serves us faithfully and strenuously will receive from us a sure reward.'[78] Obviously such a man had nothing in common with the monastic *servientes* found, for example, at St Maximin at Trier, who worked as serfs, bakers, cowherds, cooks, and launderers.[79] As *ministerialis* became the ascendant scribal word, the vernacular found its equivalent in *dienestman*,[80] which contained the essential meaning of service, like the Anglo-Saxon equivalent, *cniht* or knight. The royal chancery mentioned 'those who are called *dienestman* in German', and in Conrad III's time this was, in turn, latinized as *dienismanni*.[81]

Institutional and genealogical antecedents of the ministeriales *of 1100*

Discussion of these words and their changing usage does not in itself tell us very much about the emergence of the *ministeriales* as a professional order in Germany. Chronologically the eleventh century was crucial, because the sources are beginning to reveal them as a social group with recognized and hereditary functions, as at Bamberg. The question of origins is controversial because the surviving evidence is too thin to provide very satisfactory answers. Scholars in Germany have employed different, if related, approaches. Firstly, they have looked at antecedents stretching back to the Carolingian age for institutional realities which might have determined the emergence of the *ministeriales* as a social order. This approach employs source-material on Carolingian and Ottonian *familiae* or households or retinues which might yield

[78] MGD Henry III, 247, pp. 330 f., 1050.
[79] Ibid. 372 B, p. 512, c.1050, rewritten by c.1116.
[80] E.g. Eppo *dinstman* in B. Uhl, *Die Traditionen des Klosters Weihenstephan*, QE, XXVII. 1 (Munich, 1972), 289, pp. 233 f., 1165-8. For variant spellings in vernacular literature, see Bumke, *Studien*, ch. 4.
[81] UB Mainz i, 459, p. 367, 1114, and MGD Conrad III, 68, p. 121, 1142.

information about persons of unfree status who either fought for their lords, or administered their seigneurial patrimonies as officials. Secondly, they have looked for more direct genealogical origins, seeking the human forebears of *ministeriales* somewhere in the varied social terminology of the ninth to the eleventh centuries.

One drawback to both these approaches is that *ministeriales*' unfree status and knightly function about 1100 were not very much like the realities of the ninth and tenth centuries. Economic, political, and military opportunities changed greatly in the eleventh century, and it was these that promoted the *ministeriales* as the new knighthood of Germany. There were, of course, technical similarities relating to the maintenance of military retinues common to the whole medieval period. The precedent for endowing *ministeriales* with a hereditary economic base of fiefs does go back to the Carolingians, when vassals were given fiefs in exchange for services. Surviving the economic recession of the fourteenth century, the method still governed the relationship of magnates and knights in many parts of fifteenth-century Germany. In this sense the function and status of *ministeriales* can fairly be compared with similar situations as far back as the eighth century. But the *ministeriales* as such cannot unequivocally be derived from any of them.

The search for institutional antecedents has tended to project backwards to the ninth century a concept of *ministeriales*' service which then slowly came to fruition in the eleventh. This creates a fundamental confusion in eliding the rise of knighthood as a new social phenomenon in eleventh-century feudal Europe, including the German empire. It is, nevertheless, worth reviewing the early material, because it leaves the impression that magnates were familiar with fitting out unfree dependents as cavalrymen on a temporary or permanent basis.

Carolingian sources reveal that persons of unfree status called *fiscalini, coloni, caballarii, ecclesiastici,* and *servi* did service as cavalry, and that some of them had fiefs.[82] Tenth-century sources imply that, in East Francia, military tasks were performed by similar ranks, such as the *hiltischalken* in Bavaria, and the *liberti* and *iamundilingi* in Saxony,[83] but it is not certain if they fought as

[82] Boretius, *Capitularia* i, 25, pp. 66 f., 792-3, 49, pp. 135 f., 806-7, and 75, p. 168, 804-11.

[83] P. Dollinger, *L'Évolution des classes rurales en Bavière*, Publications de la Faculté des lettres de l'Université de Strasbourg, CXII (Paris, 1949), pp. 290 f. (and MGD

cavalry. Nor is it clear how to distinguish them from other vassals and *milites* who were low in the social scale, such as the abbot of Corvey's 'vassals of inferior condition', or the bishop of Halberstadt's *milites servi*.[84] Other sources, stretching from the ninth to the eleventh centuries, imply military services rendered to prelates by *tributarii* at Constance, *fiscalini servi* at Worms, *clientes* at Petershausen, *scaremanni* at Trier and Prüm, and *equites* at Regensburg.[85] We are told that the *servientes* 'whom we call *scaremanni*' were expected, like other members of his retinue, to fight as knights for the abbot of St Maximin at Trier. If these *scaremanni* look like embryonic *ministeriales*, the rest of the monastery's *servientes* and *scaremanni* do not.[86] In the twelfth century St Maximin still possessed *ministri vel scaremanni* who were distinct from the other *ministeriales* of the abbey.[87]

In the 1030s it was customary for the abbot of Limburg's *laszi* at Sulzbach, if they had fiefs, to ride daily wherever the abbot might command, presumably as escorts and messengers, as a service alternative to carting wine and grain as far as the Peacock Gate of Worms. The abbot also possessed the authority to promote his men into *milites* or household officials if he gave them fiefs, apparently upon a temporary basis.[88] When Bosonville was founded by the counts of Alsace in 1033, some members of the abbot's *familia* were similarly beneficed in order to render service on horseback. They were called *servientes*.[89] When Archbishop Anno of Cologne founded Siegburg in 1075, he specified that the abbot might promote *famuli aecclesiae*, or servants of his church,

---

Louis the Child, 28, p. 139, 903 for the *hengistfuotri* there). For Saxony, MGD Otto I, 11, pp. 98 f., 937.

[84] MGD Arnolf, 3, pp. 5–8, 887, with later additions, and MGD Otto III, 104, pp. 515 f., 992.

[85] Zeumer, *Formulae*, 36, p. 419, MGD Arnolf, 158, pp. 239 f., 897, *Vita Gebehardi Episcopi Constantiensis*, MGS, X, p. 588, 993, E. Wisplinghoff, 'Königsfreie und Scharmannen', *Rheinische Vierteljahrsblätter* xxviii (1963), 200–17, and Dollinger, *L'Évolution*, pp. 290, 504 f., and 508.

[86] UB Mittelrhein i, 382, p. 439, 1082–4, and MGD Henry III, 372, pp. 505–13, 1056–1116.

[87] UB Mittelrhein i, 583, pp. 538–40, 1135. Prüm Abbey's humbler 'scararii, id est ministeriales et haistaldi' were mentioned by Ex-Abbot Caesarius, ibid. ii, 135, p. 145, n. 3, 1222, and see p. 32, n. 40 above.

[88] MGD Conrad II, 216, pp. 294–6, 1035.

[89] *Notitiae Fundationis Monasterii Bosonis-Villae*, MGS, XV. 2, pp. 979 f., 1033–43.

into knights, and a later scribal revision of the text assumes that they were *ministeriales*.[90] These monastic examples can be taken to reveal ways in which the Church recruited *ministeriales* in the eleventh century.

Analogies have been drawn between the administrative offices exercised later by *ministeriales* and the employment in the tenth and eleventh centuries of seigneurial dependents in the running of estates and households.[91] In the rules which Bishop Burchard of Worms drew up for his retinue, he envisaged promoting *fiscalini* into the household offices of chamberlain, butler, seneschal, or constable.[92] This parallels the abbot of Limburg's option of appointing dependents as butlers or seneschals. At Weissenburg in Alsace it was affirmed in 1102 that 'the abbot might promote anyone from the *familia* of that place into enfeoffed *servientes*', and this was rewritten within a few years as 'he may promote into the order and rights of *ministeriales*'.[93]

Evidence from Bavaria shows, however, that such appointments were not always leading their beneficiaries towards the rank of *ministerialis*. Bishop Abraham of Freising (957-94) conferred hereditary, enfeoffed household offices upon the offspring of noblewomen who had voluntarily surrendered their personal freedom to become *censuales* of his church, arrangements confirmed for their descendants in the eleventh century.[94] Some time later, when *servi* were promoted into officials by the abbot of St Emmeram, they were merely guaranteed exemption from paying head-taxes, but nothing was said of their entering the order of *ministeriales*.[95]

These examples show that unfree dependents with fiefs to support them did indeed carry out military or administrative functions for their lords. But they hardly add up to a structure upon which the knighthood of the later eleventh and twelfth centuries could be based. Rather, the model for *ministeriales* was vassalage, as the

[90] E. Wisplinghoff, *Urkunden und Quellen zur Geschichte von Stadt und Abtei Siegburg*, vol. i (Siegburg, 1964), 8, pp. 12-16, 1075, and 95, pp. 198-201, 1223.

[91] Dollinger, *L'Évolution*, pp. 288f., Kluckhohn, pp. 16f., and Stimming, *Das deutsche Königsgut*, pp. 57-65.

[92] MGC i, 438, ch. 29, p. 643, 1023-25.

[93] MGD Henry IV, 473, pp. 642-4, 1102, and the forged MGD Regum Francorum i, 31, pp. 149f.

[94] T. Bitterauf, *Die Traditionen des Hochstifts Freising*, vol. ii, QE, V (Munich, 1909), 1226A, B, pp. 136f., 972-6, and 1458A, p. 311, 1047-53, and Störmer, *Früher Adel*, pp. 76f.

[95] Tr. Regensburg, 675, pp. 327f., c.1090-5, and 835, pp. 401f., 1148.

Bamberg code from the 1060s already showed: compurgation with the assistance of equals, hereditary fiefs in exchange for military service in Italy as well as north of the Alps, and the right to take up only the honourable household offices of seneschal, butler, chamberlain, marshal, and forester.[96]

Genealogical origins

The quest for genealogical origins has been pursued with greater vigour. Some scholars have preferred to derive the *ministeriales* from the free social classes of the ninth, tenth, or eleventh centuries. But the majority, impressed by their servile status, derive their descent from the unfree.[97] These speculations founder upon the inconclusive nature of the evidence. There are, in any case, difficulties in making clear distinctions between free and unfree social groups in medieval Germany.[98] We know, for example, a

[96] See p. 27, n. 17.
[97] The principal proponents of 'free' origins have been W. Wittich, 'Altfreiheit und Dienstbarkeit des Uradels in Niedersachsen', *VSWG* iv (1906), 1–127, P. Heck, 'Die Ursprung der sächsischen Dienstmannschaft', *VSWG* v (1907), 116–72, G. Caro, 'Zur Ministerialenfrage' in *Nova Turicensia. Beiträge zur schweizerischen und zürcherischen Geschichte* (Zürich, 1911), pp. 77–101, E.F. Otto, *Adel und Freiheit im deutschen Staat des frühen Mittelalters*, Neue deutsche Forschungen, CXXX (Berlin, 1937), and H. Dannenbauer, 'Königsfreie und Ministerialen' in his *Grundlagen der mittelalterlichen Welt* (Stuttgart, 1958), pp. 329–53. The following have defended 'unfree' origins: F. Keutgen, 'Die Entstehung der deutschen Ministerialität', *VSWG* viii (1910), 1–16, 169–95, 481–547, Kluckhohn, pp. 16–23, Stimming, *Das deutsche Königsgut*, pp. 57 ff., Ganshof, *Étude*, pp. 31–69, E. E. Stengel, 'Über den Ursprung der Ministerialität' in *Papsttum und Kaisertum. Festschrift für Paul Kehr* (Munich, 1926), pp. 168–84, U. Stutz, 'Zum Ursprung und Wesen des niederen Adels', *Sitzungsberichte der Preußischen Akademie der Wissenschaften*, Phil.-hist. Klasse, XXVII (Berlin, 1937), pp. 213–57, Dollinger, *L'Évolution*, pp. 289–92, Bosl, *RM*, pp. 25–73, supported by his 'Über soziale Mobilität in der mittelalterlichen Gesellschaft. Dienst, Freiheit, Freizügigkeit als Motive sozialen Aufstiegs' in *id.*, *Frühformen*, pp. 156–79, and 'Die Familia als Grundstruktur der Mittelalterlichen Gesellschaft', *ZBLG* xxxviii (1975), 403–24, J.-P. Ritter, *Ministérialité et chevalerie. Dignité humaine et liberté dans le droit médiéval* (Lausanne, 1955), pp. 19–25, and a good summary in J.B. Freed, 'The Origins of the European Nobility: The Problem of the Ministerials', *Viator* vii (1976), 211–41.
[98] On *liberi* Niermeyer, *Lexicon*, p. 607, abandoned hope: 'Nous renonçons à tout essai d'analyse ...' For Germany, see Dollinger, *L'Évolution*, pp. 311–82, Ritter, pp. 35–80, T. Mayer, 'Die Entstehung des modernen Staates im Mittelalter und die freien Bauern', *ZRGGA* lvii (1937), 210–88, 'Königtum und Gemeinfreiheit im frühen Mittelalter' in *id. Mittelalterliche Studien* (Lindau and Constance, 1959), pp. 139–63, and the essays edited by him, *Das Problem der Freiheit in der deutschen und schweizerischen Geschichte* VF, II (Lindau and Constance, 1955), I. Bog, 'Dorfgemeinde, Freiheit und Unfreiheit in Franken. Studien zur Geschichte der fränkischen

number of cases where *censuales* changed their status and became *ministeriales*.[99] But *censuales* were described both as free and unfree; free because they were not bound by any hereditary calling or services, place of residence, or restrictions upon contracting marriages, but unfree because they and their descendants owed an annual tribute or head-tax to their lords.[100]

There are a number of clearly attested cases where *liberi* or *ingenui*, the foremost technical terms for persons of free status, did become *ministeriales*.[101] In practice this change may not have seemed very striking, since the obligations imposed upon *ministeriales* resembled the rules of vassalage for knightly *liberi*. It might mark the knight's entry into a new retinue, or be a device for acquiring new fiefs,[102] or for placing allodial inheritances under the protection of powerful lords by receiving them back as fiefs.[103] Examples have also been preserved of *ministeriales* who were created out of unfree social categories with such labels as *mancipia*, *liti, famuli, fiscalini, homines proprii*, and *mansionarii*.[104] Here there is also difficulty in discerning what kind of restrictions, or indeed freedoms, were given up in favour of the new status. We know, for example, that the imperial *fiscalini* at Zürich enjoyed favourable

Agrarverfassung', *Jahrbücher für Nationalökonomie und Statistik* clxviii (1956), 1-80, relevant sources in Weinrich, pp. 70-2, 114-18, 278-86, and see p. 55, n. 8 below.

[99] Examples in UB Mainz i, 546, pp. 453f., 1127, UB Wirtemberg ii, 386, p. 151, 1166, and H. Kelleter, *Urkundenbuch des Stiftes Kaiserswerth*, Urkundenbücher der geistlichen Stiftungen des Niederrheins, I (Bonn, 1904), 44, pp. 59-61, 1249.

[100] For *censuales*, K. Schulz, 'Zum Problem der Zensualität im Hochmittelalter' in *Beiträge zur Wirtschafts- und Sozialgeschichte des Mittelalters. Festschrift für Herbert Helbig* (Cologne and Vienna, 1976), pp. 86-127, Reimann, pp. 44-53, and pp. 57f., nn. 19-22 below.

[101] Examples in Tr. Regensburg 804, p. 380, 1141, N. Kindlinger, *Geschichte der deutschen Hörigkeit mit Urkunden* (Berlin, 1819), 13, pp. 241f., 1170, and *Annales Stederburgenses*, MGS, XVI, p. 217, before 1180.

[102] UB Hildesheim i, 274, p. 256, 1151, and Kluckhohn, p. 36.

[103] CD Westphalia i, 192, p. 150, 1123.

[104] For *mancipia*, M. Thiel, *Die Traditionen, Urkunden und Urbare des Klosters Weltenburg*, QE, XIV (Munich, 1958), 91, pp. 63f., and 101, p. 71, 1128-35, UB Land ob der Enns i, 271, p. 711, c.1130, UB Hildesheim i, 236, pp. 215f., 1145, and UB Mainz ii, 261, pp. 467f., 1151-60. For *liti*, W. Crecelius, *Traditiones Werdinenses*, vol. ii, Collectae, III. B (Berlin, 1870), 124, p. 21, 1066-81, and UB Hildesheim ii, 249, p. 109, 1227. For *famuli*, UB Mainz i, 592, pp. 508f., 1134. For *fiscalini*, J. Escher and P. Schweizer, *Urkundenbuch der Stadt und Landschaft Zürich*, vol. i (Zürich, 1888-90), 388, pp. 273f., 1219. For *homines proprii*, Reg. Eichstätt 328, p. 106, 1129 and Mon. Boica xxxvii, 89, pp. 55f., 1140 or later (and Reimann, p. 12 n. 80). For *mansionarii*, UB Hildesheim i, 151, p. 143, 1093. Converted Jews at Cologne became *ministeriales*; UB Niederrhein i, 359, p. 246, 1147.

terms which included freedom of choice in marriage,[105] a privilege
enjoyed neither by *ministeriales* nor by serfs.

These individual transfers from a previously free or unfree status
are not very numerous in the charter evidence. In terms of human
material, therefore, we cannot really know how the retinues of
ministeriales were being recruited. But there is more which can be
inferred from evidence less specific than such charters. In a letter
of 1147 to Abbot Wibald of Corvey, Conrad III confirmed that
'the abbot may transfer them [free men] into the property of his
church as *ministeriales* and also has the power to make *ministeriales*
from the lower orders, that is, of *liti* or *censuarii*',[106] a nice balance
between the rival modern theories on genealogical origins. The
king's letter clearly confirms the trend of events indicated by the
charters recording transfers of status, and there survives an example from Corvey which bears out Conrad III's statement in practice. In 1106 two brothers who were free men gave themselves and
their considerable property at Eilenstedt to the abbot,[107] and were
very likely the progenitors of the Eilenstedt family of *ministeriales*
later prominent in another retinue, as butlers of the bishops of
Halberstadt.

It is also possible to ascertain the shift from free man to *ministerialis* in the changing composition of witness-lists to the charters
of a given region, although this can be unrewarding and inconclusive work. But dynastic toponymics in witness-lists do move into
the category of *ministerialis*, showing that the families in question
had abandoned their status as *liberi*. In some cases this must have
come about through the lords' insistence in exchange for new or
renewed titles to fiefs and offices, in others, because free men
married women who were *ministeriales*, and their children, according to German custom, would automatically inherit their mothers'

[105] Escher and Schweizer, *Zürich*, 259, pp. 143 f., 1114 and MGD Lothar III, 23,
p. 34, 1130. Since the *Chronicon Ebersheimense*, MGS, XXIII, p. 432, claims that
the German *milites* were called *fiscales regni et ministeriales principum*, and Frederick
Barbarossa confirmed that Strasburg *servientes* were exempt *iure fiscali*, MGD Frederick I, 133, pp. 223-5, 1156, this may indicate that *fiscalini* in Alsace had become
ministeriales, as at Zürich.

[106] MGD Conrad III, 181, p. 328, 1147. There is very little information about
Corvey *ministeriales* before Abbot Wibald's time; H.H. Kaminsky, *Studien zur
Reichsabtei Corvey in der Salierzeit*, Abhandlungen zur Corveyer Geschichtsschrei-
bung, IV (Cologne and Graz, 1972), pp. 171-3.

[107] UB Halberstadt i, 123, pp. 85 f., 1106.

status.[108] Sometimes the regional witness-lists can show a substantial shift from free rank to that of *ministerialis*. The Bavarian diocese of Eichstätt provides an example,[109] although in this respect it went contrary to the trend in other Bavarian bishoprics such as Freising and Salzburg.[110]

Entry into the order of ministeriales: *the later eleventh and twelfth centuries*

If the conclusions which can reliably be drawn from the early genealogical and institutional information are quite limited, the quality and variety of evidence improves towards 1100, and more can be gleaned about the circumstances under which *ministeriales* were being recruited and enfeoffed as knights. The Bamberg custumal of the 1060s already revealed the bishop's *ministeriales* as a military and administrative élite with hereditary rights, and later, when Bishop Otto (1102-39) put up several new castles to protect the temporalities of the see, he installed *ministeriales* as hereditary castellans, who took their family names from the castles.[111] Castle-building and the enfeoffment of *ministeriales* went hand in hand, and so did the recruitment of talented men as household officers. In 1127 the provost of Aschaffenburg promoted two *censuales* into *ministeriales* as hereditary butler and marshal of his household.[112] After a commission of inquiry, Provost Conrad of Mariengreden at Mainz was permitted to place Gernod of Osterhofen in one of his household offices and to give him the status of *ministerialis*, over the objections of his advocate.[113] The bishops of Würzburg were also acquiring men from the neighbouring lords, to place them specifically as butlers, seneschals, or marshals.[114] Pro-

[108] Bitterauf, *Freising*, 1711, pp. 512 f., 1123-30, and Ch. 6 below.
[109] My unpublished thesis, '*Ministeriales* and the Development of Territorial Lordship in the Eichstätt Region, 1100-1350' (Oxford, 1972), pp. 133-5.
[110] G. Flohrschütz, 'Die Freisinger Dienstmannen im 10. und 11. Jahrhundert', *Beiträge zur altbayerischen Kirchengeschichte* xxv (1967), 9-79, and J.B. Freed, 'The Formation of the Salzburg Ministerialage in the Tenth and Eleventh Centuries: An Example of Upward Social Mobility in the Early Middle Ages', *Viator* ix (1978), 67-102.
[111] *Herbordi Vita Ottonis Episcopi Babenbergensis*, MGS, XII, p. 766, and Joetze, pp. 776, 779 f.
[112] UB Mainz i, 546, p. 454, 1127.
[113] Ibid. ii, 264, pp. 470-2, 1155-62.
[114] Mon. Boica xlv, 16, pp. 31 f., 1169, and xxxvii, 146, pp. 138-40, 1189, 178, pp. 181 f., 1211, and 221, pp. 235-7, 1230.

motion of officials persisted late. In the thirteenth century, the bishops of Münster transferred the bailiff at Beckum and the justice at Königinhof, with their families, into their retinue of *ministeriales*.[115]

Men were prepared to offer cash or land or services for the rank of *ministerialis*, to assist their way out of their previous condition.[116] Three *mancipia* given to the abbot of Prüfening in Bavaria in the late twelfth century as *censuales* were given the option after three or four years of becoming his *ministeriales* on paying a suitable fee for the privilege.[117] In 1095 a *servus* of the abbot of St Trond in Lotharingia was offered a similar option. Having married a free woman, he settled his children's status by submitting them to the abbot as *censuales*, more or less a compromise between his own and his wife's degrees. In return, they were re-enfeoffed with their lands at Halmael, which they would hold for nothing should they choose to offer military service. Later they did take up the option and, after some argument, became *ministeriales* and knights of St Trond.[118]

If service and standing as *ministeriales* were attractive, not all lords were well enough endowed to enfeoff them properly. In 1134 the abbot of St Peter at Erfurt was fortunate in that the aristocratic donor of *famuli* also gave substantial lands and the seigneurial appurtenances, including serfs, so that the men could be established as *ministeriales* with hereditary fiefs.[119] The lure of fiefs was a powerful one. Before 1095, for example, the widow of a *ministerialis* belonging to one of the monasteries at Trier, but herself a free woman, was married again to a *liber*. Yet she persuaded her children by this marriage to become *ministeriales*, to qualify for her first husband's fiefs.[120]

[115] UB Münster 348, pp. 188 f., 1238, and 820, pp. 425 f., 1268.
[116] Mon. Boica ii, 17, p. 287, c.1135, and UB Hildesheim ii, 301, p. 139, c.1230.
[117] Mon. Boica xiii, 92, pp. 78 f., late 12th c.
[118] C. Piot, *Cartulaire de l'abbaye de Saint-Trond* i, Collection de chroniques belges inédites (Brussels, 1870), 21, p. 28, 1095, C. de Borman, *Chronique de l'abbaye de Saint-Trond*, Publications de la Société des bibliophiles liégeois, X and XV (Liège, 1877), i, p. 147, before 1138, and E. Linck, *Sozialer Wandel in klösterlichen Grundherrschaften des 11. bis 13. Jahrhunderts. Studien zu den familiae von Gembloux, Stablo-Malmedy und St Trond*, Veröffentlichungen des Max-Planck-Instituts für Geschichte, LVII (Göttingen, 1979), p. 167.
[119] UB Mainz i, 592, pp. 508 f., 1134, and a similar case in Tr. Passau 120, p. 97, 1121–38.
[120] UB Mittelrhein i, 389, p. 446, 1095.

The magnates sometimes found in the rank of *ministerialis* a useful solution to their peccadilloes, and new knightly families were established. The sons of a Swabian count Cuono by his mistress Bertha, an unfree woman belonging to the counts of Dillingen, fell into the latter's possession as *ministeriales* upon their father's death. They were 'most formidable in all military matters and spirited beyond measure', which qualified one of them as a close confidant of Henry IV.[121] The *ministeriales* and marshals of Menach, a substantial family in Bavaria, were descended from the powerful Count Adalbert of Bogen's illegitimate son Rudolf.[122] In another case, a nobleman called Wolfolt of Guntersberg formed a liaison with a woman belonging to the abbey of St Emmeram, and their children's future was settled by turning them over as the abbot's *ministeriales*.[123]

Some final examples illustrate further effects that the transfers of status were having in the twelfth century. At Salzburg before 1147, *censuales* were seeking, without success, to usurp the position of *ministerialis* to escape payment of their head-tax.[124] In other cases, *ministeriales* were able to prove that their conversion from *censuales* had been legitimate,[125] yet there were some who preferred to revert to paying head-tax.[126] In compensation for their oppression by an unjust advocate, the abbot of St Emmeram at Regensburg granted the rank of *ministerialis* in the 1120s to four of his serfs.[127] The result of this and similar manœuvres was that some families might persist in more than one status. Near Regensburg the Dünzlings included *liberi* as well as *censuales* and *ministeriales* of the abbots of St Emmeram and the bishops of Regensburg amongst their number.[128]

Historical perspectives in the twelfth century about the rise of ministeriales

The emergence of the new knighthood of *ministeriales* was some-

---

[121] *Casus Monasterii Petrishusensis*, MGS, XX, p. 649.
[122] Mohr, *Oberalteich*, 68, pp. 138-40, 1147, and 128, pp. 258 f., c.1234-9.
[123] Tr. Regensburg 848, pp. 409 f., 1149-55.
[124] UB Salzburg i, 286, p. 405, before 1147.
[125] Tr. Regensburg 1036, p. 528, c.1210-17, and Redlich, *Brixen*, 565, pp. 204 f., 1238.
[126] Uhl, *Weihenstephan*, 94, pp. 79 f., 1138-47, and Tr. Regensburg 1015, p. 518, 1197-1200.
[127] Tr. Regensburg 774, pp. 361 f., c.1126-9.
[128] Ibid. 880, pp. 426 f., 1159, 1014, pp. 517 f., 1197-1200, and 1019, p. 520, 1201.

thing of a social revolution in Germany, and contemporaries not-
iced its impact and commented upon its origins. Their speculations
tended to the fantastic, and contribute very little to the quest for
real origins, but they are, of course, valuable for showing how the
social standing of *ministeriales* was rated in the twelfth and thirteenth centuries.

The twelfth-century monastic chronicle of Ebersheimmünster in
Alsace ascribes the establishment of *ministeriales* in Germany to
Caesar: 'When he was ready to return to Rome, he held a meeting
in Germany, and greeting everyone, commended the lesser knights,
minores milites, to the princes, not to use them as servants, *servi ac
famuli*, but to accept their services, *ministeria*, as though they were
lords and warriors, *domini ac defensores*. And so it happened that,
amongst the other nations, the German knights belonged to the
royal fisc or were called *ministeriales* of the princes.' The chronicle
goes on to explain that the Merovingian king Dagobert II gave
property in Alsace to the bishops of Strasburg, with its dependents
or *familia* divided into three categories: 'First the *ministerialis*, who
is certainly called warrior, so noble and bellicose, that surely he is
comparable with free status.'[129] The second and third ranks were
the *censuales* and the serfs, but all three were subject to the bishop
and his officers. The derivation of knighthood from classical Rome
was, of course, a widespread literary commonplace in medieval
times. Provost Gerhoh of Reichersberg, who disapproved of ecclesiastical retinues of *ministeriales*, believed that they had been forced
upon churches by the Roman magnates of Constantine the Great's
time.[130]

Monastic foundation-stories sometimes connect the establishment of retinues of *ministeriales* with lavish gifts to their houses.
Provost Gerhard of Steterburg (1163-1209) reported that early in
the eleventh century the foundress, Frideruna of Olsburg, 'had
subjected to Our Lord all that she possessed by hereditary right in
serfs, vassals, and officials, and had most gloriously embellished
our church, according to the manner of princes, with what belonged to the glory of this world in seneschals, butlers, marshals,

[129] *Chronicon Ebersheimense*, MGS, XXIII, pp. 432f. The 12th-c. forgery recording Dagobert's gift has also survived; MGD Regum Francorum i, 70, pp. 186f.,
dated to 662.
[130] Sackur, *Gerhohi Libelli*, p. 155, and P. Classen, *Gerhoch von Reichersberg.
Eine Biographie* (Wiesbaden, 1960), pp. 40-7.

knights, and *ministeriales*'.[131] Probably he was reading a picture of the retinues in his own time back into the early eleventh century, but he was not mistaken in showing that founders and benefactors did give whole retinues of *ministeriales* to monasteries. In 1126 Count Godfrey of Cappenberg converted his family, castle, and lordship to monastic purposes, and included 105 copiously enfeoffed *ministeriales* with their wives and posterity.[132] In another endowment, the patriarch of Aquileia confirmed possession of a vast property given by the rich nobleman Diebald of Kager to Obernburg monastery in 1140, including nearly a hundred *ministeriales* of both sexes with their own possessions, and about 500 serfs with their women and children.[133] Like Gerhard of Steterburg, Henry II's twelfth-century biographer Adalbert also anachronistically assumed that *ministeriales* were included when the bishopric of Merseburg was re-established in 1004. He reported that the see was restored in its 'buildings, *ministeriales*, secular possessions, ecclesiastical belongings, and its original state of pontifical dignity'.[134] Another twelfth-century author similarly believed that the wealthy Swabian *ministeriales* of Arbon and Bollingen were descended from men given to the see of Constance by Bishop Gebhard before 995.[135]

By contrast with such sources, an eleventh-century historian, the St Gallen monk known as Ekkehard IV, who died after 1057, claimed that before his own time, the abbey's manorial bailiffs had usurped the standing of knights: 'It is written of servants, that if they fear no one, they swell with pride, and the bailiffs began to carry bright shields and arms.' Leaving others to till the soil, they took care of their fiefs, which presumably were also usurped, and trained their hounds, graduating from hunting hares and wolves to bears and boars.[136] This extraordinary passage has not quite defeated modern commentary, which suggests that it reveals, not

---

[131] *Annales Stederburgenses*, MGS, XVI, p. 200.

[132] CD Westphalia ii, 199f., pp. 5f., 1126, *Vita Godefridi Cappenbergensis*, MGS, XII, p. 519, and H. Grundmann, *Der Cappenberger Barbarossakopf und die Anfänge des Stiftes Cappenberg*, Münstersche Forschungen, XII (Cologne and Graz, 1959).

[133] UB Steiermark i, 180, pp. 188-90, 1140.

[134] *Adalberti Vita Heinrici II. Imperatoris*, MGS, IV, pp. 793f.

[135] *Casus Monasterii Petrishusensis*, MGS, XX, ch. 35, pp. 635f.

[136] H. F. Haefele, *Ekkehard IV. St Galler Klostergeschichten*, AQ, X (Darmstadt, 1980), pp. 108-10, and K.-H. Ganahl, *Studien zur Verfassungsgeschichte der Klosterherrschaft St. Gallen*, Forschungen zur Geschichte Vorarlbergs und Liechtensteins, VI (Innsbruck, 1931), pp. 117-25.

tenth-century realities, but an eleventh-century avenue into the rank of *ministerialis* which the abbots of St Gallen were not wholly able to regulate.

Another tradition suggested a biblical foundation for different statuses in Germany, deriving from the sons of Noah and other characters in Genesis. With unusual good sense Eike von Repgow rejected this in his *Sachsenspiegel*, and suggested, when touching upon *ministeriales*' rights and rank, 'in real truth servitude had its origin in force, detention and unjust power, which men have of old turned into unjust custom, and would now elevate into law'.[137] Not that this theory carries us any nearer to the social realities of the Hohenstaufen age.

Other Germans were not interested in wondering why the *ministeriales*, amongst others, were unfree. They were more concerned with giving weight and respectability to the rules they wished to impose upon their followings of *ministeriales*. For this purpose the golden age of the Carolingians was in favour in the twelfth-century monasteries. Forged charters dated to the eighth and ninth centuries confirmed abbots in their powers over their *ministeriales*, who were, at the same time, immunized from interference by the magnates who were the secular advocates of monasteries. At Klingenmünster a series of faked imperial privileges culminated in a confirmation ascribed to Archbishop Adalbert of Mainz in 1115, also a forgery.[138] Similar results were achieved at the nunnery of Erstein, whose imaginary patroness, the Empress Irmengard, was held to have disciplined the *ministeriales* in 853.[139] A document purporting to be Charlemagne's instructions about putting together military expeditions to Italy was drawn up at Reichenau Abbey about 1160. It is concerned, in part, with *ministeriales*' obligations, and the abbot probably had in mind his contributions to Frederick Barbarossa's current large-scale military adventures in Lombardy.[140]

[137] K. A. Eckhardt, *Sachsenspiegel Landrecht*, MG Fontes iuris Germanici antiqui, n.s., I. 1 (2nd edn., Göttingen, 1955), pp. 223–8, and E. Rosenstock, 'Die Verdeutschung des Sachsenspiegels', *ZRGGA* xxxvii (1916), 498–504.
[138] UB Mainz i, 462, pp. 369–71, 1115, and T. Mayer, 'Die älteren Urkunden des Klosters Klingenmünster', *MIöG* xlvii (1933), 137–85.
[139] MGD Lothar I and II, 146, pp. 330f., and P. Scheffer-Boichorst, 'Zur Geschichte der Reichsabtei Erstein', *Zeitschrift für die Geschichte des Oberrheins* xliii (1889), 283–99.
[140] MGC i, 447, pp. 661–3, and G. Klapeer, 'Zur Überlieferung der Constitutio de expeditione Romana', *MIöG* xxxv (1914), 725–32. A charter donating a *ministerialis*

Imaginary precepts from Carolingian times about *ministeriales* became an acceptable tradition in the twelfth century. Towards the end of the thirteenth, therefore, the *Deutschenspiegel* could again base the duty of *ministeriales* to accompany emperors into Italy upon the dictates of the warlike Charlemagne.[141] *Ministeriales* themselves probably thought that their rights went back to the Carolingians, if not Caesar, and appealed to the past to protect their future. In the twelfth century the abbot of Lorsch's *ministeriales* of Gundheim and Insultheim guaranteed their status, lands, serfs, and rights to the office of chamberlain by forging a charter in which their putative ancestors had voluntarily surrendered themselves to the abbey, and had it dated 781.[142]

Some time after 1100 the imperial *ministeriales* at Weissenburg in Franconia pressed into service not the Carolingian age, but Conrad II's reign, and claimed that in 1029 he had granted favourable terms concerning their fiefs, their hunting-rights in the Weissenburg Forest, and their fitting-out allowances for expeditions to Italy. The charter was phrased as a petition, duly confirmed by the emperor, and Conrad II was a convincing choice for this forgery, if he was indeed still remembered a century later for his concessions to the lesser vassals of his kingdoms.[143] This confection was preserved in a cartulary finished in 1125, which also included a charter of the 1070s, rewritten to point out the social progress of *ministeriales* in two generations. One of Henry IV's *servientes* was now adorned as a 'praiseworthy knight' who was 'favoured by us as a loyal vassal, active knight, ready and prepared day and night for our service entirely',[144] with the attributes of knighthood, in short. In a similar vein, the St Trond chronicler recorded of the abbot's knightly *servus* Guntramn at the beginning of the twelfth century that he was, amongst other things, 'most brave in battle, daring in spirit, skilled in counsel, and reliable in undertakings'.[145]

to Abbot Ulrich appears to refer to this forgery as *Lex atque iusticia nobilium Augiensium*; UB Wirtemberg ii, 380, pp. 142–5, 1163.

[141] K. A. Eckhardt and A. Hübner, *Deutschenspiegel und Augsburger Sachsenspiegel*, MG Fontes iuris Germanici antiqui, n.s., III (Hanover, 1933), pp. 110 f.

[142] K. Glöckner, *Codex Laureshamensis*, Arbeiten der Historischen Kommission für den Volksstaat Hessen (3 vols., Darmstadt, 1929–36), ii, 1147, pp. 339 f.

[143] MGD Conrad II, 140, pp. 188–91, 244, pp. 335–7, 1037, and Wipo, *Gesta Chuonradi*, p. 28.

[144] MGD Henry IV, 319, pp. 419 f., 1079.

[145] Borman, *Saint-Trond* i, pp. 83 f.

These speculations about their history, the literary phrases about knighthood, and the forgeries ascribed to earlier times, were self-conscious attempts to comprehend a new social phenomenon. By contrast, there survive records of two court-cases from twelfth-century Würzburg which illustrate the origins of *ministeriales* in more matter-of-fact terms. In the first of them, Bishop Embricho was obliged in 1131 to rescue the *ministeriales* pertaining to the huge episcopal manor at Salz from the claims of the cathedral Provost Otto that they were all *censuales* owing him head-taxes. There were indeed *censuales* at Salz as well, but Conrad of Wittig-hausen proved by the ordeal of hot iron that he and his fellows were *ministeriales*, and this was duly confirmed by the bishop. Heaven and the bishop were right. These *ministeriales* clearly were descended from the twenty-six named '*servientes* of the household at Salz' whom Queen Richiza of Poland gave to Würzburg in the original grant of 1057, not from the *mancipia* or serfs also trans-ferred.[146]

In the second case, Abbot Berengar of St Stephen's at Würzburg complained in 1136 to Bishop Embricho that a certain Sasso, his sister Gerburga, and their offspring claimed to be *ministeriales*, whereas the abbot held them to be serfs. Perhaps they had fallen upon hard times, but investigations showed that they were de-scended 'from the better and more honourable following' of Duke Otto of Swabia, who had died in 1057. His granddaughter, Duchess Adelheid of Limburg, had later transferred Sasso and Gerburga's mother, from whom all her descendants would have derived their status, to St Stephen's as *ministeriales*. Evidently this did not satisfy the monastery. In 1189 Bishop Godfrey was obliged once more to confirm that Sasso and Gerburga's children were derived, ultimately, from the 'better people' of the duchess's *familia*, and were given to the monastery by her as *ministeriales*. To resolve the dispute, the bishop took them over as his own *ministeriales*, and compensated the abbot with six other men as dependents.[147]

Finally, a report from Saxony reveals the novel position of *ministeriales* in German society and politics after 1100, and their

[146] Mon. Boica, xxxvii, 78, pp. 40f., 1131, and 67, pp. 25-8, 1057, which Rei-mann, p. 21 n. 129, defends as an original. The late 11th-c. *Brunwilarensis Monasterii Fundatio*, MGS, XI, p. 406, also reports that Queen Richiza gave to Würzburg *numerosa familiarum clientela* at Salz.
[147] UB St Stephan 114, pp. 119-21, 1136, and 207, pp. 211-13, 1189.

arrogation of judicial functions as knights, lords, and landowners. In 1146 the Pöhlde annalist noted with disapproval that they even attempted what the king could not achieve: 'This year an astonishing and hitherto unheard-of business arose in the duchy. For the *ministeriales* of the king and of other magnates, although not ordered to do so, held a meeting, and without consulting the king or other princes, themselves did justice as magistrates to all wrong-doers. The king had come to Saxony to do justice, but even he had not managed to effect this.'[148] As a force to be reckoned with, the *ministeriales* had arrived.

[148] *Annales Palidenses*, MGS, XVI, p. 82.

CHAPTER 2

The Servile Legal Status
of *Ministeriales*

Ministeriales *were unfree*

The forms of knighthood which prevailed in twelfth-century Germany came to regard the *ministerialis* as a nobleman, yet consigned him to an unfree legal status. Two phases in the history of knighthood appear to have been uneasily conjoined. In the first, the vassal *miles* of the later Carolingian world was probably subordinated to his lord as an unfree dependent, though we lack clear evidence about vassalage in that era. In the second, the functions, and *a fortiori* the status, of knighthood acquired fresh importance in the military and political history of the eleventh century. In France, where the authority of the princes was extremely fragmented, this caused a liberation of the vassal-knight and his elevation to noble rank. In Germany, where the sway of magnates was more formidable, such exaltation of status was inhibited, and lords retained a tighter rein upon their knights. The result was a form of vassalage essentially non-contractual coupled with unfree status, but the new social significance of knightly functions permitted recognition, by the mid-twelfth century, of hereditary noble rank in the French mode. It is not to be supposed that German magnates habitually reflected upon the standing of their *ministeriales* and made conscious decisions about it. The survival of written rules or custumals for retinues of *ministeriales* does, however, prove the desire by both lord and knight to define the extent and limits of service, subordination, and unfree degree.[1]

Medieval society recognized no absolute distinctions between freedom and servitude, for those commonly called free men might owe obligations such as homage and fealty with the concomitant services, while serfs were not slaves but possessed rights sometimes called liberties. The sources from twelfth and thirteenth-century

---

[1] For the German custumals, Ch. 3 below.

Germany do, nevertheless, make it plain that the knightly *minister-iales* were not considered to be free men. Their lords had heredi-tary, proprietary rights over their actual persons, services, and possessions.[2] This is, of course, a fundamental difference from knighthoods in other west European, Mediterranean, and Crusader kingdoms, where knights were free men constrained by their oaths of homage, or in the Orders of Spain, Outremer, Prussia, and elsewhere, by their monastic vows. For German *ministeriales*, their obligations were personal, hereditary, inescapable, not contractual or dependent upon oaths of homage, although these were generally given as well. *Ministeriales* were accessories of the lordship, usually named from the castle, cathedral or monastic church, or manor, at its centre, in which they were born. They could not move without leave, nor marry without consent. But they were not subject to manorial jurisdictions,[3] they hardly ever paid head-taxes, their *raison d'être* was to bear arms, and they attended the royal and pro-vincial courts as litigants, witnesses, jurors, and magistrates.[4] The unfreedom of *ministeriales* was therefore nothing like that of serfs.

Marks of unfreedom, notably hereditary ascription, were com-mon to both, but those imposed upon *ministeriales* were not insti-tutionally borrowed from serfdom, though this was several hundred years older. Rather, *ministeriales'* servitude was a strict form of vassalage descending ultimately from the Carolingian age, and in

---

[2] This was more than feudal *potestas* or *dominium*, F.L. Ganshof, *Feudalism* (London, 1952), p. 74, although lords had that as well; *Annales Steterburgenses*, MGS, XVI, p. 217, before 1180, and UB Krain ii, 80, p. 60, 1233. For the legal Latin of proprietary right over *ministeriales*; Tr. Regensburg 200, p. 149, 1143, Tr. Tegernsee 327, p. 247, 1163-73 and 387, p. 299, 1206-17, UB Mainz ii, 569, pp. 938-40, 1192, UB Krain ii, 18, pp. 13f., 1209 and 205f., pp. 163-6, 1254, Kelleter, *Kaiserswerth*, 34, pp. 50f., 1224, UB Osnabrück ii, 223, p. 170, 1227, P. Kehr, *Urkundenbuch des Hochstifts Merseburg*, vol. i, Geschichtsquellen der Provinz Sach-sen, XXXVI (Halle, 1899), 268, p. 215, 1249, UB Nürnberg 535, p. 324, 1276, Mon. Boica xlix, 370, pp. 570f., 1291, and Kluckhohn, pp. 59-67.

[3] This freedom from any seigneurial *bannus* elevated them above all other unfree social groups, except the *censuales*. The magnates recognized that *ministeriales* must themselves exercise manorial jurisdiction if their fiefs were to support them effec-tively; confirmed in F.M. Wittmann, *Monumenta Wittelsbacensia. Urkundenbuch zur Geschichte des Hauses Wittelsbach*, QE, V and VI (Munich, 1857-61), vol. i, 140, p. 340, 1281 and vol. ii, 193, p. 30, 1293.

[4] As imperial magistrates, Gislebert of Mons, p. 254, 1190. Bavarian *ministeriales* were directed as plaintiffs to the ducal *Landgerichte* in Wittmann, *Wittelsbach*, vol. i 86, pp. 204-10, 1265. See MGC iv, 1056-7, 1060-2, 1064-70, 1085-87, pp. 1095-106, 1299-309 for a series of cases in which Henry, marshal of Pappenheim sued the neighbouring counts, free lords, and *ministeriales* in the royal court for various damages.

the twelfth-century evidence about their marriages, military duties, devolution of fiefs, and transfers of allegiance, we can see that, socially speaking, they were vassal-knights first and *homines proprii* or 'owned persons' second.[5] The combination of ascription—reminiscent, it is true, of serfdom—and enfeoffment reminiscent of international knighthood, was neatly illustrated in a privilege issued by Frederick Barbarossa in 1153 for the see of Cologne, which mentions the *ministeriales* as enfeoffed or *inbeneficiati* alongside the barons, as well as *appendicii* or appurtenant, alongside the serfs.[6]

But in their economic standing and military functions the *ministeriales* did not resemble serfs, and the translation of their name as 'serf-knight' is misleading. In the German social hierarchy they were, ideologically, counted with 'the secular magistrates, lords, and knights, who should protect widows and orphans', a rank served by the lower orders which included the serfs.[7] The technically servile nature of *ministeriales'* hereditary obligations did not isolate them from the values and pursuits of knighthood everywhere in Christendom. They made up one of the forms which differed from the northern French knightly paradigm: for Castile had a knighthood without fiefs, England a knighthood without allods, southern France a knighthood without service-obligations, Italy a knighthood which was urban, Outremer, Prussia and elsewhere a knighthood which was monastic, and Germany a knighthood which was unfree.

What was the servitude of ministeriales?

If *ministeriales* were the objective appurtenances of ecclesiastical and secular patrimonies, they were not rightless chattels. The rank of *ministerialis*, individually or generally, was quite often denoted a 'liberty', this being, in the medieval mode,[8] a privilege or exemption or guarantee against some grosser form of servitude. When

[5] On the use of *homines proprii*, p. 58, n. 26.
[6] MGC i, 146, p. 205, 1153.
[7] F. Pfeiffer, *Berthold von Regensburg. Vollständige Ausgabe seiner Predigten*, Deutsche Neudrucke, Texte des Mittelalters (Berlin, 1965), vol. i, 10, pp. 140-56, and H. Stahleder, 'Das Weltbild Bertholds von Regensburg', *ZBLG* xxxvii (1974), 728-98.
[8] On the relative meanings of liberty and servitude; M. Bloch, 'Liberté et servitude personnelles au moyen âge' (1933) in id. *Mélanges historiques*, vol. i, Bibliothèque générale de l'École pratique des hautes études (Paris, 1963), pp. 286-355, D. von Gladiss, 'Christentum und Hörigkeit in den Urkunden des fränkischen und deutschen

ministeriales were said to have their *ius et libertas* or 'rights and liberty',[9] this meant rights appropriate to their way of life as unfree knights legally bound to lords. And so, in 1140, Conrad III confirmed that the bishop of Freising's *ministeriales* 'shall remain in that *libertas* which the *ministeriales* of the kingdom and of other churches have'.[10] A *ministerialis* given to the bishop of Augsburg in 1157 was to 'enjoy the liberty which the better *ministeriales* of that church are known to have',[11] and in 1259 the bishop of Halberstadt received a *ministerialis* who would 'rejoice in the free liberty which our *ministeriales* are known to enjoy'.[12] Other charters make clearer what this liberty was. *Ministeriales* given to the bishops of Würzburg 'shall freely serve the bishop of that place absolved of all servile burdens' or 'free and immune from all requisitions' or 'absolved and freed from the yoke of labour',[13] in short, that labour-services, head-taxes, or other fiscal exactions would never be required of them.

In a corroborating thirteenth-century example, a certain Wernhard of Regensburg paid a stiff fee to his lords 'in order to transfer myself to the church of Windberg, not to be assigned any head-tax,

---

Mittelalters', *VSWG* xxix (1936), 35-8, H. von Voltelini, 'Der Gedanke der allgemeinen Freiheit in den deutschen Rechtsbüchern', *ZRGGA* lvii (1937), 182-209, G. Duby, *La Société aux XIe et XIIe siècles dans la région mâconnaise*, Bibliothèque générale de l'École pratique des hautes études (Paris, 1953), pp. 118-27, 245-60, 366-96, 611-16, H. Grundmann, 'Freiheit als religiöses, politisches und persönliches Postulat im Mittelalter', *HZ* clxxxiii (1957), 23-53, K. Bosl, 'Freiheit und Unfreiheit. Zur Entwicklung der Unterschichten in Deutschland und Frankreich' in *Frühformen*, pp. 180-203, F. Merzbacher, 'Die Bedeutung von Freiheit und Unfreiheit im weltlichen und kirchlichen Recht des deutschen Mittelalters', *HJ* xc (1970), 257-83, G. Tellenbach, 'Servitus und libertas nach den Traditionen der Abtei Remiremont', *Saeculum* xxi (1970), 228-34, H.H. Hofmann, 'Sigena, oder Was ist Freiheit?' in H. Beumann (ed.), *Historische Forschungen für Walter Schlesinger* (Cologne and Vienna, 1974), pp. 194-214, H.K. Schulze, 'Rodungsfreiheit und Königsfreiheit. Zu Genesis und Kritik neuerer verfassungsgeschichtlicher Theorien', *HZ* ccxix (1974), 529-50, A. Harding, 'Political Liberty in the Middle Ages', *Speculum* lv (1980), 423-43, and p. 41, n. 98 above.

[9] As in Bitterauf, *Freising*, 1711, pp. 512 f., 1123-30.
[10] MGD Conrad III, 46, p. 78, 1140, and on these *ministeriales*, G. Flohrschütz, 'Die Freisinger Dienstmannen im 12. Jahrhundert', *Oberbayerisches Archiv* xcvii (1973), 32-339.
[11] W.E. Vock, *Die Urkunden des Hochstifts Augsburg*, Schwäbische Forschungsgemeinschaft, ser. 2A, Urkunden und Regesten VII (Augsburg, 1959), 31, p. 16, 1157.
[12] UB Hildesheim ii, 1095, p. 544, 1259.
[13] UB Land ob der Enns ii, 84, p. 121, 1096, and Mon. Boica xxxvii, 73, pp. 33 f., 1104, 89, pp. 55 f., 1140, and 178, pp. 181-3, 1211.

but to be the free *ministerialis* of that church'.[14] Another illuminating text is Frederick Barbarossa's confirmation of *libertas* to the episcopal and monastic *ministeriales* of Strasburg,[15] which consolidated the sole jurisdiction of their lords over them by exempting them from all urban jurisdictions, from fiscal demands by the empire, and from any service except to their lords.

Sources mentioning *ministeriales'* 'liberty' or exemptions are, not surprisingly, less frequent than charters specifying their services. *Ministeriales* performed their duties upon a particular legal basis, but the Latin word most often employed, *servitium*, covered all forms of service in the German social and religious spectrum: of monks to their saints, vassals to their overlords, prelates to their emperors, serfs to their landlords, as well as *ministeriales* to their owners. In the last case, the free men who became Corvey *ministeriales* in 1106 were said to have entered into the *servitium* of that abbey.[16] In 1131 the *ministeriales* given to Mainz were required to offer the same *servitium* given to their former lords.[17] A certain Eberlint, given in the twelfth century to the monastery of Ebersberg, was committed to the *servicium* owed by a *ministerialis*,[18] and so on.

In the twelfth century, the standing of *ministeriales* was defined in the custumals by the rules of vassalage, but it was also compared with the rank of *censualis*. The abbot of Tegernsee's advocate, Margrave Berthold of Istria, pointed out that *ministeriales* and *censuales* enjoyed the same immunity from alienation out of the abbot's following, except with their own consent.[19] When the status of *censualis* was granted or confirmed, it too was emphasized either as liberty or as servitude.[20] These similarities possibly betray a large-scale recruitment of *censuales*, many of whom were land-

---

[14] Mon. Boica liii, 77, p. 39, c.1250.

[15] MGD Frederick I, 133, pp. 223-5, 1156, confirming Henry V's grant of 1122; Meyer von Knonau vii, p. 195 n. 7.

[16] UB Halberstadt i, 123, pp. 85f., 1106, and see Niermeyer, *Lexicon*, pp. 964-7 for *servitium* and *servitus*.

[17] UB Mainz i, 571, p. 488, 1131.

[18] Hundt, *Ebersberg*, 54, p. 171.

[19] Tr. Tegernsee 380A, pp. 293f., 1173-86.

[20] As a liberty, Tr. Regensburg 792, pp. 372f., 1135, Mayerhofer, 'Codex Augiensium', 177, p. 126, c.1150, Redlich, *Brixen*, 498, p. 175, 1165-70, and MGC ii, 172, pp. 213f., 1222 for *liberi censuales* at Osnabrück. As servility, Tr. Regensburg 653, p. 320, c.1082-3, Piot, *Saint-Trond*, vol. i, 32, pp. 41f., 1129, and Mon. Boica vii, p. 73, 1183-1203.

owners, into the status of *ministerialis*. In other respects *ministeriales* and *censuales* were not alike. The former had hereditary and professional duties and obligations, the latter had none.[21] They might travel, reside, work, and marry as they chose,[22] so long as they surrendered heriots and paid their annual head-tax. With rare exceptions, *ministeriales* did not pay this tax. By the end of the twelfth century their status was considered to be better than that of *censualis*, largely because knighthood was the all-important avenue of economic improvement, through holding fiefs and offices. *Ministeriales* sometimes became *censuales*,[23] but the reverse was more often the case. The growing social divergence between them was demonstrated in the count of Tecklenburg's custumal drawn up in the 1220s, which said that 'if a *ministerialis* sleeps with a serf or a *censualis*, the child born of them shall be a *camerlingus*', and *camerlingi* were, according to another Westphalian source, 'halfway between *ministeriales* and men of more servile condition'.[24]

Ministeriales *in the possession of their lords*

In law *ministeriales* were unfree, their persons actually belonged from birth to their lords, they could be given away to other lords,[25] they were transferred *in proprietatem* or 'into ownership', and were frequently designated *homines proprii* or 'owned men'.[26] These realities were laboriously spelt out in 1123, when a free-born family surrendered 'the temporal freedom of the flesh to the ownership

---

[21] See p. 42, n. 100.
[22] Bitterauf, *Freising*, 1244, pp. 148f., 972-6, UB Wirtemberg i, 244, pp. 300-2, c.1094, Tr. Regensburg 802, p. 379, 1138-42, Mon. Boica xlv, 5, pp. 11-13, 1140, UB Wirtemberg ii, 356, pp. 105f., 1157, and G. Franz, *Quellen zur Geschichte des deutschen Bauernstandes im Mittelalter*, AQ, XXXI (Darmstadt, 1967), pp. 218-20, 236-8, 270-2.
[23] Mon. Boica xxxvii, 86, pp. 50-2, 1140, UB Salzburg i, 632, p. 557, after 1188, Tr. Regensburg 1015, p. 518, 1197-1200, and Wisplinghoff, *Siegburg*, 66A, pp. 149f., 1173.
[24] UB Osnabrück ii, 123, p. 92, and H. Finke, *Westfälisches Urkundenbuch*, vol. iv *Die Urkunden des Bisthums Paderborn*, 3 (Münster, 1889-94), 1233, p. 601, c.1270.
[25] Redlich, *Brixen*, 496A-C, p. 174, 1165-70 and 501, p. 176, 1170-4, and *Chronicon Affligemense*, MGS, IX, p. 414, 1091-5.
[26] Otto and Rahewin, *Gesta Friderici*, p. 90, 1149, UB Wirtemberg ii, 337, p. 61, 1152, Tr. Passau 745, p. 266, 1180-1220, Mon. Boica xxxvii, 221, p. 235, 1230, and Bayerisches Staatsarchiv Nürnberg, Hochstift Eichstätt Lehenbücher I, ff. 1-73, c.1305 for whole retinues of *homines proprii*.

and service of the Church, and gave themselves into the property of the church of Paderborn as *ministeriales*'.[27]

Proprietary right meant that, in theory at least, *ministeriales* owed their loyalty and service for life to the lords into whose *familiae* or retinues they had been born. In practice this ascription was modified in the direction of contractual vassalage because lords permitted mobility of service, and consequently of allegiance, if they themselves were not prepared to provide fiefs, as already shown in the 1060s by the Bamberg custumal.[28] Nevertheless, *ministeriales* were tied by the law to the estates, castles, and jurisdictions of their lords, and were therefore transferable as appurtenant possessions when patrimonies or lordships were given away, exchanged, purchased, inherited, pledged, or otherwise devolved. The reason why we know the rules governing the Bamberg *ministeriales* is that Bishop Gunther (1057–65) gave a large estate of his to the cathedral church and included 'the *ministeriales* belonging, *pertinentes*, to that property', whose rights were then spelled out.[29]

Many a transfer of property explicitly included the *ministeriales* in this fashion,[30] or listed them with the other appurtenances. In 1192, when Henry VI gave Haldensleben Castle and Königslutter Abbey to the archbishop of Magdeburg, he included 'the castellanies, *ministeriales*, and all the serfs of whatever condition, and all the appurtenances'.[31] If such transactions automatically transferred the proprietary right over the *ministeriales*, it was often underlined. Some time before 1158, Frederick Barbarossa had purchased Count Rapoto of Abenberg's huge Saxon patrimony, including the castle and castellans of Colditz.[32] Then, in order to secure for himself Clementia of Zähringen's marriage-portion in Swabia, Badenweiler Castle with its hundred *ministeriales*, from her husband,

[27] CD Westphalia i, 192, p. 150, 1123.

[28] In another case, Archbishop Bardo of Mainz (1031–51) appears to have provoked his *milites* and *servientes* by his incompetence as a lord, so they opted into the imperial retinue instead; P. Jaffé, *Monumenta Moguntina*, Bibliotheca Rerum Germanicarum, III (Berlin, 1866), p. 525.

[29] Full text of the grant in Jaffé, *MB*, 25, pp. 50–2.

[30] UB Mainz i, 527, p. 435, 1124, and 616, pp. 536f., before 1137, *Gestorum Treverorum Continuatio Tertia*, MGS, XXIV, p. 380, 1152–68, UB Krain ii, 5, p. 3, 1202, and H. Sudendorf, *Urkundenbuch zur Geschichte der Herzöge von Braunschweig und Lüneburg und ihrer Lande*, vol. i (Hanover, 1859), 32, p. 22, 1248.

[31] F. Israël and W. Möllenberg, *Urkundenbuch des Erzstifts Magdeburg*, vol. i, Geschichtsquellen für die Provinz Sachsen und des Freistaates Anhalt, n.s. XVIII (Magdeburg, 1937), 438, p. 574, 1192.

[32] *Arnoldi Chronica Slavorum*, MGS, XXI, p. 246.

Duke Henry the Lion, he compensated the latter out of imperial possessions in Saxony, including his *ministerialis* Adelhard of Burgdorf 'with his children and allod and fief, which he holds from the kingdom'. In return, he compensated the empire itself out of his personal possessions, including 'the castle of Colditz and Temo our *ministerialis* with his children, and all his property and fiefs, which add up to twenty manors'.[33] Such transfers had given Colditz and its castellans several changes of owner since the eleventh century. An allod belonging to Margrave Ekkehard of Meissen, it passed to Henry III and Empress Agnes in 1046,[34] and was almost certainly given by their son Henry IV, still as an allod, to Count Wiprecht of Groitzsch in the 1080s.[35] From Wiprecht it passed first to his son-in-law Count Dedo of Wettin, and then to Dedo's son-in-law Rapoto of Abenberg, from whom Frederick Barbarossa bought it back into royal ownership.

In a similar fashion the rich lordship of Schönburg and Oberwesel on the Rhine, which had originally been given in 966 by Otto I to Magdeburg, passed back, with it *ministeriales*, to Frederick Barbarossa in 1166.[36] In 1216 Frederick II gave it back to Magdeburg,[37] but reacquired it for the empire after 1232. Again the *ministeriales* there changed masters in 1278, when King Rudolf pledged it to the counts of Jülich, and in 1312, when it passed for good to the archbishops of Trier.[38] As can be seen from the Burgdorf and Colditz cases, lords were transferring not only the hereditary obediences of *ministeriales*, but also their fiefs and allods as additional appurtenances. The legal reason for this was that the ultimate proprietary right over all possessions, whether fief or allod, of men of servile status also belonged to their lords.[39] In 1126, when transferring Itter Castle, the abbot of Corvey therefore included the *ministeriales* 'and their fiefs, and the allods in their property'.[40]

The rights over *ministeriales*, then, were objective items of prop-

[33] MGD Frederick I, 199, pp. 332f., 1158.
[34] MGD Henry III, 162, pp. 204f., 1046.
[35] *Annales Pegavienses*, MGS, XVI, p. 240.
[36] MGD Otto I, 332, p. 446, 966, and MGD Frederick I, 506f., pp. 438-42 and 516, pp. 453f., 1166.
[37] J.L.A. Huillard-Bréholles, *Historia Diplomatica Friderici Secundi* (6 vols., Paris, 1852-61/repr. 1963), vol. i. 2, p. 463, 1216, and pp. 811f., 1220.
[38] G. Landwehr, *Die Verpfändung der deutschen Reichsstädte im Mittelalter*, Forschungen zur deutschen Rechtsgeschichte, V (Cologne and Graz, 1967), pp. 398f.
[39] See Ch. 5 below.
[40] CD Westphalia ii, 198, p. 4, 1126.

erty. This was once again made clear in the wills by which the childless Count Gebhard of Hirschberg in Bavaria left most of his patrimony to the see of Eichstätt late in the thirteenth century: '... our castle Hirschberg with all its rights and appurtenances, that is, the men of military condition, and the serfs of common or whatever status and condition they be, together with the universal and particular possessions belonging to that castle', followed by an inventory of the visible manorial landscape and its jurisdictions.[41] And the men of military status, very many of whom were already the bishop of Eichstätt's feoffees, duly joined his retinue when the count died in 1305. But not all of them. Those adhering to Sulzbach Castle, which had not been willed to Eichstätt, passed automatically to his nearest secular heirs, the dukes of Bavaria.[42]

The theoretical rigidity of this kind of ascription is what, in part, rendered territorial inheritances so attractive to the magnates, for their new lordships arrived with enfeoffed *ministeriales* whose automatic loyalty extended their own military and political significance overnight. We are told by a much later commentator that Margrave Ottokar of Styria (1129–64) was 'much strengthened and supported' by three substantial comital inheritances made up of 'lands, fortifications and *ministeriales*.'[43] All Styrian *ministeriales* were in turn bequeathed to the dukes of Austria in 1186, the instrument listing precisely of what rights and powers Styria, a duchy since 1180, consisted: church tithes and fifteen monastic advocacies, and ownership of the ducal manors, castles, and *ministeriales*.[44] The rights of the new duchy of Westphalia conferred upon Archbishop Philip of Cologne in 1180 were defined slightly more widely: counties, advocacies, policing of roads, manors with all their holdings, and fiefs, *ministeriales*, and serfs.[45] In 1191, when Duke Welf

---

[41] Mon. Boica xlix, 181, pp. 286–8, 1291, confirmed in 223, pp. 342–4, 1296, and 344, pp. 527–9, 1304.

[42] On the dispersal of the Hirschberg retinue, about 130 families, see my thesis, pp. 247–61.

[43] *Genealogia Marchionum de Stire*, MGS, XXIV, p. 72.

[44] UB Steiermark i, 677f., pp. 651–4, 1186, and H. Appelt, 'Zur diplomatischen Kritik der Georgenberger Handfeste', *MIöG* lviii (1950), 97–112. On the Styrian *ministeriales*, H. Dopsch, 'Ministerialität und Herrenstand in der Steiermark und in Salzburg', *Zeitschrift des Historischen Vereines für Steiermark* lxii (1971), 3–31, and F. Posch, 'Siedlungsgeschichte der Oststeiermark', *MIöG* Ergänzungsband xiii (1941), 385–679.

[45] MGC i, 279, pp. 384–6, 1180. On the Cologne *ministeriales*, W. Pötter, *Die Ministerialität der Erzbischöfe von Köln*, Studien zur Kölner Kirchengeschichte, IX

VI's Swabian patrimony, the reversion of which his nephew Frederick Barbarossa had purchased in the 1170s, eventually devolved upon his great-nephew Henry VI, it included 'lands, advocatial jurisdictions, and *ministeriales*'.[46] In the 1260s, when Abbot Hermann of Niederaltaich was struck by the inordinate number of comital patrimonies snapped up in recent decades by the dukes of Bavaria, he listed the inheritances with castles and lands, 'as well as the *ministeriales*'.[47]

The ascription of *ministeriales* to the seigneuries upon which they were born resembled that of serfs, but for the knights it did not appear unseemly or degrading, since it had its real social parallel in the customs of free vassalage. For the fiefs held and the castles garrisoned by free-born vassal-knights were also transmitted when patrimonies and lordships changed hands, and charters sometimes transferred their homages explicitly. This happened in 1166 when Frederick Barbarossa exchanged Nienburg Abbey and Freckleben Castle in Saxony, including the free men and the *ministeriales*, with the archbishop of Magdeburg, who, as already mentioned, gave him Schönburg Castle and Oberwesel, again with the free men, called vassals, and the *ministeriales*.[48] Similarly, a charter of 1244 lists '*ministeriales*, serfs, and free men, and all rights real and personal' pertaining to Laas Castle, an extensive comital property in Carniola.[49] In another case the vendor actually wrote 'to each and every one of his vassals and *ministeriales*' that since he had sold his lands to the see of Merseburg, they must offer the homage and fealty the bishop would require of them.[50] In 1254 King Ottokar of Bohemia wrote, in similar circumstances, to the *ministeriales* of the counts of Weichselburg and Preis, who had recently come by inheritance into the possession of his wife, Margaret of Babenberg, to tell them that they were being transferred to Bishop Conrad of Freising.[51]

(Düsseldorf, 1967), and J. Ahrens, *Die Ministerialität in Köln und am Niederrhein* (Leipzig, 1908).

[46] *Hugonis Chronica Continuatio Weingartensis*, MGS XXI, p. 477.

[47] *Genealogia Ottonis II. Ducis Bavariae*, MGS, XVII, pp. 377 f., and M. Spindler, *Die Anfänge des bayerischen Landesfürstentums*, Schriftenreihe zur Bayerischen Landesgeschichte, XXVI (new edn., Aalen, 1973), pp. 92-104.

[48] MGD Frederick I, 506, pp. 438-40, and 516, pp. 453 f., 1166.

[49] UB Krain ii, 127, p. 97, 1244; further examples in UB Niederrhein ii, 659, p. 387, 1274, and *Historia Monasterii Rastedensis*, MGS, XXV, p. 511, 1292.

[50] Kehr, *Merseburg*, 341, pp. 270 f., 1268.

[51] UB Krain ii, 205 f., pp. 163-6, 1254.

If the ascription and transmission of *ministeriales* were part of feudal custom in Germany, lords might also exempt them from transfer as accessories of the properties in question in order to preserve their retinues, and this they were perfectly entitled to ordain. In 1091 Henry IV did so in a gift to the see of Speyer, since the *servientes* had received valuable fiefs from his parents and himself which he did not wish to lose sight of.[52] When Duke Henry of Carinthia made enormous grants to the monastery at St Lambrecht in 1103, he included the *ministeriales* in some places and excluded them in others.[53] When Count Gerhard of Guelders founded Wassenberg out of his inheritance in 1118, he simply exluded 'my *ministeriales* with their fiefs'.[54] In 1202 the duke of Merania pledged two castles at Stein to the patriarch of Aquileia 'with all the property, serfs and their women, and all rights and appurtenances, except the *ministeriales*'.[55] Similarly, the count of Rietberg kept back three named *ministeriales* from the sale of Horstmar Castle to the bishop of Münster in 1269, and the bishop of Merseburg reserved his when he sold Dettum to the duke of Brunswick in 1280.[56] Donors might also change their minds. When Count Otto of Botenlauben sold his castle to the bishop of Würzburg in 1234, he kept back the *ministeriales* for some years, giving them to the see about 1242. Some forty individuals were listed, belonging to eight different families.[57]

Retaining the use of *ministeriales*, either for the lifetime of the donor, or for a shorter period, was not unusual.[58] When Count Gebhard of Hirschberg raised much-needed cash by selling Sandsee Castle to the bishop of Eichstätt in 1302, he exempted the garrison because he hoped shortly to be able to buy the castle back.[59] In the event, he died before he could do so, and these *ministeriales* therefore passed outright to the bishop. They had, in the meantime, owed double allegiance by arrangement between count and bishop. Lords might also desire to give lands to one recipient and the

[52] MGD Henry IV, 426, pp. 571 f., 1091.
[53] UB Steiermark i, 95, pp. 111 f., 1103.
[54] UB Niederrhein i, 289, pp. 189 f., 1118.
[55] UB Krain ii, 7, p. 5, 1202.
[56] UB Münster, 840, p. 439, 1269, and Sudendorf, *Braunschweig*, 93, pp. 58 f., 1280.
[57] Mon. Boica xxxvii, 239, pp. 260-2, 1234, and 270, pp. 299 f., c.1242.
[58] e.g. UB Wirtemberg i, 226, p. 268, 1045.
[59] Mon. Boica xlix, 312-4, pp. 481-9, 1302.

ministeriales pertaining to them to another. This is what happened in 1074 when a nobleman called Udo gave his enfeoffed *ministeriales* to the archbishop of Mainz, and all his other lands with the serfs to the monastery of Ravengiersburg.[60]

Since *ministeriales* counted as disposable property, their transfer, or exemption, could be arranged for a variety of purposes. About 1075 Count Ulrich of Ratelnberg in Bavaria gave six *ministeriales* to his wife Matilda as part of her dowry,[61] and much later, *ministeriales* figured again in the marriage-portions, jointures, and dowries settled in matrimonial treaties between the counts of Ravensberg and Tecklenburg in Saxony.[62] In 1127 Count Conrad of Laufen gave eight *ministeriales* with their children and possessions to the bishopric of Worms as an entry-fine on receiving his father's fief from that see.[63] It was possible, though rare, to buy *ministeriales* directly. In the 1080s Countess Wilcha of Sindelfingen in Swabia sold the emperor her *ministeriales* at Bernhausen and elsewhere in return for a life-pension.[64] In 1221 Abbot Cuno of Ellwangen purchased Lucgardis of Nellingen and her sons from their previous lord, to be *ministeriales* of his house.[65] More often *ministeriales* were sold as part and parcel of a lordship. In 1182 or 1183 Duke Otto of Bavaria bought Dachau Castle, the *ministeriales*, and all other appurtenances for a large cash sum from the widow of the last duke of Dachau and Merania.[66] In 1200 Count Berthold of Nimburg transferred Nimburg, his *ministeriales*, and the other appurtenances to the bishop of Strasburg 'through the medium of money'.[67] When magnates pledged their property, the *ministeriales* went too, as in 1152 when Duke Berthold of Zähringen pledged Teck Castle in Swabia to Frederick Barbarossa.[68] In the same way, the imperial *ministeriales* living in the towns repeatedly pledged and redeemed by the crown in the thirteenth century were also changing their masters.[69]

[60] UB Mainz i, 549, pp. 456 f., 1128.
[61] A. Fuchs, *Urkunden und Regesten zur Geschichte des Benedictinerstiftes Göttweig*, vol. i, Fontes Rerum Austriacarum, ser. 2, LI (Vienna, 1901), 4, p. 5, *c.* 1075.
[62] UB Osnabrück ii, 370, pp. 289-91, 1238, and 483, pp. 384-6, 1246.
[63] UB Wirtemberg i, 291, p. 374, 1127.
[64] *Annales Sindelfingenses*, MGS, XVII, p. 301.
[65] UB Wirtemberg iii, 644, pp. 119 f., 1221.
[66] *Chuonradi Chronicon Schirense*, MGS, XVII, pp. 620 f.
[67] Bloch, *Annales Marbacenses*, p. 76.
[68] MGD Frederick I, 12, pp. 22-4, 1152.
[69] Landwehr, pp. 396-448.

The *ministeriales* also had to be considered when, as so often, the ruling magnates decided to divide their territories. In 1166 the county of Liedberg in the Rhineland was divided between two heiresses, each receiving a castle 'with all the *ministeriales* and other men and all possessions and jurisdictions belonging to that castle'.[70] In 1219 the lords of Hohenlohe agreed to divide their *ministeriales* together with their castles, fiefs, and serfs, while another Franconian dynasty, the counts of Castell, decided about 1258 to divide their lands and the serfs, but not the knights.[71] When Margrave Otto of Brandenburg supervised the division of Brunswick-Lüneburg in 1267, he directed that *ministeriales* within this dominion should be divided between the dukes, but those living beyond its borders were still to be held as common property.[72] The divisions of dynastic territories occasioned much friction between the parties, their feuds sustained by the divided retinues of *ministeriales*. The two Bavarian duchies set up in 1255 by the Wittelsbach brothers were notorious in this respect.[73] In the 1160s, when the *ministeriales* themselves arranged the division between Counts Henry and Frederick of Arnsberg in Westphalia, the annalist learnedly remarked that the knights continued to set the brothers against each other, like Thyestes and Atreus.[74]

Were ministeriales *exempt from head-taxes, corvées, and heriots?*

The head-tax paid by *censuales* as the sign of their subjection was also paid to landowners by their serfs. But *ministeriales* were nearly always exempt from taxes of this kind. To force them to pay tribute like *censuales* was singled out as an injustice.[75] Archbishop Adalbert of Mainz's charter confirming a gift of *ministeriales* and lands

---

[70] UB Niederrhein i, 414, pp. 285 f., 1166.

[71] K. Weller, *Hohenlohisches Urkundenbuch*, vol. i (Stuttgart, 1899), 37, p. 19, 1219, and Wittmann, *Monumenta Castellana*, 152, p. 50, c.1258.

[72] Sudendorf, *Braunschweig*, 64, pp. 42 f., 1267.

[73] On this division, M. Spindler, *Handbuch der bayerischen Geschichte*, vol. ii, *Das alte Bayern* (2nd edn.), Munich 1977), pp. 69-72, and on the Wittelsbach *ministeriales*, G. Flohrschütz, 'Machtgrundlagen und Herrschaftspolitik der ersten Pfalzgrafen aus dem Haus Wittelsbach' in H. Glaser (ed.), *Die Zeit der frühen Herzöge. Von Otto I. zu Ludwig dem Bayern*, Beiträge zur bayerischen Geschichte und Kunst I, 1 (Munich and Zürich, 1980), pp. 42-110, and 'Der Adel des Wartenberger Raumes im 12. Jahrhundert', *ZBLG* xxxiv (1971), 85-164 and 462-511.

[74] *Annales Egmundani*, MGS, XVI, pp. 463 f., 1164.

[75] Tr. Regensburg 1036, p. 528, c.1210-17, and Redlich, *Brixen*, 565, pp. 204 f., 1238.

to the Church carefully distinguished these enfeoffed persons from 'the peasants and serfs paying the head-tax'.[76] In 1020, when a free woman married a *serviens* belonging to the church of St Adalbert at Aachen and accepted his status, it was stipulated that they paid no head-tax.[77] In 1131, when the bishop of Würzburg confirmed the relative standing of *ministeriales* and *censuales* belonging to his see, he distinguished the latter from the former as those who, by law, paid head-tax.[78] Early in the thirteenth century, the abbess of Erstein made the same simple distinction when she forbade those who paid head-taxes from trying to appropriate the status of *ministerialis*.[79] There are, nevertheless, a few cases where *ministeriales* did pay head-tax in the twelfth century, to Bavarian monastic lords at St Emmeram, Plankstetten, and Ebersberg.[80] Probably the previous status of *censualis* lies behind the families in question, who had failed to secure for themselves all the usual privileges when they became *ministeriales*. It also appears that *ministeriales* were exempt from paying for their lords' consent to their marriages. In 1092 Bishop Udo of Hildesheim admitted that his predecessors had unjustly charged for permission, a custom abrogated henceforth.[81]

Ministeriales were exempt from performing any corvées of a degrading nature, although lords did sometimes reserve the right to requisition their horses[82] or plough-teams. From 1154 the counts of Ahr in the Rhineland remitted this obligation.[83] The wives and daughters of *ministeriales* sometimes undertook household duties for their lords. According to the Weissenburg grant to imperial *ministeriales*, their daughters spent much time preparing clothing and other necessaries for the expeditions to Italy, in return for substantial compensation in stores for their larders.[84] Sometimes *ministeriales* had to be rescued from unbecoming corvées. In 1085 Bishop Erpho of Münster discovered that the abbess of Freckenhorst's *ministeriales* 'had hardly a better status than the *liti* and

---

[76] UB Mainz i, 549, pp. 456f., 1128.
[77] UB Niederrhein i, 157, p. 97, 1020.
[78] Mon. Boica xxxvii, 78, pp. 40f., 1131.
[79] MGD Lothar I and II, 146, pp. 330f., dated to 853.
[80] Tr. Regensburg 754, p. 352, *c*.1120, Reg. Eichstätt 328, p. 106, 1129, Hundt, *Ebersberg*, 85, p. 178, *c*.1180, and see Tr. Tegernsee 275, p. 208, 1149-55.
[81] UB Hildesheim i, 150, pp. 142f., 1092.
[82] *Ortliebi Zwifaltensis Chronicon*, MGS, X, p. 78.
[83] UB Niederrhein iv, 624, pp. 774f., 1154.
[84] MGD Conrad II, 140, pp. 188-91, dated 1029.

those who toil daily on the manors, and are much burdened'.[85] They were restored to more suitable rights. From time to time charters warned against corvées. Free men transferred as *ministeriales* to St Emmeram in 1141 'cannot be subjected to any servile work by any ecclesiastical or secular person'.[86] In 1231 Bishop Ulrich of Gurk promoted a family into the rank of *ministerialis*: 'We lift entirely the yoke of servility and free them from all servile work'.[87]

In order to secure the title to their inheritances, *ministeriales* were frequently subjected to fines by their lords. Were they heriots technically owed by the deceased himself, or feudal reliefs owed by the heir to enter the fief? Serfs and *censuales* commonly paid heriots in Germany, but reliefs were not very often levied amongst the free vassals. Nevertheless, in giving *ministeriales* to his chapter in 1131, Archbishop Adalbert of Mainz stipulated that their heirs must hand over their best head of cattle or their best clothing in order to succeed to their inheritances.[88] The bishops of Bamberg only required such payments, a hauberk or a horse, when fiefs passed to indirect heirs. According to the Cologne custumal, *ministeriales* owed no relief or heriot, although in 1074 there is record of Archbishop Anno having charged £3 for passing fiefs from father to son who were his *ministeriales*.[89] Other lords regularly exacted such fines; the abbess of Erstein asked for cash or valuable movables, the abbots of Zwiefalten and the counts of Ahr for horses. When *ministeriales* were transferred to the bishop of Münster in 1263, it was shown that by custom 'the daughter of a *ministerialis* dying without sons succeeds to her father's fiefs, paying a heriot something above an imperial mark in cash'. Other Saxon *ministeriales* were known to be exempt from such heriots.[90]

Were ministeriales *ever emancipated?*

If *ministeriales* were unfree then they could be emancipated, but this rarely happened. Burchard of Ursberg tells us that in 1197 Henry VI did as much for Markward, seneschal of Annweiler, to

[85] CD Westphalia i, 164, pp. 128 f., 1085.
[86] Tr. Regensburg, 804, p. 380, 1141.
[87] Mon. Carinthia i, 532, pp. 413 f., 1231.
[88] UB Mainz i, 571, p. 488, 1131.
[89] Pötter, p. 148. Mon. Boica xlv, 4, pp. 8-11, 1137 remits a heriot at Würzburg.
[90] UB Münster 707, p. 367, 1263, and 296, p. 163, 1232.

fit him for his high titles in Italy: 'At that time the emperor gave his freedom to Markward of Annweiler, his seneschal and *ministerialis*, and granted him the duchy of Ravenna with Romagna, and the march of Ancona'.[91] In a much earlier case, the *ministerialis* Liutold, who belonged to the counts of Dillingen but was himself the illegitimate son of another Swabian count, 'acquired the privilege of freedom' for himself and his posterity from Henry IV.[92] In thirteenth-century Saxony a language approaching emancipation was employed in charters which turn out to transfer *ministeriales* from one retinue to another. These are, in effect, certificates granting one freedom, that of mobility and the exchange of allegiance,[93] a right recognized long before by the bishops of Bamberg and Cologne in their custumals for their *ministeriales*. The purpose of these certificates was spelled out by Count Otto of Tecklenburg in the 1230s when he dismissed Arnold of Lüdinghausen, 'my *ministerialis*, from all liabilities owed to me, so that he may subject himself to whatever lord he wishes'.[94] Similarly, Bishop Gerhard of Münster absolved Regenbodo van then Husen in 1267 from his duties as *ministerialis* of the see, so that he could go and make a career where he chose.[95]

Genuine emancipations in the style of Markward of Annweiler's did take place in the thirteenth century. Free lords sometimes found it worthwhile to marry heiresses who were so rich that the risk of passing their status as *ministeriales* to the children was taken anyway. By 1245 a prominent Franconian nobleman, Reinhard of Hanau, had married Adelheid of Münzenberg, one of the great heiresses of the time. In 1256 they received their share of her father's patrimony, and in due course their children, Isengard and Ulrich, married into the comital houses of Weilnau and Rieneck.[96] In 1273

---

[91] Burchard of Ursberg, pp. 72 f.

[92] *Casus Monasterii Petrishusensis*, MGS, XX, p. 649.

[93] UB Osnabrück ii, 101, pp. 73 f., 1218 (bishop of Osnabrück to abbess of Herzebrock), UB Münster 374, p. 203, 1240 (count of Lippe to abbess of Freckenhorst), UB Halberstadt ii, 884, p. 148, 1253 (count of Blankenburg to bishop of Halberstadt), UB Osnabrück iii, 256, p. 182, 1262 (count of Tecklenburg to abbess of Essen), UB Halberstadt ii, 1203, p. 343, 1269 (bishop of Halberstadt to count of Wernigerode), and UB Münster 1677, p. 875, 1300 (bishop of Münster to abbess of Essen).

[94] UB Osnabrück ii, 289, p. 230, 1232-8.

[95] UB Münster 792, p. 409, 1267.

[96] UB Hanau 235, p. 178, 1245, 312 f., pp. 228-30, 1256, 400, pp. 293 f., 1265, and 463, pp. 341 f., 1272.

Reinhard decided to secure emancipation for Adelheid and the children by a royal grant. He asserted that he had not realized Adelheid was a *ministerialis*, and the king duly liberated her and their offspring 'from all the servility of *ministeriales*.'[97] In 1289 their heir, Ulrich of Hanau, thought it best to secure a much more elaborate retroactive charter for his mother, and consequently, for all her descendants.[98] In 1298 Siegfried of Eppstein, who had married Isengard of Falkenstein, another heiress descended from the Münzenbergs, successfully applied to King Albert for her liberty.[99]

Ministeriales *as noblemen*

Legally *ministeriales* were unfree persons, but during the twelfth century they came to be reckoned as noblemen, and began to be called nobles personally.[100] This was possible because nobility was a social quality, not technically a legal status like personal freedom and servitude. Since the knightly function was so highly regarded in the twelfth century, it is not difficult to see why *ministeriales* gained acceptance as nobles. Whereas *liber* and *ingenuus* were legal terms denoting free birth, *nobilis* indicated the aristocratic style of life. Of this style the *ministeriales* partook. They had hereditary patrimonies of fief and allod with the exercise of seigneurial jurisdictions over them.[101] They resided in stone towers and castles, they were entitled to judgement by their peers, and they prosecuted personal feuds and duels.[102] They entered the high offices of the Church,[103] they employed a system of forenames modelled upon

[97] Ibid. 471-80, pp. 348-51, 1273.
[98] MGC iii, 392 f., pp. 378 f., 1289.
[99] MGC iv, 37 f., pp. 33 f., 1298. See A. Schulte, *Der Adel und die deutsche Kirche im Mittelalter*, Kirchenrechtliche Abhandlungen, LXIII-LXIV (Stuttgart, 1910), pp. 314-30 for similar cases. The exchanges of status in UB Hildesheim ii, 313, p. 145, 1230-40 are probably to be explained by a mixed marriage.
[100] Tr. Passau 120, p. 97, 1121-38, UB Land ob der Enns ii, 116, p. 174, 1134, Mon. Boica iii, 66, p. 256, c.1150, UB Wirtemberg ii, 380, pp. 142-5, 1163, Mayerhofer, 'Codex Augiensium', 145, p. 117, before 1182; see O. von Dungern, 'Comes, liber, nobilis in Urkunden des 11. bis 13. Jahrhunderts', *AU* xii (1932), 200.
[101] See Ch. 5 below.
[102] See Chs. 4 and 9 below.
[103] e.g. Archbishops Arnold (1153-60) and Christian (1249-51) of Mainz, Bishops Hermann of Constance (1138-65), Conrad of Speyer and Metz (1200-24), Henry of Würzburg (1202-7), Siegfried of Augsburg (1209-27), five incumbents at Eichstätt (1223-46) and their successor Reinboto (1279-97) and many others, were born *ministeriales*. So, we are told (*Annales Stadenses*, MGS, XVI, p. 316, 1072), was

that of the free-born nobility, and they used dynastic toponymics as well as the predicate *dominus* or lord.[104]

In practice no one confused *ministeriales* with free-born nobles until the intermarriages of the fourteenth century rendered the distinction redundant. *Ministeriales'* nobility was acceptable to free-born nobles because of its strictly functional origin in the exercise of arms, and because they themselves shared some of the decorations of knighthood[105] with *ministeriales*. In Henry III's time Wipo had again aired the conceit that valour ennobled the common man,[106] and valour was, after all, a professional qualification of *ministeriales*. Since unfree status was a legal matter and the enjoyment of nobility a social one, the medieval mind did not struggle with a contradiction here.

The prestige of knightly functions conferred upon the *ministeriales* the quality of nobility which, like their castles, family names, and patrimonies, they passed on to their descendants. For this reason they were forming lineages with some of the aristocratic imagery attached to them.[107] Already in 1107, when Archbishop

Archbishop Liemar of Bremen (1072-1101), and many abbots; examples in *Walteri Historia Monasterii Marchtelanensis*, MGS, XXIV, p. 666, 1160s, *Chronicon Montis Sereni*, MGS, XXIII, p. 172, 1205, and A. Weissthanner, *Die Traditionen des Klosters Schäftlarn*, QE, X (Munich 1953), 408, pp. 397f., *c*.1220-5.

[104] W. Störmer, 'Adel und Ministerialität im Spiegel der bayerischen Namengebung bis zum 13. Jahrhundert', *DA* xxxiii (1977), 84-152. *Ministeriales'* dynastic toponymics were also based upon aristocratic usage, and usually derived from the principal castle, e.g. Dietrich of Apolda with his *munitio* and fiefs at the *villa* of Apolda in Thuringia, CD Saxony ii, 220, pp. 151f., 1150, or *dominus* Conrad of Hagen and Arnsburg, UB Mainz ii, 159, pp. 292-7, 1151, whose family then moved to Münzenberg Castle, after which they were forthwith called. The richer *ministeriales* proliferated their castles, and therefore their toponymics, through the division of inheritances, e.g. UB Wirtemberg v, 50, pp. 437f., 1240, amongst the Swabian seneschals of Waldburg, and see pp. 181f., nn. 113-15, p. 214, n. 30, p. 219, n. 54 below.

[105] J. Fleckenstein, 'Friedrich Barbarossa und das Rittertum. Zur Bedeutung der großen Mainzer Hoftage von 1184 and 1188' in *Festschrift für Hermann Heimpel*, vol. ii, Veröffentlichungen des Max-Planck-Instituts für Geschichte XXXVI. 2 (Göttingen, 1972), pp. 1023-41, and e.g. UB Niederrhein ii, 22, pp. 13f., 1208 for a duke's son who was a *miles*.

[106] Wipo, *Gesta Chuonradi*, p. 4.

[107] See *parentela* and *genus* in UB Krain ii, 205, p. 164, 1254. On families of *ministeriales*, revealing their aristocratic style, P. Zinsmaier, 'Das gefälschte Diplom König Heinrichs VII. für Johann von Scharfeneck', *MIöG* Ergänzungsband xiv (1939), 289-302, K.A. Eckhardt, *Die Schenken zu Schweinsberg*, Germanenrechte, Neue Folge, Deutschrechtliches Archiv III (Göttingen, 1953), W. Schwemmer, *Die ehemalige Herrschaft Breitenstein-Königstein*, Schriftenreihe der altnürnberger Landschaft, XIII (Nuremberg, 1965), A.M. Drabek, 'Die Waisen. Eine niederösterreichisch-

Bruno of Trier founded Springiersbach Abbey out of the bequest of Benigna, a *ministerialis* belonging to the Count-Palatine Siegfried, he tactfully called her 'born of good parentage'.[108] In the 1170s a line of Corvey *ministeriales* were called 'a knightly family' or *gens militaris*.[109] In 1188 an Alsatian *ministerialis*, Wolfhelm of Truchtersheim, was called 'a man of conspicuous manners and family, a knight by calling'[110] and a Bavarian source spoke of 'Lord Liebhard, who was a worthy and proper knight from the stock and family of Falkenstein'.[111] Much later, John of Viktring described an imperial *ministerialis* of Hohenrechberg in Swabia as 'a man of good but not free birth'.[112]

As part of Germany's military élite, *ministeriales* belonged to 'the honourable persons', including bishops and counts of the old aristocracy, who celebrated Conrad III's court at Aachen in 1145.[113] They belonged with the *militia* and vassals of free birth who attended such magnates as the bishops of Osnabrück and the counts of Hainault,[114] and were amongst the imperial *fideles* or loyal subjects who, like the princes and the *liberi*, gave Frederick Barbarossa their consent to legislation against incendiaries in 1186.[115] Towards 1200 the adjective *nobilis* had become normal for them, such as the emperor's *viri nobiles* Hugo of Warta and Rudolf of Altenburg, who were his officials in his eastern lordships,[116] or the abbot of Tegernsee's *nobilis ministerialis* Berthold of Egertshausen,[117] or Frederick *nobilis ministerialis* of Tanne, who went to Italy with Duke Philip of Swabia, and was killed in 1197 in the

mährische Adelsfamilie unter Babenbergern und Přemysliden', *MIöG* lxxiv (1966), 292–332, G. Wunder, *Die Schenken von Stauffenberg. Eine Familiengeschichte*, Schriften zur südwestdeutschen Landeskunde, XI (Stuttgart, 1972), and R. Dollinger, 'Die Stauffer zu Ernfels', *ZBLG* xxxv (1972), 436–522.

[108] UB Mittelrhein i, 415, pp. 475–7, 1107.

[109] CD Westphalia ii, 380, pp. 132f., 1176.

[110] Reg. Straßburg i, 643, p. 358, 1188.

[111] Mohr, *Oberalteich*, 104, pp. 216–20, 1188. He belonged not to the Bavarian comital house of Falkenstein but to the Diepolding *ministeriales* with the same toponymic; ibid. 102, pp. 213f., c.1184–8.

[112] F. Schneider, *Iohannis Abbatis Victoriensis Liber Certarum Historiarum*, MG schol. XXXVI. 1–2 (Hanover and Leipzig, 1909–10), vol. i, pp. 355f., for 1298.

[113] MGD Conrad III, 142, pp. 256f., 1145.

[114] CD Westphalia ii, 252, p. 41, 1146, and Gislebert of Mons, p. 300, 1194.

[115] MGC i, 318, p. 449, 1186.

[116] F. Rosenfeld, *Urkundenbuch des Hochstifts Naumburg*, Geschichtsquellen der Provinz Sachsen, n.s., I (Magdeburg, 1925), 287, p. 276, 1172.

[117] Tr. Tegernsee 365, p. 279, 1189–1206.

riots which occurred in Tuscany upon the report of Henry VI's death,[118] and others.[119]

If the knights who were *ingenui* or free-born were never mistaken for *ministeriales* who were not, scribes did frequently use the legally neutral word *nobilis* as a synonym for *ingenuus* and *liber*.[120] This confusing pratice persisted well into the thirteenth century,[121] and was to some extent encouraged by those lineages of *ingenui* who, having no comital title, used *vir nobilis* or nobleman as a distinguishing mark. In 1143 a Saxon charter had correctly placed them between the counts and the *ministeriales*, all three ranks having their dynastic toponymics.[122] The prominent Swabian dynasty of Neuffen, which later inherited the comital titles of Marstetten and Graisbach, employed *nobilis* as their title early in the thirteenth century,[123] and so did many other free-born families of knights.[124] In 1192 an Austrian ducal charter also distinguished the free-born as *nobiles*, an 'order of nobles', before those 'of the order of *ministeriales*'.[125] In 1202, when Archbishop Adolf of Cologne bound himself and his enfeoffed following to Otto IV, the men were divided into free-born *nobiles* and then his *ministeriales*,[126] and elsewhere the imperial chancery persisted in using *nobilis* for the same separation from unfree knights.[127]

Free knightly families below the rank of count were therefore sharing with the much more numerous *ministeriales* the aristocratic labels of *dominus* and *miles*, lord and knight, as well as the adjective 'noble'[128] and even the flourish *Dei gratia*, 'by the grace of God'.

---

[118] Burchard of Ursberg, p. 76.

[119] e.g. Mon. Boica xlix, 19, p. 43, 1185 and 25, p. 56, after 1195, UB Weida 28, p. 10, 1188, and UB Krain i, 157, p. 139, 1191.

[120] MGD Conrad III, 74, p. 132, 1142, UB Wirtemberg ii, 327, p. 43, 1148, UB Niederrhein i, 470, p. 330, 1179, and Mon. Boica xlix, 13, p. 35, 1180.

[121] Sudendorf, *Braunschweig*, 8, p. 6, 1225, Wittmann, *Monumenta Castellana*, 82, p. 24, 1225, and UB Halberstadt ii, 1378, p. 443, 1281.

[122] Jordan, *Urkunden Heinrichs des Löwen*, 4, p. 6, 1143.

[123] MGC ii, 52, p. 64, 1214, and 57, p. 71, 1216.

[124] e.g. UB Wirtemberg ii, 526, p. 350, 1205 and iv, 1083, pp. 145f., 1246, and UB Hildesheim ii, 193, pp. 82f., 1226 and 564, p. 227, 1240.

[125] Mon. Boica liii, 44, p. 16, 1192.

[126] MGC ii, 24, p. 28, 1202.

[127] e.g. MGC i, 329, p. 467, 1190, 366, p. 515, 1195, and ii, 279, p. 393, 1222.

[128] UB Steiermark ii, 122, p. 185, 1212 for the 'nobilis ac strenuus miles' Herrand of Wildon, Weissthanner, *Schäftlarn*, 394, p. 387, c.1217 for Gebhard of Beigarten as *domnus* and *nobilis*, and K. Dumrath, *Die Traditionsnotizen des Klosters Raitenhaslach*, QE, VII (Munich, 1938), 125, p. 102, 1243 for 'dominus Chunradus miles

In 1188 an imperial scribe simply used *nobiles viri*, or noblemen, to denote *ministeriales* between the Saxon counts above them and the townsmen of Goslar beneath them.[129] The thirteenth-century foundation story of Weissenau in Swabia also placed Duke Henry the Lion's *ministerialis*, the *dominus* Gebizo of Ravensburg, who founded Weissenau in 1145 and was assassinated in 1152, amongst the *nobiles terre* or 'noblemen of the land'.[130] As for the *Dei gratia* designation, the duke of Brabant's *ministerialis* Arnold of Wesemael called himself 'lord of Wesemael by the grace of God' in 1237, and *nobilis vir* and *miles* of Wesemael in 1240.[131] The influential Saxon *ministeriales* of Wolfenbüttel-Asseburg, who were often called *servi* and *famuli*, also called themselves seneschals of Wolfenbüttel 'by the grace of God', as well as *nobiles viri*.[132] So did another imperial officer, Henry of Pappenheim 'by the grace of God and the empire, marshal of the imperial court',[133] but the *Dei gratia* flourish was by no means confined to the greatest *ministeriales*.[134]

The genealogical memory of that age was long, but thirteenth-century scribes did remind themselves that some of their nobles were still *ministeriales*. In Austria and Styria, where there were almost no other noblemen than *ministeriales* by the end of the twelfth century, expressions such as *nobiles terre ministeriales* might still be used.[135] In 1237 the counts of Sternberg and Maltein called their knights at Laas in Carniola 'our *ministeriales* and noblemen',

de Eschelpach ministerialis', and Reimer, *Hanau*, 497 f., pp. 361 f., 1275, where the archbishop of Mainz addresses Wernher of Falkenstein as *nobilis vir*.

[129] UB Asseburg i, 26, p. 25, 1188. Clearly literature did not imitate life in the twelfth century; Bumke, *Studien*, p. 68, shows that in vernacular literature *ritter*, *kneht*, *dienestman*, and *eigen* were never confused with *hêrre*, *vrî*, and *adel*.

[130] *Historiae Augienses*, MGS, XXIV, p. 654, and Haendle, pp. 57 f.

[131] Ganshof, *Étude*, p. 93 n. 1 f., and M.-J. Tits-Dieuaide, 'Un exemple de passage de la ministérialité à la noblesse: la famille de Wesemael 1166–1250', *Revue belge de philologie et d'histoire* xxxvi (1958), 335–55.

[132] UB Hildesheim ii, 357, p. 167, 1232, and UB Asseburg i, 178–80, pp. 123 f., 1234, 217, p. 154, 1242, 486, p. 309, 1296, and 490, p. 311, 1296.

[133] W. Kraft, *Das Urbar der Reichsmarschälle von Pappenheim*, Schriftenreihe zur bayerischen Landesgeschichte, III (Munich, 1929), p. 4 n. 9, 1251.

[134] J.S. Seibertz, *Quellen der Westfälischen Geschichte*, vol. i (Arnsberg, 1857), p. 476, 1245, and UB Hildesheim iii, 609, p. 316, 1282.

[135] UB Steiermark ii, 172, p. 255, 1220, and H. Dopsch, 'Probleme ständischer Wandlung beim Adel Österreichs, der Steiermark und Salzburgs vornehmlich im 13. Jahrhundert' in J. Fleckenstein (ed.), *Herrschaft und Stand. Untersuchungen zur Sozialgeschichte im 13. Jahrhundert*, Veröffentlichungen des Max-Planck-Instituts für Geschichte, LI (Göttingen, 1977), pp. 219–44.

and in 1245, when Count Conrad of Neuburg bequeathed his property to the bishops of Freising, he stipulated that 'my men of noble condition have bound themselves to owe service to the church of Freising and its future bishops as *ministeriales* bound by oath'.[136]

In the twelfth century the continuing importance of active knighthood obviously was advancing the significance of this unfree nobility, at least at its better-known upper level. *Ministeriales* provided, for example, nearly all the personnel in the German crusading order established in 1198, the Teutonic Order, and the notable grand-master Hermann of Salza (1210-39), who transferred it to Prussia, was a Thuringian *ministerialis*.[137] As we have seen, *ministeriales* competed with the free and titled aristocracy for high places in the Church. The imperial household officers stood at the centre of German affairs,[138] and they approached a political equality with the territorial magnates. In 1183 the sixteen 'princes and nobles of the court' who swore for the emperor to the Peace of Constance with the papacy included four prelates, three dukes, two margraves, three counts, and four prominent imperial *ministeriales*; Rudolf, chamberlain of Siebeneich, Wernher of Bolanden, Cuno of Münzenberg, and Conrad, butler of Schüpf.[139] In 1213 the ten 'princes and nobles of the empire' who swore to Frederick II's commitments to the pope included Henry, marshal of Kalden and Walter, butler of Schüpf.[140]

Although they had achieved recognition as a nobility, the *ministeriales* did not agitate for the stigma of unfreedom to be lifted from them, probably because they already outstripped the *liberi* in wealth, political significance, and numbers, and reckoned their own status to be the exemplar of knighthood in the German empire. They saw personal servitude not as a degradation but as a form of

[136] UB Krain ii, 96, p. 70, 1237, and J. Zahn, *Codex Diplomaticus Austriaco-Frisingensis*, Fontes rerum Austriacarum, ser. 2, XXXI (Vienna, 1870), 145, pp. 140f., 1245.

[137] M. Hellmann, 'Bemerkungen zur sozialgeschichtlichen Erforschung des Deutschen Ordens', *HJ* lxxx (1961), 126-42, W. Cohn, *Hermann von Salza*, Abhandlungen der Schlesischen Gesellschaft für vaterländische Cultur. Geisteswissenschaftliche Reihe IV (Berlin, 1930), p. 1, and H. Patze, *Die Entstehung der Landesherrschaft in Thüringen*, Mitteldeutsche Forschungen, XXII (Cologne and Graz, 1962), pp. 352-4.

[138] Chs. 7 and 8 below.

[139] MGC i, 293, pp. 416f., 1183.

[140] MGC ii, 49f., p. 62, 1213. Wernher of Bolanden was included with *imperii magnates* in UB Steiermark ii, 204, p. 294, 1223.

vassalage which was honourable. Gislebert of Mons, however, reports an interesting case in 1188 when the count of Hainault's cousin Gerard of St Aubert successfully claimed back the knights Achard of Verli and Robert of Beaurain as his *servi*.[141] Robert denied that he belonged to Gerard, and claimed to be a *liber*. Gerard offered to prove the opposite in a trial by combat, but Robert lost his nerve and failed to appear on the day appointed. He was arrested and handed over to Gerard in chains. Gerard forced him to swear fealty 'like a man of servile condition', but Gislebert says that Robert eventually secured a reversal of the judgement against him by appeal to Henry VI's court. The solution to his problems was found, apparently, in a timely death on the Third Crusade.

[141] Gislebert of Mons, pp. 209–15.

CHAPTER 3

The Rights of *Ministeriales* in Written Custom

Rules for ministeriales *and their standardization*

The standing of *ministeriales* in German society was compounded
of personal servitude, ascription to their lords' patrimonies as accessories, and the professional functions of knighthood underlined
by the obligations of fief-holding vassalage. Duties and exemptions
were termed, in aggregate, *ministerialies'* right or *ius*, with the
scribes often employing synonyms such as *lex* or rule, *libertas* or
privilege, and *dignitas* or rank.[1] Men given with their fiefs to the
see of Passau in the mid-twelfth century 'obtained the right, *ius*, of
ministeriales in the *familia*, retinue, of St Stephen, and the complete
conditions for this order of men'.[2]

Fortunately for us these rights and duties were, in certain circumstances, written down, and more than a dozen such lists, some of
them forgeries, have survived. As we have seen, the earliest is for
Bamberg *ministeriales* about 1060, and the most elaborate is the
custumal drawn up, probably in 1165, for Archbishop Rainald of
Cologne. Shorter custumals were prepared in 1154 for Count Dietrich of Ahr's *ministeriales*, in the 1220s for Count Otto of Tecklenburg's, and in 1237 a very brief one for the counts of Sternberg
and Maltein's knights at Laas in Carniola. There are forged charters ascribed to earlier emperors purporting to lay down rules for
ministeriales; at the imperial manor of Weissenburg in Franconia,
and at the Alsatian monasteries of Klingenmünster and Erstein. The
edict manufactured at the Swabian abbey of Reichenau about 1160

---

[1] Bitterauf, *Freising*, 1711, pp. 512 f., 1123-30, Mayerhofer, 'Codex Augiensium',
57, p. 99, 1125, MGD Lothar III, 73, pp. 112 f., 1135, MGD Conrad III, 46, pp.
77 f., 1140, K. Bosl, 'Das ius ministerialium. Dienstrecht und Lehnrecht im
deutschen Mittelalter' in *Frühformen*, pp. 277-326, and K. Kroeschell, 'Recht und
Rechtsbegriff im 12. Jahrhundert' in *Probleme des 12. Jahrhunderts*, VF, XII (Constance and Stuttgart, 1968), pp. 309-35.
[2] Tr. Passau 628, p. 231, 1149-64.

pretends to regulate imperial expeditions to Italy for the entire German military élite; princes and free-born lords and vassals, as well as *ministeriales*. Early in the thirteenth century, two forgeries were prepared at Tegernsee Abbey and dated 1163 and 1193, giving imperial consent to a number of privileges claimed by the abbots, including the rights over their *ministeriales*. Probably these forgeries more or less correctly reflect twelfth-century military and social practices.

There are also a number of genuine sources which are not custumals, but preserve in passing considerable information about *ministeriales'* rights. They include three instruments drawn up by the archbishops of Cologne; for founding a covent in 1166, for ending a feud in 1182, and for concluding a political alliance in 1227. The mandate by which Duke Ottokar of Styria bequeathed his duchy to Austria in 1186 included some of the rights of his *ministeriales*. So did the monastic chronicles of Zwiefalten in Swabia for 1135 and of Kremsmünster in Austria for 1217, for their *ministeriales*. Fragments about obligations are to be found in episcopal charters from Hildesheim, Passau, Mainz, Würzburg, Salzburg, and elsewhere, monastic sources from Niederaltaich and Rott in Bavaria, and from Prüm in Lotharingia, and in town-laws from Strasburg and Basel.

Although the practices revealed in these sources are by no means uniform, apparently there was already wide consensus early in the twelfth century about what could or could not be expected of *ministeriales*. In 1114 Henry V referred to the rights of those 'who are called in German *dienestman*',[3] assuming them to be common knowledge. For this reason *ministeriales'* rights are frequently mentioned, particularly in the charters recording their creation or recruitment or transfer, without affording further details. Yet the nature of *ministeriales'* adherence to their lords meant that in theory each retinue might have its own customs based upon its lord's needs, expectations, and authority. Traces of this can be seen in a cursory comparison of comital custumals, Ahr with Tecklenburg, or episcopal, Bamberg with Cologne, or monastic, Reichenau with Klingenmünster, and so on.

Practices were becoming standardized, particularly for retinues under lords of comparable power and standing, or who lived in the same region. Since Henry IV's time customs had in many cases

[3] U B Mainz i, 459, p. 367, 1114.

been standardized by royal precept. In 1064 the Einsiedeln *ministri* were given the same customs as their neighbours, the St Gallen *servientes*, and the Ottobeuren *ministeriales* were said to have the same rights as those of Fulda and Reichenau in the twelfth century.[4] These retines belonged to abbots, and it was becoming assumed that the more prominent German houses would have the same rules for their *ministeriales*. In 1124, therefore, Henry V granted the abbot of Scheyern's *ministeriales* the same rules or *lex* as exercised under 'the other abbots in our kingdom'.[5]

The customs for bishops' *ministeriales* also drew closer, so that in 1218 Frederick II could confirm to the Chiemsee and Seckau retines all the rights 'which the *ministeriales* of the [episcopal] churches of Germany have hitherto been accustomed to obtain'.[6] Monasteries also might adopt rules from bishoprics. Ravengiersburg and Klingenmünster took the Mainz customs for their *ministeriales*, the latter via a forgery designed to protect the retinue from oppressive advocates, the former by a genuine archiepiscopal grant.[7] In 1153 at Niederaltaich Abbey, Bishop Eberhard of Bamberg confirmed the equality of the *ministeriales* with his own, specifying the matter of jurisdiction over them, their marriages, and the purchase, sale, or donation of land.[8]

The crown was responsible for assigning the rules for imperial *ministeriales* to other retinues, although the Weissenburg forgery ascribed to Conrad II is the only surviving custumal for imperial knights. *Ministeriales'* customs must have varied region by region. In 1135 Lothar III confirmed to the abbot of Wildeshausen's *ministeriales* the rights they had enjoyed in Duke Magnus Billung of Saxony's time, the last quarter of the eleventh century. They were the same customs as his own *ministeriales* enjoyed, and so did those of his son-in-law, Duke Henry the Proud of Bavaria. The same year, the emperor gave these rules to St Michael at Lüneburg's *ministeriales* as well.[9] In 1213 Frederick II gave the *ius* of imperial

[4] M G D Henry I V, 125, pp. 163 f., 1064, and M G D Charlemagne, 219, pp. 292–4, dated to 769.
[5] Mon. Boica x, 5, p. 451, 1124. M G D Henry I V, 280, p. 361, dated 1075, a late 11th-c. fabrication for Hirsau, used the same phrase, probably providing the formula for the 1124 charter.
[6] U B Steiermark ii, 161, p. 242, 1218.
[7] U B Mainz i, 462, pp. 369–71, dated 1115, and 341, p. 237, 1074.
[8] Mon. Boica xi, 43, pp. 166 f., 1153.
[9] M G D Lothar I I I, 73, pp. 112 f., and 75, pp. 116 f., 1135.

RIGHTS IN WRITTEN CUSTOM

79

ministeriales to the bishop of Gurk's knights,[10] and in 1235, when he created the duchy of Brunswick and Lüneburg, he conceded this right to the ducal retinue.[11] Without detailed information about the imperial *ius*, it is difficult to judge what such grants meant in practice. A ruling by King Henry VII in 1231 is more explicit. He extended to ecclesiastical *ministeriales* his instructions for imperial knights about the inheritance and escheat of fiefs,[12] and presumably this would have applied to the Brunswick *ministeriales* from 1235.

Such standardizations of custom in Saxony undermine the value of Eike von Repgow's assertion that it was not worth discussing *ministeriales*' rights because they were everywhere so different.[13] Standard custom was also encouraged in the twelfth century by intermarriage between retinues, by mobility of service, and by the multiple enfeoffment of *ministeriales*, and consequently of their allegiances. Already in 1092 Bishop Udo of Hildesheim indicated that there were few restrictions left about where and whom the imperial, Mainz, and Hildesheim *ministeriales* might marry.[14] Bishops were recognizing other integrations of custom. In 1085 the way in which the bishop of Münster guaranteed the abbess of Freckenhorst's *ministeriales* against oppression was to grant them the rights of his own *ministeriales*.[15] In 1111, when Bishop Ulrich of Passau left his Swabian lands to his cathedral church, the *ministri* and *servientes* there were henceforth to enjoy the same rights as the Bavarian *ministeriales* of Passau.[16] In 1140 the patriarch of Aquileia accredited the rights of his own *dienstmanni* to the *ministeriales*

[10] Mon. Carinthia i, 442, p. 338, 1213.
[11] MGC ii, 197, p. 264, 1235.
[12] Ibid. 310, p. 423, 1231.
[13] Eckhardt, *Sachsenspiegel Lehnrecht*, p. 82; on the Saxon *ministeriales*, Haendle, *Dienstmannen Heinrichs des Löwen*, E. Molitor, *Der Stand der Ministerialen vornehmlich auf Grund sächsischer, thüringischer und niederrheinischer Quellen*, Untersuchungen zur deutschen Staats- und Rechtsgeschichte, CXII (Breslau, 1912), A. Heinrichsen, 'Süddeutsche Adelsgeschlechter in Niedersachsen im 11. und 12. Jahrhundert', *Niedersächsisches Jahrbuch für Landesgeschichte* xxvi (1954), 24–116, and L. Fenske, 'Ministerialität und Adel im Herrschaftsbereich der Bischöfe von Halberstadt während des 13. Jahrhunderts' in J. Fleckenstein (ed.), *Herrschaft und Stand*, pp. 157–206.
[14] UB Hildesheim i, 150, pp. 142 f., 1092.
[15] CD Westphalia i, 164, pp. 128 f., 1085, and see K. Poth, *Die Ministerialität der Bischöfe von Münster* (Münster, 1912).
[16] Mon. Boica xxix. A, 438, p. 224, 1111.

just acquired by the monastery at Obernburg,[17] and in 1224 Count
Otto of Ravensberg accepted the bishop of Paderborn's rules for
his *ministeriales*.[18] But Eike von Repgow was not mistaken in
pointing out the potential variety in customs, since individual lords
were at liberty in law to impose rules of their own devising upon
their *ministeriales*, because they were unfree.

Committing rules to writing: the Bamberg custumal about 1060

Ministeriales were subjected to rules not under a contract, but
because of their servile birth. Customs did, nevertheless, give contractual colouring to the connection of lord and *ministerialis*. This
is plain to see in the written lists. *Ministeriales* were obliged to offer
service and obedience without question, but lords could expect
efficiency only if their retinues understood what customs were traditional, reasonable, and above all, hereditary. The Bamberg rules
were already hereditary in the mid eleventh century, and twelfth-
century sources also take for granted that rights and status were
heritable.[19]

The Bamberg custumal[20] shows that sons or near male relatives
could expect to inherit fiefs, the latter by offering a heriot. It shows
that *ministeriales* were not expected to serve at all unless they received fiefs, and if they did not, then they were at liberty to seek
service as knights under other lords. Their duties were military and
administrative; on campaigns north and south of the Alps, and in
the bishop's five household offices of seneschal, butler, chamberlain, marshal, and forester. The custumal was concerned with discipline and security; for the bishop against conspiracies by *ministeriales*, for the *ministeriales* against the hazard of violent death, in
which case the family's recompense was £10, a large sum. In these
respects, the heritability of fiefs, the administrative and military
nature of service, and discipline under household and wider law,
all the later custumals follow Bishop Gunther's example, so that by
1231 Bishop Ulrich of Gurk might refer in a quite perfunctory
fashion to 'all the rights of *ministeriales*, either about fiefs or about

[17] UB Steiermark i, 180, pp. 188–90, 1140.
[18] UB Münster 541, p. 290, 1224.
[19] e.g. MGD Lothar III, 73, pp. 112f., 1135.
[20] Jaffé, *MB*, pp. 51 f.

patrimony or about penalties', without feeling the need to give any
details.[21]

The surviving custumals: the see of Cologne

Of the surviving custumals, Archbishop Rainald of Cologne's list
is by far the longest.[22] Probably it was drawn up in 1165 before
the ill-starred imperial expedition to Italy planned for 1166. The
archbishop was the architect of this campaign, upon which he
greatly distinguished himself and his knights, and was the mightiest
prince to die of the malarial infection which decimated the German
army in 1167 and brought the expedition to an inglorious close.
His custumal began by obliging his *ministeriales* to swear him
fealty, and to defend the confines of the see and Cologne's property
beyond its boundaries. He also provided for the military expeditions to Italy. Notice was to be given a year and a day in advance,
and *ministeriales* with fiefs worth more than five marks a year were
obliged to go. Knights with fiefs of lesser value might stay behind,
but had to give up half the revenue of their fiefs in commutation
of service, as war-tax or *herstura*.

In a real emergency, when the bishopric or territories of Cologne
were invaded, even *ministeriales* not yet enfeoffed were expected to
turn out, 'to assist their lord archbishop in defending the land and
to follow him in arms to the boundaries of the see'. This is what
happened in 1240 when Archbishop Conrad summoned the Westphalian *ministeriales* from across the Rhine to withstand a sudden
onslaught by the duke of Brabant: '... since, according to the
obligations of your fealty to us and the church of Cologne, you
should come if necessary prepared with horses and arms as military
assistance, to receive back for your services fitting remuneration
and lasting favour'. The invasion was beaten off.[23]

The custumal is greatly concerned with discipline. The archbishop tried absolutely to forbid duels amongst Cologne *ministeriales*, 'whatever one might do to another'. Duels between Cologne
knights and imperial *ministeriales* were permitted, and were to take

[21] Mon. Carinthia i, 532, pp. 413 f., 1231.
[22] Weinrich, pp. 266–78, and H. von Loesch, 'Das kürzere Kölner Dienstmannenrecht', *ZRGGA* xliv (1924), 298–307.
[23] E. Winkelmann, *Acta Imperii Inedita Saeculi XIII. et XIV.* (2 vols., new edn.,
Aalen, 1964), vol. i, 666, p. 532, 1240, and Waitz, *Chronica Regia Coloniensis*, p.
277 f.

place before the emperor or the archbishop, depending on who had issued the challenge. The archbishop might deprive *ministeriales* of their possessions for other unspecified misdemeanours, and if they failed to recover grace within a year, they were expelled from the retinue. Those falling into debt upon Italian expeditions, for which they were paid extra from the archbishop's treasury, were liable to be sent home. In arbitrary homicides amongst the *ministeriales* the murderer was obliged to regain the archbishop's grace within a year and a day. If it was not forthcoming, he was imprisoned for life beneath the archbishop's palace for his own protection from 'his enemies, whom he earned for himself by the death of the murdered man', in short, the victim's kinsmen and friends. Only at Christmas, Easter, and the Feast of St Peter, the see's patron, would he be allowed out on three-day parole to try to arrange accommodation for the crime. Should he flee or escape from confinement, then he lost all rights and was to be killed out of hand as an outlaw, even if dragged from sanctuary.

The archbishop sought to protect his *ministeriales* from excommunication by other Cologne clerics 'unless by chance they have unjustly seized or usurped for themselves the tithes or possessions of the Church'. Other cases brought for misdemeanours against the clergy were to be heard in an annual court held by the archbishop's chaplain. The archbishop also forbade the free lords of the diocese to cite his *ministeriales* before their own courts. They should bring their grievances against them to his court.

Next, the custumal is concerned with the administration of the archbishop's estates and household. The two chief *ministeriales* of the see were the advocate and the chamberlain. They were exempt from Italian expeditions: 'Indeed these two must remain at home, the advocate to collect and conserve the revenue of the episcopal manors, and the chamberlain the revenue from the tolls and mint'. Evidently Archbishop Rainald changed his mind. The advocate Gerhard of Heppendorf did go with him and in Rome, witnessed Frederick Barbarossa's gift of Andernach on the Rhine as the archbishop's reward for his victory at Tusculum in May 1167.[24] The advocate was also the archbishop's principal judicial officer, and was paid with the revenues of twelve manors. The other *ministeriales*, 'especially those who are senior amongst them', were obliged to serve as the household officers for six weeks at a time on a rota

[24] U B Niederrhein i, 426, pp. 296 f., 1167.

system. In 1169 the office of advocate, which hitherto had been an annual appointment, was enfeoffed perpetually to Gerhard of Heppendorf and his descendants in exchange for homage.[25]

The custumal included the grants made by the archbishop for various purposes: the fitting-out allowances for Italian expeditions, the victuals for murderers seeking forgiveness within their time-limit of a year and a day, and new attire, or six marks a head, for thirty knights at each of the great feasts at Cologne, Christmas, Easter, and St Peter's Day. The clothing was of luxury quality, including furs and leatherwork. Undoubtedly the heaviest call upon the archbishop's resources was for Italian campaigns. Since the fitting-out allowance was ten marks plus clothing, horses, and other equipment, and the rate of pay in Italy a mark a month, the expeditions were very expensive. For Frederick Barbarossa's fifth expedition, which set out in 1174, Rainald's successor Archbishop Philip borrowed at least two thousand marks from the city of Cologne, and from Count Engelbert of Berg, who was still owed his money in 1189.[26]

Finally, the Cologne custumal confirmed hereditary right by primogeniture to the *ministeriales*' fiefs and offices. Nothing was said about heriots or reliefs, but a century earlier they had, apparently, been charged £3 per inheritance.[27] Younger brothers without fiefs but possessing war-horses, shields, and lances were put on probation, after saying their prayers in Cologne Cathedral, and offering fealty and service as knights to the archbishop at his palace. After a year's service the archbishop was obliged to find them new fiefs. Those not acceptable were offered mobility of service, and might enter other retinues. Magnanimously the archbishop recognized their duty to fight for their new lord and to defend his castles even in feuds against the see, but they were to refrain from pillage and arson in opposing the archbishop.

The surviving custumals: Ahr in the Rhineland

No other source matches the Cologne custumal in its detail and precision. In 1154 the archbishop's vassal Count Dietrich of Ahr

---

[25] Ibid. 434, p. 304, 1169; Gerhard was called *advocatus curie nostre* in 445, p. 312, 1173.

[26] Ibid. 452, p. 318, 1174, 455, pp. 319 f., 1176, and 517, p. 362, 1189.

[27] Pötter, p. 148.

had already issued a custumal guaranteeing his *ministeriales'* rights,[28] concerned mainly with fiefs and with discipline. Fiefs were hereditary to sons, or failing them, to daughters, brothers, and sisters. If they had no fiefs as yet, then the heriot was a horse with saddle and bridle. If it was their second fief, then they had to pay over its value, reckoned by their peers, and a hauberk if they had one, as the heriot. If *ministeriales* died without heirs of this kind, then widows enjoyed the usufruct of fiefs, but their children by further marriages had no ultimate right to them. New fiefs given to young *ministeriales* who died before they had issue reverted to the count absolutely. Hereditary rights were curtailed if the heir was physically incapacitated or mentally unsound.[29] The fief was then delegated to another *ministerialis* who could fulfil the services expected, but he had to maintain the unfortunate one so that the count might not be accused of dishonourably neglecting his men. The fiefs carried the military obligations of supporting the count on campaign under his own lords, the archbishop of Cologne and the emperor, and being ready at all times to garrison his castles, fulfilling both duties at the count's expense. If horses were lost in his service, the count replaced them. As at Cologne there was probation for young *ministeriales*, their fathers providing their outfits, the count finding their food and the winter-fodder for their horses.

Count Dietrich graded the penalties for misdemeanours. Breach of the custumal itself entailed expulsion from the retinue, and fellow-knights were expected to become the enemies of such felons. Those who wounded or killed another *ministerialis* without excuse fell absolutely into the count's power, losing his protection and their fiefs. Those who despoiled the count's property were fined £2, and so were those who oppressed their fellows, in which case the count received a third of the fine, exacted by their peers. Lesser, unspecified offences were also compounded by fines of five shillings to the count, except in brawls where the knights pulled each others' hair or hit each other. Then the fine was £1, the guilty party being convicted by two other knights, either *ministeriales* or *liberi*.

Count Dietrich left no sons, and his indirect heirs, the counts of Nürburg and Hochstaden, decided to hold the county, castle, *mini-*

---

[28] U B Niederrhein iv, 624, pp. 774 f., 1154.

[29] U B Salzburg iii, 984, pp. 532–4, 1242 for a *ministerialis*, Ulrich of Reisberg, who was insane. He had brothers to look after him.

steriales, and nearly all the appurtenances in common. Their sons, Count Gerhard of Nürburg and Count Lothar of Hochstaden, renewed this arrangement in 1202, updating some of the rights of the *ministeriales* who performed garrison duty in Ahr.[30] The fiefs dependent upon these offices were now to descend to sons, daughters, or near relatives of either sex without heriots being charged. The knightly garrison had the right to hunt in Ahr Forest and to be buried in Ahr churchyard. If one of the counts was accused of injuring a *ministerialis*, the other count judged the case. *Ministeriales* accused of injuring the counts were tried in the castle, and convicted offenders were obliged to regain grace within a year and a day or, presumably, suffer expulsion from the retinue.

The surviving custumals: Tecklenburg in Westphalia

The concern about fiefs, penalties, and services was repeated when Count Otto of Tecklenburg, another Cologne vassal, issued a custumal for his *ministeriales* in the 1220s.[31] Here too the enfeoffed *ministeriales*, except those in real need, were expected to garrison the count's castles for four weeks a year, with two weeks' notice and at their own expense. In exchange, the *ministeriales* had evidently been able to demand that the count take their counsel before he required their military services in the field. In addition, the count offered protection to his knights, even a refuge in his own castle when necessary.

Fiefs were hereditary in both lines, and to collateral heirs. The heriot, the best horse or half a mark, was due to the count or his chamberlain within a year and a day. If inheritances were to be divided between brothers, then the youngest received the family *domus* or castle. The hereditary expectations of families were protected in that fiefs could not be alienated by *ministeriales* without their relations' consent. Count Otto in later years referred to this right when *ministeriales* gave fiefs to monasteries; the alienations followed 'the rules of our *ministeriales* and the declarations approved'.[32] The rules also protected the count's ultimate proprietary

---

[30] U B Niederrhein iv, 646, pp. 791-3, 1202. By 1214 six families of *ministeriales* garrisoned Ahr, ibid. ii, 46, p. 24, including the burgraves and seneschals of Ahr.

[31] U B Osnabrück ii, 123, pp. 89-92, and R. Froessel, *Das Ministerialenrecht der Grafen von Tecklenburg* (Münster, 1907).

[32] U B Osnabrück ii, 255, pp. 200 f., 1230, and 347, pp. 268 f., 1236.

right to his *ministeriales*' allods, which it was forbidden to alienate without his consent. As at Cologne and Ahr, the count provided for the expenses of *ministeriales* conducted across the Alps to Italy, or elsewhere on imperial service.

Miscreant *ministeriales* were to be judged by their peers, but the count was not obliged to accept sentences he disapproved of. *Ministeriales* out of favour had to regain grace within a year and a day, and could appeal to the bishop of Osnabrück, another of the count's overlords, against an unfavourable sentence. The count would confiscate all possessions and withdraw his protection for serious offences: entering the countess's bed-chamber without lights or unaccompanied by the chamberlain, entering his treasury similarly unaccompanied, or conspiring against his life and honour. Evidently the Tecklenburgs feared the fate of Count Hermann of Winzenburg and his wife. In 1152 the Winzenburg and Hildesheim *ministeriales* conspired successfully to slay them at night in their bed, and to purloin their treasure, said to total the vast sum of £6,000.[33] Winzenburg Castle was not so far from Tecklenburg, and the tale must have frightened all the Saxon counts. The Tecklenburg *ministeriales* were protected too. If oppressed by more powerful knights, they might appeal to the count, who would share out the appropriate fine. *Ministeriales*' serfs and other servants were exempt from the count's courts, since the knights would themselves exercise manorial jurisdiction over them, and their carts, when loaded with provisions, were exempt from the count's tolls.

The surviving custumals: Laas in Carniola

Ministeriales belonging to the ruling margraves and dukes of Austria, Styria, Carinthia, and Carniola, to their comital vassals, and to the Bavarian bishops who owned extremely extensive lands in the eastern marches, were involved not only in the German colonization of those regions as military garrisons, but also in the economic organization of forest and valley as manorial lords on their own account. The most notable example was the Kuenring family in Lower Austria, with their numerous castles, towns, monasteries, manors, and forests.[34] At Laas in Carniola, surrounded by the

[33] *Annales Palidenses*, MGS, XVI, p. 86.
[34] K. Brunner, 'Die Herkunft der Kuenringer', *MIöG* lxxxvi (1978), 291-309, A. Kusternig and M. Weltin (ed.), *Kuenringer-Forschungen*, Jahrbuch für Landeskunde

Slovene population, the counts of Sternberg and Maltein maintained a garrison of *ministeriales*, and confirmed their father's custumal for them in 1237.[35] Much briefer than the comital custumals of Ahr and Tecklenburg, it guaranteed descent of fiefs and allods in the male and female lines, and when they failed, to cousins. The *ministeriales* were to exercise manorial jurisdiction over their serfs, except those taken as robbers worthy of hanging. Such cases were to go before the court of the lord of Carniola, at that time the duke of Austria. The counts renounced requisitions for their own upkeep, and other levies in cash and kind, from their *ministeriales*, but reserved the right to fine them five shillings for minor offences.

Rights and obligations of ministeriales *preserved in other sources*

Details about *ministeriales*' duties and rights have been preserved in a variety of other sources which serve to confirm the information contained in the five authentic custumals. In 1092, for example, one of Bishop Udo of Hildesheim's charters remitted the tax on *ministeriales*' marriages unjustly levied by his predecessors.[36] In 1111, Bishop Ulrich of Passau's donation showed that his *ministeriales* were exempt from enfeoffment to, or exchange with, other lords except by imperial mandate.[37] This safeguard is all we know about the rights of *ministeriales* in the margraviate of Namur created in 1184.[38] The deed recording the Bishop of Bamberg's

von Niederösterreich, n. s. XLVI-VII (Vienna, 1981), J. Gründler, H. Wolfram, K. Brunner, and G. Stangler (ed.), *Die Kuenringer. Das Werden des Landes Niederösterreich*, Katalog des Niederösterreichischen Landesmuseums, n. s., CX (2nd edn., Vienna, 1981), and H. Helbig and L. Weinrich, *Urkunden und erzählende Quellen zur deutschen Ostsiedlung im Mittelalter*, vol. ii, AQ, XXVI. B (Darmstadt, 1970), pp. 446-508. For the significance of the *ministeriales* in the Saxon marches, H. Schieckel, *Herrschaftsbereich und Ministerialität der Markgrafen von Meissen im 12. und 13. Jahrhundert*, Mitteldeutsche Forschungen, VII (Cologne and Graz, 1956), Schulze, *Adelsherrschaft*, pp. 105-207, D. Claude, *Geschichte des Erzbistums Magdeburg bis in das 12. Jahrhundert*, vol. ii, Mitteldeutsche Forschungen, LXVII. 2 (Cologne and Vienna, 1975), pp. 257-79, G. Winter, *Die Ministerialität in Brandenburg* (Munich and Berlin, 1922), and O. von Heinemann, *Codex Diplomaticus Anhaltinus*, vol. i (Dessau, 1867-73), 362, p. 273, 1151, 486, p. 354, 1164, and 658, p. 484, 1188.

[35] UB Krain ii, 96, pp. 70f., 1237.
[36] See p. 79, n. 14.
[37] See p. 79, n. 16.
[38] MGC i, 298, p. 423, 1184.

purchase of Rimbach in 1125 reveals in passing that the *ministe-riales* there would lose their inheritances if they did not marry amongst Bamberg *ministeriales* in the future.[39] In 1246 Abbot Henry of Rott in Bavaria also warned the *ministeriales* recently bequeathed to his house to marry within his retinue, as well as guaranteeing them against involuntary subinfeudation or alienation to other lords.[40]

In 1131 Archbishop Adalbert of Mainz's grant of *ministeriales* to his chapter makes only one right explicit. The possessions of *ministeriales* dying without heirs would lapse to their lords, but surviving heirs would receive them on paying the heriot.[41] The same right was enjoyed by the Aquileian *ministeriales*. In 1251, when Patriarch Berthold left Windischgrätz to his cathedral church, 'all the *ministeriales*, castellans, and vassals shall have the *ius* or right of Aquileian *ministeriales* in everything', though only the *con-suetudo feudorum* or 'custom about fiefs' was actually spelt out; '... that no fief or allod can be vacated or given up while any man or woman of the kindred should survive to possess it'.[42]

In 1135 Ortlieb of Zwiefalten recorded in his chronicle three of the rules which applied to the monastery's *ministeriales*.[43] The abbot disciplined them for offences or derelictions of duty, and if necessary could apply to the advocate, the duke of Bavaria, for further assistance against their contumacy. If their horses were lost in the abbot's service through no fault of their own, then he re-placed them or remitted services due from their fiefs for up to three years. The heriot owed for a fief was a horse.

In 1166 Archbishop Rainald of Cologne and Countess Hilde-gund of Ahr founded a new convent at her castle of Meer.[44] Her lands and *ministeriales* were also given to the house, but with her consent the archbishop and his successors, not the nuns, took com-mand over the *ministeriales* in all matters, including their customs and their fiefs. This was probably a device to protect the convent from their unruliness. The *ministeriales* were to serve the countess for her lifetime, and she would continue to receive the heriots. The knights were permitted to enter Meer as canons, and to give or sell

[39] U B Wirtemberg i, 285, p. 365, 1125.
[40] Mon. Boica i, 28, pp. 384 f., 1246.
[41] U B Mainz i, 571, p. 488, 1131.
[42] U B Steiermark iii, 88, pp. 153 f., 1251.
[43] *Ortliebi Zwifaltensis Chronicon*, MGS, X, ch. 9, pp. 77 f.
[44] U B Niederrhein i, 415, pp. 286-8, 1166.

their fiefs to the house. Rainald's successor Archbishop Philip confirmed these transactions in 1176.[45]

Archbishop Philip was also responsible in 1182 for the settlement
between the abbot of Siegburg and the counts of Sayn, which
included their *ministeriales*.[46] The counts were forbidden to avenge
the homicides and injuries committed by Siegburg *ministeriales*
against their own men without first consulting the abbot. In intermarriages of Sayn and Siegburg *ministeriales*, the children were to
be divided equally between the lords. In feuds between the counts
of Sayn and the counts of Berg, who were advocates of the abbey,
the Siegburg *ministeriales* were to be immune from attack, unless
they were known to be in arms on the advocates' behalf.

Quite different in scope were the instruments issued by Duke
Ottokar of Styria in 1186, leaving his duchy to the dukes of Austria, in which he outlined safeguards for his *ministeriales* when they
passed to their new lord.[47] They were not to be oppressed, they
were to be free within Styria to sell or give away their property,
and the household officers amongst them were to retain their posts
under the Austrian dukes. Should the Austrian line die out, as it
did in 1246, the Styrian *ministeriales* were at liberty to choose a
new duke. This right they exercised in 1251 when they confirmed
Ottokar of Bohemia as their duke, and in more dubious circumstances, when they sought intervention from Rudolf of Habsburg
in 1276 and Adolf of Nassau in 1295.[48]

At the beginning of the thirteenth century, the abbot of
Kremsmünster in Upper Austria apparently had difficulty in con-
trolling his *ministeriales*. In 1217 Duke Liutpold of Austria restored
the abbot's authority over them, and immunized them from interference by any secular jurisdiction.[49] Their allegiance was restricted
by forbidding them to accept fiefs from anyone but the abbot or
emperor. They were to marry only amongst themselves, or amongst
imperial *ministeriales*.

In 1227 a political treaty between the bishoprics of Cologne and

[45] Ibid. 453 f., pp. 318 f., 1176.
[46] Wisplinghoff, *Siegburg*, 70, pp. 155-8, 1181 or later.
[47] U B Steiermark i, 677 f., pp. 651-4, 1186.
[48] See Ch. 9 below.
[49] *Bernhardi Liber de Origine et Ruina Monasterii Cremifanensis*, M G S, XXV p.
645, and U B Land ob der Enns ii, 397, pp. 589-91, 1217, releasing the house from
the ducal *Landrichter*, Ortolf of Volkensdorf.

Osnabrück,[50] which was never actually put into effect, proposed to evict Count Otto of Tecklenburg from all his possessions for his supposed part in the plot which brought about Archbishop Engelbert of Cologne's murder in 1225. It also proposed to acquire the count's *ministeriales* for the churches. Tecklenburg Castle with its manors would revert to Cologne as a confiscated fief, and the count's Osnabrück fiefs to that see. Four Osnabrück *ministeriales* were to be enfeoffed as garrison in Tecklenburg Castle, as well as Cologne *ministeriales*. All the count's allods and *ministeriales* were to be divided equally between Cologne and Osnabrück, and intermarriages between the two divisions were to be encouraged, to strengthen the bond of alliance between their new episcopal lords. No compensatory exchanges of wives and children, the usual practice in marriages into other retinues,[51] would be required. Furthermore, the *ministeriales* were to be free to choose under which of the rules they preferred to serve, those of Tecklenburg, Cologne, or Osnabrück. Finally, a committee of twelve *ministeriales*, six from each church, would settle all disputes between Osnabrück and Cologne knights, who would have ultimate right of appeal to the bishops. Had these proposals been enforced, then Cologne's occupation of Tecklenburg Castle, the confiscation of the county's other resources, and the close connection between the Osnabrück, Tecklenburg, and Cologne *ministeriales*, would have furthered the long-lasting ambitions of the archbishops of Cologne to expand their Westphalian ducal authority north of the River Lippe. In the event the counts survived the feud, and an uneasy peace was arranged in 1236.

In another archbishopric, that of Salzburg, a handful of charters permit some sort of reconstruction of *ministeriales*' rights. When Bishop Altmann of Trent bequeathed Hohenburg Castle with his *ministeriales* to Salzburg in 1142, he stated that they were to have the rights of Salzburg *ministeriales*, without telling us what they were.[52] Later charters do reveal a few of the Salzburg rules; for example, that *ministeriales* might transfer their allods and fiefs only

---

[50] UB Osnabrück ii, 231, pp. 178 f., 1227; on the *ministeriales* of these districts, J. Prinz, *Das Territorium des Bistums Osnabrück*, Studien und Vorarbeiten zum Historischen Atlas Niedersachsens, XV (Göttingen, 1934), pp. 108-27, and W. Hillebrand, *Besitz- und Standesverhältnisse des Osnabrücker Adels*, Studien und Vorarbeiten zum Historischen Atlas Niedersachsens, XXIII (Göttingen, 1962).

[51] See Ch. 6 below.

[52] UB Salzburg ii, 207A, pp. 303 f., 1142.

to other Salzburg knights, or to monasteries owned by Salzburg.[53] In 1246 Gurkfeld Castle was transferred by the counts of Bogen to the archbishop, with its *ministeriales* who acquired the Salzburg rules about marriages and fiefs, the latter being hereditary in both lines, as well as the guarantee that archbishops would not forcibly alienate them or their possessions from the retinue.[54]

From other surviving fragments about *ministeriales'* rights, we learn that at Strasburg, the bishops' principal *ministeriales* required their arms to be prepared by the city armourers before Italian expeditions, or other imperial campaigns.[55] In 1169 the bishop of Würzburg mentioned the rights of his *ministeriales*, but revealed only their exemption from paying any kind of tax to the cathedral advocate, the count of Henneberg.[56] At Prüm Abbey the misdeeds of the lords of Daun, a powerful family consisting of free men, Trier *ministeriales*, and Prüm vassals, moved Ex-Abbot Caesarius, in his commentaries upon the Carolingian land-register which he was copying out in 1222, to enlarge upon what was permitted to an enfeoffed *ministerialis*. He was forbidden to marry outside the abbot's retinue, an offence only to be reconciled by transferring the wife and children into the abbot's possession. The abbot also conceded 'from good and pious custom' that daughters of *ministeriales* without male heirs would inherit the fiefs.[57] Two generations later, the town-law of Basel mentions in passing that *ministeriales* who wished to become the bishop's active knights must pay a fee of £5. For misdemeanours they were liable to be locked up in the Red Tower of St Ulrich until they regained their lord's grace.[58]

Customs recorded in forgeries

The authentic custumals were drawn up for bishops and counts without reference to the emperor. The forgeries looked higher, and were manufactured to give the semblance of imperial approval to the obligations of *ministeriales*. The results were similar to the

[53] Ibid. iii, 967, pp. 516 f., 1241.
[54] Ibid. 1095, pp. 639 f., 1246.
[55] F. Keutgen, *Urkunden zur städtischen Verfassungsgeschichte*, Ausgewählte Urkunden zur deutschen Verfassungs- und Wirtschaftsgeschichte, I (new edn., Aalen, 1965), 126, ch. 111, p. 101.
[56] Mon. Boica xxxvii, 111, pp 91–3, 1169.
[57] UB Mittelrhein i, pp. 149 f. n. 2.
[58] Keutgen, *Urkunden*, 132, ch. 12, pp. 115 f., 1260–2.

genuine custumals, and lend credence to the forgeries as records of twelfth-century practices. At Weissenburg in East Franconia the imperial *ministeriales* claimed to be entitled to grants in cash and kind towards Italian expeditions, and to have the right to hunt, fish, and cut hay in the Weissenburg Forest.[59] Young *ministeriales* went on probation for a year, and received fur coats before taking their fiefs of three royal *mansi* in extent, or being released to serve another lord.

If the Reichenau source refers in reality to the abbot's vassals about 1160,[60] then those with large fiefs, ten *mansi* in extent, were obliged to go on Italian expeditions, as well as *ministeriales* with five *mansi*, who would get fitting-out allowances in cash and horses. *Ministeriales* with the household offices got double, £10 each and four horses, a trotter, a war-horse, a hack, and a pack-horse. Clearly the Erstein source was designed for quite a different purpose,[61] to shore up the abbess's disintegrating authority over her *ministeriales*, and in the text, it was regretted that the fragility of her sex required protection from their disobedience. They were forbidden to marry outside the retinue, or to exchange or sell their allods, on pain of losing their fiefs and their rights as *ministeriales*. Incumbents of other jurisdictions were warned not to claim any authority over them, and *censuales* were forbidden to try to enter their ranks. Knightly status must be proved by descent, or by charters of donation as *ministeriales*. The Klingenmünster forgery also was devised to protect the abbot's sole authority over his *ministeriales*, and went on to mention financial penalties to be exacted should they be killed or seriously wounded.[62]

The Ottobeuren forgery, which purports to give the Fulda and Reichenau rules to the monastery's *ministeriales*, mentions their right to be judged and condemned only by a court of their peers.[63] A list of manorial customs forged for the abbot of Ebersheimmünster's estates and serfs mentioned that the household knights who looked after the monastic lands ought to be enfeoffed with incomes.[64] But the most accomplished of all these fabrications

[59] M G C i, 451, pp. 678 f.
[60] Ibid. 447, pp. 661-3.
[61] M G D Lothar I and II, 146, pp. 330 f.
[62] U B Mainz i, 462, pp. 369-71.
[63] M G D Charlemagne 219, pp. 292-4.
[64] A. Dopsch, 'Die Ebersheimer Urkundenfälschungen und ein bisher unbeachtetes Dienstrecht aus dem 12. Jahrhundert', *M I ö G* xix (1898), 613, ch. 9.

were the charters drawn up at Tegernsee Abbey early in the thirteenth century and ascribed to Frederick Barbarossa and Henry VI.[65] They immunized the Tegernsee *ministeriales* from coercion by the secular advocates, the counts of Andechs and margraves of Istria, yet the abbot might if he chose cite refractory *ministeriales* before the advocate's court at Warngau.[66] If *ministeriales* were to be deprived of fiefs, then the reasons must be given in that court. As usual, unlicensed marriage outside the Tegernsee retinue was forbidden on pain of depriving the offspring of their inheritances.

Drawing up custumals and forging edicts for *ministeriales* appears not to have been a widespread practice, probably because human memory over the generations and pragmatic innovations of custom within the retinue did not seem to require the written word. But some lords did find pressing reasons for putting pen to parchment. The abbot of Kremsmünster and the abbess of Erstein, for example, needed to restore their authority over their *ministeriales*. The abbot of Reichenau wanted to commit all his vassals, *ministeriales* included, to their obligations for the imperial campaigns in Italy. Archbishop Henry of Cologne aspired to take over the county of Tecklenburg and its *ministeriales*. Countess Hildegund of Ahr and Duke Ottokar of Styria wanted to protect their *ministeriales*' rights when they passed to new masters.

More numerous are the manorial custumals and related materials which recorded the renders, jurisdictions, labour-services, and all other things due to landlords from their estates. In form and content these sources[67] are not related to *ministeriales*' custumals, although one of their chief purposes, to make rights, customs, and obligations explicit, was the same.[68] One preoccupation of the counterfeit sources from Erstein, Klingenmünster, and Tegernsee was to protect *ministeriales* from outside jurisdictions or oppressive advocates. This may well explain their appeal to imperial precept, because it was a widespread monastic practice in the eleventh and twelfth centuries to revise or forge imperial grants, or to apply for

[65] Mon. Boica vi, 17, pp. 174–80 and 31, pp. 195–201, dated to 1163 and 1193.

[66] This claim was based upon an authentic grant, MGD Frederick I, 160, pp. 274–6, 1157, and real practices, Mon. Boica vi, 13, pp. 167 f., 1140.

[67] e.g. MGD Conrad II, 216, pp. 294–6, 1035, Dollinger, *L'Évolution*, pp. 493–512, UB Mainz i, 443, pp. 349–51, 1109, and Franz, *Quellen*, pp. 158–64, 198–210, 258–62.

[68] As Archbishop Anno of Cologne had stated in UB Niederrhein i, 192, pp. 123 f., 1057.

new ones, exempting monastic houses, possessions, and all their
dependents from high-handed advocates.[69]

Defending ministeriales' *rights*

Whether they were written down or not, evidence has survived for
the vigilance which needed to be exercised in defence of *ministeriales*' rights. In 1063 the Bamberg *ministeriales* refused to fulfil their
military obligations when Bishop Gunther's agent tried to call up
half their number for the campaign to Hungary projected by the
imperial regents. The *ministeriales* correctly replied that this was
not the custom; only a third ought to go, at the expense of the
other two-thirds. In the event they all tried to get out of their
duties, pleading the lateness of the summons, the widespread
absence of knights, and such poverty and distress in the bishopric
that their horses were too emaciated for service.[70] In spite of such
contretemps, Bishop Otto of Bamberg (1102-39) was praised by
one of his biographers for preserving inviolate the proper rights of
his *ministeriales* and vassals,[71] and a few years later, Bishop Eberhard (1146-72) was soliciting ducal protection for his *ministeriales*
far away in Swabia, whose rights were under attack by the local
lords.[72]

Before 1100 the abbot of St Emmeram acquired men for his
retinue 'with all the rights of *ministeriales*, which no one ought to
infringe at all'.[73] But infringed they were, and at Regensburg early
in the thirteenth century, a family of *ministeriales* had lost their
rights 'through the evil of these times',[74] the conflicts over the
German throne. In this case the oppressor was an unjust advocate.

[69] MGD Henry IV, 473, pp. 642-4, 1102 and 476, pp. 647-50, 1102-4; MGD
Henry III, 372, pp. 505-13, 391, pp. 541f., and MGD Henry IV, 159, pp. 206-8,
reworked by 1116, and E. Wisplinghoff, *Untersuchungen zur frühen Geschichte der
Abtei S. Maximin bei Trier*, Quellen und Abhandlungen zur mittelrheinischen Kirchengeschichte, XII (Mainz, 1970), pp. 143-76.
[70] Erdmann and Fickermann, *Briefsammlungen*, 18, pp. 211-13 and 35, pp. 233f.,
1063. The see had in truth been devastated by feuds, 63, pp. 110f., 67, pp. 114f.,
and 70, pp. 117f., 1061-2.
[71] *Herbordi Vita Ottonis Episcopi Babenbergensis*, MGS, XII, ch. 36, p. 765.
[72] UB Nürnberg, 53, pp. 37f., 1147-52.
[73] Tr. Regensburg 674, p. 327, c.1090-5.
[74] Ibid. 1026, p. 523, 1201-10; other cases in CD Westphalia i, 164, pp. 128f.,
1085, UB St Stephan 114, pp. 119ff., 1136 and 207, pp. 211f., 1189, and UB Land
ob der Enns ii, 227, pp. 331f., 1166.

At times *ministeriales* might turn on their oppressors. It was reported that the motive for Count Sigehard of Burghausen's murder in 1104 at Regensburg was his denigration of *ministeriales*' rights, and more specifically that 'he enacted some unjust judgement over these *clientes*'.[75] In the see of Utrecht, where the bishops were continually threatened by their quarrelsome *ministeriales*,[76] the Egmont annalist admitted that in 1159 they rose 'to conserve their rights', transferred their allegiance to the count of Guelders, and besieged the bishop in his castle. But we are not told in what ways the *ministeriales* thought that the rules had been broken.[77]

Like Bishop Eberhard of Bamberg, lords often had to take steps to protect their *ministeriales* from surreptitious or open attacks on their status by neighbouring magnates. At Tegernsee, for example, they tried to poach the abbot's *ministeriales* into their own retinues.[78] In 1173 Frederick, count-palatine of Bavaria, had to return the *ministeriales* of Arnhofen whom he had taken over forcibly.[79] At the same time the abbot called upon his advocate, Margrave Berthold of Istria, to defend his *ministeriales* of Hartpenning and Ottmarshart from the claims of ownership to them made by Frederick, lord of Sigmertshausen. The next generation of these families also had to be defended from the same claimant.[80] In similar circumstances Bishop Gero of Halberstadt rescued his *ministerialis* Dietrich and his offspring from Count Hoyer of Wöltingerode in 1163, and gave them, with their rights confirmed, to the monastery of Huysburg.[81] In 1170 the abbess of Altmünster rescued Otwig of Weinheim and his descendants from an advocate who sought to deprive them of their rights as *ministeriales*. The Weinheims, originally of free status, had belonged for four generations to the abbesses as *ministeriales*.[82] In 1186 the bishop of Osnabrück complained that his advocate Count Simon of Tecklenburg had deprived him of four *ministeriales* and intended to appeal to the emperor,[83] but we are not informed of the outcome. Small wonder

[75] G. Waitz, *Annales Hildesheimenses*, MG schol. VIII (Hanover, 1878), p. 51.
[76] See p. 232, nn. 38–41.
[77] *Annales Egmundani*, MGS, XVI, pp. 461 f., 1159.
[78] Tr. Tegernsee 301, pp. 228 f., 1157–63, and 327, p. 247, 1163–73.
[79] Ibid. 331, p. 252, 1173.
[80] Ibid. 380A, B, pp. 293 f., 1173–1217.
[81] UB Halberstadt i, 264, pp. 227 f., 1163.
[82] UB Mainz ii, 330, pp. 559–61, 1170.
[83] UB Osnabrück i, 385, p. 306, 1186.

that charters and other sources frequently forbade alienation of
ministeriales by enfeoffment or any other method out of their lords'
retinues, unless by prior consent of the parties.

It was a temptation for the aristocratic advocates of regular and
secular churches to try to compel ecclesiastical *ministeriales* to offer
them military services, or to pay them taxes. In 1229 Duke Henry
of Limburg as advocate of Siegburg renounced fiscal levies from
the abbot's *ministeriales*.[84] Through genuine imperial privileges as
well as forgeries confected in their writing-offices, the German prelates continually exempted themselves from improper interference
by their advocates. In 1142 Conrad III obliged Count-Palatine
Otto of Bavaria to renounce any kind of judicial authority over
Bishop Otto of Freising's *ministeriales*.[85] In 1189, when Count
Poppo of Henneberg, burgrave of Würzburg and advocate of St
Stephen's Abbey there, objected to Bishop Godfrey's exchange of
ministeriales with the abbot, the bishop replied that advocates had
no authority in such matters, and reminded the count not to exact
any services from such people.[86] In a more serious quarrel Bishop
Frederick of Merseburg laid an interdict in 1270 upon the lands of
Margrave Dietrich of Landsberg, in part because 'he compelled the
vassals and *ministeriales* of our church, belonging to us spiritually
and temporally, to unjust and hitherto uncustomary exactions'.[87]
It was also a temptation for the territorial lords to try to recruit,
or if necessary to expropriate, the *ministeriales* in their lands who
belonged to other lords, in pursuit of greater political homogeneity.
In 1286 Duke Albert of Austria and Styria tried to forestall this
sort of manœuvre when Carinthia was enfeoffed to Count Meinhard of Görz and Tirol. Meinhard was forbidden to buy up the
castles and possessions of Albert's *ministeriales* there, or otherwise
to oppress them.[88]

*What do the custumals and associated sources reveal about German
knighthood, 1060–1250?*

The surviving custumals, forgeries, and other materials stretch over
two centuries when the German militias of *ministeriales* were being

[84] Wisplinghoff, *Siegburg*, 99, pp. 207 f., 1229, confirmed in 109, pp. 218-20, 1243.
[85] M G D Conrad III, 83, pp. 145-9, 1142.
[86] U B St Stephan 207, pp. 211 f., 1189.
[87] Kehr, *Merseburg*, 365, pp. 296-8, 1270.
[88] M G C iii, 373, pp. 355 f., 1286.

entrenched as a powerful order in society. If we cannot assume that customs preserved in writing were *ipso facto* put into practice, still there emerges a convincing picture of knighthood, especially in the lower Rhineland and in Westphalia, where the archbishop of Cologne was the principal magnate and since 1180, himself duke of Westphalia.[89] A great deal can be inferred about the anxieties and frictions amongst lords and knights. The most important single concern of the *ministeriales* was to ensure inheritance of fiefs within their kindreds. Lords desired to deploy the resources available for enfeoffment to their best advantage, and from time to time this might conflict with hereditary claims by *ministeriales*. But the books of fiefs compiled towards 1300 and later, which succeeded the custumals as the chief sources of information about *ministeriales'* hereditary rights, show the commitment of lords to interpretations of inheritance favourable to knights.[90]

Broadly speaking, lords were not anxious about their *ministeriales'* ability to fulfil their obligations in military and administrative affairs, except upon the complicated and onerous imperial ventures into Italy for which special measures had to be taken. Military and official functions were the purposes and privileges of life for which *ministeriales* were brought up. However, lords were more concerned about discipline: not only did they fear conspiracies and misdemeanours committed by their *ministeriales*, but they were also intent on conserving their retinues and their resources in fiefs, allods, and above all, future manpower, under close supervision. This is why prohibitions against alien marriages contracted without permission were so often repeated. In spite of attempts to bend the custom in certain cases, it was accepted that *ministeriales* belonged to their mothers' lords.[91] Unless specific arrangements were agreed to the contrary, these lords would, through alien marriages, gain

---

[89] MGC i, 279, pp. 384-6, 1180.

[90] H. Rothert, *Die Mittelalterlichen Lehnbücher der Bischöfe von Osnabrück*, Osnabrücker Geschichtsquellen, V (Osnabrück, 1932), B. Diestelkamp, *Das Lehnrecht der Grafschaft Katzenelnbogen*, Untersuchungen zur deutschen Staats- und Rechtsgeschichte, n. s., XI (Aalen, 1969), H. Hoffmann, *Das älteste Lehenbuch des Hochstifts Würzburg 1303-1345*, Quellen und Forschungen zur Geschichte des Bistums Würzburg, XXV (Würzburg 1972), E. Grünenwald, *Das älteste Lehenbuch der Grafschaft Oettingen*, Schwäbische Forschungsgemeinschaft, ser. 5. ii (Augsburg, 1976), K.H. Spiess, *Lehnsrecht, Lehnspolitik und Lehnsverwaltung der Pfalzgrafen bei Rhein im Spätmittelalter*, Geschichtliche Landeskunde, XVIII (Wiesbaden, 1978), and Bayerisches Staatsarchiv Nürnberg, Hochstift Eichstätt Lehenbücher I, ff. 1ʳ-340ᵛ.

[91] On these rules, Ch. 6 below.

future generations of *ministeriales* with their inheritances from unwary lords who had not, from whatever cause, prevented their knights from taking brides outside their retinues. The abbot of Tegernsee invoked imperial sanction for the penalty he intended to exact against this practice: 'If anyone should contract a marriage outside the company of the monastery's *ministeriales*, then all his patrimony with the fiefs acquired from this church shall, upon his death, fall to the monastery absolutely and without contradiction.'[92] Discipline was difficult to maintain because *ministeriales* were part of a military nobility addicted to feuds, which they were prepared to launch even against their own lords if they considered it justifiable.[93] For rich lords another problem was to supervise their *ministeriales* who lived far afield in the vast medieval empire. The archbishops of Cologne, for example, owned *ministeriales* throughout the lower Rhineland and Westphalia, the bishops of Bamberg in Franconia, Bavaria, Carinthia, and elsewhere, and the archbishops of Mainz along the Main and Rhine valleys, and further afield in Hesse and Thuringia.[94]

Apart from their anxieties about the loss of fiefs and allods by their children or collateral descendants, *ministeriales* were also afraid of being transferred into other retinues where they might become liable for less advantageous obligations. Repeatedly they were protected from this kind of alienation without their own consent. When secular lords died without direct heirs, the *ministeriales* had little choice but to pass to new lords, and to see the old retinue disbanded. This is what happened in 1305, when Count Gebhard of Hirschberg's *ministeriales* were dispersed, the majority to the bishops of Eichstätt, the minority to the dukes of Bavaria.[95] In 1099 it was said that Count Ulrich of Passau's *ministeriales* objected to entering Count Berengar of Sulzbach's retinue by inheritance.[96]

From the charter evidence we are well informed about the devolution of fiefs and allods, the offices which *ministeriales* held, and the consequences of their marriages.[97] But the custumals are more

---

[92] See p. 93, n. 65.
[93] See Ch. 9 below.
[94] Pötter, pp. 21–69, UB Land ob der Enns i, 69, p. 313, 1150–9 for the Bamberg *ministeriales* from the three duchies gathering in Regensburg, and UB Mainz i and ii, *passim*.
[95] See my thesis, pp. 247–61.
[96] *Fundatio Monasterii Baumburgensis*, MGS, XV. 2, p. 1062.
[97] See Chs. 5–7 below.

revealing about certain of the *ministeriales'* preoccupations, and the violent tenor of their lives. Few were rich, and it appears that they had difficulties in finding their military equipment, clothing, and horses. Expensive to acquire and maintain, lords undertook to supply or replace a certain number of horses, sometimes making sure of receiving them back as heriots. The business-like tone of the custumals, the brutal manners which might end in homicide, the poverty of life in the grim stone towers punctuating the German hillscape, must mean that the majority of *ministeriales* were not acquainted with the cultured mentality of knighthood familiar to a tiny handful of talented or literate individuals, some of whom themselves composed verse.[98] The fantastical representations of knighthood displayed in the vernacular poetry of the Hohenstaufen epoch were almost wholly the work of clerics and professionals at a small number of princely courts, clerical households, and urban milieux, to which the *ministeriales'* knightly sense of identity or *esprit de corps* owed next to nothing.

The custumals nevertheless hint at solemn rites and days for all *ministeriales*; formal investitures with fiefs, court-hearings with oath-taking and sentences, the armed columns setting out for Italy, and at Cologne, the young Rhenish and Saxon *ministeriales* arriving in the city,[99] saying their prayers in the cathedral, then crossing to the palace to offer fealty to their archbishop, who might be one of the great veterans of imperial politics such as Rainald of Dassel, Barbarossa's chief adviser, Philip of Heinsberg, the first duke of Westphalia, Adolf of Altena, the mainstay of Otto IV, or Engelbert of Berg, regent in Germany for Frederick II.

---

[98] J. Bumke, *Ministerialität und Ritterdichtung. Umrisse der Forschung* (Munich, 1976), is less enthusiastic about the *ministeriales'* contribution than P. Kluckhohn, 'Ministerialität und Ritterdichtung', *Zeitschrift für deutsches Altertum* lii (1910), 135-68. See also G. Kaiser, 'Minnesang, Ritterideal, Ministerialität' in H. Wenzel (ed.), *Adelsherrschaft und Literatur*, Beiträge zur älteren deutschen Literaturgeschichte, VI (Berne and Frankfurt, 1980), pp. 181-208.

[99] Weinrich, pp. 276-8, ch. 12.

CHAPTER 4

Ministeriales as Vassal-knights and Retainers

Ministeriales *in the magnate retinue: the* familia *or household*

The custumals and other sources examined in the last chapter re-vealed a great deal about the rights which lords reckoned to exer-cise, and obligations which *ministeriales* expected to perform, as well as a number of rules, rites, and customs governing the lives of knights and their families. The custumals were drawn up with whole retinues in mind, and sought to combine *ministeriales'* com-pulsory membership of unfree *familiae* with their professional func-tions as vassal-knights into a formal pattern of association between lord and man. *Ministeriales* belonged to an emergent *ordo* in Ger-man society, as discussed in Chapters 1 and 2, and to kindreds with quite complicated rules about marriage, inheritance, and land-holding, as we shall see in Chapters 5 and 6. Between *ordo* and family stood the magnate retinue to which all *ministeriales* must belong. The structure of these retinues shows that two distinct in-stitutions were being combined in the eleventh century: the legally disciplined *familia*, and vassal-knighthood which was pre-dated by the former. In the 1060s the Bamberg custumal shows the *ministe-riales* bound by both, but the practices of vassalage proved stron-ger than the bonds of *familiae*, and in the twelfth century actually permitted the erosion of retinues, some of which were disintegra-ting in the thirteenth.

Familia had no very precise definition, and can inelegantly be translated as household, or retinue, or aggregate dependents of a lord.[1] Used without qualification, *familia* might cast a wide net, to include kindred, friends, and advisers, as well as military retainers of whatever status, clerics high and low,[2] and all those in some

---

[1] Niermeyer, *Lexicon*, pp. 407 f., discerns eleven meanings of the word.
[2] *Vita Burchardi Episcopi*, MGS, IV, ch. 17, p. 840, and Kelleter, *Kaiserswerth*, 16, pp. 24 f., 1184.

way bound or obliged to a lord and protected by him, including
the mass of serfs. To one of the imperial abbots in Hainault,
Alexander III wrote in 1173 of his *familia* with 'its *ministeriales*
and everyone living from your bread, the castellans and their equals
with their own households and *ministeriales*, and the [abbot's]
household of clerics, scholars, and canons'.[3] Some sources specified
that the *familia* included both free and unfree, such as the abbot of
Stablo's 'entire *familia*, servile and free-born, belonging under his
protection' in 987.[4] In 1115 the Mainz *familia*, consisting of free
nobles as well as the *ministeriales*, begged or forced Henry V to
release their archbishop from confinement.[5] In Landgrave Louis of
Thuringia's *familia* collected at Schmalkalden for the crusade of
1227, the Reinhardsbrunn chronicler included four counts, eighteen
named knights, many of them *ministeriales* including the four household officers, Rudolf, butler of Vargula, Henry, marshal of Ebers-
burg, Hermann, seneschal of Schlotheim, and Henry, chamberlain
of Fahner, a handful of priests and chaplains, and yet more knights
and clerics.[6] In other cases *familia* was intended to embrace only
the unfree dependents,[7] and when Ortlieb of Zwiefalten and the
Ebersheimmünster chronicler described their monastic *familiae* early
in the twelfth century, they referred to the *ministeriales*, *censuales*,
and serfs in turn.[8] Yet others wanted a clearer distinction of
knights from peasants, so they mentioned the *ministeriales* before
the *familia humilior* or *familia curtis*, meaning serfs.[9]

Scribally, *familia* was not proving satisfactory because it was so
vague. A refinement of the twelfth century was therefore to call the
retinue of *ministeriales* the *familia ministerialium* of the lord in

---

[3] *Iacobi de Guisia Annales Hanoniae*, MGS XXX. 1, pp. 217 f., and the Augsburg
familia in *Gerhardi Vita S. Oudalrici Episcopi*, MGS, IV, p. 390, and *Uodalscalcus
de Egino et Herimanno*, MGS, XII, p. 437, 1097 for a *ministerialis ex potiori familia
beatae virginis Mariae*.

[4] MGD Otto III, 33, p. 433, 987.

[5] Waitz, *Chronica Regia Coloniensis*, p. 56.

[6] *Cronica Reinhardsbrunnensis* MGS, XXX. 1, p. 611, and Patze, *Entstehung*,
pp. 326–38 on these officers.

[7] MGD Conrad II, 216, pp. 295 f., 1035, Dollinger, *L'Évolution*, pp. 243 f., and
Anselmi Gesta Episcoporum Leodiensium, MGS, VII, p. 205 which distinguishes the
ingenui from the *familia* of Liège.

[8] See p 35, n. 69, p. 47, n. 129. Lorsch Abbey's *familia* also included the *ministeriales* with the serfs; Glöckner, *Codex Laureshamensis*, vol. i, p. 423, 1110–11.

[9] UB Mainz i, 616, p. 536, before 1137, and UB Niederrhein ii, 81, p. 45, 1219.

question, or variations of this phrase.[10] By similar devices Otto of
Freising depicted Count Sigehard of Burghausen's assassins as 'the
princes' *familia* who are called *ministeriales*', and the Cologne custumal called the archbishop's *ministeriales* 'knights of his *familia*',
which Gislebert of Mons expanded to *ministeriales* 'under a prince's
advocacy or from his own *familia*'.[11] Scribes experimented with
other words such as 'following', 'clientage', 'consortium', 'college',
and 'society',[12] but none of them caught on, no doubt because they
were as imprecise as *familia* itself.

The *familia* governed by its lord was the legal community into
which *ministeriales* were born, the social body through which they
performed their obligatory services, and the juridical institution
within which they might find defence and redress.[13] But the familial
communities of *ministeriales* did not, in reality, turn out to be
closed groups of people, in spite of the technically rigid dependence
upon their lords which hereditary servile status had imposed upon
them. The integrity of *familiae* was continually being eroded by
mobility of service, inter-marriage of *ministeriales*, multiple enfeoffment and homage, and the devolution amongst the lords themselves of the patrimonies, castles, and lordships to which their *ministeriales* pertained. Except in the case of external marriages,
through which fiefs, allods, and future generations of knights would
be alienated for good from their lords, the *familiae* of *ministeriales*
were not as rigorously supervised or contained as lordly authority
might in law permit. In 1118 Count Conrad of Wettin did try to
confine the abbess of Gerbstedt's *ministeriales* to her service exclusively,[14] but on balance the majority of lords favoured a much
laxer attitude. The Bamberg and Cologne custumals permitted mo-

---

[10] UB Wirtemberg i, 285, p. 365, 1125, ii, 386, pp. 151 f., 1166, UB Salzburg i,
348, p. 753, *c.* 1131, Tr. Passau 628, p. 231, 1149-64, Busley, *Neustift*, 6, pp. 10 f.,
1152, UB Land ob der Enns ii, 224, pp. 327 f., 1163, *Chronicon Eberspergense*,
MGS, XX, p. 15, 1184, and Mon. Boica xiii, 24, p. 193, 1194.

[11] Otto of Freising, p. 318, 1104, Weinrich, p. 276, ch. 11, *c.* 1165, and Gislebert
of Mons, p. 254, 1190.

[12] MGD Henry IV, 329, p. 432, *c.* 1081 for *obsequium*, UB Halberstadt i, 146,
p.112, 1109-20 and MGC i, 447, ch. 6, p. 662, *c.* 1160 for *clientela*, Kindlinger, 10,
p. 237, 1156 and UB Wirtemberg ii, 386, pp. 151 f., 1166 for *consortium*, Tr. Tegernsee
380A, p. 293, 1173-86 for *collegium*, and UB Krain i, 157, p. 139, 1191 for *societas*.

[13] Bishop Burchard of Worms (1000-25) was concerned that justice should be
available to all members of his *familia*; *Vita Burchardi Episcopi*, MGS, IV, ch. 20,
pp. 843 f.

[14] CD Saxony ii, 55, pp. 46-9, 1118.

bility of service so that fiefs would not have to be found for every-one. Lords might benefit from mobility, recruiting a wider spectrum of talent and strategic alliances, while expelling the unruly, the incompetent, or the unwanted. In feudal custom there were diffi-culties about having more than one lord to serve, but multiple enfeoffment was so common by the end of the twelfth century that Wernher of Bolanden, the richest imperial *ministerialis* of the day, had forty-four lords apart from the emperor himself.[15]

Multiple allegiance

Many an ambitious *ministerialis* organized multiple allegiance, such as the Styrian knight Ottokar, castellan of Graz, who sought in 1190 to secure his future on the eve of the duchy's devolution to new lords, the dukes of Austria. He transferred his allodial castle of Neuglaneck as a fief to the archbishop of Salzburg, who accepted his son Ulrich as a Salzburg *ministerialis* and rewarded father and son with new fiefs.[16] The imperial *ministeriales* also did homage to and received new fiefs from their neighbouring magnates, if not on the scale of Wernher of Bolanden. To name only a handful, Ber-nard of Trebsen was Margrave Dietrich of Meissen's vassal by 1204, Henry of Salach was the bishop of Würzburg's from 1221, and Conrad, butler of Schmalnegg, was Godfrey of Hohenlohe's from 1244.[17]

Later in the thirteenth century the bishop of Osnabrück's *mini-steriales* of Bramsche arranged, with his consent, to become her-editary castellans of the counts of Ravensberg and Tecklenburg, and of the bishops of Münster as well.[18] Similarly, the bishop of Eichstätt's *ministerialis* Henry of Hofstetten was also the count of Hirschberg's castellan and butler, and from 1276, the duke of Bavaria's castellan at Geyern.[19] In that region in the 1280s, the

[15] Metz, *SG*, pp. 55-8, H. Werle, 'Ministerialtät und Heerschildordnung' in F.L. Wagner (ed.), *Ministerialität im Pfälzer Raum*, Veröffentlichungen der Pfälzischen Ge-sellschaft zur Förderung der Wissenschaften, LXIV, (Speyer, 1975), pp. 69-74, and UB Mainz ii, 691, pp. 1130 f., 1194-8 for the Bolanden fiefs from Mainz.

[16] UB Steiermark i, 701, pp. 688-91, 1190.

[17] CD Saxony iii, 78, pp. 64 f., 1204, Mon. Boica xxxvii, 200, pp. 208 f., 1221, and Weller, *Hohenlohe*, 209, pp. 119 f., 1244.

[18] UB Osnabrück iii, 517, p. 360, 1274, 615, p. 434, 1278, and iv, 252, p. 164, 1289 and 308, p. 201, 1291.

[19] Wittmann, *Wittelsbach*, vol. 1, 124, pp. 305 f., 1276, Reg. Eichstätt 950, p. 294, 1282, and Mon. Boica xlix, 255, pp. 392 ff., 1297.

burgrave of Nuremberg's *ministeriales* of Dietenhofen made careers
for themselves by taking new allegiances where they could. Otto of
Dietenhofen served the burgrave as a magistrate, Rüdiger was the
count of Hirschberg's castellan at Sandsee, another Rüdiger was the
bishop of Eichstätt's marshal and castellan at Wernfels, and his
brother Frederick was the same bishop's castellan at Arberg, all of
them with appropriate fiefs.[20] The result of multiple allegiance was
that princes such as the bishops of Eichstätt had numerous enfeoffed
vassals amongst the imperial *ministeriales* and those of the neighbouring lords, notably the dukes of Bavaria, the burgraves of Nuremberg, and the counts of Hirschberg, Oettingen, Graisbach, and
Hohentrüdingen in the thirteenth century.[21] Knightly families which
were prolific were constrained as much by necessity as ambition to
compete for places in these retinues. Cadet branches of the Eichstätt
ministeriales of Muhr transferred their primary allegiances to Bavaria, Oettingen, and Hirschberg, and also acquired the patrimonies of Konstein, Oberndorf, and Stopfenheim by judicious marriages. At home the elder branch divided the family lands, built
another castle called Neuenmuhr, and sought new offices from the
bishops.[22]

Books of fiefs are not common before the fourteenth century, so
we are not well informed about the twelfth-century origins of
multiple enfeoffment. But some illuminating charters have survived.
By the 1160s the bishop of Naumburg's *ministerialis* Hugo of
Schönburg had twenty other lords, an abbot, six counts, two burgraves, and eleven free-born noblemen. Before 1186 he arranged,
with Bishop Udo's advice and permission, for all the fiefs he held
from them to be divided up amongst his five sons.[23] The nature of
multiple allegiances much depended upon the standing of the *ministeriales* involved, and the political circumstances in which the new
homages were sworn. In 1250, when the titles to Austria and Styria
were still in doubt after the death of their childless duke in 1246,

[20] UB Nürnberg 674, p. 396, 1282, Mon. Boica xlix, 150, p. 244, 1286, and Reg.
Eichstätt 983, p. 304, 1284, 1062, p. 322, 1289, and 1135, p. 346, 1295.
[21] See my thesis, pp. 156-68, 175 f., 219-25, 286-345, 376-9, 386-401.
[22] Ibid. pp. 151, 265 f., 276, 358, 377, 386, 393.
[23] Rosenfeld, *Naumburg*, 334, pp. 314 f., 1161-86; W. Schlesinger, *Die
schönburgischen Lande bis zum Ausgang des Mittelalters*, Schriften für Heimatforschung, II, (Dresden, 1935), and *Die Landesherrschaft der Herren von Schönburg*,
Quellen und Studien zur Verfassungsgeschichte des Deutschen Reiches, IX. 1
(Münster and Cologne, 1954).

the most formidable Styrian *ministerialis*, Ulrich of Liechtenstein, submitted to the nearest territorial lord, the archbishop of Salzburg, in what amounted to a substantial military treaty of mutual obligation, sealed by dynastic alliances. Ulrich opened all his castles to the archbishop, promised the aid of a hundred armed men, married off his son and heir to the daughter of one of the archbishop's richest *ministeriales*, and transferred his own daughter into the archbishop's ownership as the wife of another leading Salzburg *ministerialis*.[24] The Liechtensteins were themselves a political power to be cultivated, and the handsome financial settlements which went with the treaty make it clear that they were bought by the archbishop. Lesser families also changed military allegiance to try to make a better living. In 1268 the Davensberg brothers, who belonged to the free-born lords of Holten in Westphalia, offered their services to Count Godfrey of Arnsberg in his current feuds, to include armed men, ten fully-equipped mounts, and the use of their fortifications. In return they were entitled to whatever ransoms and loot they could take. Evidently they did not do well. By 1298 Hermann of Davensberg was bankrupt, and had to be rescued by his lord Wicbold of Holten, who, providentially, had just been elected archbishop of Cologne. Wicbold paid his debts, turned him and his heirs by a new homage into Cologne knights with a money-fief, and opened Davensberg Castle to future archbishops and their officials.[25]

If Wernher of Bolanden deferred to the emperor and Hugo of Schönburg to the bishop of Naumburg as their principal lords, formal liege-homage to the lord entitled to service and loyalty before all others was not practised in Germany. By a different device *ministeriales* in the Rhineland sometimes offered to subject their castles to new lords, using the German equivalent of the word liege.[26] But this did not apply to their persons. On the contrary, *ministeriales* who submitted 'liege castles' to new lords sometimes

[24] UB Steiermark iii, 70-2, pp. 131-6, 1250.
[25] UB Niederrhein iv, 670, pp. 805 f., 1268 and ii, 1010, p. 594, 1298, and *Catalogi Archiepiscoporum Coloniensium*, MGS, XXIV, p. 357.
[26] V. Henn, *Das ligische Lehnswesen im Westen und Nordwesten des mittelalterlichen Deutschen Reiches* (Munich, 1970) W. Janssen, 'Burg und Territorium am Niederrhein im späten Mittelalter' in H. Patze (ed.), *Die Burgen im deutschen Sprachraum*, vol. i, VF, XIX (Sigmaringen, 1976), pp. 322-4, and UB Niederrhein ii, 773, p. 455, 1282 for 'castrum de Oye, esse lygiam domum, quod vulgariter Ledegehuse dicitur'.

specified that their personal loyalty was reserved to their original lords.[27]

The technically involuntary adherence of *ministeriales* to the *familiae* into which they had been born was therefore being eroded by the practices of vassalage. Lords permitted mobility of service when they were not themselves prepared to grant adequate fiefs. In the Cologne retinue, where Archbishop Rainald's custumal stipulated primogeniture, younger brothers could not always count upon being accepted as active knights with new fiefs, and might be dismissed to seek new lords. Lords were prepared for their *ministeriales* to take new allegiances and fiefs, and could be persuaded to change the membership of their retinues to suit the new homages. In 1238, for example, the bishop of Gurk agreed to exchange *ministeriales* with the counts of Ortenburg: the bishop's *ministerialis* Ulrich of Liemberg held his chief castle as a fief from the counts, and in order not to deprive his four sons of their opportunity to inherit it, the bishop gave them to Count Hermann; in exchange he received four Ortenburg *ministeriales*, the knights of Hungerberg, for his own retinue.[28]

In addition to these strictly feudal considerations, alien marriages were also a potent agent in rearranging the composition of retinues, because brides, children, and less often husbands, were exchanged amongst the magnates to balance out the demographic and tenurial consequences of such matches. The most common compromise was the equal division of the offspring between the lords of the parties contracting matrimony.[29] Retinues might also exhibit signs of disintegration during political crises. When Duke Henry the Lion was deprived of Saxony and Bavaria in 1180, Arnold of Lübeck reported that 'many of his *ministeriales* such as Henry of Weida, Liupold of Herzberg, Liudolf of Peine, and many others who had been brought up by him from the cradle and whose fathers had served him without any question, abandoned him and transferred themselves to the emperor', taking their strongholds with them, as another chronicler noted.[30] Innocent III encouraged the same kind

---

[27] UB Niederrhein ii, 239, pp. 123 f., 1239 and 322, p. 168, 1247, and UB Münster 906, pp. 471 f., 1271.

[28] Mon. Carinthia ii, 556, pp. 22 f., 1238.

[29] Ch. 6 below.

[30] *Arnoldi Chronica Slavorum* MGS, XXI, p. 137 and *Chronicon Montis Sereni*, MGS, XXIII, p. 158.

of treason against Philip of Swabia, and when circumstances changed again, absolved the imperial *ministeriales* in 1211 from their oaths of loyalty to Otto IV.[31] The evaporation of Hohenstaufen authority from Germany after 1245 encouraged the imperial *ministeriales* to make terms with new lords, or to drift amongst the knights of whom the dukes of Bavaria complained that 'one does not know to whom they belong'.[32]

Condominium over ministeriales

The boundaries of *familiae* were pierced by the exercise of joint-lordship or condominium, not only over individual *ministeriales* and their families—for examples of multiple allegiance can be found everywhere[33]—but over whole retinues or sections of them. Upon examination it turns out that in nearly every case where condominium was exercised or claimed, the joint lords were not formally sharing the actual ownership of individuals, retinues, or portions of retinues. One lord was the legal owner of the *ministeriales* in question, the other sharing with him certain rights or jurisdictions or services due from them. The ancient political connection of the imperial office with the German church meant that ecclesiastical resources, including the services of enfeoffed knights, were at the disposal of emperors.[34] Since episcopal *ministeriales* therefore stood close to the crown, emperors liked to emphasize their function as corporations loyal to the dynasty, particularly in those sees where imperial influence was strong, notably Speyer, Worms, Bamberg, and Würzburg.[35] The relationship of imperial

[31] Holder-Egger, *Monumenta Erphesfurtensia*, p. 209.

[32] Wittmann, *Wittelsbach*, vol. i, 123, pp. 296-305, 1276 and 168, pp. 413-23, 1287.

[33] *Notitiae Fundationis Monasterii Bosonis-villae*, MGS, XV, 2 p. 979, 1123 (Bencelin *ministerialis* in Alsace), Uhl, *Weihenstephan*, 225, p. 184, 1157-62 (*ministeriales* of Lappach in Bavaria), and UB Wirtemberg ii, 477, p. 289, 1193 and Jordan, *Urkunden Heinrichs des Löwen*, 129, pp. 186 f., 1194 (Sulgen brothers in Swabia).

[34] J. Ficker, 'Ueber das Eigenthum des Reichs am Reichskirchengute', *Sitzungsberichte der Kaiserlichen Akademie der Wissenschaften*, phil.-hist. Classe, LXXII, (Vienna, 1872), pp. 55-146, 381-450, L. Santifaller, *Zur Geschichte des ottonisch-salischen Reichskirchensystems*, Abhandlungen der österreichischen Akademie der Wissenschaften, phil.-hist. Klasse, Sitzungsberichte, CCXXIX (Vienna, 1954), Metz, *Das Servitium Regis*, and the Concordat of Worms confirming imperial overlordship of German ecclesiastical temporalities, MGC i, 107 f., pp. 159-61, 1122.

[35] H. Fichtenau, 'Bamberg, Würzburg und die Stauferkanzlei', *MIöG* liii (1939), 241-85, K. Bosl, 'Würzburg als Reichsbistum' in *Aus Verfassungs- und Landesgeschichte. Festschrift für T. Mayer*, vol. i (Lindau and Constance, 1954), pp. 161-81,

with episcopal *ministeriales* was encouraged by intermarriages and cross-enfeoffment with lands and offices.[36] But emperors did not actually claim in law to own bishops' *ministeriales* jointly. On the contrary, they rather rigorously applied the rules and restrictions about marriages, divisions of children, and the devolution of fiefs, allods, and offices between the imperial and episcopal retinues.

Imperial condominium over bishops' *ministeriales* was an informal practice, its nature outlined by Frederick Barbarossa in a charter favouring a family of Würzburg *ministeriales*. Bodo, son of the bishop's *vicedominus* Herold, 'who, while he lived, always faithfully served us and the empire', was called the emperor's loyal friend, and 'so that from friendship he may be made more familiar to us, and from esteem he may become more esteemed', he was further connected to the imperial circle by marriage to one of the Hohenstaufen *ministeriales*.[37]

The empire was also entitled to military services from *ministeriales* belonging to the richer abbeys, but this right was sometimes remitted.[38] In one case, Hilwartshausen Abbey in Saxony, Conrad III did state that when the empire owned monasteries, it also owned the *ministeriales*, their services, and their fiefs, but this claim was

---

F. Geldner, 'Das Hochstift Bamberg in der Reichspolitik von Kaiser Heinrich II. bis Kaiser Friedrich Barbarossa', *HJ* lxxxiii (1964), 28–54, MGD Frederick I, 396, pp. 271 f., 1163, and Weinrich, pp. 278–86, 1168. When the bishop of Naumburg listed *ministeriales imperii et nostri*, CD Saxony ii, 559, p. 385, 1190, or the bishop of Speyer *ministeriales tam inperii quam ecclesie*, UB Wirtemberg iii, 808, p. 303, 1232, they referred to the meeting of two retinues, not to one jointly owned. As Philip of Swabia's treaty with Speyer showed, their retinues of *ministeriales* were separate; MGC ii, 447, pp. 617 f., 1198.

[36] Bosl, *RM*, pp. 218–87, Reimann, pp. 137–86, and Mon. Boica xxxvii, 215, p. 225, 1228. Bosl, pp. 58–62, 468–76, defends the view that in Bavaria a handful of *ministeriales* had been enfeoffed under joint-lordship by the dukes and emperors, but G. Kirchner in 'Staatsplanung und Reichsministerialität', *DA* x (1953-4), 450–67, supposes that *regnum* refers, not to the German kingdom but to the Bavarian realm or duchy, so that, in this context, *ministerialis regni* simply means 'Bavarian *ministerialis*'. Kirchner's view is supported by sources which denote ducal Bavarian *ministeriales* by such terms as *fidelis noster ministerialis regni*, UB Land ob der Enns ii, 380, p. 556, c. 1212, or *ministerialis regni Bavariae*, Mon. Boica iii, 137, p. 284, c. 1220. Also controversial is what Frederick II intended when he conceded to the Brunswick-Lüneburg ducal *ministeriales* the privileges of imperial *ministeriales*; MGC ii, 197, p. 264, 1235.

[37] MGD Frederick I, 153, pp. 263 f., 1155–6.

[38] MGD Conrad III, 167, pp. 302-04, 1147 (Lorsch), 266, pp. 460 f., 1151 (Kitzingen), and Mon. Boica xxix, A, 520, p. 402, 1171 (Ottobeuren).

waived by his successor in 1156.[39] As we have already seen, joint-lordship over the *ministeriales* belonging to Meer nunnery from 1166 confirmed their real ownership to the house and their services to the archbishops of Cologne.[40] In 1181, when Frederick Barbarossa founded a monastery at Waldsee in Swabia, he sought to avoid ambiguity by giving the *ministeriales* of Waldsee outright to the dukes of Swabia, the canons having no claims upon them.[41]

Many cathedral and monastic churches were protected by imperial edict from any exercise of secular advocates' authority over their retinues of *ministeriales*, unless requested for some specific purpose by the prelates who owned them. One lord might nevertheless have powers over another's *ministeriales* by virtue of some office or jurisdiction. In Bavaria the *Landgerichte* or regional magistracies under the dukes' judges also had jurisdiction over the *ministeriales* belonging to the eight bishops of the duchy, and in Regensburg, the ancient ducal capital, the dukes had residual judicial powers over the bishops' *ministeriales* and townsmen in the thirteenth century.[42]

In the see of Eichstätt the bishops' *ministeriales* could not in practice be exempted from the advocates' authority because Bishop Gebhard (1125-49) and his brother, Count Hartwig of Grögling and Dollnstein, who was the secular advocate,[43] were jointly responsible for enfeoffing a new retinue of about seventy *ministeriales* out of their dynastic and ecclesiastical resources situated in the borderland of Bavaria, Franconia, and Swabia.[44] Successive bishops, advocates, and *ministeriales* co-operated until 1225, when the cathedral church began to throw off the advocate's influence in a twenty-year feud.[45] But a large number of the *ministeriales* still served both lords until the beginning of the fourteenth century. In 1300 the bishops possessed about sixty families of *ministeriales*, the

---

[39] MGD Conrad III, 77, pp. 136-8, 1142, and MGD Frederick I, 138f., pp. 231-4, 1156.

[40] UB Niederrhein i, 415, pp. 286-8, 1166.

[41] UB Wirtemberg ii, 426, pp. 213f., 1181.

[42] Mon. Boica liii, 57, p. 25, 1230.

[43] P. Fried, 'Zur Herkunft der Grafen von Hirschberg', *ZBLG* xxviii (1965), 82-98.

[44] E. Klebel, 'Eichstätt zwischen Bayern und Franken' in *Probleme der bayerischen Verfassungsgeschichte*, Schriftenreihe zur bayerischen Landesgeschichte, LXII (Munich, 1957), pp. 341-4, and my thesis, pp. 124-9.

[45] MGC ii, 187, pp. 228f., 1234, Reg. Eichstätt 706, p. 216, 1239, Mon. Boica xlix, 46, pp. 85-7, 1245, and my thesis, pp. 139-49.

advocates, by then calling themselves counts of Hirschberg, about 120, of whom nearly a hundred also held fiefs from the bishops. When the last count died in 1305, the majority of his *ministeriales* were transferred into the bishop's retinue, and the Eichstätt book of fiefs compiled at about that time shows that joint-lordship over Hirschberg *ministeriales* before 1305 must have been repaired after the feud by numerous individual acts of enfeoffment.[46] For a long time the counts and bishops had shared rights over their respective *ministeriales*, but neither party claimed formal joint-ownership of the other's retinue.

At Regensburg it appears that the two ecclesiastical princes, the abbot of St Emmeram and the bishop, also exercised joint-lordship over some of their *ministeriales*, who were called in 1085 'the *servientes* of St Peter and St Emmeram'.[47] In the tenth century both churches had one head, and the titles and lands of bishop and abbot were not formally separated until the 970s.[48] Their tradition of joint-lordship persisted much later. In 1141 Berthold of Treitersberg, son of an imperial *ministerialis* but himself belonging to the bishop through his mother's ascription, could only obtain succession to his father's allodial property by transforming it into an eccesiastical fief. But it was to be held of the abbot, not the bishop.[49]

Vassalage, homage, and fiefs

The *familia ministerialium* was a military establishment of knights enfeoffed with lands, castles, revenues, and offices, operating according to the customs of vassalage.[50] Strictly speaking *ministeriales* owed service not by the feudal contract but by birth. They did nevertheless reinforce their bonds by customary oaths of homage

[46] See p. 97, n. 90.
[47] Tr. Regensburg 655, p. 321, 1085.
[48] R. Budde, 'Die rechtliche Stellung des Klosters St. Emmeram in Regensburg zu den öffentlichen und kirchlichen Gewalten', *AU* v (1913), 153-238.
[49] Tr. Regensburg 805, p. 381, 1141 and 826, p. 395, 1147.
[50] G. Droege, *Landrecht und Lehnrecht im hohen Mittelalter* (Bonn, 1969), pp. 111-17, 186-8, W. Martini, *Der Lehnshof der Mainzer Erzbischöfe im späten Mittelalter* (Düsseldorf, 1971), G. Bradler, *Studien zur Geschichte der Ministerialität im Allgäu und in Oberschwaben*, Göppinger akademische Beiträge, L, (Göppingen, 1973), and V. Rödel, *Reichslehenswesen, Ministerialität, Burgmannschaft und Niederadel*, Quellen und Forschungen zur hessischen Geschichte, XXXVIII (Darmstadt and Marburg, 1979).

and fealty. They had the right to give counsel to their lords, and fulfilled an array of judicial and administrative tasks for them.[51] Military aid they gave in the form of garrison-duties, and active service as cavalry in the field. They were bound to protect their lord's life, honour, and possessions, and expected in return that he would defend them from their enemies and avenge their injuries. In return for fealty and service they received hereditary fiefs in land, or other forms of maintenance such as money-fiefs,[52] and expected to be judged by their peers. Except in the matter of hereditary ascription, *ministeriales'* style of life followed the patterns of secular knighthood everywhere in western Christendom.[53] For this reason they were almost at one with the much smaller class of free-born knights in Germany, and shared the values of knighthood which began to pervade the highest social ranks of the empire by the twelfth century. The high nobility, the free knights, and the *ministeriales* were often viewed as belonging to one knighthood, 'the order of knights' as a charter of 1139 put it, including in this *ordo* a duke, two counts, and five prominent *ministeriales* belonging to the archbishop of Cologne.[54] In 1146 the bishop of Osnabrück referred to his *militia* or knighthood, 'whether free men or *ministeriales*', and permitted them, in the way of aristocratic patrons, to donate their fiefs to the monastery of Gertrudenberg.[55]

[51] Chs. 7 and 8 below.
[52] Kluckhohn, pp. 72-9 on heritablity of fiefs. In the 13th c. castle-guard was paid for by money-fief at Harzburg (Metz, *SG*, pp. 122-33 for the Goslar *Vogteigeldlehnrolle* of 1244) and Gurkfeld, UB Salzburg iii, 1095, pp. 639 f., 1246. Cologne *ministeriales* were *vassali de pecunia*, UB Niederrhein ii, 1010, p. 594, 1298. *Ministeriales* and others at Rimpar in Franconia received annual pensions from the bishop of Würzburg from 1213, Mon. Boica xxxvii, 186, pp. 192-4. Imperial revenues enfeoffed to *ministeriales* are discussed in E. Müller, 'Kuningstoph 1282 und Koningesstope 1308 u. ff.', *AU* xi (1929-30), 423-34. Paid troops who were not *ministeriales* were used in the empire; P. Schmitthenner, *Das freie Söldnertum im abendländischen Imperium des Mittelalters*, Münchener historische Abhandlungen, 2nd ser., Kriegs- und Heeresgeschichte, IV (Munich, 1934), and H. Grundmann, 'Rotten und Brabanzonen. Söldner-Heere im 12. Jahrhundert', *DA* v (1942), 419-92. *Ministeriales* did receive cash-payments upon Italian expeditions, but not north of the Alps until the 13th c., and then very irregularly. Our knowledge of their remunerations is scanty, but see MGC ii, 338, pp. 446 f., 1242.
[53] A. Borst (ed.), *Das Rittertum im Mittelalter*, WF, CCCXLIX (Darmstadt, 1976), S. Harvey, 'The Knight and the Knight's Fee in England', *Past and Present* xlix (1970), 3-43, P. van Luyn, 'Les milites dans la France du XIe siècle. Examen des sources narratives', *Le Moyen Âge* lxxviii (1971), 5-51, 193-238, and J. Flori, 'Chevaliers et chevalerie au XIe siècle en France et dans l'Empire germanique', ibid. lxxxii (1976), 125-36.
[54] UB Niederrhein i, 330, pp. 220 f., 1139. [55] UB Osnabrück i, 272, p. 217, 1146.

Twelfth-century chronicles also assumed that free and unfree knights belonged to one military and social community. The Lorsch chronicler reported that when, many years before, Archbishop Adalbert of Bremen had tried to confiscate the abbey by means of letters sent out in the king's name, the knights of the church, *ministeriales* and free-born noblemen, took to arms and built fortifications to defend the abbot.[56] The Admont chronicler recalled that free lords and *ministeriales* were the *fideles* of Archbishop Gebhard of Salzburg (1060-88),[57] and Gislebert of Mons reported the same of the counts of Hainault's fellow-knights and counsellors.[58] He also spoke of princes, noblemen, *ministeriales*, knights, and clerics associating at Mainz for Frederick Barbarossa's celebrations there in 1184.[59] Another chronicler reported for 1195 that the German magnates arrived in Italy 'with the whole knighthood or *militia* of nobles and *ministeriales* and knights of their households'.[60] Knight, vassal, and *fidelis* were labels shared by *ministeriales* and free men, such as Archbishop Philip of Cologne's feudatories 'whether of the nobles or the *ministeriales* of the church'.[61] We are told that when the bishop of Halberstadt died in 1201, 'the vassals of the church, free-born knights as well as *ministeriales*, the lesser and the greater', were desolated.[62]

In theory homage was not required of *ministeriales* as a preliminary to their receiving fiefs, because their obligation to serve their lord was not a contract. Initially a distinction was therefore drawn in some of the German regions between fiefs depending upon real homage and fiefs given to *ministeriales*. The Goseck chronicler indicated that when monastic lands were enfeoffed to free men and *ministeriales* in the 1090s, it was the former who did homage for them.[63] In 1131 Lothar III pointed out that Abbot Wibald of Stablo's *ministeriales* held their fiefs by no real right of

[56] C. Erdmann, *Die Briefe Heinrichs IV*, MG Deutsches Mittelalter, i (Leipzig, 1937), 2-4, pp. 6-8, 1065, Glöckner, *Codex Laureshamensis* i, p. 393, and *Annales Weissemburgenses*, MGS, III, p. 71.
[57] *Vita Gebehardi et Successorum eius* MGS, XI, p. 36.
[58] Gislebert of Mons, pp. 300, 327f., and L. Genicot, 'Le premier siècle de la "curia" de Hainaut, 1060 env.-1195', *Le Moyen Âge* liii (1947), 39-60.
[59] Gislebert of Mons, pp. 155f.
[60] Chroust, *Kreuzzug Friedrichs I.*, p. 112.
[61] UB Niederrhein i, 527, p. 368, 1183-90, and similar usage in 511, p. 359, 1188, Mon. Boica xlix, 27, p. 60, 1208, and UB Münster, 707, p. 367, 1263.
[62] *Gesta Episcoporum Halberstadensium*, MGS, XXIII, p. 115, 1201.
[63] *Chronicon Gozecense*, MGS, X, p. 150.

benefice.[64] Such fiefs were sometimes designated as dependent upon the lord's court or household, instead of depending upon the act of homage, and were therefore called *hovelen* or house-fiefs in the vernacular.[65] In his *Sachsenspiegel*, Eike von Repgow claimed incorrectly that these were the only form of fief to which *ministeriales* were entitled.[66]

This contrast between fiefs quickly ceased to correspond with reality, since *ministeriales* were taking fiefs by real homage from their own and other lords as well,[67] so that by the end of the twelfth century the bishop of Verden's *ministeriales* were said to be 'enfeoffed in feudal law' like any other vassals.[68] Count Siboto of Falkenstein's land-register drawn up in late twelfth-century Bavaria drew no distinction at all between fiefs held by his free knights and his *ministeriales*. All of them were called 'his men who have done homage to him for various fiefs'.[69] In Brabant too, the free-born nobles and the *ministeriales* enjoyed the same rights in feudal custom over their fiefs,[70] but sometimes *ministeriales* themselves appear to have preferred to hold fiefs by servile rather than feudal tenure, probably to safeguard their descent to heirs. Shortly before 1200 Burchard of Essem, a *ministerialis* belonging to the abbey of St Michael's at Hildesheim, acquired extensive property from other *ministeriales*, and arranged for its devolution amongst his descendants by stipulating the forms which their tenure from the abbot ought to take. The principal legatees would inherit it as real fief, *in beneficium* and *iure feodi*, the residual legatees in part as servile fief,

[64] MGD Lothar III, 35, pp. 57 ff., 1131.
[65] MGC ii, 310, p. 423, 1231, and UB Halberstadt ii, 676, p. 13, 1238, 886, p. 149, 1254, and 1233, p. 358, 1271.
[66] Eckhardt, *Sachsenspiegel Lehnrecht*, pp. 81 f.
[67] UB Niederrhein i, 402, pp. 277 f., 1160, UB Wirtemberg ii, 386, p. 151, 1166, UB Halberstadt i, 445, pp. 396 f., 1208 and 508, pp. 454-6, 1219, UB Steiermark ii, 191, p. 276, 1222, Reg. Straßburg ii, 1029, p. 67, 1234, UB Münster 373, pp. 202 f., 1240, and Wittmann, *Monumenta Castellana*, 123, p. 38, 1244.
[68] MGC i, 367, p. 516, 1195.
[69] Noichl, *Codex Falkensteinensis*, 106, pp. 68-70, before 1189, for 'viri sui qui fecerunt ei hominium pro beneficiis variis', of whom more than half appear elsewhere in the Codex as Count Siboto's *ministeriales*. Imperial letters of enfeoffment also confirmed to free lords and to *ministeriales* the same terms about real fiefs; compare the *ministerialis* Wernher of Bolanden's hereditary rights in both lines in MGD Frederick I, 517, pp. 455 f., 1166 with the free lord Arnold of Dorstadt's almost identical rights 'per rectum feodum secundum morem Theutonicum' in 522, pp. 462 f., 1167.
[70] MGC ii, 279, pp. 392 f., 1222.

iure ministerialis, in part as real fief in exchange for homage, *iure hominii*.[71]

Ministeriales were, in short, collecting fiefs by several titles, of which *ius ministerialium*, persisting into the fourteenth century, was but one. The Osnabrück *ministerialis* Hugo the Bear, for example, held by real fief or *jure feodi*, by manorial tenure or *jure villicationis*, and by hereditary rent or *jure pensionali*.[72] Six *ministeriales* transferred to the bishop of Osnabrück by the count of Tecklenburg in 1236 also held their fiefs under three differing titles; fiefs *jure ministerialium*, real fiefs or *feodalia*, and fiefs incumbent upon their garrison-duty in castles.[73] In 1269 the knight Stephen of Wischel similarly accepted three hereditary titles to fief from his lord, Count Dietrich of Cleves. Kervenheim Castle was to be held *iure feodali* as a real fief, the lands pertaining to the castellan's office at Monreberg Castle to be held partly as fief in return for castle-guard or *iure castrensis feodi*, and partly as servile fief, *iure bonorum ministerialium*.[74] Fiefs attached to a castle, or to the office of castellan, or to the duties of castle-guard, formed a separate tenurial category widespread in Germany.[75] Its purpose was to ensure that the functions of a castellan in command of a castle, or of castle-guard by other knights, were actually fulfilled by *ministeriales* or their deputies in return for the fiefs granted. In consequence, Butler Henry of Hofstetten-Geyern's fiefs from the bishop of Eichstätt listed in 1297 included not only hereditary fiefs *iure feodi* and fiefs for life *iure precario*, but also those sustaining garrison-duty at Nassenfels and Hirschberg Castles, fiefs revocable at any time.[76]

As a form of tenure, fief in return for castle-guard was of great significance in the military world of the *ministeriales* and their masters. In the 1250s Bishop Dietrich of Gurk tried to evict the heirs of Otto of Strassburg from that castle, the most important in the bishopric, by enfeoffing another *ministerialis*, Nicholas of Liem-

---

[71] UB Hildesheim i, 522, 526, and 531, pp. 499–509, 1196–7.

[72] UB Osnabrück ii, 109, pp. 80 f., 1219, and 230, pp. 176 f., 1227.

[73] Ibid. 351, p. 272, 1236, iii, 359, p. 248, 1267, and iv, 544, p. 344, 1299, where Osnabrück fiefs were still being held *jure ministerialium*.

[74] UB Niederrhein ii, 598, p. 350, 1269.

[75] e.g. Mon. Boica xxxvii, 328, pp. 369 f., 1255 for *castrense feodum* of a castle held *a manu nostra* of the bishop of Würzburg, and xlix, 118, p. 181, 1282, for *ius castellanie quod vulgariter burchvt* (castle-guard) *dicitur*, and 312, pp. 481–5, 1302 for *feodum illum quod purklehen* (castle-fief) *dicitur*.

[76] Mon. Boica xlix, 255, pp. 392–4, 1297.

berg, with half the castle for life plus an enormous fief *ad ius quod purchuot dicitur*, 'by the title which is called castle-guard'.[77] In 1278 the Hildesheim *ministerialis* Hildemar of Oberg sold his castle at Huden for a large sum to his bishop, who entirely rebuilt it. The castle continued to be Hildemar's hereditary but revocable fief, and he was appointed the castellan with residence there, an office not alienable without the bishop's consent.[78] Effective castle-guard was essential to the security of all the territorial magnates, so they showed concern about the proper uses of fief in exchange for castle-guard. In 1278, when the bishop of Würzburg's *ministerialis* Herbord of Schwanfeld desired to sell a fief to the abbess of Heiligenthal, it turned out that it belonged to Herbord's office as castellan at Werneck Castle. The bishop permitted the sale, but required Herbord to convert one of his allods into the equivalent castellan's fief for sustaining garrison-duties at Werneck.[79]

Tenure of fiefs *iure ministerialium*[80] was dying away in face of other titles, especially that of real homage, 'the true title of fief completely and without reserve' as the bishop of Münster put it when enfeoffing *ministeriales* with the Königinhof in 1268.[81] For castles a separate category often seemed appropriate, and in other cases, tenure *iure ministerialium* was not necessarily suitable or desirable. Already in 1120 the archbishop of Mainz conceded new tenure to two *ministeriales* at Erfurt, in exchange for previous tenure as *ministeriales*.[82] In a striking case the archbishop of Bremen insisted upon the abolition of *ministeriales'* tenure in favour of real homage throughout the country of Stade in 1219. The archbishop forced the incumbent, the Welf Count-Palatine Henry of Brunswick, to recognize that Stade was not an allodial county, but a fief from Bremen. He was anxious to press home one of the consequences, to make the count-palatine's *ministeriales* in Stade into Bremen's rear-vassals. The *ministeriales* were therefore asked to swear fealty to Bremen, 'and the lands which hitherto they had

[77] Mon. Carinthia ii, 617, pp. 68 f., 1254–8.

[78] *Chronicon Hildesheimense*, MGS, VII, pp. 863, 867, and UB Hildesheim iii, 487, pp. 259 f., 1278; upon Hildemar the bishop conferred the castle 'titulo castrensis mansionis, quod borechsathe vulgariter nuncupatur'.

[79] Mon. Boica xxxvii, 421, pp. 489 f., 1278.

[80] e.g. UB Hildesheim iii, 652, pp. 340 f., 1283 for 'iure feodali ministerialium quod vulgariter dicitur hovelen'.

[81] UB Münster 820, pp. 425 f., 1268.

[82] Keutgen, *Urkunden*, 92, pp. 57 f., 1120.

held from the palatine by right as *ministeriales* or *iure ministeriali-*
tatis, they now received from him as real fiefs *iure feodali'*.[83]

Restrictions upon ministeriales *about fiefs*

As the custumals showed, the chief purpose of granting fiefs to
ministeriales was to ensure military services.[84] A problem for lords
was that feoffees sought fiefs as hereditary patrimonies to ensure a
reasonable economic future for their families, and were inclined to
lose sight of the service originally incumbent upon the grant. Provost Gerhoh of Reichersberg went so far as to reject altogether the
enfeoffment of ecclesiastical possessions to laymen whose business
was violence and whose motive was to devour the substance of the
Church, but his ungrateful[85] strictures were quite out of touch with
realities in Germany.[86] Lords were well aware that they must enfeoff *ministeriales* if they were to protect their lands, to survive the
rigours of their feuds, and to cut a figure in the dangerous politics
of the empire. What they did try to do was to regulate the proportion of their assets which they could afford to hand over to their
vassals without undue impoverishment. Under pressure from
greedy knights, the abbot of Reinhardsbrunn announced a prohibition upon enfeoffment which could be bent to his convenience,
'that no abbot of this monastery shall presume to grant any of the
lands and possessions belonging to it to any free man or *ministe-*
rialis for military service'.[87]

Ecclesiastical landlords sought imperial edicts or reworked their

---

[83] Lappenberg, *Hamburg*, 432, pp. 375 f., 1219.

[84] Lords also desired administrative services, see Ch. 7 below; in 1254 Bishop
Iring of Würzburg conferred a fief upon Liupold *magister coquinae* of Rothenburg
'ut vos nostris serviciis strictius obligemus', without giving further details, Mon.
Boica xxxvii, 327, p. 369.

[85] MGD Conrad III, 81, pp. 143 f., 1142 encouraged *ministeriales* to give their
lands to Reichersberg.

[86] Sackur, *Gerhohi Libelli*, pp. 136-202, Classen, pp. 40-7, and J. Semmler, *Die*
Klosterreform von Siegburg. Ihre Ausbreitung und ihr Reformprogramm, Rheinisches
Archiv, LIII (Bonn, 1959), pp. 306-11, who shows that Siegburg and its associated
houses were not hostile to *ministeriales*, as has previously been thought. However,
the 12th-c. historian of Petershausen claimed that, in the late 10th-c., the founder
had thought it best not to give *ministeriales*, who might simply oppress the monastery; *Casus Monasterii Petrishusensis*, MGS, XX, ch. 32, p. 635. Another 12th-c.
monk, Henry of Melk, was also suspicious of German knighthood and its designs
upon the possessions of the Church; Störmer, *Früher Adel*, vol. ii, pp. 482-6.

[87] UB Mainz i, 607, pp. 526 f., 1136, or later.

diplomas from earlier emperors, to provide themselves with the sort of restrictions they desired. The abbot of Fulda's lands, for example, were only to be enfeoffed to *ministeriales* who properly were owed reward for defending that house.[88] From Henry II, dead for a century, the abbess of Kaufungen conjured the words; 'We ordain that fiefs of *ministeriales* should not be augmented out of the prebends established for the nuns, nor should what they possess by right be diminished'.[89] Other monasteries approached the living for their requirements. In 1135 Lothar III granted to Abbot Anno of St Michael's at Lüneburg that 'all fiefs which free man have acquired in whatever fashion from the abbot, we take back wholly into the possession of the church, ordaining that no future abbot shall presume to give out any fief unless to *ministeriales* of the church'.[90] In 1145 Conrad III protected the abbot of Schaffhausen's lands on stricter terms, that 'you and your successors may not give anything in fief nor create any knights unless with the monks' advice'.[91] In 1151 the king imposed a prohibition similar to Reinhardsbrunn's upon the nunnery of Kitzingen, since it owed no military service to the empire. Here there had been a usurpation, since the Bamberg *ministerialis* Hartwig of Erlach had wrongfully claimed a military fief from the abbess.[92]

In some places it seemed almost too late to save the church lands. At the end of the eleventh century it was said that Goseck Abbey and the bishopric of Hildesheim were already quite impoverished by enfeoffments to *ministeriales* and to free vassals.[93] At Hilwartshausen Abbey in 1156, Frederick Barbarossa endeavoured to repair the damage. The *ministeriales* were permitted to retain fiefs which could be proved to have been rightfully granted or inherited up to 1125. The rest were scrutinized, usurpations were cancelled, and none of the fiefs legally granted after 1125 might in future be sold, exchanged, subinfeudated, pledged, or otherwise alienated from Hilwartshausen. In addition, fiefs of *ministeriales* dying without legitimate heirs were to revert to the abbey.[94] At Kremsmünster the monk Bernard, recounting the calamities of his

[88] Interpolation about 1150 into MGD Otto II, 104, p. 118, 975.
[89] MGD Henry II, 521, p. 673, dated to 1015.
[90] MGD Lothar III, 75, pp. 116 f., 1135.
[91] MGD Conrad III, 130, pp. 234–7, 1145.
[92] Ibid. 266, pp. 460 f., 1151.
[93] See p. 112, n. 63.
[94] MGD Frederick I, 138, pp. 231–3, 1156.

house, claimed that it was Abbot Manegold who had been extravagant in handing out the monastic resources far and wide to the *ministeriales* of the region late in the twelfth century.[95]

If it was thought proper to enfeoff *ministeriales* for the defence of churches such as Fulda, Lüneburg, and Hilwartshausen, some bishops were proving more careless than their chapters might wish. In 1203 the Osnabrück canons appealed to the papal legate to restrain Bishop Gerhard from alienating the see's resources by enfeoffing noblemen with lands and revenues 'which should not, however, be conceded unless to *ministeriales*'.[96] In a similar vein, the bishop of Passau was warned in 1222 not to sell or enfeoff resources without the advice and consent of the canons and *ministeriales*.[97] In 1259 the Eichstätt chapter tried to prevent the bishop from giving fiefs to knights who were not *ministeriales* of their church, but to no avail.[98]

Whatever the restrictions, large-scale enfeoffment of ecclesiastical lands, revenues, and castles to the military laity was inevitable. So were usurpations of fiefs, and consequent wrangles between *ministeriales* and their lords.[99] In reality the German Church had, ever since Carolingian times, been endowed with lands so extensive that several institutions could later be founded upon them: firstly, the independent ecclesiastical principalities themselves,[100] many of which survived the Reformation and the Thirty Years' War, lasting until their dissolution in 1803; secondly, a number of dynastic ter-

---

[95] *Bernardi Liber de Origine et Ruina Monasterii Cremifanensis*, MGS, XXV, p. 650.

[96] UB Osnabrück ii, 21, p. 14, 1203.

[97] MGC ii, 277, p. 391, 1222.

[98] Mon. Boica xlix, 66, pp. 109-11, 1259.

[99] e.g. *Chronicon Ebersheimense*, MGS, XXIII, p. 449, 1213.

[100] A. Hauck, *Die Entstehung der geistlichen Territorien*, Abhandlungen der Sächsischen Gesellschaft, phil.-hist. Klasse XXVII. 18 (Leipzig, 1909), M. Stimming, *Die Entstehung des weltlichen Territoriums des Erzbistums Mainz*, Quellen und Forschungen zur hessischen Geschichte, III (Darmstadt, 1915), H. Aubin, *Die Entstehung der Landeshoheit nach niederrheinischen Quellen* (2nd edn., Bonn, 1961), von Guttenberg, *Die Territorienbildung am Obermain*, H.-W. Klewitz, *Studien zur territorialen Entwicklung des Bistums Hildesheim*, Studien und Vorarbeiten zum Historischen Atlas Niedersachsens, XIII) (Göttingen, 1932), W. Heinemann, *Das Bistum Hildesheim im Kräftespiel der Reichs- und Territorialpolitik*, Quellen und Darstellung zur Geschichte Niedersachsens, LXXII (Hildesheim, 1968), E. Klebel, 'Landeshoheit in und um Regensburg', *Verhandlungen des Historischen Vereins von Oberpfalz und Regensburg* xc (1940), 5-61, Spindler, *Handbuch* ii, pp. 66-9, 593-601 and the literature cited there, and MGC ii, 73, pp. 86 ff., 1220, 156, pp. 192-4, and 171, pp. 211-13, 1232.

ritories which were, for the most part, constructed out of ecclesiastical fiefs subsequently usurped; and thirdly, a good proportion of
the knightly nobility of *ministeriales* and their descendants,[101] the
late medieval *Ritterschaft* or knighthood, which subsisted upon
thousands of small fiefs granted out by the Church between the
eleventh and the fourteenth centuries. Some of the princes of the
Church had, nevertheless, tried to exercise caution. When Archbishop Conrad I (1106–47) entered Salzburg in 1106 supported by
a thousand armed men, the powerful party of *ministeriales* who
had favoured the fallen imperial candidate eventually gave way,
and sought to renew the titles to their fiefs with the new master.
But Conrad would confirm only those bestowed by his papalist
predecessors, and the rest, declared to have been 'seized by violence
or usurped by fraud', were lost to the unlucky claimants.[102] In
similar circumstances his hard-pressed successor, the Alexandrine
archbishop Conrad II (1164–8), defending Salzburg from the schismatic emperor, refused to enfeoff more lands and tithes to the
knights he badly needed, and instead, rewarded them in kind for
their services.[103]

Oaths of loyalty

Just as they might hold real fiefs and do homage for them, so
ministeriales customarily swore oaths of fealty to their lords. Since
ministeriales were unfree and their services involuntary, such oaths
were not necessary in law to bind them to their duties, but they
were often required as an additional safeguard.[104] In 1290 Herman
of Asbeck therefore 'swore fealty because he is a *ministerialis* of
our church' to the abbess of Herford.[105] When *ministeriales* were

[101] S. Bachmann, *Die Landstände des Hochstifts Bamberg* (Bamberg, 1962), E.
Riedenauer, 'Kontinuität und Fluktuation im Mitgliederstand der fränkischen Reichs-
ritterschaft' in *Gesellschaft und Herrschaft. Festgabe für K. Bosl* (Munich, 1969),
pp. 87–152, R. Sprandel, 'Die Ritterschaft und das Hochstift Würzburg im
Spätmittelalter', *Jahrbuch für fränkische Landesforschung* xxxvi (1976), 117–43, F.L.
Wagner (ed.), *Ministerialität im Pfälzer Raum*, and A. Gerlich (ed.), *Geschichtliche
Landeskunde. Ministerialitäten im Mittelrheinraum*, Veröffentlichungen des Instituts für
Geschichtliche Landeskunde an der Universität Mainz, XVII (Wiesbaden, 1978).
[102] *Vita Chunradi Archiepiscopi Salisburgensis*, MGS, XI, p. 66.
[103] *Vita Gebehardi et Successorum eius*, MGS, XI, p. 46.
[104] e.g. Weinrich, p. 266, c. 1165 at Cologne.
[105] Franz, *Quellen*, 149, p. 388, 1290.

transferred into new retinues, or a new master came into his inheritance, then oaths of loyalty were also the custom.[106] In 1235
Frederick II commanded the *ministeriales* in the county of Stade,
the Brunswick fief from Bremen, to 'submit the oath of fealty after
the custom of the empire',[107] to the new duke of Brunswick. In
1276, when Count William of Jülich converted the burgraves of
Hammerstein, who were Cologne *ministeriales*, to his allegiance,
they 'took the oath of fealthy and homage to him'.[108]

In addition to these oaths of loyalty, *ministeriales* were often
required to swear to fulfil other purposes of their lords. In 1165
Frederick Barbarossa required the *ministeriales* as well as the clergy
and all vassals in every German diocese to swear fealty to his
anti-pope Paschal III.[109] In 1172 Archbishop Philip of Cologne
announced to the Pisans that the *ministeriales*, amongst other Germans, had promised their services by oath for the forthcoming
Italian expedition. In 1189 the imperial *ministeriales* swore on oath
to Henry VI for the same purpose.[110] These oaths were a sign of
the *ministeriales'* increasing political significance, and that was why
Innocent III felt it necessary to absolve the imperial *ministeriales*
from their allegiance when he turned against Otto IV in 1211.[111]

Ministeriales continually swore oaths to guarantee that their
lords would fulfil undertakings of a political or financial or domestic nature.[112] Such oaths were a regular part of the legal business
undertaken by *ministeriales* for their masters.[113] In 1229, for example, four *ministeriales* of each party swore to uphold the treaty
of mutual military aid drawn up between the counts of Oettingen

[106] L. Sloet, *Oorkondenboek der Graafschappen Gelre en Zutfen* (The Hague,
1872), 184, pp. 182 f., 1076-99, *Cronica Reinhardsbrunnensis*, MGS, XXX. 1, p. 597,
1221, and Gislebert of Mons, pp. 275, 300, 1192 and 1194, where the Hainault
ministeriales also did homage, with their masters, to the bishops of Liège for the
margraviate of Namur, the Liège fief to the counts of Hainault.
[107] MGC ii, 198, p. 265, 1235, and see p. 116, n. 83 above.
[108] UB Niederrhein ii, 692, pp. 404 f., 1276, and similar transactions in 686, p.
400, 1275, 843, p. 499, 1288, and 958 f., p. 567, 1295. Previous fealty was sometimes
declared to have been dissolved when *ministeriales* transferred into new retinues,
e.g. UB Hildesheim ii, 955, p. 477, 1254.
[109] MGD Frederick I, 481 f., pp. 398-401, 1165.
[110] Waitz, *Chronica Regia Coloniensis*, pp. 122, 144.
[111] See p. 107, n. 31.
[112] e.g. UB Wirtemberg iii, 655, p. 131, 1222, and a reported misuse of such oaths
in *Uodalscalcus de Egino et Herimanno*, MGS, XII, p. 437, 1097.
[113] Ch. 7 below.

and the bishops of Würzburg.[114] For similar purposes nine named
Salzburg *ministeriales* promised in 1250 to assist the count of Plain,
a prominent vassal of the archbishop, against the dukes of Bavaria.[115] In 1236 'all our *ministeriales* belonging to us by reason of
homage' swore to the peace-treaty between the counts of Arnsberg
and Rietberg, a wise precaution because they must have been active
in the hostilities; 'holding up their right hands in the manner of
knights, they promised to guard inviolably the oath given'.[116]

Also in the manner of knights, *ministeriales* might seek to place
restrictions upon their oaths of fealty, and commonly reserved loyalty to the empire or their lord's overlord, or refused to fight
against knights related to them, 'because I cannot bear arms
against them for the sake of my honour', as one of them put it.[117]
We have already seen that the Stade *ministeriales* reserved loyalty
to their lord's lord in 1219, and the *ministeriales* in the archbishop
of Salzburg's proprietary bishoprics at Gurk, Chiemsee, Seckau,
and Lavant similarly reserved loyalty from their bishops to the
archbishop as overlord, and to the emperor as ultimate lord.[118]
After some disagreement, the form of oath to be sworn by the
Gurk *ministeriales* to the archbishop was settled in 1232: 'I swear
that I will assist and support my lord the Bishop of Gurk in good
faith and without deceit to maintain and fulfil the oath which he
has taken to the Archbishop of Salzburg, so help me God'.[119]

In theory *ministeriales'* loyalty was the monopoly of their lords,
so these reservations of fealty, as well as the oaths themselves,
indicate that knightly customs of vassalage were eroding the stricter
law of unfree *familiae* in this respect. In his biography of Conrad
II, Wipo had already outlined the strict principle in a famous
passage about Duke Ernest of Swabia's abortive rising against the
emperor in 1027. The Swabian counts abandoned the duke on the
grounds that the fealty of free men could not possibly extend to

[114] Mon. Boica xxxvii, 216, pp. 226f., 1229.
[115] UB Salzburg iv, 12, pp. 11–13, 1250.
[116] UB Niederrhein iv, 657, pp. 798f., 1236, and another treaty ending feuds
between Count Meinhard of Görz and Bishop Egno of Brixen, sworn by four named
ministeriales on each side, in UB Krain ii, 112, pp. 85–7, 1241.
[117] See p. 114, n. 74.
[118] Mon. Carinthia i, 442, p. 338, 1213, 445f., pp. 341–4, 1214, and UB Steiermark ii, 161, p. 242, 1218, and so Frederick II could call the Salzburg *ministeriales*
his *fideles*, as in UB Salzburg iii, 943, pp. 495f., 1239.
[119] Mon. Carinthia i, 538, pp. 418–20, 1232.

joining in hostilities against the crown. Only if they had been servile, *servi*, then 'we should not be permitted to separate ourselves from you [the duke]'.[120] This rule applied to *ministeriales*, who were therefore encouraged to think more highly of their own lord's authority than the emperor's, as Henry the Lion's *ministeriales* were said to have done,[121] at least until his fall in 1180. On occasion *ministeriales* were not afraid to stage riots against the emperor's person and entourage, in defence of their lords' or their own interests, as at Mainz in 1115, Utrecht in 1123, and Augsburg in 1132.[122]

Counsel, advice, and consent

In feudal custom, lords sought advice and consent from their vassals, and this included their *ministeriales*. Gislebert of Mons named forty-five free noblemen and *ministeriales* who regularly counselled the counts of Hainault in the later twelfth century, calling them 'most trustworthy knights'.[123] Advice from *ministeriales* was appropriate to every kind of political and administrative act. When the countess of Ortenburg and her sons gave lands to Baumburg Abbey in 1190, the act was authorized by seventeen of their *ministeriales*, who were said to have distinguished themselves by their sage counsel.[124] When Duke Ottokar of Styria renewed the market-rights at Enns in favour of Regensburg, he did so with the advice of his most powerful *ministeriales*, who apparently constituted his permanent council; his seneschal Herrand of Wildon, his marshal Hartnid of Orth, from the famous island-fortress in the Traunsee, Gundechar of Steyr, Otto of Volkensdorf, and his chamberlain Ortolf of Gonobitz.[125] The *esprit de corps* of the Styrian *ministeriales* was exceptional, and in 1237 Frederick II, who had temporarily taken possession of the duchy, announced that he would heed 'the communal counsel of the greater *ministeriales* of Styria'.[126]

[120] Wipo, *Gesta Chuonradi*, p. 40.
[121] Helmold of Bosau, p. 242, 1149, Burchard of Ursberg, pp. 53 f., 1176, and Jordan, *Heinrich der Löwe. Eine Biographie*, pp. 41, 189.
[122] Waitz, *Chronica Regia Coloniensis*, p. 56, 1115, Ekkehard of Aura, pp. 360-2, 1123, and Jaffé, *MB*, 260, pp. 444-7, 1132.
[123] Gislebert of Mons, pp. 327 f.
[124] Mon. Boica ii, 11, pp. 193 f., 1190.
[125] Mon. Boica liii, 43, p. 13, 1191-2.
[126] UB Steiermark ii, 354, p. 463, 1237.

When Philip of Swabia was seeing to a peace-treaty between the
bishop of Regensburg and the duke of Bavaria, he imposed it 'by
counsel of the better barons and *ministeriales* of the land', without
whose agreement and participation such an act would, of course,
be nugatory.[127] It might prove unwise to ignore the *ministeriales*.
In 1216 Frederick II attempted to give two of the richest nunneries
in Germany, the Obermünster and the Niedermünster at Regensburg,
to Bishop Conrad in exchange for the towns of Nördlingen and
Oehringen. The king had to cancel the exchange under pressure
from the abbesses, who claimed that no such act could be valid
without the consent of their *ministeriales*, which was not forthcoming.[128] His grandfather, however, had passed Niederaltaich
Abbey in 1160 to the bishop of Bamberg without a hitch, 'the
advocate and *ministeriales* benignly consenting'.[129]

Consent was frequently given in the form of swearing with or for
the lord, to fulfil his military, fiscal, or political commitments.[130]
In 1120, for example, twelve of Conrad of Zähringen's *ministeriales*
guaranteed his oath to respect the laws he had granted to his new
town-foundation at Freiburg.[131] Count Berengar of Sulzbach, who
was enjoined by his mother and wife, both of them substantial
heiresses, to endow monasteries out of their inheritances, was held
to the purpose by twelve of his *ministeriales*, who had sworn with
him to observe these wishes. After some hesitation, and a warning
from the *ministeriales* about their collective peril of falling into
perjury, he founded Baumburg and Berchtesgaden before he died
in 1125.[132] In Frederick Barbarossa's time the Cologne *ministeriales* swore to uphold the archbishop's alliances against Henry the
Lion,[133] and in 1202 twenty of them, representing their entire community, swore their support for Archbishop Adolf's treaty with
Otto IV against Philip of Swabia.[134] The practical importance of
involving the *ministeriales* can be seen in another notorious case,

[127] Mon. Boica xxix. A, 582, p. 525, 1205-06.
[128] UB Wirtemberg iii, 581, pp. 33 f., 1215, and MGC ii, 57, pp. 70-2, 1216.
[129] MGD Frederick I, 306, pp. 121 f., 1160.
[130] e.g. UB Krain, ii, 225, p. 179, 1256.
[131] Keutgen, *Urkunden*, 133/i, p. 118, 1120.
[132] *Fundatio Monasterii Baumburgensis*, MGS, XV-2, pp. 1061-4, and R. van
Dülmen, 'Zur Frühgeschichte Baumburgs', *ZBLG* xxxi (1968), 3-48.
[133] Israël and Möllenberg, *Magdeburg*, 324, p. 423, 1167, and UB Halberstadt i,
283, pp. 246 f., 1178.
[134] MGC ii, 24, pp. 28 f., 1202.

when the bishop of Passau endeavoured in the 1220s to put an end to Count Conrad of Wasserburg's interference with the traffic on the Danube, exercised from his castle of Viechtenstein. In 1224 the count was obliged to pledge the castle to the bishop with the consent of the castellan and *ministeriales*, who committed themselves to obey the bishop, and finally submitted to the new arrangements in 1227.[135]

The military undertakings of *ministeriales*

Above all else *ministeriales* were knights enfeoffed to fight for their lords as loyal vassals. In 1147 Conrad III said of the Lorsch *ministeriales* that of old they had held fiefs from the abbot in return for military service,[136] and as we have seen, the abbey's chronicler had ascribed to them a proper knightly zeal in defending Abbot Ulrich when he was threatened with forcible eviction in 1065.[137] This affair passed off without a fight, but the endless feuds and confrontations of the Salian and Hohenstaufen age could prove more hazardous to *ministeriales*. When Duke Lothar of Saxony, the murderous Count Hermann of Winzenburg, and the counts of Cappenberg took Münster in 1121, 'the aforesaid duke carried off captive almost all the town's defenders, nobles as well as *ministeriales*'. It was said that in remorse for this affray, in which the cathedral had been burned down, the counts turned Cappenberg into a monastery.[138] Saxon *ministeriales* also did badly at the beginning of the thirteenth century when the Stedinger peasants expelled the Oldenburg and Bremen knights who garrisoned their countryside. Some were beaten up or even killed, and their castles burned down. The count of Oldenburg's *ministeriales* redeemed themselves when they beat off attacks upon the town by the Stedinger in 1232 and 1233,[139] and the archbishop of Bremen's knights had their revenge when the Stedinger were overthrown and massacred in 1234.

At about the same time, Count Frederick of Zollern in Swabia was complaining of the loss of Achalm Castle during the revolt

[135] UB Land ob der Enns ii, 450, 457 f., and 464, pp. 652 f., 659-65, and 670 f., 1224-7.
[136] MGD Conrad III, 167, pp. 302-4, 1147.
[137] See p. 112, n. 56.
[138] Waitz, *Chronica Regia Coloniensis*, pp. 59 f.
[139] *Historia Monasterii Rastedensis*, MGS, XXV, pp. 504-7.

against Frederick II, and sought help from the emperor: 'All my servants and eight of my *ministeriales* were wounded, tortured, and imprisoned by the marshal and the lord of Neuffen. Besides, they robbed me and my men of arms and mounts worth a hundred marks. In the assault no one brought help to any of my retinue'.[140] More fortunate in its outcome was the ingenious exercise by which the archbishop of Bremen's *ministeriales* recaptured Bremervörde Castle from his Welf enemy, Count-Palatine Henry of Brunswick, in 1218. Disguising themselves as pilgrims, the *ministeriales* claimed they were on their way to visit Otbert, a peasant faith-healer with a wide reputation who lived in the next village. Under this cover they swarmed into the castle and expelled the Welf garrison.[141]

The lords or relatives of *ministeriales* killed in the field might commemorate them by pious donations. During the troubled years of Conrad III's reign, for example, the counts of Wolfratshausen gave property to Diessen Abbey in memory of their *ministerialis* Magenso, 'who was killed at the siege of Valley Castle', and one of the count of Andech's *ministeriales* gave lands for his brother Liutold of Hausen, 'who was killed on campaign with his lord, Count Berthold'.[142]

In the extensive wars between the territorial magnates, the *ministeriales* are everywhere reported to have borne the brunt of battle. In 1229, for example, Archbishop Albert of Magdeburg was victorious over the margraves of Brandenburg, who had attacked his see. 'Hastily collecting an army of his *ministeriales*', he caught the margraves trying to cross the River Plane and chased them off, taking loot and captives. Just the reverse occurred in 1240. Archbishop Wilbrand's *ministeriales* having devastated the Havelland, Margrave Otto trapped them recrossing the rivers, many were drowned as the bridge at Plaue collapsed, seventy of them were wounded in the fray, many were captured, and the rest fled.[143] Such feuds might bring forward notable field-commanders. During the succession-wars which overwhelmed the landgraviate of Thuringia after 1247, the claims of Margrave Henry of Meissen were sustained in the field by Rudolf, butler of Vargula, who defeated

[140] UB Wirtemberg iii, 863, p. 361, 1235.
[141] *Annales Hamburgenses*, MGS, XVI, pp. 382 f.
[142] W. Schlögl, *Die Traditionen und Urkunden des Stiftes Dießen 1114–1362*, QE, XXII (Munich, 1967), 6, pp. 9–11, 1140, and 9, pp. 13–15, 1137–47.
[143] *Gesta Archiepiscoporum Magdeburgensium*, MGS, XIV, pp. 421 f., and Waitz, *Chronica Regia Coloniensis*, p. 279.

the Thuringian counts in 1248, burning their manors and taking four of them captive. In 1263, once the margrave had secured Thuringia itself, Rudolf once more took to arms with a hundred knights and, in another victory, captured Duke Albert of Brunswick, who had assaulted the margrave's territory.[144]

These battles were dangerous. After 1260, when the townsmen of Strasburg in Alsace rose against their new bishop, Walter of Hohengeroldseck, 'the canons, knights, and *ministeriales* of the church' fled to his camp, but they were badly defeated at the Battle of Hausbergen in 1262. More than sixty *ministeriales* were killed, and over seventy were captured and carried off to Strasburg. After a plot to free them had failed, they were said to have released themselves by abandoning the bishop's cause. After his death in 1263, of chagrin it was thought, the canons managed to patch up a new peace.[145]

In another case, the bitter wars of the 1270s and 1280s between the bishops of Hildesheim and the dukes of Brunswick, the worst blow fell in 1279 when the dukes captured about seventy Hildesheim *ministeriales* at the siege of Campen Castle. The chronicler told how the church was so cast down that scarcely any hope of recovery could be entertained. However, Bishop Siegfried managed not only to set the dukes against each other but also to capture many of their own knights. These were exchanged with his captured *ministeriales*, so that 'again he armed himself for the defence of the church', prudently reinstalling them in such castles as were left to him.[146]

From the Mediterranean to the Baltic German *ministeriales* were dying on campaign, but from day to day the less bloody task was to make castles secure.[147] *Ministeriales* lived in fortified houses or towers, which often were allodial property of their own, or they shared residence in the larger castles, which belonged to their

[144] Holder-Egger, *Monumenta Erphesfurtensia*, pp. 102, 105, 241 f., 768 f., 1248-63.

[145] *Ellenhardi Bellum Waltherianum*, MGS, XVII, pp. 105-14, and A. Hessel, 'Die Beziehungen der Straßburger Bischöfe zum Kaisertum und zur Stadtgemeinde in der ersten Hälfte des 13. Jahrhunderts', *AU* vi (1916-18), 266-75.

[146] *Chronicon Hildesheimense*, MGS, VII, pp. 863-7 and UB Hildesheim iii, 515, pp. 275 f., 1279.

[147] e.g. the four principal Salzburg castellans, Liutwin at Hohensalzburg, Durinc at Werfen, Eberhard at Leibnitz, and Siegfried at Friesach in UB Salzburg ii, 265, p. 376, 1147-52, or the count of Ravensberg's *milites castellani in Ravenesberg et ministeriales* in UB Osnabrück ii, 153 f., pp. 113-15, 1223-4.

lords.[148] For security reasons lords frequently required *ministeriales* to give up their allodial castles as fiefs,[149] but in the 1140s the bishop of Brixen permitted the opposite, and Frederick of Rodeneck converted the fief upon which he had built his castle into an allod, compensating the bishop with another property.[150] The larger castles, upon which the safety of lords and their territories was based, were enfeoffed to *ministeriales* on strict terms. The abbot of Stablo's castle at Logne, the chief fortification in his territory, with its hill, valleys, jurisdiction, and town, was protected by a series of imperial diplomas from grasping advocates 'along with all the fiefs and households which pertain to the custody of this castle'. Custody was entrusted to the abbot's *ministeriales*, one of whom received a fief worth £5 annually to hold the new tower built there in 1138.[151]

The bishops of Halberstadt suffered similar anxieties about their castles at Alvensleben, Gatersleben, and Emersleben. The first two were recovered from Henry the Lion's *ministeriales* in 1180,[152] and were entrusted to Halberstadt knights. Alvensleben was bought back from Seneschal John of Alvensleben in 1248, with the proviso that it was never to be pledged, enfeoffed, or otherwise alienated from the church of Halberstadt. Similar intentions were expressed about Emersleben, without the opportunity of carrying them out until 1263.[153] In 1262 the *ministerialis* John of Gatersleben and his five sons renewed their title to their castle on careful conditions; they held it 'by right of fief called *hovelen* or house-fief in the vernacular, and we can or ought not to alienate, pledge, or sell it to anyone' except the bishop. The castellans were bound to defend Gatersleben with all their strength, and were always to belong to Halberstadt as *ministeriales*, if necessary by arranging exchanges of

[148] The *ministeriales* on garrison-duty in the home castle of the last count of Hirschberg belonged to eight different families of knights: Mon. Boica xlix, 181, pp. 286-8, 1291, 223, pp. 342-4, 1296, and 344, pp. 527-9, 1304.

[149] UB Niederrhein ii, 482, p. 270, 1259 where Hermann, butler of Ahr, gave up Kuchenheim Castle to the archbishop of Cologne, and Mon. Boica xlix, 118f., pp. 181-4, 1282 where Albert, seneschal of Pfünz, gave up Pfünz Castle to the bishop of Eichstätt.

[150] Redlich, *Brixen*, 457, pp. 160f., 1140-7.

[151] MGD Lothar III, 119, pp. 190-3, 1137, MGD Conrad III, 5, pp. 8-11, 1138 and 40, pp. 64-6, 1140, and MGD Frederick I, 1, p. 3, 1152. On castle-guard at Logne, Ganshof, *Étude*, pp. 179f., and Linck, pp. 67-73.

[152] *Gesta Episcoporum Halberstadensium*, MGS, XXIII, p. 109.

[153] UB Halberstadt ii, 793, pp. 90f., 1248, 842, pp. 122f., 1251, 1023, pp. 243f., 1261, 1075, p. 276, 1263, and 1081, pp. 280f., 1263.

persons descended from mixed marriages. Should Gatersleben heirs not wish to take up their option as active Halberstadt *ministeriales*, then the castle would revert without compensation to the bishop.[154] In spite of these wearisome precautions, Emersleben and Gatersleben had, once more, to be recovered by force for the bishop in 1324.[155]

In another case, Bishop Conrad of Freising endeavoured to secure Gütenworth Castle by enfeoffing it to Albert of Gütenworth and his eldest son, who was committed to marriage within the *domus et familia*, 'the house and retinue', of Freising, to ensure that his heirs would remain Freising *ministeriales*. Marriage outside the retinue entailed forfeiture of the castle from the Gütenworth family. Bishop Conrad further stipulated that Albert and his sons must reside for life in the ambit of Gütenworth as 'our faithful castellans'.[156]

The political importance of these arrangements was amply shown in the case of the fortress at Neuburg on the Inn, in Bavaria. It belonged to Countess Agnes of Andechs-Merania, who transferred it to her husband, the last Babenberg duke of Austria. Enfeoffed by them to her *ministerialis* Rapoto of Essenbach, it was successfully defended by him against the dukes of Bavaria, for long after the houses of Babenberg and Andechs-Merania had passed away.[157] Neuburg was thus one of the very few Bavarian comital patrimonies to elude the dukes' claims as heirs in the thirteenth century. Owing to Rapoto's tenacity, it was preserved as an Austrian enclave until modern times.

Lords also employed their *ministeriales'* castles as gaols. When Henry IV took hostages from the defeated Saxon nobility in 1075, two of the youngest were imprisoned in one of Eberhard of Hagen's castles. Lampert of Hersfeld tells a long story about how they were clever enough to take advantage of Eberhard's indulgence or carelessness, and much to his fury escaped in 1076.[158] In the celebrated case of Richard Cœur de Lion, the duke of Austria entrusted the king to his *ministerialis* Hadmar of Kuenring, who locked him up in Dürnstein Castle. Transferred to Henry VI's custody, he was

[154] Ibid. 1040, pp. 253 f., 1262, and 1197, pp. 339 f., 1268.
[155] *Gesta Alberti II. Episcopi Halberstadensis*, MGS, XXIII, p. 124.
[156] UB Krain ii, 282, pp. 219 f., 1261. Bishop Egno of Brixen similarly enfeoffed Werso of Stein with Veldes Castle, envisaging descent in the male or female lines, to Werso's own children or to his sister's, ibid. 141, pp. 107 f., 1247.
[157] Spindler, *Anfänge*, p. 49.
[158] Lampert of Hersfeld, pp. 274-6.

given the burgrave of Trifels as his gaoler. The German magnates
were quite often captured during their feuds, imprisoned, and later
ransomed. In 1233, for example, when Bishop Eckbert of Bamberg
was on his way back from harrying the duke of Carinthia's lands,
he fell into the hands of the duke's *ministerialis* Henry of Finken-
stein, who incarcerated him in his castle. After a time the bishop
was ransomed.[159]

Since *ministeriales* possessed castles, they were strong enough to
refuse their proper obedience, if they chose. This was a perennial
irritation in territorial politics. The archbishop of Cologne's stronghold at Rheineck, for example, was enfeoffed to burgraves who
virtually betrayed him in 1275 by doing homage to the see's enemy,
the count of Jülich. By the end of the century, the burgraves had
received other fiefs and castles from Jülich,[160] and posed a real
threat to Cologne. All that the archbishop could do was to insist
in 1300 that Rheineck was 'unconditionally the allodial, unham-
pered, liege, and open castle' of his church, and that the burgrave,
who had to be a Cologne *ministerialis*, should hold it as a hereditary fief.[161]

In the annual round of local affairs, the military and administrative significance of castles large and small was paramount. Towards
the end of the thirteenth century, the bishops of Eichstätt rebuilt
their castles and entrusted them to their household officers, making
them responsible, at the head of their sub-castellans, for defending
the bishops' manors and gathering the incomes; the marshal at
Wernfels, the butler at Arberg, and the chamberlain at Mörnsheim.
Since this worked well, the system was extended to new acquisitions
under Abenberg, Hirschberg, and Sandsee Castles. But a generation later, when the bishop was involved in feuds with his own and
other lords' *ministeriales*, he had to bring them down by confiscating or destroying their castles, notably Stauf, Erlingshofen, Nassenfels, and Sommersdorf.[162]

The richer *ministeriales* were strong enough to take an independent line when they chose. No one could match Wernher of Bolanden, 'a very shrewd man enriched by seventeen castles of his own
as well as many manors, and recipient of 1100 knightly homages',

[159] *Continuatio Scotorum*, MGS, IX, p. 626.
[160] UB Niederrhein ii, 686, p. 400, 1275 and 1032, p. 606, 1299.
[161] Ibid. iii, 1, pp. 1 f., 1300, and Pötter, p. 114.
[162] See my thesis, pp. 201-15, 260-78, 306 f.

or Cuno of Münzenberg, 'a rich and judicious man possessing castles, estates, and many vassal-knights',[163] but most of the imperial *ministeriales* also had armed retinues of their own knights.[164] A survey of the imperial *ministeriales* enfeoffed in the borderland of Swabia, Franconia, and Bavaria in the thirteenth century shows that they owned approximately the following numbers of knightly families: the butlers of Reicheneck and Königstein twenty-five, the marshals of Pappenheim twenty-four, Hilpoltstein fourteen plus another fourteen by inheritance from the Sulzbürgs about 1266, Sulzbürg-Wolfstein a residue of thirteen, Rindsmaul of Grünsberg and Schönberg ten, Kropf of Emetzheim and Flüglingen eight, Stauf seven, and Burgsalach four.[165] Like the burgraves of Rheineck, some of them proved unreliable to their lord. In 1247 Godfrey of Sulzbürg abandoned Frederick II for the papal party,[166] and so, a little later, did Walter, butler of Klingenberg, whose wife and children were heirs to the Reicheneck name and Königstein estates. When he changed his mind, the pope wrote in disgust to the bishop of Eichstätt that he had returned to the Hohenstaufen cause 'like a dog to its vomit'.[167]

Ministeriales often proved to be disobedient or treacherous vassals, and because they were armed they were dangerous. When their lords were away, they might more readily make trouble. During the Second Crusade, Conrad III wrote to his son from Jerusalem about the royal *ministeriales* who were refusing their obligations, or so he had heard, and urged measures to be taken against them.[168] When Frederick Barbarossa, then duke of Swabia, arrived back in Germany from the same expedition, he had some of his *ministeriales* hanged for breaking the peace during his absence.[169] Evidently Frederick II was enraged by the number of imperial *ministeriales* who had supported his son's rebellion against him, and in the peace-legislation proclaimed at Mainz in 1235, he out-

[163] Gislebert of Mons, p. 162.
[164] e.g. J. F. Boehmer and F. Lau, *Urkundenbuch der Reichsstadt Frankfurt*, vol. i (new edn., Frankfurt, 1901), 111, p. 57, 1236, UB Wirtemberg iv, 1107, pp. 169f., 1248, and UB Hanau, 446, p. 331, 1269.
[165] See my thesis, pp. 159–73, 177–9, 369–74.
[166] UB Nürnberg 335, p. 203, 1247.
[167] Reg. Eichstätt, 773, pp. 240f., 1254.
[168] MGD Conrad III, 196, pp. 355f., 1148.
[169] Otto and Rahewin, *Gesta Frederici*, p. 90, 1149.

lawed *ministeriales* who gave aid and counsel to sons against fathers.[170]

Contemporary writers did, nevertheless, ascribe the knightly principles of military loyalty to the *ministeriales*. The Reinhardsbrunn chronicler, for example, recounted that in 1172, when Frederick Barbarossa was supposed to have visited Landgrave Louis of Thuringia at Neuenburg Castle, the emperor remarked that such a fine edifice did not appear to have very solid walls. The landgrave undertook to rebuild them that very night. Next morning the astonished emperor found all around an encampment of helmed and mail-clad men, with their shields and swords. 'Seeing therefore *ministeriales*, knights, armed men, and other nobles, all subject to his [the landgrave's] dominion, he was astounded and cheerfully admitted never having seen a more valuable or stronger wall'.[171] Dismissed as fabulous by his modern editor,[172] this story was invented or included by a chronicler sensitive to political reality. Perhaps it was to poke fun at the artlessness of princes, but there is no doubt that knightly loyalty and reliability had a valid place in the calculations of the magnates of the Hohenstaufen era.

Ministeriales *and the observance of knightly customs*

Military tasks and the mechanics of feudal aid and counsel were sustained by the knightly code of values, of loyal assistance and service reinforced by oaths, at least when lord and *ministerialis* were not feuding with one another. This prevailing mentality can be found not only in self-conscious tales such as that of Barbarossa's visit to Neuenburg Castle, but is taken for granted in some of the driest charters. In 1064 the king instructed the abbot of Einsiedeln's *ministri* that 'they shall always fulfil their debt of

---

[170] MGC ii, 196, ch. 18, p. 245, 1235. Such strictures did not deter *ministeriales* in 1281 from backing Dietrich of Thuringia against his father, Landgrave Albert, Holder-Egger, *Monumenta Erphesfurtensia*, pp. 286 f., and *Cronica Reinhardsbrunnensis*, MGS, XXX. 1, pp. 630 f. See M. Wellmer, 'Eine süddeutsche Proscriptionsliste im Staatsarchiv Wolfenbüttel' in *Aus Verfassungs- und Landesgeschichte. Festschrift für T. Mayer*, vol. ii (Lindau and Constance, 1955), pp. 105-24 for a list, probably 1235, of Swabian *proscripti*, including *ministeriales* who had backed Henry VII's revolt, as well as other wrong-doers.

[171] *Cronica Reinhardsbrunnensis*, MGS, XXX 1, p. 539.

[172] O. Holder-Egger, 'Studien zu thüringischen Geschichtsquellen', *Neues Archiv* xxi (1896), 714.

service and obligation of fidelity.'[173] When the bishop of Paderborn granted a fief in 1103 to a certain Wulfer, 'he received his fief and as long as he possesses it, shall render loyal and competent service like the other *ministeriales*.'[174] In 1128, when Lothar III rewarded his *ministerialis* Conrad of Hagen, the stated motive was 'on account of his great and assiduous devotion and maintenance of the most faithful service'.[175]

In much the same tone, Archbishop Eberhard of Salzburg explained in 1232 what lords should do for *ministeriales*, in this case the bishop of Gurk's knights who were his rear-vassals: he took them 'into his favour, choice, faith, and grace to advance, enfeoff, support, and defend them in everything just like *ministeriales* of the church of Salzburg'.[176] In 1241 the same prelate made this programme specific when the castellans of Reisberg begged for his protection and became his *ministeriales*.[177] In return for swearing fealty and giving him their castle as a fief from Salzburg, he promised to rescue their relatives who had been incarcerated by the Styrian *ministerialis* Hartnid of Orth, and to wage war upon him until he disgorged the Reisberg fiefs which he had seized.

Although we know that *ministeriales* robbed their lords, launched feuds against them, betrayed them to their enemies, and even assassinated them,[178] the knightly principles of loyalty, mutual assistance, and supportive vengeance were alive too. *Ministeriales* ran considerable risk of captivity, mutilation, or death in their lords' service. Early in the 1120s Count Conrad of Wettin claimed that his second cousin, Margrave Henry of Meissen, was supposititious, and the rumour was put about by the count's *ministerialis* Hildolf, forebear of the knights of Zörbig. When the margrave's men caught Hildolf, they mutilated him frightfully and the count undertook a war of revenge against them. It went badly, for he was himself captured and chained up at Kirchberg Castle. He was released upon Henry's unexpected death in 1123, and succeeded him

[173] MGD Henry IV, 125, pp. 163 f., 1064.
[174] CD Westphalia i, 174, pp. 135 f., 1103.
[175] MGD Lothar III, 14, pp. 17 f., 1128. The other motive was to make sure that Henry V's *ministeriales* backed the crown, not his private heirs, the Hohenstaufen brothers.
[176] Mon. Carinthia i, 538, p. 419, 1232.
[177] UB Salzburg iii, 968, pp. 517-19, 1241.
[178] Ch. 9 below.

as margrave.[179] At the end of the century, in a feud between Landgrave Henry of Thuringia and Margrave Albert of Meissen, the latter took Wunnenfels Castle and blinded the castellan. To avenge this atrocity the landgrave wasted the margrave's lands.[180]

Lords regarded wars of revenge to be necessary to their retinues' sense of security, and consequently, to their own. In Swabia one such feud grew out of all proportion to its origin. We are told that in 1164 Count-Palatine Hugo of Tübingen descended upon the Welf *ministeriales* at Möhringen for unspecified misdemeanours, pulled down their castle, and hanged them. Thereupon Duke Welf and his son attacked the count-palatine, who successfully appealed for military support from Duke Frederick of Swabia, the emperor's nephew. In this traditional division of Swabian allegiances, the Welfs at first did poorly. After 900 of the 2,200 men they put into the field has been captured, they submitted to a truce. But when the war was renewed, they took four of the count-palatine's castles, obliged Duke Frederick to abandon him, forced him to submit in 1166, and with imperial consent, kept him in custody for a year.[181]

In return for such displays of supportive vengeance, the *ministeriales* expressed exasperation when their lords fell victim to captivity or violent death. After the notorious murder of Archbishop Engelbert of Cologne by Count Frederick of Isenburg in 1225, the Cologne *ministeriales* pursued justice with alacrity. The Reinhardsbrunn chronicler says that the highest *ministeriales* of his retinue took his bloodstained clothing to exhibit at the royal court, and cried out for vengeance from the princes of the empire.[182] When the count's brothers, the bishops of Münster and Osnabrück, were brought to trial at Liège for their supposed part in the conspiracy, Emo of Wierum tells us that when the Cologne *ministeriales* indicted Bishop Dietrich of Münster, his own *ministeriales* sprang

---

[179] *Chronicon Montis Sereni*, MGS, XXIII, pp. 140 f., and *Chronicon Gozecense*, MGS, X, p. 147, *c.* 1085 for compensation obtained for a *ministerialis* blinded by an enemy.

[180] *Cronica Reinhardsbrunnensis*, MGS, XXX. 1, p. 553, 1193-4. *Ministeriales* were not above blinding their own foes; UB Salzburg ii, 463, pp. 627 f., 1189.

[181] E. König, *Historia Welforum*, Schwäbische Chroniken der Stauferzeit, I (Sigmaringen, 1978), pp. 60-7. Otto of St Blasien (Hofmeister, *Chronica*, pp. 20 f.) reports a slightly different version in which, of the three *ministeriales* taken at Möhringen, two belonged to the count-palatine and were let go, and the third, belonging to Duke Welf, was hanged. Such selective mercy would also have angered the Welfs.

[182] *Cronica Reinhardsbrunnensis*, MGS, XXX. 1, p. 603.

forward to his defence, but bloodshed was avoided.[183] Since the bishop could not satisfactorily clear himself, he was deposed and died soon afterwards. Count Frederick was proscribed, and all his *ministeriales* were released from their fealty to him.[184] Eventually he was captured and broken upon the wheel.

A recurrent hazard for *ministeriales* was imprisonment by their lords' enemies in the violent rivalries of local, territorial, and imperial politics.[185] During the civil wars after 1245, the imperialist Duke Otto of Bavaria's procurator in the papalist Rhineland, Conrad of Alzey, was unfortunate enough to fall into the hands of the papal faction, and was delivered to the burgrave of Nuremberg. The duke requested his release, but the archbishop of Mainz warned the burgrave not to let him go, since he was proscribed as an outlaw, at least in the eyes of the papalists. The duke's petition was refused.[186] Normally prisoners could expect to be ransomed, but since their lords were always short of cash, they or their families had to find the money. This is what happened later to another of the Alzeys, the seneschal Walter, who was besieged and captured in 1260. For a high ransom of 400 marks he was released by his custodian, Count Emicho of Leiningen.[187] In an earlier case, Henry the Lion's seneschal Jordan of Blankenburg was captured during the abortive invasion of Holstein in 1190. His ransom was fixed very high, at 600 marks 'because he was so rich', double the rate for the count of Schwerin taken prisoner at the same time.[188] In 1268 the knights of Rautenberg, who were Hildesheim *ministeriales*, were obliged to raise 120 marks to free Siegfried of Rautenberg from Count Henry of Wohldenberg. They had to sell off a considerable proportion of their allods, to which the bishop of Hildesheim handsomely agreed.[189]

Apart from the mentality of their class and profession, it was the oath of fealty which committed *ministeriales* to the honourable

[183] *Emonis Chronicon*, MGS, XXIII, pp. 510f., 1226.
[184] *Catalogi Archiepiscopi Coloniensium*, MGS, XXIV, p. 355.
[185] Magnates also threatened to detain their weaker rivals' *ministeriales* as hostages for future good behaviour; MGC ii, 39f., pp. 48-50, 1212, UB Niederrhein ii, 85, p. 47, 1220, and UB Osnabrück ii, 483, pp. 384-6, 1246.
[186] R. von Stillfried and T. Maercker, *Monumenta Zollerana. Urkundenbuch zur Geschichte des Hauses Hohenzollern*, vol. ii (Berlin, 1856), 44-6, pp. 18f., c. 1245.
[187] *Annales Wormatienses*, MGS, XVII, pp. 64f.
[188] *Arnoldi Chronica Slavorum*, MGS, XXI, p. 180, and Haendle, pp. 3-10.
[189] UB Hildesheim iii, 189f., pp. 93f., 1268.

behaviour of loyal knights, 'those who by homage, whether they
are free men or unfree, adhere to their lords.'[190] The oaths might
be taken either upon entry into active military service, as at Cologne, or upon *ministeriales*' attaining their majority: in 1269 one of
Count Dietrich of Cleves' *ministeriales* promised for his children
that 'when they shall reach years of discretion, I will ensure that
they take the oath of fealty owed to that lord'.[191] The principles
of honour underlined by oaths had certain consequences. In a
Saxon chronicle about the princes of Brunswick put together in the
1270s, the problems of *ministeriales*' honour and the conflict of
loyalties in the perilous world of imperial politics were considered.
We are informed that long ago, when Henry V invaded Saxony in
1112, the Margravine Gertrude of Brunswick was obliged to hand
over some of her *ministeriales* as hostages, including Widekind of
Wolfenbüttel. The emperor was impressed with him, and invited him
to enter imperial service. Widekind replied: 'If I violate my debt of
faith to my lady, before God I shall be guilty of sin, I shall have
slighted my reputation and honour, and I shall displease the regal
dignity of yourself'.[192] The emperor accepted this, sent him back
to Saxony, and enfeoffed him all the same with portions of the
imperial fisc there, offices which the Wolfenbüttel family probably
did actually administer in the thirteenth century.[193]

No doubt this legend, ascribed to a distant past, was composed
as a compliment to the Wolfenbüttel-Asseburg family, which had
recently returned from service under the Hohenstaufen to its ancient allegiance to the house of Brunswick. It nicely balances for
the record the demands made upon the family by their initial Brunswick connection, and the wider imperial horizon opened to Seneschal Gunzelin of Wolfenbüttel at the beginning of the thirteenth
century. The Wolfenbüttels had been close to Duke Henry the Lion,
who appointed Eckbert the guardian of his family and retinue when
he left for Palestine in 1172.[194] The Wolfenbüttels were not amongst
the *ministeriales* who abandoned Henry the Lion in 1180, though
they did back their own relatives, the *ministeriales* of Dahlum and
Wenden, in a feud with the ex-duke in 1192. In spite of this quarrel

[190] MGC i, 447, ch. 4, p. 662, *c.* 1160.
[191] See p. 114, n. 74.
[192] *Chronicae Principum Brunsvicensium Fragmentum*, MGS, XXX. 1, pp. 22 f.
[193] Metz, *SG*, pp. 37 f.
[194] *Arnoldi Chronica Slavorum*, MGS, XXI, p. 116.

they remained high in favour at Brunswick, and when Otto IV claimed the imperial crown in 1198, he appointed Gunzelin his chief secular counsellor and seneschal of the empire.[195] Victor in a notable campaign which cleared the Hohenstaufen garrisons out of Saxony,[196] he was one of the ambassadors to Innocent III in 1209 who finally secured Otto's recognition as emperor-elect.[197]

The seneschal was one of the very few imperial *ministeriales* who did not desert Otto IV for Frederick II in the years after 1211. At the first signs of disaffection in Saxony, he fortified and garrisoned Nordhausen and Mühlhausen for Otto IV, stuck to him after his fall in 1214, and witnessed the dying emperor's will in 1218, under which he received custody of more Welf castles.[198] With Otto's death there could remain hardly a shadow of disloyalty in Gunzelin's resuming his office as imperial seneschal under Frederick II. Until his death in the 1250s he served the Hohenstaufen interest in Saxony, where he was the most powerful *ministerialis*, and in Tuscany, where he was imperial legate. With the collapse of Hohenstaufen hegemony in Germany, all the imperial *ministeriales* had to weigh up the advantages of new allegiances. Since Gunzelin's wife had been a Hildesheim *ministerialis*, their offspring inclined at first to the bishops, from whom they held the county of Peine,[199] but their future was settled when Duke Albert of Brunswick, Henry the Lion's great-grandson, seized their principal castles and invited or constrained them back into Welf service. By the 1270s they were marshals of the duchy.[200] In fact and fable the Wolfenbüttels had therefore reconciled with honour the conflicting demands upon their fealty as *ministeriales* over the generations.

There were further social consequences of the *ministeriales'* commitment to knightly values. One was the growing importance attached to knightly descent as such, the sense of noble family of which *ministeriales* were becoming aware,[201] and which was con-

[195] Holder-Egger, *Monumenta Erphesfurtensia*, pp. 209f., and Haendle, pp. 40-6.
[196] *Arnoldi Chronica Slavorum*, MGS, XXI, pp. 217f., 1206.
[197] MGC ii, 33, p. 42, 1209.   [198] Ibid. 42, pp. 51-3, 1218.
[199] UB Asseburg i, 292, pp. 202f., 1258. Part of the agreement was that Bishop John of Hildesheim (1257-61) would pay some of the Wolfenbüttel debts; *Chronicon Hildesheimense*, MGS, VII, p. 862.
[200] UB Asseburg i, 289, pp. 197-200, 1254-8, 377, p. 249, 1275, and 395, p. 259, 1280.
[201] See pp. 70f., nn. 104-5, 108-11, MGD Lothar I and II, 146, pp. 330f., actually c. 1200 for *ministeriales'* status *ab attavo*, and UB Salzburg iii, 783, pp. 310-12, 1223 for *ministeriales* who were *de militari prosapia*.

sciously encouraged by the imperial court.[202] Another was the aristocratic notion of judgement by peers, under their lords' direction, for misdemeanours and in other adjudications.[203] Another was admiration for *ministeriales* who distinguished themselves in tournaments and carried off the prizes, such as the landgrave of Thuringia's knight Waltram of Sättelstedt at Merseburg in 1227.[204] Also in 1227, in one of the more bizarre undertakings of the age, the Styrian *ministerialis* Ulrich of Liechtenstein claimed that he successfully challenged the knighthood of Friuli, Carinthia, Styria, Austria, and Bohemia to a series of jousts in honour of Venus, whom he impersonated by wearing false braids, a white dress, and silk gloves over his armour. In 1240 he embarked upon a similar enterprise, but this time attired as King Arthur.[205]

Penalties for breaking the knightly code

When the rules of vassalage or the code of knighthood were broken, unpleasant penalties were likely to be imposed. In 1111, for example, when the castellan of Salzburg caught the *ministerialis* largely responsible for armed unrest against Archbishop Conrad, he had him blinded.[206] The Hainault *ministerialis* Robert of Beaurain was, as we have seen, imprisoned for failing to turn up for a judicial duel,[207] and Gislebert of Mons reported another case

[202] MGC i, 140, p. 197, ch. 10, 1152 and 318, ch. 20, p. 451, 1186. See E.F. Otto, 'Von der Abschließung des Ritterstandes', *HZ* clxii (1940), 19–39, P. Bonenfant and G. Despy, 'La noblesse en Brabant aux xiie et xiiie siècles', *Le Moyen Age* lxiv (1958), 27–66, J. Fleckenstein, 'Zum Problem der Abschließung des Ritterstandes' in H. Beumann (ed.), *Historische Forschungen für Walter Schlesinger* (Cologne and Vienna, 1974), pp. 252–71, and 'Zur Frage der Abgrenzung von Bauer und Ritter' in R. Wenskus, H. Jahnkuhn, and K. Grinda (eds.), *Wort und Begriff Bauer*, Abhandlungen der Akademie der Wissenschaften in Göttingen, phil.-hist. Klasse, 3rd ser., LXXXIX (Göttingen, 1975), pp. 246–53.
[203] Crecelius, *Werden*, 103, p. 6, 1050–63, *Charta Pacis Valencenensis*, MGS, XXI, p. 608, 1114, MGD Charlemagne 219, p. 294, actually c. 1160, and Mon. Carinthia i, 536, pp. 415f., 1232.
[204] *Cronica Reinhardsbrunnensis*, MGS, XXX. 1, p. 608, and M. Weltin, *Die 'Laaer Briefsammlung'. Eine Quelle zur inneren Geschichte Österreichs unter Ottokar II. Přemysl*, Veröffentlichungen des Instituts für österreichische Geschichtsforschung, XXI (Vienna etc., 1975), 17f., pp. 103f., 27f., p. 108, and 56f., p. 122, 1262–4 which mention tournaments held in Austria and Carinthia.
[205] R. Bechstein, *Ulrichs von Liechtenstein Frauendienst*, Deutsche Dichtungen des Mittelalters, VI and VII (Leipzig, 1888), i, pp. 178–86 and ii, pp. 173–6.
[206] *Vita Chunradi Archiepiscopi*, MGS, XI, p. 69.
[207] See p. 75, n. 141.

where one of the bishop of Strasburg's knights failed to appear in 1191 at the royal court at Hagenau for a duel with the imperial marshal Henry of Kaiserslautern. By sentence of the royal assembly, the knight 'was deprived of his honour and his lands and his wife'.[208] At about this time Count Siboto of Falkenstein was preparing a grim punishment for his disobedient *ministerialis* Rudolf of Piesting. He requested another vassal, Ortwin of Merkenstein, to kill him or at least to blind him, offering Rudolf's fiefs as the reward.[209]

Ministeriales were aware that broken faith might entail, in feudal custom, confiscation of fiefs and loss of their lords' protection, and in imperial law, personal proscription as outlaws losing allods and all legal rights, as well as excommunication by the Church.[210] In the thirteenth century, in the long struggles of the Austrian and Styrian *ministeriales* against their dukes, the knights saw their lands harried, offices confiscated, castles razed, and their very persons imprisoned, exiled, or executed.[211] In 1202, when the Würzburg *ministeriales* of Rabensburg assassinated their new bishop, Conrad of Querfurt, they got away with temporary exile, their lands were confiscated, their castle was destroyed, and ecclesiastical penances were imposed upon them.[212] But when Abbot Bertho of Fulda was killed by nine of his *ministeriales* in 1271, the ringleaders were rounded up and executed.[213] In 1281, when the count of Oldenburg decided to break his contumacious *ministerialis* Lothar Mundel of Linebroke, 'he drove him with his entire kindred out of his dominions, seized all their chattels and lands, and dishonourably expelled them as fugitives'.[214]

In another case, Archbishop Eric of Magdeburg laid siege in 1292 to Neugattersleben Castle, held by a faction of his *ministeriales* who objected, not without justification, to his having pledged

[208] Gislebert of Mons, pp. 214f., 268.
[209] Noichl, *Codex Falkensteinensis*, 183, pp. 163f., c. 1180-90.
[210] For excommunications see, e.g. UB Salzburg ii, 262, p. 374, 1147-64, and Reg. Eichstätt 1620, pp. 501f., before 1317.
[211] Ch. 9 below.
[212] A. Wendehorst, *Das Bistum Würzburg. Die Bischofsreihe bis 1254*, Germania Sacra, n.s., Die Bistümer der Kirchenprovinz Mainz, I. 1 (Berlin, 1962), pp. 195-9, and G. Beckmann, 'Die Pappenheim und die Würzburg des 12. und 13. Jahrhunderts', *HJ* xlvii (1927), 17-56.
[213] W. Heinemeyer, *Chronica Fuldensis. Die Darmstädter Fragmente der Fuldaer Chronik*, *AD* Beihefte, I (Cologne and Vienna, 1976), pp. 129-33.
[214] *Historia Monasterii Rastedensis*, MGS, XXV, p. 510.

the see's rights in Lusatia to his brother, Margrave Otto of Brandenburg. Apparently the *ministeriales* survived the siege, but the archbishop got the better of them when his brother staged their captain's assassination in the Dominican Church at Magdeburg, whence he was dragged out by the hair.[215] If the penalties which lords preferred to impose were severe, violent, and exemplary, the imperial butler Walter of Limburg was lucky in 1237 to get off with a warning for having backed King Henry's revolt against Frederick II in 1234. The butler had attacked the lords of Hohenlohe, who remained loyal to the emperor. Frederick II now required Walter to give extensive property to the Hohenlohes in compensation. His further good behaviour was secured under pain of strict penalties in imperial and feudal law: 'I should become an outlaw which is called *êlos et rehtlos*, without honour and rights in the vernacular, and all my possessions, both allod and fief, would fall to the pleasure of the lord emperor, and my other fiefs which I hold from other lords would revert to them'.[216]

[215] *Gesta Archiepiscoporum Magdeburgensium*, MGS, XIV, p. 425.

[216] UB Wirtemberg iii, 891, pp. 390f., 1237. Huillard-Bréholles, *Dipl. Friderici II*, vol. iv. 2, pp. 760-6, 1235, shows that Godfrey of Hohenlohe had already taken custody of castles from the rebels, including Walter of Limburg.

CHAPTER 5

The *Ministeriales* and their Lands

Fiefs and allods

Appraising what the legal servitude of *ministeriales* meant (Ch. 2), and examining their rights and obligations preserved in the custumals and other texts (Ch. 3), reveal a great deal about their rank in German medieval society. Probably the *ministeriales* were not themselves concerned with these problems except when their status was threatened, or their rights infringed. Their social standing, their effectiveness as knights, and the future of their families turned upon other considerations which were their more conscious preoccupations; the possession of lands and offices with revenues, and the arrangement of marriages. Since their castles and lands, fief and allod, were hereditary, and their marriages were subject to their lords' consent, these questions were intertwined to a degree. The manorial economy and the fruits of office determined what *ministeriales* could invest in stone towers, military equipment, and retainers of their own, what marriages they could make for their children, and to what extent they could patronize the religious culture of their time.

The most extensive single category of information we possess about *ministeriales* concerns their possession of land and other real property. It is accumulated in charters, cartularies, land-registers, books of fiefs, books of donation, and similar materials drawn up principally by monastic and cathedral churches, recording the gifts, exchanges, and sales by *ministeriales* and others to these corporations, or the *ministeriales'* acquisition of ecclesiastical property, nearly always as fief, in exchange for services or cash, or both. From this it is possible to construct a remarkably clear picture of the terms upon which *ministeriales* held property, although the evidence is one sided because so much of it concerns gifts just about to go out of *ministeriales'* possession into the hands of the

Church. However, there are numerous charters of enfeoffment, exchange, and confirmation to *ministeriales* from their secular and ecclesiastical lords, and other miscellaneous regulations about their fiefs and allods issued mainly by the imperial court. In addition, *ministeriales* themselves issued charters, testaments, or letters of reversion about the tenurial status of their possessions.[1]

Ministeriales were principally sustained by the hereditary fiefs which were the reward for their service and fealty, and provided the economic basis for the future of their families. Fief was tenure, for the proprietor was the lord who granted the fief to the *ministerialis*. But *ministeriales* themselves possessed allods as proprietors, distinguished from fief by such terms as *allodium, proprietas, patrimonium, hereditas, predium*, or *proprium*,[2] although all these words, even *allodium* itself, can also be found, depending on the context, applying to fief, and the neutral word *bona*, goods or possessions, to either.[3] It is likely that nearly everywhere in Germany the extent and value of *ministeriales*' fiefs were much greater than those of their allods. According to the rules for the imperial *ministeriales* at Weissenburg in Franconia, their fiefs were to be three royal *mansi* in extent, and the Reichenau forgery about military service mentioned fiefs of ten and five *mansi*.[4] But these hints from questionable sources convey no firm idea of what was needed to sustain a militarily active knightly family in the twelfth century. Some

[1] e.g. Mon. Boica xlix, 73, pp. 116f., 1264, 148, pp. 241f., 1285, and 255, pp. 392-4, 1297.

[2] In the following examples the terms are applied to allodial property: *predium* in MGD Conrad III, 50, p. 84, 1140 and Busley, *Neustift*, 35, p. 35, 1160-70, *allodium* in Tr. Regensburg 812, pp. 386f., 1143-9, *proprietas* in ibid. 934, p. 466, 1179, *hereditas* in Lappenberg, *Hamburg*, 284, p. 251, 1189, *patrimonium* in UB Hildesheim i, 526 and 531, pp. 504-9, 1196-7; and UB Niederrhein ii, 1045f., pp. 616f., 1299 for allods 'ad me iure proprio quod vulgariter Eygen dicitur pertinentibus'.

[3] In MGD Conrad III, 77, pp. 136-8, 1142 *bona* referred to *ministeriales*' fiefs; in MGC ii, 30, p. 35, 1209 *bona* 'sive patrimonialibus sive feudalibus' to their fiefs and allods. See Metz, *SG*, pp. 58f. for a discussion of *allodium* which was fief, and Mon. Boica xxxvii, 429, pp. 501f., 1279 for an *allodium* held by *ministeriales* from Würzburg *in feodum*. See Uhl, *Weihenstephan*, 102, pp. 87f., 1138-47 for *predia* possessed *hereditario iure* and other *predia* possessed *beneficiaro iure* by the Freising *ministerialis* Isanrich, chamberlain of Lohkirchen. If 'allod' sometimes meant 'fief', 'fief' sometimes meant 'allod'; see Mohr, *Oberaltaich*, 127, pp. 257f., c.1231-4 where Ulrich of Rain resigned a *benefitium* 'quo proprietario iure possidebat', which was transferred to his cousin Baldwin 'in veram possessionem', and Reg. Eichstätt 1621, p. 502, 1317 where the Eichstätt marshal Rüdiger of Dietenhofen possessed 'duo feoda ad me iure proprietatis et dominii pertinencia'.

[4] MGC i, 447, pp. 661-3, and 451, p. 678.

142 GERMAN KNIGHTHOOD 1050-1300

ministeriales were fabulously rich in fiefs, such as Wernher of Bolanden in the Rhineland or Henry of Weida in the Saxon and Thuringian marches, while others complained of their poverty, hunger, and debts.[5] As we have seen in the previous chapter, multiple enfeoffment and the acquisition of new fiefs by real homage were practices well advanced in the twelfth century.

Allodial property

Ministeriales were the proprietors of allods which they inherited or purchased, such as the Münster knight Henry of Rechede's house 'which I held of no one, but possessed by right of property'.[6] Over allods they enjoyed extensive rights of disposal which could not, of course, apply to their fiefs. These rights were illustrated when, some time before 1147, the Freising *ministerialis* Fritilo of Schweinersdorf had purchased an allod for £10 from the Church, 'to have it by hereditary right or to give it to whomsoever he might wish'. He took the latter option and gave it to Weihenstephan Abbey, to secure his daughter Gebirga a place there.[7]

There was, however, a catch to these rights. Since *ministeriales* were unfree, their dealings as allodial proprietors were not unfettered, because the ultimate proprietary right even to their allods was thought to reside with their lords. In other words, lords really owned everything that their servile dependents owned. For this reason *ministeriales* were required to ask permission to alienate allod as well as fief, and in some cases, to offer their lords compensation for parting with the former as well as the latter. About 1135 Archbishop Conrad of Salzburg permitted his *ministerialis* Henry of Nassau to give two *mansi* at Wolfsdorf to Admont Abbey. One was an allod 'which was his *predium*', the other a fief 'which he had *in beneficium* from the church of Salzburg'.[8] In 1221,

[5] K. Bertau, 'Versuch über Wolfram', *Jahrbuch für fränkische Landesforschung* xxxvii (1977), 35 f. Wolfram appears to have been a *ministerialis* belonging to the counts of Wertheim; M.F. Richey, *Studies of Wolfram von Eschenbach* (Edinburgh and London, 1957), pp. 27-9. On debts, F. Peeck, *Die Reinhardsbrunner Briefsammlung*, MG Epistolae selectae, V (Weimar, 1952), 96, p. 80, after 1130.
[6] UB Münster 902, p. 470, 1271, and see Uhl, *Weihenstephan*, 220, p. 179, 1156-7 for Reginhalm of Altfalterbach's *predium* 'quicquid hereditario vel empticio iure possederat'.
[7] Uhl, *Weihenstephan*, 140A, B, pp. 118f., 1147.
[8] UB Steiermark i, 157, p. 159, c.1135, and Kluckhohn, pp. 67-72 on lords as ultimate allodial proprietors.

when the bishop of Constance's *ministerialis* Berthold of Bankhol-
zen wanted to sell allod and fief to Salem Abbey, the see was
compensated for both. The bishop also claimed that 'because he
was a *ministerialis* of our church, Berthold could not for himself
confer property, whether allod or fief, upon the aforesaid monastery', and the bishop acted for him.[9] Twenty years later, when the
Styrian *ministerialis* and Salzburg vassal Frederick of Pettau
wanted to give lands to Sittich Abbey, it was discovered that allod
and fief could be devolved only to other members of the Salzburg
familia or to the monasteries owned by Salzburg, which Sittich was
not.[10] In the last resort, everything a *ministerialis* possessed in fiefs
and allods counted as part of his lord's collection of rights,[11] and
explicit consent was therefore necessary to legalize the alienation of
both types of possession.

Allods of *ministeriales* were sometimes called *inwarteseigen*, internal or intrinsic property, signifying confinement, like their owners, to a particular retinue or *familia*.[12] The rules were spelled out
when Archbishop Adalbert of Bremen acquired the royal *serviens*
Nanno with all his possessions at Weende in 1064; Nanno's powers
over his *predium* allowed him to give it away, sell it, exchange it,
enfeoff it or grant it by some other precarial contract, or leave it to
his heirs, as long as any such transaction involved other dependents
of the archbishop, and no one beyond his retinue or household.[13]
When this proviso was circumvented with lords' consent, then *ministeriales'* rights of disposal were the same as for free men.[14]

[9] CD Salem 122, pp. 160f., 1221.
[10] UB Salzburg iii, 967, pp. 516f., 1241.
[11] Therefore the *bona* of *ministeriales* were confirmed to the archbishop of Cologne in MGC i, 146, p. 205, 1153, with the other possessions of the see.
[12] P. Puntschart, 'Das "Inwärts-Eigen" im österreichischen Dienstrecht des Mittelalters', *ZRGGA* xliii (1922), 66-102, E. Klebel, 'Freies Eigen und Beutellehen in
Ober- und Niederbayern', *ZBLG* xi, (1938), 45-85, H. Dubled, 'Allodium dans les
textes latins du moyen âge', *Le Moyen Âge* lvii (1951), 241-6, M. Soenen, 'A propos
de ministeriales brabançons propriétaires d'alleux aux xiie et xiiie siècles' in *Hommage
au professeur Paul Bonenfant 1899-1965* (Brussels 1965), pp. 139-49, and H. Ebner,
Das Freie Eigen. Ein Beitrag zur Verfassungsgeschichte des Mittelalters, Aus Forschung und Kunst, II (Klagenfurt, 1969).
[13] MGD Henry IV, 120, p. 159, 1064; also 115, p. 152, 1063 on Bremen's familial
property.
[14] e.g. in MGD Henry III, 118, p. 149, 1043 and 133, p. 167, 1045, the scribe AA
used for margraves the forms adopted in 210f., pp. 279f., 1048 and 248, p. 331,
1050 by scribe WA for *ministeriales*; see D. von Gladiss, 'Die Schenkungen der
deutschen Könige zu privatem Eigen', *DA* i (1937), 80-137, and H.C. Faussner, 'Die

In spite of the safeguard which their ultimate proprietary right guaranteed them, lords preferred to reward and sustain their *ministeriales* with fiefs rather than allods because the former carried, at least in principle, obligations of military or other services.[15] Still, allodial grants were sometimes considered to be appropriate. Shortly before 1100 Archbishop Hermann of Cologne gave his *ministerialis* Albero an allodial manor at Honnef 'in free possession'. In 1101 Albero chose to sell it to the abbot of Siegburg.[16] In 1123 Henry V gave a forest in the Rhineland outright to his *ministerialis* Eberhard of Hagen, mentioning that 'We do this without diminution of the kingdom', i.e. of royal property,[17] since the allod would still be subject to the crown's ultimate proprietary right as Eberhard's owner.

To be effective in law, the acquisition, exchange, or alienation of allods by *ministeriales* required the permission or participation of their lords.[18] In 1231 King Henry permitted Conrad of Weinsberg to exchange seven allodial manors with the bishop of Würzburg, stating that 'since the aforesaid Conrad of Weinsberg is our *ministerialis*, he cannot and should not alienate his inherited property unless by our permission, and by the plenitude of our counsel we give him full and free authority to confer the said manors upon the said church'.[19] Put a different way, the counts of Schaumberg in 1303 allowed their seneschal Henry to give to Göttweig Abbey property *der sein recht aigen ist und von uns inwert aigen*, 'which is his real property and our intrinsic property'.[20] In the reverse transaction, the bishop of Osnabrück's *ministerialis* Eilhard of Harste bought an allod in 1218 from the chapter of Enger. The chapter transferred the proprietary right to Osnabrück, and Bishop Adolf conferred it upon Eilhard.[21]

Verfügungsgewalt des deutschen Königs über weltliches Reichsgut im Hochmittelalter', *DA* xxix (1973), 345-449.

[15] As in MGD Frederick I, 138, pp. 231-3, 1156.

[16] Wisplinghoff, *Sieburg*, 19, pp. 40-3, 1101-2.

[17] Mon. Boica xxix.A, 447, pp. 244f., 1123. In 1189 the bishop of Würzburg gave his *ministerialis* Wolfram of Zabelstein an allod in place of a surrendered fief, ibid. xxxvii, 145, pp. 137f.

[18] As in UB Wirtemberg ii, 477, p. 289, 1193 or UB St Stephan 271f., pp. 296-300, 1257.

[19] UB Wirtemberg iii, 791, pp. 286f., 1231, and the same principle spelled out by Philip of Swabia in M. Krühne, *Urkundenbuch der Klöster der Grafschaft Mansfeld*, Geschichtsquellen der Provinz Sachsen, XX (Halle, 1888), 17A, pp. 670f., 1201.

[20] Fuchs, *Göttweig*, 234, pp. 245f., 1303.   [21] UB Osnabrück ii, 93, pp. 68f., 1218.

Another illuminating example bears out the notion of a distinction between real allod and *ministeriales*' intrinsic allod, on lines similar to the abortive distinction between fiefs by homage and *ministeriales*' fiefs, a distinction collapsing in the twelfth century.[22] In 1179 Abbot Arnold of Burtscheid purchased an allod at Weiler from the four sons of William of Nisweiler for forty marks. The abbot prudently remarked that they could not have had the true ownership or seisin 'because they are not free', but *ministeriales* belonging to Duke Henry of Limburg. In careful language the abbot described ownership as *usucapium possessionis huius quod theotonica exprimitur lingua Sala*, 'usucapion of this possession which is expressed as seisin in the German language'. The way out was to pay the purchase-price to the Nisweiler brothers, and to redeem the usucapion from the duke for a further four marks, or 10 per cent.[23] Such scrupulous caution was not usual in acquiring allods from *ministeriales*, but the abbot was correct in seeing that in the German legal universe, the duke was the ultimate proprietor of his *ministeriales*' allods, and that his rights ought to be taken into account.

More often lords were obliged to defend the principle of intrinsic property because their *ministeriales* would not respect it. In 1209 an imperial decree forbade the bishop of Trent's *ministeriales* to alienate allod, and indeed fief, without consent 'because churches are thus reduced to excessive poverty'.[24] At about this time the abbess of Erstein was trying to prevent unlicensed sales or exchanges of allods by threatening to deny her *ministeriales*' fiefs to their heirs.[25] The counts of Tecklenburg sought to forestall similar lapses by declaring that 'our *ministeriales* can no more alienate hereditary property than what is enfeoffed to them by us'.[26] In 1254 the dukes of Bavaria and the bishop of Bamberg attempted, once more, to forbid alienation of *proprietates que inwartes eigen dicuntur*, 'properties which are called intrinsic allod', without lords' consent.[27] The *Schwabenspiegel* law-book, composed in the 1270s, also tried to preserve lords' interest in their *ministeriales*' allods by

---

[22] See pp. 113 f., nn. 68–71.
[23] UB Niederrhein i, 470, p. 330, 1179.
[24] MGC ii, 30, p. 35, 1209.
[25] MGD Lothar I and II, 146, pp. 330 f., c 1200
[26] UB Osnabrück ii, 123, p. 91, 1220–30.
[27] MGC ii, 461, p. 633, 1254.

claiming that they could never fall into the hands of the king or otherwise escape the power of their lords, a manifest archaism.[28]

Alienations of fief and allod

Lords were not necessarily hostile to the alienation of *ministeriales'* fief and allod. On the contrary, they frequently sought to improve the endowments of their monastic foundations by encouraging them. But they did very often require compensation for alienated fiefs, for example, by converting *ministeriales'* allods into fiefs,[29] and they always expressed their right to give consent to alienations.[30] Permission was implied when *ministeriales* employed their lords' charters, seals, and witnesses to effect the actual transfer. In 1140 it was Conrad III who conferred his *ministerialis* Baldwin's allods and fiefs upon Weissenohe Abbey, and in 1166 Frederick Barbarossa did the same for Godfrey of Hörzhausen's and Ortolf of Dierschhofen's gifts to Indersdorf and Biburg.[31] Gifts, sales, and exchanges were made secure by this simple expedient of requesting the lord to issue or authenticate the charters, as Lothar III did when Bevo of Gronau gave a substantial fief to Bursfeld in 1134.[32] These joint arrangements could become quite elaborate. In 1198 Count Rudolf of Habsburg issued four charters effecting Wernher and Cuno of Ailingen's gift of all their possessions to Kreuzlingen Abbey, including a letter to the bishop of Constance explaining that he confirmed the donation and would allow no one to obstruct it. Some of the lands were transferred by the count with Wernher's assent, some by Wernher himself with the count's authority.[33] Gifts might be held up, or stand in hazard of invalidation, if permission were not sought in due form. In the 1140s this endangered a

[28] K.A. Eckhardt, *Schwabenspiegel Kurzform*, vol. i, MG Fontes iuris Germanici antiqui, n.s. IV.1 (Hanover, 1960), p. 102.

[29] UB Niederrhein ii, 217, pp. 112f., 1237, UB Osnabrück iii, 655, pp. 464f., 1279, and Mon. Boica xxxvii, 402, p. 465, 1276, where Henry of Zabelstein 'dedit nobis [bishop of Würzburg] in restaurum, quod vulgo vrsaze dicitur, villam ...'

[30] Weissthanner, *Schäftlarn*, 344, p. 343, 1198-1200 for 'consensu et licentia domni sui'.

[31] MGD Conrad III, 50, p. 84, 1140, and MGD Frederick I, 510 and 512, pp. 444-7, 1166.

[32] MGD Lothar III, 65, pp. 101f., 1134, and other examples of lords acting for *ministeriales* in UB Hildesheim i, 196, p. 179, 1131, 200, pp. 183f., 1132, 222, pp. 201f., 1140 and 225, pp. 203f., 1141 (Hildesheim), Wisplinghoff, *Siegburg*, 44, pp. 94f., 1138-9 (Cologne), and UB Hildesheim iii, 159, pp. 78f., 1267 (Brunswick).

[33] UB Wirtemberg ii, 504-7, pp. 324-7, 1198.

donation from the *ministeriales* Engilmar and Adelheid to St Peter's at Salzburg, which had taken place 'without the consent and permission' of their lord, Count Frederick of Peilstein. All went well after Archbishop Conrad's intercession with him.[34] Careful records and repeated confirmations were sometimes felt to be necessary to the long-term stability of *ministeriales'* gifts. When the Bavarian *ministerialis* Rafold of Schönberg gave allods to Raitenhaslach, the monastery petitioned both Conrad III and Frederick Barbarossa to confirm the act. It was also necessary to seek confirmation from Henry the Lion, who was lord of Rafold's nephew and heir, Berthold of Löwenstein.[35] Berthold surrendered his expectations, and Duke Henry renounced 'whatever rights and authority we are seen to have in this matter'. In other words, monastic beneficiaries thought it wise to avoid claims from anyone connected with the donors as lords or relatives. Fears of such obstructions explain why the church of St Mary at Aachen secured Conrad III's consent to a gift of allod from one of its own *ministeriales*, for he had purchased it from a free man whose relatives might have claimed some compensation.[36]

Exploiting their lands

Almost without exception the lands which *ministeriales* possessed were hereditary fiefs and allods, although life-fiefs were sometimes accepted,[37] and a very few tenurial agreements have survived which were explicitly non-feudal leases for one or more lives.[38] The richer

[34] UB Salzburg i, 283A–C, pp. 403 f., before 1147.

[35] MGD Conrad III, 202, pp. 365–7, 1149, MGD Frederick I, 468, pp. 379 f., 1164, and Jordan, *Urkunden Heinrichs des Löwen*, 72, pp. 105 f., 1166. The allods in question were in origin imperial gifts to Rafold's forebears; MGD Henry III, 261, pp. 347 f., 1051, and MGD Henry IV, 318, pp. 418 f., 1079.

[36] MGD Conrad III, 186, p. 335, 1147; see Krühne, *Mansfeld*, 37, pp. 24 f., 1283 where the abbess of Gerbstedt secured the renunciation of rights by the advocate and all relatives when she bought property from one of her own *ministeriales*.

[37] e.g. *Chronicon Ottenburanum*, MGS, XXIII, p. 623, after 1197, UB Hildesheim i, 700, p. 667, 1217, and UB Halberstadt ii, 714, p. 37, 1242.

[38] UB Hanau 81, pp. 57 f., 1144, Uhl, *Weihenstephan*, 285, pp. 230 f., 1166–72 and 331, p. 270, 1197–1203, and Mon. Carinthia i, 382, p. 281, 1200. In Schlögl, *Dießen*, 5, pp. 108 f., 1173–81 the margrave of Istria's Bavarian *ministeriales* have lands 'ad sustentationem vitae, quod vulgo lipgedinge vocatur' and 'ad tempus vitae suae detinendam'. See G. Rüthning, *Oldenburgisches Urkundenbuch*, vols. ii–iv (Oldenburg, 1926–8), ii, 28, p. 14, c.1181–3 for the *palus* or marshlands held of Archbishop Siegfried or Bremen by his *ministerialis* Frederick of Mackenstedt 'iure

ministeriales might subinfeudate fief or allod,[39] but the majority subsisted directly upon their portions of the manorial landscape, exploiting 'the right and use both in village and country with the appurtenances belonging to them', as the Gatersleben brothers said of their substantial fief from the bishops of Halberstadt.[40] Such appurtenances might include serfs[41] or other dependents,[42] tithes[43] and rents,[44] woods[45] and other rights in woodland such as timber and pannage,[46] hunting rights,[47] river tolls,[48] vineyards,[49] the patronage of parish churches,[50] small townships,[51] and manorial jurisdictions over their villages.[52]

Scores of charters reveal cumulative information about the manorial rights which *ministeriales* possessed and exploited. In the majority of cases the inclusive inventory of appurtenances is a scribal formula, not an accurate survey of the properties in question, as in Henry IV's confirmation in 1105 of his *ministerialis'* Gertrude of Boppard's gift of three manors with all their adjuncts to St Pantaleon at Cologne.[53] In others, the tally is a true or

---

Hollandrico vendere sive suis usibus reservare', and UB Salzburg iii, 687, pp. 194 f., 1215 where the Salzburg *ministeriales* of Bergheim received property for three lives 'iure civitatis nostre, quod in vulgari purchrecht dicitur'.

[39] UB Mainz ii, 691, pp. 1130 f., 1194-8, Lappenberg, *Hamburg*, 429, p. 372, 1219, and UB Nürnberg, 764, p. 449, 1288.

[40] UB Halberstadt ii, 1197, p. 339, 1268.

[41] Tr. Regensburg 955, pp. 481 f., 1181 and 1037 f., pp. 528 f., c.1210-17, and Tr. Tegernsee 249, p. 188, 1147.

[42] Mentioned in MGC ii, 287, pp. 402 f., 1224 and 304, pp. 481 f., 1231, and Mon. Boica xlix, 168, p. 266, 1289 and 274, pp. 425 f., 1300.

[43] UB Osnabrück ii, 166, p. 121, 1223.

[44] UB Niederrhein iv, 649, p. 794, 1221.

[45] Mon. Boica xxxvii, 398, p. 461, 1275.

[46] Wisplinghoff, *Siegburg*, 80, p. 172, 1205, and see UB Wirtemberg ii, 550, pp. 382 f., 1210 for a dispute about them.

[47] UB Wirtemberg iv, 1206, pp. 275 f., 1251.

[48] E. Krausen, *Die Urkunden des Klosters Raitenhaslach*, QE, XVII (Munich, 1959), 13, pp. 16 f., after 1158.

[49] Wisplinghoff, *Siegburg*, 65, pp. 146 f., 1166-74.

[50] UB Niederrhein ii, 609, pp. 360 f., 1271, and UB Nürnberg 829, p. 493, 1292.

[51] Mon. Boica xlix, 352, p. 542, 1305 mentions Freystadt, founded by the imperial *ministeriales* of Hilpoltstein some time in the later thirteenth century, and ibid. 295, pp. 454-6, 1301 for Kipfenberg, which belonged to the Kropf of Flüglingen family.

[52] Wittmann, *Wittelsbach*, ii, 193, p. 30, 1293 for their confirmation to the Bavarian *ministeriales*.

[53] MGD Henry IV, 491, pp. 668 f., 1105; on this family, F.-J. Heyen, *Reichsgut im Rheinland. Die Geschichte des königlichen Fiskus Boppard*, Rheinisches Archiv, XLVIII (Bonn, 1956), pp. 74-85.

approximate record of realities. In 1275, for example, the Cologne *ministerialis* Gozwin of Rodenberg renewed with the archbishop the title to his castle there, 'with the mills, holdings, fields, pastures, woods, and all appurtenances, game-rights, fisheries, jurisdictions and incomes whatsoever, including the magistracy called *vrigrachaf* or free-county in the vernacular, and all my possessions situated in the said jurisdictions, with all my men, whether in the town of Menden [Gozwin was bailiff of Menden as well as burgrave of Rodenberg] or beyond, belonging either to the manor or to the office of magistrate, as well as the serfs and others of whatever condition', with further concessions and revenues.[54]

Disputes about property and revenues

Possessing land appears to have had contradictory psychological effects upon medieval noblemen; the desire to increase their property by laying hands upon other people's, and the desire to divest themselves of property for pious purposes. No doubt secular greed and religious remorse might be aroused and reconciled in one and the same individual. In 1279, for example, a rich and successful imperial *ministerialis*, Henry of Hilpoltstein, who had in his time been the butler of Nuremberg and had married off his four sons to heiresses, was persuaded by the bishop of Eichstätt to pay a penitential visit to Rome, and to give three manors to the church 'as recompense to those whom I have injured'.[55] To redeem unspecified sins, the count of Oldenburg's *ministerialis* Oltmann of Beverbäke was moved in 1258 to give his fief at Ohmstede to Hude Abbey.[56] Obstreperous knights might be persuaded into pious courses by their devout womenfolk. About 1215, after a long quarrel, another imperial *ministerialis*, Henry of Johannisdorf, gave back property which he had wrongly withheld from the abbot of Ranshofen. By his mother's mediation he added a bit more in expiation, and the transaction enabled his sister to enter the house as a nun.[57] Some ladies were more worldly. The Mainz *ministerialis* Embricho of Steinheim's donations to Eberbach and Tiefenthal

---

[54] UB Niederrhein ii, 689, pp. 402 f., 1275.
[55] Mon. Boica xlix, 100, pp. 151 f , 1279.
[56] Rüthning, *Oldenburg* iv, 280, pp. 126 f., 1258.
[57] Mon. Boica iii, 177, pp. 303 f., c.1215.

Abbeys were later claimed back by his daughters, without success.[58]

Churches were sometimes compelled to recognize usurpations, and accepted graceful compromises. In 1136, for example, the abbot of Mariengreden at Mainz agreed to let the archbishop's *ministerialis* Roho keep the lands he had seized, on payment of an annual rent.[59] Not so the Mainz *ministeriales* who had taken hold of the abbot of Ravengiersburg's property as their fiefs, which the archbishop obliged them to disgorge in 1128,[60] nor the Essen *ministeriales* who unjustly seized some of the abbess's houses and were forced by the archbishop of Cologne to give them back.[61] In another case, the bishop of Münster's *ministerialis* Frederick of Warendorp was dispossessed in 1238 of a manor belonging to Iburg Abbey which he claimed to have bought in good faith from its bailiff, who then absconded. The abbot would have none of this, even when Frederick took to violence to defend his spurious title, nor would his bishop, who excommunicated him. In the end Frederick had to give the manor back.[62] The prominent Styrian *ministerialis* Herrand of Wildon, on the other hand, who had seized the abbot of St Lambrecht's forest as a fief, made good his claim with support from his lord, the duke of Austria.[63] So did the *ministerialis* Henry of Seebrunn to a property at Wendelsheim which the canons of Marchtal claimed was theirs, since he had the backing of his lord, Count-Palatine Rudolf of Tübingen.[64]

These wrangles were endless. Bavarian *ministeriales* tried to undo a transaction between Count Arnold of Dachau and the abbot of Weihenstephan, who had bought a valuable property from him about 1160. Originally the count had acquired the land from his *ministerialis* Tragboto of Hohenkammer, but after his death his children boldly claimed it as a paternal inheritance and sued the abbot for it. The abbot won the case, but prudently offered some compensation in cash and kind for the family's claims.[65] Perhaps

[58] UB Mainz ii, 284, pp. 498-500, 1161-5.
[59] Ibid. i, 611, pp. 530f., 1136.
[60] Ibid. 549, pp. 456f., 1128.
[61] UB Niederrhein i, 347, p. 235, 1142.
[62] UB Osnabrück ii, 380, pp. 298f., 1238.
[63] UB Steiermark ii, 56f., pp. 94-8, 1202.
[64] *Waltheri Historia Monasterii Marchtelanensis*, MGS, XXIV p. 667, before 1190.
[65] Uhl, *Weihenstephan*, 243, pp. 197-9, 1162-72. Claims of a similar nature were settled in Wisplinghoff, *Siegburg*, 46, pp. 97-9, 1139, CD Salem 20, pp. 32f., after 1176, and CD Saxony ii, 445, p. 308, 1180 and 525, pp. 363f., 1186.

the more blatant spirits were tenacious of spurious claims because they knew that some sort of compensation might be offered for the sake of peace. In 1290 Count Conrad of Wildberg permitted a vassal to give valuable tithes at Nüdlingen to St Stephen's Abbey at Würzburg. But they were appropriated by the bishop of Würzburg's marshal, Henry of Lauer, in spite of certificates from the count, the bishop, and the papal *curia* proving that he had no title to them at all. After some twenty years of painful altercation, the marshal accepted a substantial cash-sum and the abbot was at last put in possession of the tithes.[66]

Land-gifts as the vehicle of piety

The evidence abounds with disputes over property and revenues between churches and *ministeriales*, but it also bears witness to their conventions of piety,[67] as a result of which many were eager to give land, cash, or other benefits, especially to monastic foundations. Churchmen were well aware of their conflicting motives, and the informative account by Provost Gerhard of Steterburg (1163-1209) of his administration shows his foresight both in acquiring donations from *ministeriales* and in defending his church from their claims.[68] The richest *ministeriales* might endow new houses in their entirety,[69] and a handful of them were noted patrons of the religious reforms of the age; Henry of Dornick at Xanten under St Norbert's early guidance,[70] Ulrich of Königstein

---

[66] UB St Stephan 316, pp. 353f., 1290, 343-5, 347, pp. 389-93, 1301-2, and 365-9, pp. 420-5, 1313, and another tithes dispute, between the imperial *ministeriales* of Bretten and Maulbronn Abbey, in UB Wirtemberg iii, 786, p. 280, 1231.

[67] Stated in UB Salzburg ii, 234, pp. 336f., 1145-7.

[68] *Annales Stederburgenses*, MGS, XVI, pp. 208-30, 1164-94.

[69] e.g. UB Mainz i, 558, p. 471, 1129 and 602, pp. 521f., 1135 (Kirchheimbolanden), MGD Conrad III, 36, pp. 58-60, 1139 (Zwettl; see Gründler etc., pp. 161-83), *Historiae Augienses*, MGS, XXIV, pp. 647-59, 1145 (Weissenau), MGD Frederick I, 38, pp. 63-6, 1152 (Alteburg, moved to Arnsburg in 1174), von Heinemann, *Anhalt*, 625, pp. 461f., 1181-3 (Heiligenrode), UB Weida 32, p. 11, 1193 (Mildenfurth), UB Hildesheim i, 581, pp. 556f., 1203 and 655, pp. 626f., 1212 (Escherode), CD Saxony iii, 99f., pp. 81f., 1206 (Dörschnitz), UB Osnabrück ii, 263, p. 206, 1230 and 287, pp. 227f., 1232 (Harste, later moved to Rulle), UB Steiermark ii, 280, p. 376, c.1230 and 302, pp. 403f., 1233 (Stainz), UB Wirtemberg iv, 964, pp. 10f., and 968, pp. 16f., 1241 (Baindt), Reg. Eichstätt 754, p. 234, 1249 (confirming Seligenporten), and UB Niederrhein ii, 459, pp. 254f., 1258 (Marienthal).

[70] UB Niederrhein i, 280, pp. 182f., 1116, and 290, p. 190, 1119, and Semmler, pp. 54f.

at Engelthal,[71] Jutta of Weida-Gera at Cronschwitz, and John of Ravensburg at Löwenthal. The latter two *ministeriales* took regular orders themselves.[72]

Other houses not actually founded by *ministeriales* received essential support from them. The shadowy but immensely rich Mainz *serviens* Wignand, who paid for building the new monastery at Hirsau in 1092, also bought huge estates to subvent Count Burchard's recent foundation at Comburg,[73] where he was eventually buried and revered as a benefactor. When the counts of Saffenberg founded Klosterrad, the principal subscriber was their *ministerialis* Embricho *de Meinscozen*, who donated his lands and entered the monastery with all his family about 1106. Their attempts to dominate the house aroused discord, especially when Embricho's son Hermann aspired to the abbacy in the 1120s. This he failed to achieve, but he was an able churchman, and ended his career as bishop of Schleswig (1138-48).[74] In another case, the archbishop of Trier founded Springiersbach in 1107 out of the bequest by Benigna, a *ministerialis* belonging to the see's advocate, and her son Richard became first abbot.[75] Several other houses were established or refounded upon generous donations by *ministeriales*.[76]

If some *ministeriales* were keen to enter monasteries themselves,[77] the majority were content to give portions of their fief and allod.[78] So widespread was the practice that their lords found it

---

[71] H. Grundmann, *Religiöse Bewegungen im Mittelalter* (3rd edn., Darmstadt, 1970), pp. 223-8, Reg. Eichstätt 730, p. 224, and UB Nürnberg 295, pp. 173-6, 1240.

[72] Grundmann, *Bewegungen*, pp. 191, 235, and 249 n. 118.

[73] *Historia Hirsaugensis Monasterii*, MGS, XIV, p. 257, 1092, UB Mainz i, 377, pp. 279 f., after 1090, and UB Wirtemberg i, pp. 391 f.

[74] *Annales Rodenses*, MGS XVI, pp. 688-733, 1104-57.

[75] UB Mittelrhein i, 415, pp. 475-7, 1107.

[76] Semmler, p. 51 on Siegburg's priory at Hirzenach (1109), founded upon donations by Erlolf of Sternberg (as MGD Conrad III, 211, pp. 379-81, 1149 shows); H. Wartmann, *Urkundenbuch der Abtei Sanct Gallen*, vol. iii (St Gallen, 1875-82), 889, pp. 103-5, 1244 for the refoundation of Maggenau by the St Gallen chamberlain Rudolf of Glattburg; and UB Wirtemberg iv, 1125, p. 190, 1249 for Kirchheim refounded by the Teck *ministeriales*.

[77] MGD Lothar III, 40, pp. 64-6, 1132, *Chronicon Ebersheimense*, MGS, XXIII, p. 445, 1137, UB Salzburg ii, 184, p. 271, before 1139, UB Mainz ii, 62, pp. 118-20, 1144, Uhl, *Weihenstephan*, 220, p. 179, 1156-7, MGD Frederick I, 206, pp. 345 f., 1158, UB Wirtemberg ii, 419, p. 205, 1179, and Weissthanner, *Schäftlarn*, 396, pp. 389 f., 1218-20.

[78] The monastic books of gifts (*Traditionsbücher*) published in the old and new series of 'Quellen und Erörterungen zur bayerischen Geschichte' show the enormous generosity of Bavarian *ministeriales* to the monasteries there.

expedient to issue regulations laying down terms for their donations to individual monasteries. Often the lords gave general permission to donate to the houses they or their families had founded
or patronized.[79] In most cases the donors were exempted from
providing the compensation to which lords were, strictly speaking,
entitled for lands alienated. Some patrons might persuade other
lords to allow their *ministeriales* to give lands. The margrave of
Styria's permission to donate to his foundation at Gleink was
followed by the bishop of Bamberg's, and eventually by the duke
of Bavaria's, for their *ministeriales* too.[80] In 1192 Duke Conrad of
Swabia agreed with his brothers that all Hohenstaufen *ministeriales*
might make donations to Marchtal.[81] The duke of Austria's permission in favour of St Florian in 1202 was followed by the duke
of Bavaria's in 1209.[82]

In many cases lords were really seeking subscribers for new monastic ventures, like Bishop Gebhard of Eichstätt for his brothers'
foundation at Plankstetten.[83] In 1160 Spital on the Semmering
Pass was largely endowed in advance by seven of the margrave of
Styria's *ministeriales*, who handsomely provided wide estates, vineyards, and a town. The foundation-charter permitted all Styrian
ministeriales to give of their patrimony, and confirmed the endowment already made.[84] In 1251 the bishop of Gurk stipulated
that his *ministeriales* might give a quarter of their possessions
to his foundation at Studenitz, but on second thoughts imposed
a limit of six *mansi*.[85] In a similar way the Saxon nunnery of
Osterholz, founded in 1185, was subvented by donations from the
Bremen *ministeriales* which continued into the thirteenth century.[86]

---

[79] Kluckhohn, pp. 69–71, D. von Gladiss, *Beiträge zur Geschichte der staufischen
Reichsministerialität*, Historische Studien, CCXLIX (Berlin, 1934), pp. 22–6, Ritter,
pp. 60 f., MGD Conrad III, 81, pp. 143 f., 1142, UB Osnabrück i, 272, p. 217, 1146,
UB Wirtemberg ii, 347, pp. 78 f., 1154, Jordan, *Urkunden Heinrichs des Löwen*, 31,
pp. 45 f., 1155, Weissthanner, *Schäftlarn*, 157, pp. 157 f., *c.* 1170–5, UB Mainz ii, 458,
pp. 743–5, 1183, and UB Nürnberg 553, p. 334, 1277 and 872, p. 516, 1294.
[80] UB Land ob der Enns ii, 111, p. 116, 1125, 113, pp. 169–71, 1128, and 420,
pp. 620 f., 1220.
[81] *Walteri Historia Monasterii Marchtelanensis*, MGS, XXIV, p. 670.
[82] UB Land ob der Enns ii, 336, p. 487, 1202 and 364, pp. 524 f., 1209.
[83] Reg. Eichstätt 350, p. 111, 1138 and 492, p. 157, 1191.
[84] UB Steiermark i, 406, pp. 394–6, 1160 and MGD Frederick I, 518, pp. 457 f.,
1166. Later, *ministeriales* oppressed this house; Helbig and Weinrich, *Ostsiedlung* ii,
134, pp. 502–6, 1211.
[85] Mon. Carinthia ii, 599, p. 54 and 602, p. 57, 1251.
[86] Lappenberg, *Hamburg*, 334, pp. 292 f., 1202 and 454, p. 399, 1222.

ministeriales who founded houses sought for subscribers amongst
their fellows. In the 1180s Folknand of Staufen's foundation at
Adelberg received support from Duke Welf of Tuscany's Swabian
ministeriales,[87] and in 1233 Duke Frederick of Austria authorized
his Styrian *ministeriales* to make donations from their patrimonies
to Liutold of Wildon's recent foundation at Stainz.[88] *Ministeriales*
might retain their rights of donation despite their own transfer
to new lords. In 1234 the abbot of St Gallen confirmed that the
ministeriales he had acquired from the count of Toggenburg could
continue to favour the Hospital at Bubikon with their gifts.[89]

In some cases *ministeriales* were unloading encumbered properties disguised as charity to the Church. They were acceptable for
their long-term value or convenience once the encumbrances were
paid off. In a complicated death-bed transaction Weihenstephan
Abbey took over a property at Reichersdorf from the Freising
ministerialis Aribo of Langenbach, who had pledged it for £12
some time previously. The abbot paid off £4 when he received the
property, and transferred responsibility for the rest of the debt,
together with a compensatory land-grant at Ismaning, to an obliging cleric from whom the Ismaning property would also revert to
the abbey once he had paid off the outstanding £8. A contentious
claim by Aribo's brother Rudolf was settled by giving him a further
small sum, about 4 per cent of the original debt.[90]

As well as donations, exchanges of lands with monasteries required lords' consent, again because they were the ultimate proprietors of such lands. In 1157 Frederick Barbarossa permitted his
ministeriales to exchange lands up to three *mansi* in extent with the
monasteries of Walkenried and Pforta.[91] In other cases the lords
effected exchanges for their *ministeriales*, as the bishop of Hildesheim did for Siegfried of Gladebeck and Schraudolf of Weende in
1184.[92] In a slightly different arrangement Liupold of Hoheneck in
1165 assisted his lord, the margrave of Styria, with an exchange of
property for a devout purpose. The margrave wished to found a
charterhouse at Seitz upon Liupold's lands, because its remote and

[87] UB Wirtemberg ii, 440, p. 236, c.1185.
[88] UB Steiermark ii, 307, pp. 409 f., 1233.
[89] Escher and Schweizer, *Zürich*, 493, p. 364, 1234.
[90] Uhl, *Weihenstephan*, 97, pp. 81-4, 1138-47.
[91] MGD Frederick I, 171, pp. 291 f., and 177, pp. 299 f., 1157.
[92] UB Hildesheim i, 428, pp. 416 f., 1184.

mountainous situation was suited to the purposes of the Carthusian order. In exchange Liupold received four manors and other lands as his hereditary property.[93]

Cathedral churches too were the beneficiaries of *ministeriales*' gifts, which sometimes had conditions attached to them. The cathedral chapter of Salzburg accepted donations from *ministeriales* outright,[94] or as a gamble on their death without heirs,[95] or for conversion into life-fiefs,[96] or in exchange for fiefs.[97] The Passau chapter accepted gifts on similar terms. In one case the gift was to be enjoyed by the donor for life, and then by his widow and son at a fixed annual rent, before the canons might have free disposal of it.[98] In another case the donor, his wife, and all their posterity would have possession for a fixed rent, but the canons would acquire the gift outright should heirs fail, a nice balance between the religious and dynastic sentiments of the knightly order.[99] Passau also accepted lands and serfs from the *ministerialis* Engelbert of Struben should he not return from the Second Crusade. This speculation failed, for Engelbert was back in Passau by 1150.[100] It was common, therefore, for *ministeriales* to retain use of their gifts as feoffees of the beneficiaries, as did the count of Guelders' *ministerialis* Sigebodo, who gave an allod to Wassenberg in 1118 and received it back in fief.[101]

Pious motives were so compelling that it was not unknown for knightly families to dispose of nearly all their property to the Church, in spite of leaving direct issue as legitimate heirs. In the thirteenth century the imperial *ministeriales* of Sulzbürg in Bavaria ruined themselves by a combination of family partitions and generosity to religion. By the 1240s the brothers Conrad and Godfrey of Sulzbürg had divided their patrimony into roughly equal shares. Conrad's disappeared by sale to Heilsbronn Abbey, and to his daughters' husbands, both of whom were imperial *ministeriales* of

[93] UB Steiermark i, 485, pp. 452-4, 1165.
[94] UB Salzburg i, 389, p. 465, 1167-88.
[95] Ibid., 284, p. 404, 1125-47.
[96] Ibid., 386, p. 464, 1167-88.
[97] Ibid. 390A, p. 466, 1167-88.
[98] Tr. Passau 563, p. 211, 1130-50.
[99] Ibid. 725, p. 261, 1194.
[100] Ibid. 620 and 624, pp. 228f., 1147-50.
[101] UB Niederrhein i, 289, p. 189, 1118, and other examples in Busley, *Neustift*, 6, pp. 10f., 1152 and 19, p. 21, 1156.

Hilpoltstein. Their gains included the castle of Lower Sulzbürg and about half of the Sulzbürg retinue of knights. Conrad died in 1266, leaving no surviving sons. With the other share Godfrey and his wife Adelheid had founded the nunnery of Seligenporten by 1249, and left the residue to their sons Ulrich and Godfrey. Ulrich devised nearly all of it to the Teutonic Order before his death in 1286, virtually disinheriting his only daughter, who did, however, make a good marriage later on, arranged by her maternal uncles, who were also well-to-do imperial *ministeriales*. Ulrich even sold the castle of Upper Sulzbürg, and the money was paid to the Teutonic Order. The remnant left to his younger brother Godfrey was Wolfstein Castle. Abandoning the very name of Sulzbürg, which was used by his Hilpoltstein cousins who possessed Lower Sulzbürg, he was obliged by poverty to seek new fiefs as castellan serving the bishop of Eichstätt and the count of Hirschberg. In spite of such setbacks, Godfrey and his descendants were able so to repair their secular fortune that they could re-establish title to Upper Sulzbürg as an imperial fief in 1353, and survive as territorial lords of Wolfstein, eventually with the rank of count of the Holy Roman Empire, until their demise in 1740.[102]

The purpose of pious donations

Apart from the intangible benefits of religion, pious gifts were sometimes motivated by specific aims in this world or the next. In 1119 the Würzburg *ministeriales* Wolfram of Ansbach and his uncle Dietrich gave cash, lands, and serfs to St Stephen's so that Wolfram's brother Gumbert might become a monk there.[103] In 1292 the four brothers of Stauf, imperial *ministeriales*, gave their two sisters, already entered as nuns at Seligenporten, a manor for life which would ultimately pass to the abbey.[104] *Ministeriales* quite often bought places for themselves or their kindred in monasteries or chapters by such methods.[105]

[102] See my thesis, pp. 161-4, 187f., 238, 372-4. The Teutonic Order was a popular recipient of *ministeriales'* generosity; D. Wojtecki, 'Der Deutsche Orden unter Friedrich II.' in J. Fleckenstein (ed.), *Probleme um Friedrich II*. VF, XVI (Sigmaringen, 1974), pp. 187-224, and Mon. Boica xlix, 110, pp. 166-8, 1281.
[103] UB St Stephan 77, pp. 86f., 1119.   [104] UB Nürnberg 832, p. 495, 1292.
[105] Busley, *Neustift*, 24, pp. 24f., 1143-58, Mayerhofer, 'Codex Augiensium', 25, p. 93, *c.*1150, and Mon. Carinthia i, 411, p. 301, 1206-12. Poverty was sometimes admitted as a motive for taking refuge in monasteries; Uhl, *Weihenstephan*, 294, pp. 237f., 1174-80.

A comprehensive picture of what *ministeriales* wanted was afforded by one of the archbishop of Salzburg's charters for Seckau in 1197. Apart from permitting their donations, he gave them the right of burial there, and leave to enter their sons and daughters into its ranks.[106] The bishop of Würzburg conferred the right of burial at Lambach upon his *ministeriales* in 1155, the bishop of Hildesheim at Dorstadt in 1174.[107] Most of the donors did not specify what they expected in return for their gifts, or what the beneficiaries ought to do with them. Late in the twelfth century a rich Würzburg *ministerialis* called Rutwic left £50 in silver to the cathedral church and to Bronnbach Abbey, merely advising its distribution amongst their clergy and other ecclesiastical establishments without further obligations.[108]

Sometimes *ministeriales* did get festive masses and vigils celebrated in exchange for their gifts,[109] and when the count of Frontenhausen's *ministerialis* Conrad of Rettenberg left an income from land to Raitenhaslach about 1190, it was 'for one anniversary mass to be said each year on St Emmeram's day'.[110] In 1218 Conrad of Pfahlheim gave his manor there to his lord, the abbot of Ellwangen, so that perennial lights might shine over two of the abbey's altars after his death.[111] Soon after 1220 the Austrian *ministeriales* Dietrich and Adelheid of Bühel gave land to Lambach to pay for daily masses in its Holy Trinity chapel, and sought papal confirmation of their gift.[112] For a different purpose the margrave of Styria, about 1100, gave a chapel and lands to Garsten for the soul of his slain *ministerialis* Otto, at the bereaved mother's request.[113] The reward of piety was thought to have included a percentage of miraculous cures.[114]

---

[106] UB Steiermark ii, 22, p. 50, 1197. The right of Salzburg *ministeriales* to be buried at Salzburg's monasteries went back at least to 1139; UB Salzburg ii, 194 f., pp. 278–84.

[107] UB Land ob der Enns ii, 183, p. 274, 1155, and UB Hildesheim i, 367, p. 350, 1174.

[108] Mon. Boica xlv, 25, pp. 44–6, c.1182–95.

[109] UB Niederrhein i, 316, pp. 209 f., 1133 at Brauweiler; before 1251 the Goldeggs had founded masses at St Peter's in Salzburg, UB Salzburg iv, 15, pp. 14 f.

[110] Dumrath, *Raitenhaslach*, 99, p. 82, c.1190.

[111] UB Wirtemberg iii, 606, pp. 68 f., 1218.

[112] UB Land ob der Enns ii, 442 f., pp. 640–2, c.1222.

[113] Ibid. 86, p. 123, c.1100.

[114] In MGS iv see *Miracula S. Bernwardi*, chs. 3 and 11, pp. 782–6, and *Miracula S. Cunegundis*, ch. 69, p. 827.

Donations and exchanges were commonly in the form of land, vineyards, serfs or other unfree men, and cash,[115] but other important items of property such as bridges sometimes changed hands for devout ends. In 1134 a free man and a *ministerialis* of the counts of Rebgau co-operated to buy the bridge at Vöcklabruck, to give it to the church of Salzburg.[116] This may well have inspired the imperial *ministerialis* Frederick of Rohr to do something about the bridge further downstream at Wels before he left secular life to become a canon at Reichersberg. In 1138 he gave land to Bishop Embricho of Würzburg, who remitted the tolls in exchange, and placed the bridge under the civic authority of Wels.[117]

The crusades also inspired *ministeriales* to transfer possessions to the Church before their departure,[118] sometimes in order to find the means to get to the East. To equip himself for the Second Crusade, the Salzburg *ministerialis* Poppo of Biber sold his property at Getzendorf to Admont for a horse and £32 in cash.[119] For the same crusade the Freising *ministerialis* Henry of Hohenbrunn entrusted his allods and serfs to Weihenstephan Abbey for a grant of £30. If he returned, he would not be obliged to pay off the debt, and he would receive most of the property back as a fief for life.[120] In 1208 the Thuringian *ministerialis* Henry the Bearded of Tunna pledged part of his allodial woodlands at Ettersburg to Reinhardsbrunn for cash towards his crusading costs.[121]

Ministeriales also paid for new ecclesiastical buildings, as we have seen at Hirsau in the 1090s. The abbot of St Emmeram's knight Gerold of Aiterhofen built a chapel dedicated to the Holy Sepulchre, and a Hildesheim knight called Berthold built a church

---

[115] Lands, *censuales*, and vineyards donated to Brixen in Redlich, *Brixen*, 515–21, pp. 182–4, 1178–89; in Tr. Regensburg 1012, p. 516, 1197–1200 the Bavarian *ministerialis* Liutold of Kelheim was executor for a vineyard left by his father to St Emmeram's at Regensburg; and Uhl, *Weihenstephan*, 221, p. 180, 1156–8 for serfs given to Weihenstephan.

[116] UB Land ob der Enns ii, 116, p. 174, 1134.

[117] J. Lahusen, 'Zum Welser Brückenprivileg', *MIöG* xxxi (1910), 361–74; in Schlögl, *Dießen*, 16, pp. 21–3, 1150–7 and 22, pp. 31 f., 1158–73 *ministeriales* gave their shares in the Reichenhall salt-pans to Diessen Abbey.

[118] Redlich, *Brixen*, 470, p. 165 and UB Mainz ii, 97, pp. 187 f., both 1147.

[119] UB Steiermark i, 338, pp. 324 f., before 1147.

[120] Uhl, *Weihenstephan*, 134, pp. 112 f., 1147.

[121] CD Saxony iii, 125, pp. 99 f., 1208. In 1209 he was, for a few months, grand-master of the Teutonic Order.

at Beelte in honour of St Bernward of Hildesheim.[122] Others might content themselves with paying for new altars, as Walter, butler of Klingenberg, did at Prozelten in 1258.[123] But the Cologne *ministerialis* Burgrave Godfrey of Drachenfels made the cathedral chapter pay for what they needed from him, stone from Drachenfels Hill for building the new cathedral, and use of the pathway from the quarry to the Rhine.[124] In this great undertaking everyone showed remarkable lack of perseverance,[125] and probably the burgrave was partly to blame.

Ministeriales *as monastic advocates*

One consequence of *ministeriales'* involvement with the German monastic establishment as benefactors was their function as the secular advocates and protectors of churches. This gave rise to many abuses. In 1189, for example, Archbishop Conrad of Mainz dismissed his *ministerialis* Gislebert of Rüdesheim from the advocacy of Aulhausen Abbey for his excesses, and paid him off by returning the vineyards at Oestrich which his father, the *vicedominus* Conrad, had given to the nuns.[126] In 1250 the bishop of Bamberg complained to his colleague at Würzburg about the extortionate practices of the advocate of Theres Abbey, the Würzburg *ministerialis* Wolfram of Zabelstein, and offered to buy the office back.[127]

Some of the monastic foundation-charters spelled out what was expected of *ministeriales* as advocates. At Bockeln, the Saxon house founded in 1152 by Henry the Lion's *ministerialis* Liemar, the advocate was granted important powers of high jurisdiction. Liemar 'bequeathed the protection of that place which they call advocacy to his heirs in all succeeding generations, though not as a fief [from the abbot], so that the eldest of them should administer it, not to

---

[122] Tr. Regensburg 876, p. 423, 1156 and UB Hildesheim i, 529, pp. 506f., 1197; other examples at Erfurt and Hersfeld in UB Mainz ii, 18, pp. 27–9, 1140 and 24 pp. 39f., 1138–41.

[123] *Notae Brotseldenses*, MGS, XXX.2, p. 1485.

[124] UB Niederrhein ii, 570, p. 331, 1267 and 652, pp. 381–4, 1273.

[125] Work was abandoned in the 15th c., and the cathedral was not completed until 1880.

[126] UB Mainz ii, 518, pp. 853 f., 1189, and Hirsch, pp. 158–72 on these jurisdictions.

[127] Mon. Boica xxxvii, 307, p. 344, 1250.

exact services from the serfs or to make use of any of the monastic possessions, but only to prosecute in public trial cases of theft, murder, and rape, unless the abbot should ask him from time to time to carry out some other business'.[128] In 1157, when Frederick Barbarossa conferred the advocacy of the new monastery at Peternach upon his *ministerialis* Conrad of Boppard and his heirs, 'without exaction or extortion of any service, they shall always maintain and protect that place and all the possessions belonging to it unimpaired by any disturbance'.[129] When the castellan of the imperial dynasty's birthplace, Folknand of Staufen, founded Adelberg in 1181, the emperor confirmed the advocacy to this *ministerialis* and subsequently to whoever should be custodian of Hohenstaufen Castle, a practical measure of protection since the monastery was hard by.[130]

The Church in Germany was indebted to the *ministeriales* not only for their donations but also for their talents. A fair number of them rose to bishoprics and abbacies,[131] and to high office in the Teutonic Order. In 1238, when Advocate Henry of Weida-Gera's wife Jutta founded Cronschwitz and entered it as abbess, he left for the Baltic crusade and became Master of Prussia, and their sons took over the secular offices he had administered for Frederick II as an imperial *ministerialis*.[132] Those not called to the religious life might join pious confraternities, as some of the Cologne *ministeriales* did under the guidance of the monks of Zülpich in 1190.[133] Less conventional were those who found release going in procession as flagellants in 1261.[134] And in an act of charity if not prudence, the duke of Bavaria's *ministeriales* of Wildenstein attempted

---

[128] UB Hildesheim i, 280, p. 264, 1152.

[129] MGD Frederick I, 167, p. 286, 1157.

[130] UB Wirtemberg ii, 428, p. 216, 1181; further examples of *ministeriales'* functions as monastic advocates in Stumpf-Brentano, *Acta Imperii* iii, 406, pp. 570 f., 1192, UB Salzburg iii, 571, pp. 48-50, 1203 and iv, 16 and 18, pp. 16-18, 1251, and CD Saxony iii, 344, pp. 243 f., 1225.

[131] Early examples of abbots in *Vita Altmanni Episcopi Pataviensis*, MGS, XII, p. 243, and *Walteri Historia Monasterii Marchtelanensis*, MGS, XXIV, p. 666; for incomplete lists of bishops, Schulte, pp. 61-73, 349-52.

[132] UB Weida 75, pp. 38 f., 1241-9. On other Thuringian *ministeriales* in the Order, see D. Wojtecki, *Studien zur Personengeschichte des Deutschen Ordens im 13. Jahrhundert*, Quellen und Studien zur Geschichte des östlichen Europa (Wiesbaden, 1971), pp. 78-80, 123-233.

[133] UB Niederrhein i, 526, pp. 367 f., 1190.

[134] *Continuatio Sancrucensis Secunda*, MGS, IX, p. 645.

to give refuge to Jews during the 1298 massacres, and had their
castle burned down for their pains.[135]

[135] *Annales Osterhovenses*, MGS, XVII, p. 552; on these knights, G. Voit, *Die
Wildensteiner*, Sonderheft der Mitteilungen der altnürnberger Landschaft (Nuremberg, 1964).

CHAPTER 6

Ministeriales and Marriage

Lords and their ministeriales' *marriages*

Landed property providing manorial revenues was the chief economic support of *ministeriales'* families in Germany, a heritable foundation which might be improved over the generations by military or administrative talent, multiple enfeoffment, and politic marriages. If the everyday history of knightly wedlock in medieval Germany is almost unknown to us,[1] we are well informed about the regulations which their lords applied to *ministeriales'* marriages as legal undertakings. The reason for this is that many a match was contracted between *ministeriales* from different retinues, and the lords of the parties were interested in making sure that they would not lose by such technical breaches of the *familia*.

Knightly marriage was, amongst other things, a mechanism for the legitimate devolution of real property in fiefs and allods, as well as the titles and offices which *ministeriales* might hold.[2] Generally, *ministeriales'* property and titles were inherited in the paternal line, but the ownership or ascription of children passed through the female line. Potentially this was the cause of much anxiety and dissension amongst the lords, for the children of a male *ministerialis* contracting marriage in another retinue would belong by law to their mother's lord, meaning that the latter would not only expand his man-power, but also, when such children came into their paternal inheritance, he would gain the ultimate proprietary right over these new resources as lord. Since it was not possible or desirable to enforce marriages within one retinue, lords of male *ministeriales* might risk serious losses by their marriages, unless steps were taken to mitigate the consequences of maternal ascription and the passage of persons, castles, fiefs, allods, and offices into alien retinues. The

---

[1] There is a cautionary tale in *Annales Stederburgenses*, MGS, XVI, p. 229, 1194, where the Hildesheim *ministerialis* Amelung of Hemstide's wife ran amok and killed him.
[2] On titles and offices, Chs. 7 and 8 below.

early and widespread practice of matrimony between different *fam-iliae* of *ministeriales* compelled lords to impose measures which accommodated the interests of both sides to the principle of maternal ascription, or circumvented it altogether.

Ascription of *ministeriales by female descent*

In the German empire custom dictated that servile status was handed on through the female line,[3] meaning that the right of possession of *ministeriales* belonged to their mothers' lords. As Frederick Barbarossa put it in 1155 for one of Duke Frederick of Swabia's *ministeriales*: 'She pertained to him and was his *minister-ialis*, and the sanction of the law has and serves this purpose, that children follow the mother's condition and, where the mother belongs, the children belong also'.[4] Unless arrangements were made to the contrary, a mixed marriage would thus transfer the children with their inheritances to the bride's lord. Late in the twelfth century the monks of Niederaltaich complained that Count Adalbert of Bogen 'had alienated the *ministeriales* of our church from us by extrinsic marriages',[5] and the dukes of Bavaria and bishops of Regensburg regularly envenomed their incessant quarrels by enticing contumacious *ministeriales* owned by the other party into matrimony with brides from their own retinues.[6] The bishops had, by this method, lost control of Teisbach Castle some time before 1237, because the Regensburg *ministerialis* to whom it was enfeoffed had married into the ducal *familia*, and his heirs were therefore ducal *ministeriales*. Not until 1253 did the dukes agree to give the castle back to the bishop.[7] Extrinsic marriages without consent were offensive to lords, and in 1274 King Rudolf endeavoured to prevent the Salzburg, Passau, and Regensburg *ministeriales* from such presumption.[8]

In the natural course of events, alienations through extrinsic

[3] Confirmed in MGC ii, 279, ch. 7, p. 393, 1222.
[4] MGD Frederick I, 153, pp. 263 f., 1155-6, so in CD Saxony iii, 358, p. 253, 1226 Dietrich of Ruhlhausen was the landgrave of Thuringia's *ministerialis*, but his wife, and therefore his children, belonged to the emperor. Kluckhohn, pp. 79-91 on *ministeriales'* marriages.
[5] Mon. Boica xi, p. 21.
[6] Wittmann, *Wittelsbach*, vol. i, 5, pp 14-19, 1213, and 102, pp. 244-51, 1272.
[7] Ibid. 26, pp. 57-60, 1237, and 52, pp. 118-23, 1253.
[8] Mon. Boica xxix. B, 116, pp. 510-12, 1274.

marriages would take effect only in the next generation, which may explain why lords often took time to catch up with them. In 1177 it was recorded that Eberhard of Ketschendorf, son of a Bamberg *ministerialis*, 'had transferred through his mother into the *familia* of St Kilian [Würzburg].'[9] In 1183 the abbot of St Emmeram rounded up the descendants through female lines of his *ministeriales* of Aiterhofen. They were the *ministeriales* of Sunzing and Radlkofen, 'by maternal lineage the progeny of St Emmeram's *ministeriales*' who were obliged to return to the abbot's retinue and to give him some of the property they had inherited at Aiterhofen as a fine.[10] Just as cross-marriages cracked the integrity of retinues and detached fiefs and castles, so they could secure new allegiances transmissible to the next generation and beyond. This is what Duke Louis of Bavaria tried to ensure in 1286 when he took homage from one of the count of Montfort's *ministeriales*, Conrad of Eberstal. His castle became a ducal fief and he was committed to serving the duke as a *ministerialis*, but above all, he was to marry into the ducal *familia* of *ministeriales*, the bride to be picked by the duke himself.[11]

Lords might try to get the better of each other through extrinsic marriages, but they were not hostile to female ascription in principle. In 1206, for example, it enabled the bishop of Würzburg to drive a bargain with the abbot of Kremsmünster, whose *ministerialis* Hartwig of Pütenbach had married Adelheid of Harde, who belonged to Würzburg. It followed that the children also belonged to the bishopric, 'to which they are held both by hereditary right and maternal succession'.[12] To avoid a long wrangle, the bishop conceded some of the offspring to the abbot's ownership, since Würzburg had, in any case, made a net gain by the marriage.

Such compromises after the event were common, but not all lords liked to take the risk. When the bishop of Bamberg bought Rimbach from the abbot of Hirsau in 1125, it was outlined 'that if any of the *ministeriales* of that estate takes a wife from there, and has a son by her, the son obtains the father's inheritance, but a son born to a mother from outside will not aspire to possess the paternal inheritance'.[13] In effect, the bishop sought a safeguard against

---

[9] Reimann, p. 6.   [10] Tr. Regensburg 971 f., pp. 490 f., 1183.
[11] Wittmann, *Wittelsbach*, vol. i, 162, pp. 398-400, 1286.
[12] UB Land ob der Enns ii, 350, pp. 503 f., 1206.
[13] UB Wirtemberg i, 285, p. 365, 1125.

extrinsic marriages without consent by disinheriting the offspring in advance. A similar threat by the abbess of Quedlinburg was circumvented by the archbishop of Mainz in 1155. 'A certain Reinold, *ministerialis* of the church of Quedlinburg, contracted marriage with a *ministerialis* of the church of Mainz, the daughter of Dietrich of Hofgeismar called Matilda, so that the progeny born of her can, following the law, obtain neither allod nor fief which Reinold has from the church of Quedlinburg, because these offspring belonged to the church of Mainz.'[14] The way out was to give the children to Quedlinburg, and the abbess gave other *ministeriales* to Mainz in compensation. A century later the Bavarian lords imposed the same sanction against the bishop of Bamberg's *ministeriales*: 'If any of the *ministeriales* of the church should marry a wife from an alien *familia* without consent, and without obtaining a division of the children, what shall be the law on this? It was declared and approved that the fiefs held from the church should by law be forfeit.'[15]

These anxieties were understandable. The strength and integrity of military retinues of *ministeriales* based upon fiefs was the true measure of the magnates' political standing in Germany. In taking steps to discipline *ministeriales* about extrinsic matches, they ensured that their retinues would not be eroded and their fiefs lost. In 1192 the bishop of Verden complained in the royal court that fiefs to his *ministeriales* had passed by extrinsic marriages to sons not therefore belonging to him.[16] If extrinsic marriages were inevitable, lords tried to insist upon consultation, permission, and other safeguards, such as specifying which other retinues would qualify, or in supervising the devolution of inheritances, or in dividing the ownership of progeny with the lord of the other retinue.[17]

Since it was not easy to keep track of all the marriages in a large retinue, some lords authorized considerable latitude in the hope that losses would be balanced by gains. In 1092 Bishop Udo of Hildesheim simply permitted his *ministeriales* to marry as they chose, like those, he thought, belonging to the emperor or the

[14] UB Mainz ii, 202, pp. 367 f., 1155.
[15] MGC ii, 461, pp. 633 f., 1254.
[16] MGC i, 352, p. 501, 1192.
[17] Huillard-Bréholles, *Dipl. Friderici II.* i/2, pp. 817 f., 1220 for imperial confirmation that the bishops of Würzburg and Bamberg had drawn up a general agreement about intermarriages and divisions of offspring.

archbishop of Mainz.[18] In this he was almost certainly mistaken, but it is true that emperors and bishops favoured freedom of choice within specified retinues, carrying an equal or approximate division of offspring. In 1192, for example, Henry VI confirmed such an arrangement with Mainz, intermarriages to be followed by divisions of children with their inheritances.[19] By their own acts emperors were confirming matrilinear ascription.[20] In 1196, when dealing with a sale by *ministeriales* to Maulbronn Abbey, Henry VI mentioned that 'this knight and his wife are declared to be from different *familiae*, for the knight is a *ministerialis* of the church of Reichenau, and his wife and the children born of her are known to be *ministeriales* of Count Conrad of Calw and his brother'.[21] In 1234 Frederick II recognized the usual consequences of matrilinear ascription in the Mainz marshal Siegfried of Frauenstein's marriage into the imperial *familia*. So he gave Siegfried's son and heir to Mainz, since 'on his mother's side he ought to be a *ministerialis* of the empire, and would therefore lose his father's fief, which is held from that church'.[22]

Dividing the ownership of children in cross-marriages

In order to prevent the depletion of their retinues through extrinsic marriages, lords might agree to general treaties dividing progeny in advance,[23] or to specific arrangements for individual matches. In general treaties the details varied. The agreement of 1197 between Bishop Ekkehard of Gurk and Duke Berthold of Merania envisaged the equal division of children, and an only child's right to inherit the paternal fiefs and allods.[24] Philip of Swabia's regulations for the Bavarian and Regensburg retinues awarded a sole heir to the father's lord, obliging him or her to marry into the retinue of the mother's lord, and then dividing the next generation of children.[25] In 1262, however, Duke Henry of Bavaria and

---

[18] UB Hildesheim i, 150, pp. 142 f., 1092.

[19] UB Mainz ii, 569, pp. 938-40, 1192. Mainz already recognized that in cross-marriages *allodia et beneficia altrinsecus* from both sides ought to be divided, ibid. 490, p. 801, 1186.

[20] MGD Frederick I, 168 f., pp. 288 f., 1157.

[21] UB Wirtemberg ii, 500, pp. 317 f., 1196.   [22] CD Nassau 453, p. 303, 1234.

[23] e.g. UB Mainz ii, 490, pp. 799-803, 1186 and Mon. Boica xlix, 45, p. 84, 1243.

[24] Mon. Carinthia i, 369, pp. 271-3, 1197.

[25] Mon. Boica xxix. A, 581, pp. 522 f., 1205, and a similar arrangement between the bishop of Bamberg and the margrave of Istria in Schlögl, *Dießen*, 6, pp. 109-12, 1192.

Bishop Otto of Passau would not entrust the ownership of a single child to the other on such long terms. So they imposed joint-lordship for a generation; '... a sole heir, however, shall be communal, and the offspring born of him or her shall be divided'.[26] If the duke of Austria's treaty with the bishop of Freising stated simply that 'heirs born of them [their *ministeriales*] and the possessions will be divided equally',[27] the bishops of Naumburg and Merseburg weighted the division in favour of the mother's lord, who would acquire the eldest child as well as the majority in an unequal number of children.[28]

Another device was to make arrangements for individual cases. In 1155, for example, when a daughter of the imperial marshal, Henry of Pappenheim, married the rich Würzburg *ministerialis* Bodo, Frederick Barbarossa arranged with the bishop that should an only child be born to them, he or she should belong to Würzburg in order to qualify for the paternal fiefs. The rule of maternal ascription was reversed under imperial aegis to avoid the standard penalty in mixed marriages, forfeiture of fiefs. The emperor also provided for a division should there be several children, and this is what happened.[29] Bodo's descendants included the Würzburg *ministeriales* called *de foro* and of Rabensburg, and the imperial castellans of Nordenberg and Stollberg.[30] In a later case, the Salzburg *ministerialis* Gerhoh of Bergheim married Bertha of Lonsdorf, who belonged to Passau. Salzburg would acquire the first two children, Passau the third, and the remainder would be divided equally.[31] In the 1220s Bishop Conrad of Hildesheim adopted a more conciliatory view of his *ministerialis* Henry of Hohenhameln's match with a Brunswick *ministerialis*, accepting only one child for Hildesheim but permitting the others to qualify for their father's episcopal fiefs.[32]

It was sometimes appropriate to deal in grandchildren. In 1236

---

[26] Wittmann, *Wittelsbach*, vol. i, 79, pp. 190-3, 1262.
[27] UB Krain ii, 80, p. 60, 1233.
[28] Kehr, *Merseburg*, 274, p. 218, 1251.
[29] MGD Frederick I, 153, pp. 263f., 1155-6.
[30] Beckmann, pp. 17-56, and Reimann, pp. 154-70.
[31] UB Salzburg iii, 666, p. 171, 1213.
[32] UB Hildesheim ii, 26, pp. 15f., 1221-7. Duke Otto of Brunswick later exchanged another child of this marriage with Hildesheim, ibid. 695, p. 350, 1243. Other examples of division applied to individual matches in Mon. Carinthia i, 461, p. 352, 1216 and 500, pp. 384f., 1225, and Mon. Boica xlix, 327, p. 503, 1303.

Duke Bernard of Carinthia gave Hemma, granddaughter of Liebhard of Karlsberg, to the abbess of Göss, stipulating that she should marry back into his retinue, with an equal division of her children between himself and the abbess.[33] In another case the duke of Bavaria agreed with the bishop of Eichstätt to divide the offspring when Reinboto of Meilenhart's daughters, who were Bavarian *ministeriales* through their mother, should come to marry. The Meilenhart family was poor, but since the girls were the bishop's nieces, he undertook to portion them out of Eichstätt's resources. The duke's concession of half their progeny in advance was intended to compensate the see for its outlay.[34]

A more drastic measure was to acquire the bride for her husband's lord, so that there could be no argument about ascribing the offspring. Lothar III imposed this solution upon Königslutter Abbey in 1135. 'We wish that if a woman of the church's *familia* should marry our *ministerialis* or servant ... she will remain in perpetuity with her husband under our jurisdiction'.[35] Dukes Louis and Henry of Bavaria, who had divided their inheritance into two independent jurisdictions in 1255, adopted Lothar III's idea in 1262. Their *ministeriales* might intermarry, the ownership of brides always being transferred to their husband's lord.[36] Much earlier, about 1105, the abbot of Hersfeld's *serviens* Vinnolt of Dageboldshausen arranged for his bride, who belonged as *ministerialis* to the counts of Arnsberg, to be transferred to the abbot's retinue.[37] In 1207 the duke of Austria gave Adelheid of Traun to the bishop of Würzburg when she married the bishop's *ministerialis* Dietrich of Bühel, on condition that there would still be a division of their children. But the couple was childless, and they bequeathed Bühel to Lambach Abbey.[38]

In spite of all their precautions, it is evident that quite often the lords only took the trouble to catch up with their *ministeriales'*

[33] Mon. Carinthia iv, 2116, p. 230, 1236.

[34] Mon. Boica xlix, 370, pp. 570f., 1291.

[35] MGD Lothar III, 74, p. 115, 1135.

[36] Wittmann, *Wittelsbach*, vol. i, 76, pp. 181–5, 1262.

[37] H. B. Wenck, *Urkundenbuch zu dem dritten Bande von Wencks Hessischer Landesgeschichte* (Frankfurt, 1803), 44, pp. 53 f., 1105 or later, and a similar case in Wisplinghoff, *Siegburg*, 105, pp. 214 f., 1238.

[38] Mon. Boica xxxvii, 172A, B, pp. 174–6, 1207 and UB Land ob der Enns ii, 442, p. 640, c.1222; on the *ministeriales* of this region, P. Feldbauer, *Der Herrenstand in Oberösterreich. Ursprünge, Anfänge, Frühformen*, Sozial- und wirtschaftshistorische Studien (Munich, 1972).

extrinsic marriages after the event. Then they arranged exchanges
between the retinues to rectify the balance, as King Henry and the
archbishop of Magdeburg agreed in 1230,[39] or as the bishops of
Brixen contracted from time to time with their episcopal col-
leagues.[40] As long as the essential requirement of compensation
was fulfilled, lords did not necessarily exchange *ministeriales* from
the families actually involved in extrinsic marriages, but might
choose other families to whom a transfer of allegiance was conven-
ient and acceptable.[41] In 1238 the bishop of Strasburg gave Eberhard and Dietrich, butlers of Wersauerhof, and their posterity to
the bishop of Speyer so that Beatrice, daughter of the Speyer
chamberlain Albert of Uttenheim and wife of the Strasburg marshal Egelolf of Mundlingen, and their children might now belong
to Strasburg.[42] In a similar exchange, the abbess of Quedlinburg
received the abbot of Fulda's knights Henry and Bernard of Ditt-
furt, and gave the granddaughters of her seneschal, Gertrude and
Matilda of Goslar, to Fulda instead.[43] Alternatively, lords might
agree to release *ministeriales* to another retinue without exchange
of persons, but with a monetary compensation.[44]

Patrilinear ascription when ministeriales *married free women*

The custom of maternal ascription with the compromise of dividing
or exchanging offspring did not apply when *ministeriales* married
free women, as quite often happened.[45] If there was feeling in
favour of passing on the mother's free status, it was eventually
rejected by imperial enactment. In 1190 Bishop Rudolf of Verden
inquired of Henry V I's court 'whether the children of *ministeriales*
of the church, born of free mothers, ought to belong to the church
through their fathers, or ought to remain free through their
mothers?' The answer was that they must follow into their fathers'

[39] Huillard-Bréholles, *Dipl. Friderici II.* iii, pp. 428 f., 1230.
[40] Redlich, *Brixen*, 431, pp. 150 f., c.1110-22, 458, p. 161, 1140-7, 481, p. 168, 1156-64, 512, p. 181, 1177-8 and 550, p. 197, 1220.
[41] e.g. UB Salzburg iii, 617, pp. 109 f., 1208 and Mon. Carinthia i, 501, p. 385, 1225.
[42] Reg. Straßburg ii, 1057, pp. 75 f., 1238, and similar examples in UB Hildesheim i, 706 f., pp. 671 f., 1218, and UB Halberstadt ii, 792, pp. 89 f., 1248.
[43] UB Halberstadt ii, 683, pp. 18 f., 1239.
[44] Tr. Tegernsee 369, p. 281, 1189-1206, and UB Hildesheim i, 689, pp. 658 f., 1216.
[45] e.g. UB Mainz ii, 651, pp. 1057 f., 1196.

condition, and this was confirmed by Otto IV in 1209.[46] The *Sachsenspiegel* also mentioned that in marriages which combined the two statuses, the children would always be *ministeriales*, and claims that this rule had been applied by Archbishop Wichmann of Magdeburg in the later twelfth century.[47]

Although steps were sometimes taken to mitigate it,[48] paternal ascription can be seen at work in the Hagen-Arnsburg family, forebears of the Münzenberg dynasty so powerful under the Hohenstaufen. Henry IV's prominent *serviens* Cuno of Arnsburg married Matilda, daughter of Count Eberhard of Bilstein. Their daughter and heiress Gertrude married another rich imperial *ministerialis*, Eberhard of Hagen, and their sons Conrad and Eberhard were high in favour with Henry V, Lothar III, and Conrad III. Gertrude may have been considered a free person like her mother, but her sons were not. They inherited the status and ascription of their father and grandfather as imperial *ministeriales*.[49]

Another early case concerned Ruotbert, son of a *ministerialis* belonging to the abbot of St Emmeram, who had married a free woman called Adelheid. All the posterity of their daughter Liutgard 'shall belong to the service of St Emmeram, just as her father Ruotbert was a *ministerialis* of this church'. Here the patrilinear ascription was traced over four generations.[50] When they married *ministeriales*, free women evidently realized that their children were unlikely to maintain free status. The free woman Richardis of Ouren even encouraged her children by her second marriage, to a *liber* like herself, to become *ministeriales* of St Mary at Trier, to qualify themselves for her first husband's fief. He had been a *ministerialis* of that church.[51] In another illuminating case, a free woman called Bertha refused to accept that her sons should become *ministeriales* of her husband's lord, Ortolf of Rultingen. By transferring herself as a *censualis* to the cathedral church of Passau, she

---

[46] MGC i, 329, pp. 467 f., 1190, and ii, 30, p. 35, 1209.

[47] Eckhardt, *Sachsenspiegel Landrecht*, pp. 256 f., Israël and Möllenberg, *Magdeburg*, 447, pp. 580 f., and W. Barkhausen, 'Die Gesetzgebung Wichmanns von Magdeburg', *DA* iv (1940-1), 495-503.

[48] In an early text, Mon. Boica xxxvii, 64, pp. 21-5, 1036, a Würzburg *ministerialis* was married to a *libera* 'ut libertate sua et eodem beneficio cum posteritate sua potiretur'. The source was reworked in the 12th c., and it is unclear when and to whom these conditions in reality were applied.

[49] See p. 35 n. 63.

[50] Tr. Regensburg 710, p. 339, after 1100.

[51] UB Mittelrhein i, 389, p. 446, 1095.

ensured that her children would also qualify as Passau *censuales*. Still, her husband Liutold and the Passau chapter were obliged to compensate Ortolf with land and cash, and even then, should he produce heirs, they might claim three of Bertha's boys as their ministeriales.[52] A similar solution was found for descendants of Tegernsee Abbey's *ministerialis* Richer of Schaftlach and his wife Gisela, a free noblewoman. Their posterity, one of whom was called an *ingenua*, always a term for free status, were eventually confirmed as *censuales* of Tegernsee.[53]

Although the Hagen-Arnsburg family appears to have inherited much of the Bilstein lands,[54] free dynasties sometimes tried to prevent their resources from passing to *ministeriales* by inheritance. In 1182 Judith, daughter of Count Siboto of Falkenstein's brother Count Herrand, was required to resign her rights to Falkenstein and Herrandstein since she had married the Regensburg *ministerialis* Nizo of Raitenbuch.[55] Another member of this comital house, Adelheid of Neuburg, married the Austrian *ministerialis* Henry of Kuenring, and their daughter and heiress Euphemia followed suit, marrying Rudolf of Pottendorf some time before 1257. In the 1240s Adelheid's brother Count Conrad of Neuburg had given all his property to the see of Freising, but in the 1260s Euphemia tried to get some of it back again for her sons. The judges appointed to the case discovered that Adelheid had renounced all her rights to the Neuburg lands when she married a *ministerialis*, and they claimed that 'if a *nobilis* or *liber* marries a *ministerialis* of the Church or of the duke of Austria, then the children follow into the rank of *ministeriales* and have no right or access to the possessions of free men'.[56] But the second half of this judgement would not have found general acceptance in Germany.

These cases of exclusion from comital inheritances may reflect the idea that free noblewomen were disparaged by marrying *ministeriales*. But knightly status obviously provided an acceptable matrimonial asylum for some of them, such as Sophia of Orlamünde in

[52] Tr. Passau 745, pp. 266f., 1180–1200.
[53] Tr. Tegernsee 188, pp. 150f., 1126–7, and 409, p. 313, 1217–42.
[54] Kropat, pp. 77f.
[55] Noichl, *Codex Falkensteinensis*, 157, pp. 135f., 1182.
[56] Zahn, *CD Austriaco-Frisingensis*, 145 and 148, pp. 140–4, 1245–6, 187, p. 193, 1257, and 262, 265 and 267, pp. 282–90, 1266–7.

her marriage to Henry, advocate of Weida,[57] who was probably richer than her father although he was a count. In 1153, when Frederick Barbarossa divorced his queen Adela, daughter of Margrave Diepold of Vohburg, she was married off to one of Duke Welf of Tuscany's prominent Swabian *ministeriales*, Diether of Ravensburg.[58] Such intermarriages were not very frequent before the fourteenth century, but the richest and most distinguished *ministeriales* continued to acquire high-born brides. In 1195 the younger Wernher of Bolanden married Hildegard of Eppstein,[59] whose brother Siegfried was archbishop of Mainz from 1200 to 1230. In Frederick II's time the imperial butler Walter of Limburg married a countess of Helfenstein,[60] and at the end of the thirteenth century King Albert married off one of his cousins to the most formidable Austrian *ministerialis*, Liutold of Kuenring.[61]

When free men married *ministeriales*,[62] there was no impediment to the children's coming into maternal inheritances, because they themselves belonged to their mothers' lords. This is what happened to Frederick of Hausen, the noted minnesinger, whose mother was an imperial *ministerialis*.[63] As we have seen, it was possible to apply to the imperial court for emancipations,[64] or to come to an accommodation with the bride's lord. In 1263, when Albero of Matsch married the Brixen *ministerialis* Sophia of Velturns, he arranged with the bishop that their first-born child would enjoy free status, but the rest would, by custom, be Brixen *ministeriales*.[65]

---

[57] UB Weida 112, p. 58, 1258. See also the free but impoverished Callenberg family; the sisters married Würzburg and Bamberg *ministeriales*, the brother sold Callenberg Castle to the bishop of Würzburg, Reimann, pp. 25 f. n. 153 f.

[58] Burchard of Ursberg, p. 26, and H. Decker-Hauff, 'Das Staufische Haus' in *Die Zeit der Staufer, Katalog der Ausstellung im Württembergischen Landesmuseum* (Stuttgart, 1977), vol. iii, p. 351.

[59] *Annales Remenses et Colonienses*, MGS, XVI, p. 733.

[60] In UB Wirtemberg v, 1322, p. 89, 1255 their son was mentioned by his *avunculus*, Count Ulrich of Helfenstein.

[61] J. von Frast, *Liber Fundationem Monasterii Zwetlensis*, Fontes rerum Austriacarum, ser. 2. iii (Vienna, 1851), p. 200. King Ottokar of Bohemia, during his tenure as duke of Austria, married off his illegitimate daughter Elizabeth to Henry of Kuenring-Weitra, Gründler etc., p. 45.

[62] e.g. Bitterauf, *Freising*, 1711, pp. 512 f., 1123-30, and UB Salzburg i, 50, p. 608, after 1139 and 57, p. 613, 1122-47.

[63] H-J. Rieckenberg, 'Leben und Stand des Minnesängers Friedrich von Hausen', *Archiv für Kulturgeschichte* xliii (1961), 163-76.

[64] See pp. 68 f., nn. 96-9.

[65] K. Fajkmajer, 'Die Ministerialen des Hochstiftes Brixen', *Zeitschrift des Ferdinandeums für Tirol und Vorarlberg*, 3rd ser., lii (1908), 190.

Penalties and safeguards in extrinsic marriages

Lords were not necessarily opposed to the mobility amongst retinues which mixed marriages entailed, and the consequent exchanges of persons, talents, fiefs, offices, castles, and allods might work to their advantage. Where important castles and fiefs were concerned, lords could impose safeguards against extrinsic marriages. In 1203 Bishop Gerhard of Osnabrück would only confirm Walter of Oldenburg's fiefs to his two sons if, upon reaching the age of twelve, they swore to marry, later on, within the Osnabrück retinue of *ministeriales*. The penalty would be forfeiture of fiefs, to be transferred to the other brother, and a thirty-mark fine.[66] Similarly, Sueder of Ringenberg's children were required to obtain Bishop Otto of Münster's consent to their marriages, on pain of losing their castle.[67] Less specifically, the provost of Aschaffenburg had confirmed in 1127 that the offices of butler and marshal of his household would be hereditary in the male line so long as the incumbents took wives within his retinue.[68]

Other lords took a less drastic view. They might accept extrinsic marriages as *faits accomplis*, and demand compensation of some kind for permitting the offspring to inherit parental fiefs and allods. Noth, *serviens* of St Alban at Mainz whose wife Kriemhilt belonged to St Mary at Trier, feared that his children might be deprived of their title to his allods, so he converted them, five *mansi* and two mills, into fiefs from St Alban's in 1092.[69] As we have already seen,[70] Conrad III's *ministerialis* Pecelin of Treitersberg, whose wife belonged to Regensburg, made the same arrangement in 1141 for their son Berthold. Pecelin's allodial property was converted into hereditary fief from the church, with Berthold as heir. The provost of Marchtal's *ministerialis* Riwin of Oberwachingen adopted a comparable solution later in the twelfth century. Having married outside the *familia*, he resigned an allod to the provost so that his fief at Oberwachingen might pass to his son.[71] The Salzburg *ministerialis* Otto of Weingarten also had to give an allod to the archbishop in order to be confirmed in his fief, because his wife

[66] UB Osnabrück ii, 16, pp. 9f., 1203.
[67] UB Münster 619, p. 327, 1257.
[68] UB Mainz i, 546, pp. 453f., 1127.
[69] Ibid. 382, pp. 284f., 1092.
[70] See p, 110, n. 49.
[71] *Walteri Historia Monasterii Marchtelanensis*, MGS, XXIV, ch. 33, p. 670.

was not from the Salzburg *familia*.[72] In a different arrangement the
children of Adeldegen, *ministerialis* of the cathedral church at Bamberg, and Petrissa, *censualis* of Lorch Abbey, were permitted to
become *ministeriales* of Duke Frederick of Rothenburg, to qualify
for Adeldegen's valuable ducal fiefs. Petrissa was actually the
duke's niece and Conrad III's grand-daughter, since her father was
Duke Frederick's illegitimate half-brother Gislebert of Höttingen.[73]

When all else failed, lords could resort to reprisals against *ministeriales* who had contracted unsuitable matches. The penalties
included loss of favour, withdrawal of rights and privileges, confiscation of fiefs, and exclusion of the children from inheritances.[74]
In 1137 the monastery of Holy Faith at Bamberg confiscated its
ministerialis Bertolf's fief from his sons because they belonged to
an alien lord through their father's extrinsic marriage.[75] The abbot
of Diessen voiced a general warning when accepting new *ministeriales* as a gift to his house in the 1120s; 'They and their sons and
daughters and their posterity have the rights of *ministeriales* in
perpetuity, unless they afterwards lose their rights by an intervening
marriage'.[76] Undoubtedly this is what had happened to the sons
of Jordan of Adersheim, a *ministerialis* of Steterburg Abbey, for
when they laid claim to their father's fief the provost, after long
conversations with their uncle, cast them off, with some monetary
compensation, as too dubious a case.[77] In 1239 the Salzburg *ministerialis* Charles of Gutrat was deprived of fiefs and other possessions in Styria because he had married outside the archbishop's
familia without licence, but the probability of receiving new fiefs
was held out, should he or his heirs recover the archbishop's
favour.[78]

In another notorious case Bishop Hermann of Würzburg engaged
in a long feud to break one of his principal *ministeriales*, Marshal
Henry of Lauer, whose wife appears to have been a *ministerialis*
belonging to the bishop's most dangerous territorial rival, Count
Poppo of Henneberg. In 1231 Henry was deprived of the marshal's

[72] UB Salzburg ii, 381, p. 529, 1165-6.
[73] UB Wirtemberg ii, 386, pp. 151 f., 1166, and Decker-Hauff, pp. 350, 357 f.
[74] Kluckhohn, pp. 82 f.
[75] Joetze, p. 555.
[76] Schlögl, *Dießen*, 2, pp. 4 f., 1122-3.
[77] *Gesta Praepositorum Stederburgensium Continuata*, MGS, XXV, p. 722, 1269.
[78] UB Salzburg iii, 944, pp. 496 f., 1239.

office, of Niederlauer Castle and his position as castellan in Salzburg and Osterburg Castles, and of much of his fief and allod, as well as all his own vassals. Obviously he was being punished both for taking up arms against his lord and for his extrinsic marriage into the enemy's camp. The confiscated offices and possessions were conferred upon Henry's nephews, Volker and Bodo of Eberstein, and the Lauers were permitted to retain Burglauer Castle as an episcopal fief only on condition that Henry's son would marry back into the Würzburg retinue.[79]

In 1303 Bishop Conrad of Eichstätt dealt less harshly with his *ministeriales* of Muhr, who had earned his rancour and indignation by contracting an extrinsic match without his consent. Ulrich of Muhr had married Elizabeth of Reichenbach, who belonged to the bishop of Würzburg. Their parents, Conrad of Reichenbach and the elder Ulrich of Muhr, had to promise to supplicate the see of Würzburg for an equal division of the progeny, and Bishop Conrad used the opportunity to increase the Muhrs' military obligations as the penalty. The younger Ulrich was committed to garrison-duty in continual residence in one of the bishop's key castles, Abenberg, Arberg, Wernfels, or Gundelsheim, with a suitable salary. The elder Ulrich was to provide two fully-equipped war-horses at his own expense, when the see required them. He also promised never again to arrange marriages for his offspring without the express consent and licence of his lord.[80]

Marriage and the devolution of rights and possessions

Marriages within or beyond the retinue directed the descent of *ministeriales'* fiefs, offices, allods, revenues, castles, vassals, and movables. Division of inheritances rather than primogeniture,[81] and the right of female succession to fiefs as well as allods, were the custom in Germany. Since fiefs and offices entailed the performance of military and administrative duties, it was sometimes stated that women should be excluded from inheriting them. But it was

---

[79] Mon. Boica xxxvii, 229, pp. 245-7, 1231, and Reimann, pp. 105-11.

[80] Mon. Boica xlix, 326, pp. 501 f., 1303.

[81] J. Geier, *Die Traditionen, Urkunden und Urbare des Klosters Asbach*, QE, XXIII (Munich, 1969), 38-40, pp. 115-18, 1288, where the three Sonnberg brothers, Austrian *ministeriales*, divided their *patrimonium* or *hereditas paterna*. In UB Osnabrück ii, 185, pp. 138 f., 1224, Bishop Adolf of Osnabrück required his knight Eilhard of Harste to give up a portion of his hereditary fiefs to his younger brother Hartmann.

more common for women to inherit or transfer title should no direct male heir be available. In 1171 the archbishop of Mainz agreed with his childless *ministerialis* Embricho, count of the Rheingau, that his title, office, and lands would go to his sister's son Wolfram of Stein, who eventually founded a new line of Rhinegraves on this basis.[82] In 1263, when the church of Nordhausen transferred *ministeriales* to the bishop of Münster, he agreed to preserve their custom of daughters' succeeding to paternal fiefs if no sons survived,[83] since it was understood that husbands, sons, or guardians of heiresses could fulfil functions dependent upon fiefs.

This is what happened when the imperial *ministerialis* Henry of Hilpoltstein collected four heiresses of other imperial castles for his sons. They took command in the names of their wives literally, adopting their toponymics and calling themselves Henry of Haimburg, Hermann of Breitenstein, and Henry and Hilpolt of Sulzbürg.[84] In another case a daughter of the rich Salzburg *ministerialis* During of Stöffling married one of the Ortenburg *ministeriales*, Conrad of Steinkirchen, with the equal division of offspring agreed between the lords. Conrad in time received all the Stöffling fiefs in his wife's name, since she was the only surviving descendant. Her rights to them were resigned in 1259 to their daughter Margaret, since she was the Salzburg *ministerialis* under the division of the children. She had married a Salzburg *ministerialis* herself, and it was he, Conrad of Kallham, who was committed to carrying out the military services incumbent upon the fiefs.[85]

It still happened that women were, on occasion, excluded from inheriting fiefs. In 1157 Frederick Barbarossa forbade Hertwic of Thann's daughter Margaret to take over his fief from the abbot of St Emmeram, claiming that female succession to fiefs was not customary for Regensburg *ministeriales*.[86] In 1230 King Henry enjoined 'that in general no woman can succeed her brother to any fief by hereditary claim', though this was actually designed to exclude women from inheriting the four household offices of the abbess of Quedlinburg. The next year, in an enactment for Nien-

[82] UB Mainz ii, 339, pp. 575 f., 1171, and p. 198, n. 104 below. Stein Castle was therefore known as Rheingrafenstein from the 13th c.

[83] UB Münster 707, p. 367, 1263.

[84] Mon. Boica xlix, 100, p. 151, 1279. The marriages had taken place in the 1260 s.

[85] UB Salzburg iii, 882A, B, pp. 425-7, 1232, and iv, 33, pp. 30 f., 1255 and 42, pp. 42 f., 1259.

[86] MGD Frederick I, 158, pp. 271-3, 1157.

burg Abbey, his court confirmed that *ministeriales'* fiefs might descend to daughters and sisters as well as sons and brothers.[87] So these decisions were taken pragmatically. In 1148 the royal court at Nuremberg had upheld Abbot Wibald of Stablo's enfeoffment of a son-in-law as the better heir than a sister's son when it came to devolving his *ministerialis* Widerich's fief at Neundorf, and the nephew was fined for persisting in his claim.[88] In 1237 Frederick II permitted Philip of Falkenstein to leave to his daughters 'the possessions which he holds in fief from the empire and us, since he has no sons',[89] and on a smaller scale, the abbot of St Michael at Hildesheim's *ministerialis* Burchard of Essem took similar precautions when it was agreed that should descent through his sons fail, then his fiefs might pass to his daughter's descendants.[90] But this is not what happened to the imperial butler Conrad of Winterstetten's fief from the archbishop of Salzburg, although it was originally a Winterstetten allod sold to the archbishop many years before. When Conrad died in 1243 without legitimate male heirs, the archbishop passed it not to the heiress, Irmengard of Schmalnegg, but to the duke of Bavaria as a lapsed Salzburg fief.[91]

Apart from their residual rights to inherit fiefs and allods, women also had claims upon their paternal property in the form of marriage-portions and endowments. About 1200 the abbot of Kremsmünster instructed his *ministerialis* Hartwig of Pütenbach to give serfs to his sister Hildegard, wife of Bernard of Achleiten, as her portion. They in turn renounced all other claims to the Pütenbach possessions.[92] In much grander circumstances the Styrian *ministerialis* Liutold of Wildon, having matched his daughter Gertrude to the Austrian *ministerialis* Albero of Kuenring, had the bishop of Passau, one of his lords, transfer Steyreck Castle and other Wildon fiefs to them and their heirs. Should Albero and Gertrude die childless, this marriage-portion would revert to the Wildons.[93] A similar endowment sealed the military treaty between Ulrich of Liechtenstein and Archbishop Philip of Salzburg in 1250.

[87] MGC ii, 298, p. 412 and 310, p. 423, 1230-1.
[88] MGD Conrad III, 6, pp. 526 f., 1148.
[89] Huillard-Bréholles, *Dipl. Friderici II.*, v. 1, pp. 149 f.; sons followed later.
[90] See p. 114, n. 71.
[91] Wittmann, *Wittelsbach*, vol. i, 35, pp. 76 f., 1243
[92] UB Land ob der Enns ii, 322, p. 469, c.1200.
[93] Ibid. iii, 92, p. 97, 1241.

Ulrich committed his son Ulrich to espouse the archbishop's *ministerialis* Cunegunde of Goldegg. The elder Ulrich assigned to them his castle of Murau with twenty vassals and suitable revenues, and the archbishop provided an income of £10 a year. Cunegunde's father Conrad of Goldegg guaranteed them resources worth £30 a year, and he was entrusted with a large sum by the archbishop to buy more property for the young couple. Finally, Ulrich himself promised his bride a wedding-gift of a hundred marks.[94]

Since women were entitled to endowments and wedding-gifts from their husbands or their husbands' families, as well as marriage-portions from their fathers or their nearest male relatives, both of which they might keep for life, widows were valued as matrimonial speculations. The bishop of Würzburg's *ministerialis* Gisela of Hemmersheim was generously endowed both by her father and her first husband, Godfrey of Seinsheim, which enabled her to bid for a lucrative post for her second husband, the bishop's butler Otto, who was appointed *scultetus* or magistrate of Heidingsfeld. She outlived him to marry a third time.[95]

Disputed claims and escheats

Claims upon the possessions of deceased *ministeriales* gave rise to much dissension, not only amongst the secular heirs themselves but also when they were unwilling to recognize their departed relatives' gifts of the family lands to the Church. Late in the twelfth century, after the demise of a *ministerialis* called Etich who had given his fief to the abbess of Kühbach in Bavaria, his mother Judinta seized it back again and had to be compensated before she would disgorge it.[96] In 1172 the abbot of Ilsenburg in Saxony was obliged to pay off two Hildesheim *ministeriales* who laid claim to a property 'by maternal succession' which had earlier been given to his church.[97] In 1185 it was revealed that long ago the Bavarian *ministerialis* Wernher of Fecking had given to St Emmeram's the hill at Fecking, but after his death, his son Conrad had reoccupied it and then sold

[94] UB Steiermark iii, 72, pp. 135 f., 1250.
[95] Mon. Boica xxxvii, 357 f., pp. 409-13, 1263 and 391, pp. 453 f., 1275.
[96] E. von Oefele, 'Traditionsnotizen des Klosters Kühbach' in *Sitzungsberichte der phil.-hist. Classe der Akademie der Wissenschaften zu München 1894* (Munich, 1895), pp. 285 f.
[97] UB Hildesheim i, 354, pp. 338 f., 1172.

it to a powerful neighbour, Eberhard of Abensberg, who was now building a castle upon it. The abbot foresaw much trouble from this, and prudently repurchased the property from Eberhard at a greatly inflated price.[98] In another dispute, the *ministerialis* who founded the Cistercian nunnery at Harste having died, his brother Walraf claimed back some of the lands given to the nuns, who had to buy him off.[99]

Naturally, families of *ministeriales* wrangled amongst themselves about their inheritances. In 1234 Frederick II had to restore to Henry of Ravensburg's sons 'not only the fiefs but also the allods to which they ought to succeed', and of which they had been despoiled by their relations.[100] Since offices were hereditary, brothers might quarrel over which of them was actually to exercise them. About 1242 the bishop of Worms was petitioned to settle just such a dispute about one of his household offices.[101] In another case the Halberstadt *ministerialis* Ulrich of Aderstedt sold his lord a fief in 1271, but two of his relations refused to recognize the sale and forcibly reoccupied the fief. Bishop Volrad excommunicated them, and the affair was not settled until 1279, when John of Aderstedt received cash in compensation for his claims.[102]

When quarrelsome relatives were evenly matched, they might decide upon a division of the patrimony, a solution imitating princely practice in Germany. After long feuds with the dukes of Bavaria in which their possessions had already been badly depleted, the imperial marshals of Pappenheim, with much recrimination, divided their lands, castles, and retinue in 1279. Henry kept the lands north of the Danube with Pappenheim Castle itself. Hildebrand retired to Biberbach Castle and its attendant manors south of the river.[103] In an uneven contest the weaker member of the family would have to settle for less. In 1310 Margaret, granddaughter of the prominent Bavarian *ministerialis* Henry, butler of Hofstetten-Geyern, claimed her share of Geyern Castle and its appurtenances, and of the Hofstetten lands, from the butler's three younger sons, who were in possession now that their father was

---

[98] Tr. Regensburg 978, p. 496, 1185.
[99] UB Osnabrück ii, 437, pp. 343 f., 1243.
[100] UB Wirtemberg iii, 856, p. 354, 1234.
[101] Winkelmann, *Acta Imperii*, vol. i, 677, p. 536, c.1242.
[102] UB Halberstadt ii, 1233, p. 358, 1271, 1256, p. 372, 1272, and 1345, pp. 424 f., 1279.
[103] See my thesis, pp. 169-73.

dead. Since their elder half-brother, Margaret's father, was also deceased, they got the better of the adjudication; the castle itself, all the fiefs from the duke of Bavaria which went with it, and half the Hofstetten allods. So Margaret received the other half of the allods and a substantial cash-grant, which enabled her to make a good marriage to the imperial *ministerialis* Henry of Dürrwangen, advocate of Nuremberg and Rothenburg.[104]

If *ministeriales* should die without any recognized heirs,[105] male or female, then their possessions escheated to their lords, as Archbishop Adalbert of Mainz had pointed out to his *ministeriales* who held fiefs from Ravengiersburg Abbey.[106] When Bishop Bernard of Hildesheim endowed the monastery of St Godehard in the 1140s, he arranged that the possessions of his own *ministeriales* who died without heirs would escheat not to the see but to the abbey. In this way he might augment his foundation's resources without immediately depleting his own.[107] Escheats gave rise to discord. In 1228 the abbess of Göss complained that Duke Bernard of Carinthia had withheld from her the escheated lands of her *ministeriales* dying without heirs.[108]

Mortality, female inheritance, and family partitions

Mortality amongst lines of *ministeriales*, reckoned by the social criteria of paternal descent and dynastic toponymics, was high. In 1285 the Erfurt chronicler noted exceptional mortality amongst the nobility and *ministeriales* of Thuringia.[109] Of approximately seventy families of *ministeriales* enfeoffed in the second quarter of the twelfth century by Bishop Gebhard of Eichstätt and his brother Count Hartwig of Grögling, some thirty had died out by about 1220, and less than thirty were left by the end of the thirteenth century.[110] In a few cases we know for certain that their patrimonies passed by female inheritance to other knightly families, so the

---

[104] Ibid. pp. 253-5.
[105] Tr. Passau 725, p. 261, 1194 specifies heirs *de cognatione illa* for the Passau *ministerialis* Regenger.
[106] UB Mainz i, 549, p. 456, 1128.
[107] *Chronicon Hildesheimense*, MGS, VII, p. 855.
[108] Mon. Carinthia iv, 1945, p. 167, 1228.
[109] Holder-Egger, *Monumenta Erphesfurtensia*, pp. 287 f.
[110] See my thesis, pp. 125 f., 219-21, 223 f., 355-61, 375-7, 379 f.

demise of male lines was profitable for *ministeriales* connected with them by marriage. For this reason the richer *ministeriales* of the region closed their ranks against adventurers; in the later thirteenth century the *ministeriales* of Hilpoltstein, Hofstetten-Geyern, Kropf of Flüglingen, and Sulzbürg-Wolfstein intermarried seven times within two generations, apart from contracting three other matches which brought them entire patrimonies, Breitenstein, Haimburg, and Kipfenberg, by female inheritance. Actually, these families were not quite good enough for their even more distinguished neighbours, the imperial marshals of Pappenheim and the *ministeriales* of Königstein, who sought alliances further afield in Swabia and Franconia with the other families of imperial household officers, such as the butlers of Schüpf-Klingenberg and the chamberlains of Münzenberg.

As long as heiresses could be found, male primogeniture or even the descent of family possessions in the male line did not appear essential to the continuing prominence of *ministeriales'* families. Sometimes the right of eldest sons to fiefs and offices was made explicit, but it was exceptional. It was, for example, laid down for military fiefs held from the see of Cologne, for the fiefs of Ahr Castle, and for the household offices of Benediktbeuern Abbey and the see of Salzburg.[111] Amongst the Tecklenburg *ministeriales*, the family castle would pass to the youngest son.[112] Quite simply, primogeniture never recommended itself in Germany as the preponderant legal principle until early modern times. The medieval landed families, whether territorial magnates, free lords, or knightly *ministeriales*, were inclined to divide their possessions and titles amongst all their sons. In the thirteenth century, the imperial butlers of Schüpf founded new and separate lordships at Limburg, Klingenberg, and Neukastel, and so did the imperial advocates of Weida at Gera, Plauen, and Greiz.[113] The imperial seneschal in Saxony, Gunzelin of Wolfenbüttel, whose chief residence was his Hildesheim fief of Peine Castle, built new castles for his sons and grandsons at Asseburg, Staufenburg, and Heiningen, and their descendants built or inherited or were enfeoffed with yet more

[111] Weinrich, p. 276, UB Niederrhein iv, 646, pp. 791–3, 1202, and MGC iii, 186, pp. 173 f., 1278 and 274, p. 266, 1281.
[112] UB Osnabrück ii, 123, pp 89–92, 1220–30.
[113] Bosl, *RM*, pp. 376–83, 528–38.

castles endowed with appurtenances at Hinnenburg, Moringen, Salza, and Lechede.[114]

The affluent imperial seneschals in the Rhineland made comparable divisions of their possessions into the lordships of Bolanden, Falkenstein, and Hohenfels early in the thirteenth century. Later, Philip of Falkenstein and his sons showed that subdivisions could safely be made, on the strength of the lavish inheritance brought in by Philip's wife, Isengard of Münzenberg. Philip was already rich, but his marriage really secured the future of his line as significant territorial lords. As we have seen, the prominence of the imperial *ministeriales* of Münzenberg was founded upon the combination of the Arnsburg, Bilstein, and Hagen patrimonies, enriched with fresh imperial land-grants in the twelfth century.[115] But a hundred years after Cuno of Hagen had built Münzenberg Castle as his principal residence,[116] his line resolved into heiresses. Philip and Isengard of Falkenstein secured the lion's share. He was confirmed in his father-in-law's office of imperial chamberlain with its extensive fiefs, and in the lordship of Königstein, which was a fief from the counts of Nassau.[117] Furthermore, he was able to exclude or buy out the claims of geographically more distant heirs, the imperial marshals of Pappenheim and the *ministeriales* of Weinsberg and Schönberg.[118] A fair proportion passed, inevitably, to Adelheid of Münzenberg and her husband, the free lord Reinhard of Hanau, yet Philip got the better of them after long wrangles, and was able to occupy all the principal castles of the former 'dominion of Münzenberg', that is, Assenheim, Hagen (now Dreieichenhain), and Münzenberg.

With these gains behind him, Philip had already decided in 1263 upon a division between his sons Philip and Wernher, although the details were changed several times in the following years.[119] In

[114] UB Asseburg i, 180, pp. 124–9, c.1234 and 214, p. 153, 1241 for Peine, 172, p. 119, 1234 for Asseburg, 210 f., pp. 150 f., 1240 for Heiningen, 281, p. 193, 1254 for Staufenburg, 409 f., pp. 266–8, 1281 for Hinnenburg, 515, p. 327, 1300 and ii, 583, 590 and 594, pp. 26–30, 1304 for Asseburg, Moringen, Salza, and Lechede.

[115] See p. 170.

[116] From the 1150s he called himself of Münzenberg, e.g. MGD Frederick I, 153, pp. 263 f., 1155–6.

[117] CD Nassau 658, p. 396, 1257, and UB Hanau 337, pp. 247–9, 1258.

[118] CD Nassau 647, p. 392, 1256, and UB Hanau 568 f., pp. 406–9, 1278 and 671, pp. 481 f., 1288.

[119] CD Nassau 742, p. 439, 1263, 769, p. 454, 1266, 815 f., p. 480, 1271 and 930, p. 554, 1277.

time, the younger Philip's chief residences were Falkenstein, the imperial castles of Trifels and Anebos, and Caub, which he converted into a fief from the counts-palatine of the Rhine in 1277.[120] Wernher, who resided in Münzenberg, Assenheim, and the imperial castles of Calsmunt and Nürings, also settled upon a division of his share for the benefit of his three children in 1294. It was made up of the four chief castles or *domus* of the Münzenbergs, Hagen, Assenheim, and Münzenberg, which were allods although the manors appurtenant were imperial fiefs, and Königstein, which was the Nassau fief.[121] The original Falkenstein patrimony, itself a subdivision of the vast Bolanden inheritance, had thus passed down to the elder line, and the matrilinear acquisition, Münzenberg with its antecedent Hagen-Arnsburg basis, somewhat depleted by the free dynasty of Hanau, to the younger.

[120] Ibid. 921 f., pp. 546-9, 1277.
[121] UB Hanau 747, pp. 542-4, 1294.

CHAPTER 7

The Household, Judicial, and Administrative Offices of *Ministeriales.* Knighthood and the Towns

The four principal household offices

In the world of feudal vassalage, knights owed their lords not only military support or *auxilium* but counsel or *consilium* in their peacetime affairs. It followed that lords drew upon their retinues for administrative services, and since these tasks were profitable, enterprising *ministeriales* were eager for office. As a rule the four ancient household offices of marshal, chamberlain, butler, and seneschal[1] also stood at the summit of territorial administration such as it was, and they were nearly always filled by knights who were *ministeriales.*[2] Under some lords they were overtaken by other officers who achieved greater prominence, such as the advocates of the archbishops of Cologne[3] or the *vicedomini* of the dukes of Bavaria.[4] In most cases we know nothing about the actual functions of these officers beyond what can be inferred from the title itself. However, in 1150 Abbot Wibald of Corvey did get Conrad III to enact that the Corvey seneschals and butlers were responsible for providing all the victuals and entire subsistence that the abbey would need, and that 'they should, from the revenues of their lord, see after the retinue and sustain his knights in everything'.[5]

[1] Scribal Latin rendered seneschal or steward as *dapifer*; Gislebert of Mons, p. 336 for *dapifer qui vulgariter senescalcus dicitur.* For butler, *pincerna* almost drove out *buticularius*, on which U B Nürnberg 115, p. 81, 1204-24.

[2] But Henry IV's seneschal Moricho, p. 31, n. 33, p. 33, n. 53 and Frederick II's marshal Anselm of Justingen, *Notae Sancti Emmerammi* MGS XVII, p. 574, were free-born noblemen.

[3] Weinrich, p. 270, and Pötter, pp. 71-85.

[4] A clerical title in origin, *vicedominus* was frequently applied to secular officials, Niermeyer, *Lexicon,* pp. 1093-5. On the Bavarian *vicedomini*, Spindler, *Anfänge*, pp. 128-30, 156-8.

[5] MGD Conrad III, 221, pp. 390-4, 1150.

Traditionally marshals were responsible for the military business of household and camp,[6] and chamberlains for their lords' treasure and movables. It is, nevertheless, clear that all the household offices carried *ad hoc* combinations of juridical, military, and fiscal duties. They provided hereditary titles in prominent families of *ministeriales*, and it was up to their lords to make what they wanted of them. It is also clear that some families or individuals were talented administrators, while to others the titles were honorific ornaments.[7] Resourceful or favoured families might acquire more than one of the household offices, such as the Tannes, who were imperial seneschals and butlers,[8] the Blankenburgs, who were seneschal and butler to Henry the Lion,[9] and the Wiesbachs, who were the archbishop of Salzburg's marshal and chamberlain.[10] As hereditary fiefs the household offices might pass by primogeniture or to the son 'whom we shall distinguish as the most apt and suitable for this office'.[11] Like other fiefs they might fall to collaterals and females when direct male heirs failed. In this way Philip of Falkenstein, already seneschal of the empire, acquired the office and fiefs of imperial chamberlain through his deceased father-in-law, Ulrich of Münzenberg, in 1257. Much earlier the monks of St Trond had attempted to exclude the nephew of their recently expired seneschal Hezilo from his office, but without success, 'and what belonged to the office of seneschal, he obtained'.[12]

Into the fourteenth century the custom prevailed that magnate households contained 'the four principal offices' as imperial enactments called them, although some made do with three, and others had five or six. With some exaggeration the biographer of the Welf family claimed that their household had been 'ordered in the regal fashion, so that the five curial offices, that is, the functions of

---

[6] The marshal's authority on campaign in Italy is mentioned in $M\bar{G}C$ i, 173, pp. 239-41, 1158.

[7] A. von Wretschko, *Das österreichische Marschallamt im Mittelalter* (Vienna, 1897), Kluckhohn, pp. 146–219, K. Lübeck, 'Die Hofämter der Fuldaer Äbte', *ZRGGA* lxv (1947), 177-207. Reimann, pp. 90–115, and E. Klafki, *Die kurpfälzischen Erbhofämter mit einem Überblick über die bayerischen Erbhofämter*, Veröffentlichungen der Kommission für geschichtliche Landeskunde in Baden-Württemberg, ser. B. Forschungen, XXXV, (Stuttgart, 1966).

[8] See p. 214, n. 30.

[9] Haendle, pp. 3-10.

[10] UB Salzburg iv, 417, pp. 484-6, 1270.

[11] Mon. Boica xxix, A, 581, p. 523, 1205, and alia, 343, pp. 524-6, 1304.

[12] Borman, *Saint-Trond* i, pp. 227f., 1136.

seneschal, butler, marshal, chamberlain and standard-bearer were carried out by counts or their equivalent'.[13] It is true that the imperial court and the households of bishops had honorary officers who were dukes or counts,[14] but the active officers were knights, nearly always *ministeriales*. In the imperial household, with its need to administer and defend the fisc scattered throughout Germany, the four curial titles were multiplied by enfeoffment to more than one family of *ministeriales*, on a regional basis.[15]

Imperial directives took an establishment of four household offices as the norm, as in 1278, when King Rudolf reformed the abbot of Benediktbeuern's household.[16] Some of the powerful magnates appointed a fifth official, the *magister coquinae* or master of the kitchen. Amongst others, the archbishops of Salzburg,[17] the dukes of Limburg[18] and Merania,[19] the abbot of Berchtesgaden,[20] and the bishops of Regensburg,[21] Worms,[22] and Bamberg[23] did so. Gislebert of Mons claimed that the counts of Hainault had had six offices at the end of the eleventh century,[24] and the archbishops of Cologne and the bishops of Würzburg, who were also dukes, had six in the thirteenth.[25] The imperial household too had a master of the kitchen, the office enfeoffed to the *ministeriales* of Rothenburg and Nordenberg in Franconia. The *Sachsenspiegel* also preserved the notion that the offices which *ministeriales* ought to hold were those of seneschal, marshal, chamberlain, or butler.[26] The Reich-

---

[13] König, *Historia Welforum*, p. 4.   [14] Kluckhohn, pp. 206–8.

[15] See pp. 214, n. 30, 217, n. 44, 220, n. 59.

[16] MGC ii, 68, pp. 80f., 1219, 298, p. 412, 1230, 282, pp. 396f., 1223, 332, p. 443, 1240, 358, p. 465, 1250, and for Benediktbeuern, iii, 186, pp. 173f., 1278.

[17] Krausen, *Raitenhaslach*, 221, pp. 183f., 1255 and 243, pp. 199f., 1259.

[18] UB Niederrhein ii, 269, p. 139, 1242.

[19] Schlögl, *Dießen*, 36A, pp. 48–51, 1231.

[20] UB Salzburg iv, 21, p. 20, 1252.

[21] H.-P. Mai, *Die Traditionen, die Urkunden und das Älteste Urbarfragment des Stiftes Rohr 1133–1332*, QE, XXI (Munich, 1966), 12, pp. 156–8, 1209.

[22] H. Boos, *Urkundenbuch der Stadt Worms 627–1300* Quellen zur Geschichte der Stadt Worms. I (Berlin, 1886), 118, pp. 91f., 1213.

[23] Joetze, pp. 792f.   [24] Gislebert of Mons, pp. 10f.

[25] Cologne had a *magister coquinae* as well as the advocate, Wisplinghoff, *Siegburg*, 80, p. 172, 1205 and 90, p. 191, 1218; Würzburg had a *vicedominus*, Reimann, pp. 91–3, and a *scultetus curie*, Mon. Boica xxxvii, 308, p. 346, 1250 and 409, p. 473, 1277.

[26] Eckhardt, *Sachsenspiegel Lehnrecht*, pp. 81f; normally the household officers were not required to renew their titles upon the death of their lords, but all lesser offices fell vacant automatically, and were subject to new appointment and enfeoffment.

enau rules on military expeditions confected about 1160 claimed that such 'special officials' should get more than the other knights in stipends, raiment, and mounts.[27]

The hereditary titles do not in themselves equip us with much knowledge of their function and purpose. Painstaking researches have sometimes revealed the system, or lack of it, by which a group of *ministeriales* with household titles administered the territories of their lords.[28] When the bishops of Eichstätt appointed new men to their household offices towards the end of the thirteenth century and enfeoffed them with refurbished castles, each of them was made responsible, with almost identical functions, for administering a section of the episcopal possessions.[29] Much earlier, in the administration of imperial lands, Henry of Lautern was known successively as marshal, chamberlain, and butler without these changes making any perceptible difference to his exercise of office over Kaiserslautern and its estates.[30] Titles distinguished individuals rather than functions. In the first half of the thirteenth century, therefore, the marshal of Pappenheim, the butler of Winterstetten, the seneschal of Falkenstein, and the chamberlain of Münzenberg fulfilled similar administrative tasks in large portions of the imperial fisc in Bavaria, Swabia, the Rhineland, and Franconia respectively.

Surviving accounts, audits, cadastral surveys, books of fiefs, and other sources provide some information about these administrative offices. There is nothing to compare in Germany with the rich fiscal and judicial records of the Angevin and Capetian realms, but a few prominent imperial *ministeriales* did have notes taken down. They include Wernher of Bolanden's book of fiefs, originating before 1200,[31] the marshal of Pappenheim's survey of the Neuburg crown-lands about 1214,[32] a list of the imperial towns' tax-liability

---

[27] M G C i, 447, ch. 11, p. 663.

[28] H. Aubin, *Die Verwaltungsorganisation des Fürstentums Paderborn im Mittelalter* (Berlin and Leipzig, 1911), Spindler, *Anfänge*, pp. 50–7, 149–69, and Pötter, pp. 71–108.

[29] See my thesis, pp. 201–15, 261–78.

[30] M G C i, 303, p. 431, 1185, 326, p. 465, 1188, 342, p. 490, 1191, 345, p. 492, 1192, and K.-P. Westrich, 'Die Königspfalz Lautern im 12. und 13. Jahrhundert' in F.L. Wagner (ed.), *Ministerialität im Pfälzer Raum*, pp. 75–83.

[31] Metz, *SG*, pp. 52–76. A. Eckhardt, 'Das älteste Bolander Lehnbuch. Versuch einer Neudatierung', *AD* xxii (1976), 317–44, reckons the surviving version to be later in date.

[32] Kraft, *Urbar der Reichsmarschälle*, Metz, *SG*, pp. 77–93, and Weikmann, pp. 328–31.

for 1241,[33] Gerhard of Sinzig's war-account presented in 1242,[34] the advocate of Nuremberg's survey of crown-lands in his neighbourhood about 1300,[35] and the burgrave of Rheinfelden's accounts for 1303-6.[36] The first four of these were investigated, with related sources, by Wolfgang Metz, providing the best modern account of imperial *ministeriales* as officials in Germany, but he does not credit the Hohenstaufen dynasty with planning a standardized or centralized administration of imperial lands through their *ministeriales*.[37] What was done in each region of the German kingdom depended upon the variable nature of imperial estates and revenues there, and the personal skills or political standing of the *ministeriales* to whose charge the portions of the fisc were consigned.[38] Evidently King Rudolf (1273-91) was not impressed by what these men had achieved during the years of Hohenstaufen eclipse and of rival claimants to the throne after 1245. He launched a new policy of resuming the imperial fisc, offices were confiscated from *ministeriales*, and their commissions were given to members of the free-born nobility.[39]

Household offices remained prestigious and desirable, largely by virtue of the fiefs, incomes, and castles which went with them. When Bishop Hartmann of Augsburg, the last of his line, bequeathed the county of Dillingen with its lands and *ministeriales* to

[33] MGC iii, pp. 1-6, 1241, and Metz, *SG*, pp. 98-115. Possibly Conrad, butler of Winterstetten, or, according to Weinrich, p. 510, the chamberlains of Münzenberg had the list drawn up.

[34] MGC ii, 338, pp. 446f., 1242, and Metz, *SG*, pp. 116-21.

[35] MGC iii, 644, pp. 627-31 and UB Nürnberg 1073, pp. 632-7, *c.* 1300.

[36] MGC iv.2, 1204, pp. 1252-9, 1303-6, and A. Hessel, *Jahrbücher des Deutschen Reiches unter König Albrecht I. von Habsburg*, Jahrbücher der deutschen Geschichte (Munich, 1931), pp. 192f.

[37] Metz, *SG*, pp. 134-52. He also maintains, pp. 6-51, that the list of revenues in *Das Tafelgüterverzeichnis*, MGC i, 440, pp. 646-9 and Weinrich, pp. 188-90, was given its final form by a *ministerialis* working for Henry VI, possibly William of Aachen, in the 1180s. See his discussion of its prototypes in *Das Servitium Regis*, pp. 21-44, and the literature and controversies cited there.

[38] H. Niese, *Die Verwaltung des Reichsgutes im 13. Jahrhundert* (Innsbruck, 1905), pp. 168-209, 243-67, W. Kraft, 'Über Weißenburg und den Weißenburger Wald in ihren Beziehungen zu den Marschällen von Pappenheim', *Jahrbuch des Historischen Vereins für Mittelfranken* lxvi (1930), 145-74, H. Helbig, 'Verfügungen über Reichsgut im Pleißenland' in H. Beumann (ed.), *Festschrift für Walter Schlesinger*, vol. i, Mitteldeutsche Forschungen LXXIV.1 (Cologne and Vienna, 1973), pp. 273-85, and pp. 213, nn. 21, 24-8, 214, n. 30, 217, n. 44 below.

[39] T. Schön, 'Die Landvögte des Reiches in Ober- und Niederschwaben bis 1486', *MIöG* Ergänzungsband vi (1901), 280-92, and Kaiserswerth in MGC iii, 264, pp. 257f., 1280.

his see in 1258, he stipulated that 'amongst them, the more prominent [five families were named] who function as *ministeriales* we incorporate to the rightful participation in the four offices of our church'.[40]

Ministeriales *in other offices*

Apart from the privileged household places, the German magnates disposed of a variety of other appointments to their *ministeriales*.[41] In 1141 the bishop of Basel met Conrad III at Strasburg accompanied by eight of his officials: the four household officers, his *scultetus* or magistrate, toll-master, and mint-master, and the *vicedominus*,[42] whose administrative function was similar to that of the four household officers in their fiscal and territorial administrations. The town magistrate, usually called *scultetus* or *iudex*,[43] and the regional magistrate in the rural *Landgericht*, called *iudex provincialis* in the thirteenth century,[44] exercised functions which appear to have been as prestigious and profitable as those of household officer, *vicedominus*, or monastic advocate. The archbishops of Mainz evidently promoted the situations of *scultetus*, chamberlain, and *vicedominus* over all others in their household and territorial administration in the twelfth century. A *vicedominus*, chamberlain, and *scultetus* for the Rhineland possessions resided in Mainz itself,[45] another *vicedominus* at Aschaffenburg supervised the see's lands in the Main valley, while the *vicedominus* at Rusteberg Castle and the *scultetus* at Erfurt were responsible for the Thuringian and other outlying archiepiscopal possessions.[46] In the

[40] U B Wirtemberg v, 1512, pp. 278-81, 1258.

[41] Kluckhohn, pp. 219-37. Not all officials were *ministeriales*; M G D Frederick I, 7, p. 14, 1152 for the advocate at Soest who was a *liber*, Tr. Passau 1312, p. 416, 1220-40 for a Passau chamberlain who was a *censualis*, and Mon. Boica xxxvii, 353, p. 404, 1262 for the Würzburg *buticularius* and chamberlain who were *cives*.

[42] M G D Conrad III, 57, pp. 96-101, 1141, and secular *vicedomini* who were *ministeriales* at Hildesheim, U B Hildesheim i, 150, p. 143, 1092, at Worms, Boos, *Worms*, 63, p. 55, 1127, at Regensburg, U B Land ob der Enns ii, 90, p. 127, 1107 and 115, p. 174, *c.* 1130, and at Eichstätt, Reg. Eichstätt 1521, pp. 475 f., 1313.

[43] Reimann, pp. 118-24 on Würzburg's *scultetus*, and Mon. Boica xxxvii, 235, pp. 255 f., 1233 for the bishop's *scultetus* of Mellrichstadt.

[44] Spindler, *Anfänge*, pp. 152-4, 165 f., M G C iii, 345, p. 330, 1283, and p. 193, n. 69 below.

[45] U B Mainz ii, 603, pp. 993-5, 1194.

[46] Stimming, *Entstehung*, pp. 52-9, and B. Witte, *Herrschaft und Land im Rheingau*, Mainzer Abhandlungen zur mittleren und neueren Geschichte, III (Meisenheim, 1959), pp. 95-111, 228 f., on the archiepiscopal *vicedomini*.

1180s the Thuringian *vicedominus* and *scultetus* were brothers, the latter also being the archbishop's marshal.[47] In the 1190s a similar arrangement prevailed in another Thuringian family of Mainz's knights, the *ministeriales* of Apolda, one of whom was the *vicedominus* while his brothers were the archbishop's chamberlain and butler.[48]

Tolls, mints, and markets were supervised by *ministeriales*,[49] and so was much of the manorial substructure under the titles of provost, advocate, official,[50] or bailiff. *Villici* or bailiffs governed manors, and more often were serfs rather than *ministeriales*. Yet the latter were quite frequently appointed, particularly in Saxony. Some time before 1176 one of the abbot of Corvey's *ministeriales* called Herenfrid 'was the first man of knightly family to administer that manor [Haversforde], which previously had always been administered by serfs'.[51] In 1195 discord arose between the see of Minden and the *ministeriales* 'who are officials or bailiffs of the bishop' over what they were obliged to pay yearly from the manors they administered for the church. An imperial enactment subjected them to proof of their estimates, if necessary, by the ordeal of hot iron.[52] In the thirteenth century the abbesses of Herford with their entourage sometimes went on tours of inspection of their Westphalian manors. They met the bailiffs, several of whom were *ministeriales*, were entertained by them, and transacted legal and fiscal business with them before moving on to the next manor.[53]

Conrad III's magistrate and advocate at Aachen, Dietrich of Düren, was also called *villicus de Aquisgrani* or bailiff of Aachen,[54]

[47] UB Mainz ii, 467, pp. 762 f., 1184 and 519, p. 856, 1189.

[48] Ibid. 570, pp. 940-2, 1192 and 578, pp. 953-5, 1193.

[49] UB Wirtemberg i, 291, p. 374, 1127 for the Worms *thelonearius*, Tr. Passau 543, p. 205, 1136 for the Passau *monetarius*, UB Mainz ii, 318, p. 545, 1169 for the Erfurt *magister fori*, Boehmer and Lau, *Frankfurt*, 33, p. 17, 1194 for Cuno of Münzenberg's appointment to the imperial mint at Frankfurt, and Mai, *Rohr*, 12, pp. 156-8, 1209 for the Regensburg *theolonarius*.

[50] Tr. Regensburg 792, p. 372, 1135 and 804, p. 380, 1141 for the *miles* and *ministerialis* Eggibert of Hexenagger, who was the abbot of St Emmeram's *prepositus* and *officialis*; and Mon. Carinthia i, 193, pp. 156 f., *c.* 1156 and UB Münster 193, p. 105, 1223, where *ministeriales* were advocates over serfs.

[51] CD Westphalia ii, 380, pp. 132 f., 1176.

[52] MGC i, 366, pp. 515 f., 1195; for the Minden *ministeriales*, von Heinemann, *Anhalt*, 617, p. 458, 1182.

[53] Franz, *Quellen*, 149, pp. 384-92, 1290.

[54] MGD Conrad III, 5 f., pp. 11-13, 1138, 44, p. 74, 1140, 64, p. 113, 1141, 120, p. 215, 1144, and D. Flach, *Untersuchungen zur Verfassung und Verwaltung des*

and there were other imperial bailiffs in the Rhineland at Boppard, Andernach, and Remagen.[55] The extensive procuracy of the imperial fisc along the Rhine and Mosel exercised for Frederick II by Gerhard of Sinzig was also called his *baiolatio* or bailiwick.[56] The title of advocate recurred amongst *ministeriales* who looked after their lords' possessions. The most prominent in Germany were the advocates of Weida, a prolific dynasty which supervised vast imperial estates in the east in the thirteenth century.[57] They ranked with the officials of the household as the most powerful *ministeriales* of the empire. At Cologne the advocate outranked all other offices, a hereditary fief in the Heppendorf family from 1169: 'Of all the *ministeriales* of St Peter, none may pronounce judgement in place of the archbishop save the advocate of Cologne', who was remunerated for his labours by the revenues of twelve manors.[58]

The title of advocate also applied to noblemen with protective jurisdiction over the monastic and cathedral churches of Germany, and their manorial possessions. As we have seen, *ministeriales* became advocates of monasteries, some of which they had founded themselves.[59] In the 1130s Lothar III regulated the advocacies of St Mary at Brunswick and of Königslutter, which belonged to him and his heirs. He decreed that these offices would be administered by imperial *ministeriales* without any hereditary claim as vassals, who would hold the court three times a year and receive entitlements out of the incomes of the houses.[60] Before 1219 the bishop of Halberstadt enfeoffed his *ministerialis* Dietrich of Reveningen as advocate of Kaltenborn, and in 1238 the abbess of Hohenholte was confirmed in her right of choosing her advocate amongst the bishop of Münster's *ministeriales*, who would not have the standing of hereditary vassal.[61] Before 1252 the bishop of Speyer's *ministerialis*

Aachener Reichsgutes, Veröffentlichungen des Max-Planck-Instituts für Geschichte, XLVI (Göttingen, 1976), pp. 244–80.

[55] Metz, *SG*, p. 38; other towns were under the protection of imperial *ministeriales* without a particular title, C D Salem 139, pp. 176–8, 1225, and U B Wirtemberg iv, 1178, p. 246, 1251 and v, 1598, p. 359, 1260.

[56] M G C ii, 55, pp. 66 f., 1216 and 307, pp. 421 f., 1231.

[57] U B Weida 33, p. 12, 1193–1280, 66, pp. 31 f., 1237, and 252, pp. 122 f., 1290.

[58] Weinrich, p. 270, Pötter, pp. 71–85, and UB Niederrhein i, 434, p. 304, 1169.

[59] See pp. 151, n. 69, 160, nn. 128–30.

[60] M G D Lothar III, 67, pp. 103–5, 1134 and 74, pp. 113–16, 1135. The Augsburg *ministerialis* and chamberlain Arnolf was temporary advocate of the cathedral church there; Vock, *Augsburg*, 33, p. 16, 1162.

[61] U B Halberstadt i, 511, pp. 457–61, 1219 and U B Münster 350, p. 190, 1238.

Henry of Enzberg had acquired the advocacy of Maulbronn Abbey in pledge for £330 from the Cistercians themselves. When he was paid back, he surrendered all claim 'to the entire advocacies belonging to that monastery, with all their rights, customs, renders, services, forfeits, taxes or whatever is due, whether over the abbey or over the granges and manors of those brothers'.[62] In other cases *ministeriales* were appointed to deal not with the economic or fiscal but with the legal business of a given house. In 1215 Frederick II decreed that court-cases in which Klosterroth in Swabia became involved should be settled by the seneschal of Waldburg as judge, and in 1231 similar arrangements were made by which the burgrave of Kaiserswerth would deal with cases in which the abbess of Essen's people became involved.[63]

Ministeriales *as magistrates and in legal business*

Except in a very few instances,[64] *ministeriales* were not debarred by their personal unfreedom from administering the law in all its forms, imperial and civil law, feudal law, urban and mercantile custom, the rules of campaign and camps, the law of advocacy over the Church, and the rules of *Landfrieden*, the peace-keeping truces and associations. Under Frederick II the chief justiciars of the imperial court in Germany were free-born noblemen,[65] although for generations *ministeriales* had delivered opinions and approved and passed sentences in the imperial court, in general cases[66] as well as those concerning *ministeriales*. In 1227 the bishop of Liège asked in the royal court that the count of Flanders' suit against him over the margraviate of Namur should be judged by the imperial *ministeriales*, who duly took counsel with the princes present and delivered sentence.[67] In a notable case on feudal custom, the abbey of St Remigius at Rheims complained to Conrad III's court at Frankfurt in 1149 about usurpations of its German

---

[62] U B Wirtemberg iv, 1231, p. 300 and 1237, pp. 305 f., 1252.

[63] Ibid. iii, 574, p. 25, 1215, and U B Niederrhein ii, 174, pp. 89 f., 1231.

[64] e.g. M GC ii, 279, ch. 1, p. 393, 1222 and 196, ch. 20, p. 245, 1235.

[65] U B Wirtemberg iii, 876, p. 374, 1236, and Wartmann, *St. Gallen*, 889, pp. 103 ff., 1244.

[66] Krieger, pp. 419-24, Gislebert of Mons, p. 254, 1190, and M GC i, 367, p. 516, 1195.

[67] *Aegidii Aureaevallensis Gesta Episcoporum Leodiensium*, M GS, XXV, p. 121, and *Annales Floreffienses*, M GS, XVI, p. 626.

possessions by the *ministerialis* Albert of Cusel, who had refused to appear in Rheims to answer the charges against him. The king therefore asked his *ministerialis* Conrad of Hagen 'what the rule of law held concerning this controversy. He replied, with everyone assenting, that all vassals, whether free men or *ministeriales*, must answer in their lord's principal domicile' to accusations of this nature.[68]

Everywhere in Germany *ministeriales* acted as judges, commissioners, and arbitrators for their own lords, for the Church, for the emperor, for neighbouring princes, and for their fellow knights, as well as exercising their own manorial jurisdiction over their lands, villages, and serfs. In the twelfth and thirteenth century the more formidable of the territorial princes organized their jurisdiction over homicide, theft, rape, pillage, and other serious offences into regional magistracies known as *Landgerichte*, and in these jurisdictions their *ministeriales* acted as judges and advisers.[69] As duke of Austria, King Ottokar of Bohemia required his *ministeriales* to attend the *Landgericht* 'to help the court'.[70] If the *Landgerichte* were rural in character, the larger towns had their own magistrates, most of whom were *ministeriales*, such as the archbishop of Mainz's *sculteti* at Mainz, Fritzlar, and Erfurt.[71] In 1225 Bishop Engelbert of Osnabrück agreed with his townsmen that their magistrate would be a *ministerialis* chosen by him and approved by them.[72]

As knights, *ministeriales* were also judges of their peers in their lord's household in its guise as a feudal court,[73] and as vassals they also delivered opinions and sentences and settled disputes about

[68] MGD Conrad III, 210, pp. 377-9, 1149. Suit of court to the lord's house was confirmed for Lotharingia in MGC ii, 279, chs. 2-3, p. 393, 1222.

[69] Mon. Boica xxxvii, 86-8, pp. 50-5, dated to 1140 and 178, p. 181, 1211, UB Land ob der Enns ii, 378, pp. 547-50, 1212, Busley, *Neustift*, 26, p. 102, before 1214, UB Salzburg iii, 861, pp. 402 f., 1231, and see Spindler, *Handbuch*, vol. ii, pp. 59-64 and Hirsch, pp. 158-72, 185-203. On the Westphalian forms of these jurisdictions, see p. 199, n. 108.

[70] MGC ii, 440, ch. 26, p. 607, 1256-61.

[71] UB Mainz ii, 467, pp. 762 f., 1184, 603, pp. 993-5, 1194, and 647, pp. 1052-4, 1196. One of the victims of the Erfurt disaster of 1184, when the building in which the royal court had assembled suddenly collapsed, precipitating several princes of the empire into a sewer, was 'ministerialis et quidam civitatis officialis, qui vribode dicitur'; *Chronicon Montis Sereni*, MGS, XXIII, p. 159.

[72] UB Osnabrück ii, 196, pp. 146 f., 1225.

[73] Tr. Regensburg 899, p. 440, 1169, UB Hildesheim iii, 604, pp. 313 f., 1282, and Joetze, p. 564, 1176 (Bamberg *ministeriales* in Carinthia).

fiefs granted out even to counts, free lords, and free-born knights.[74] The imperial enactment of 1222 on feudal custom in Lotharingia had stated that 'in feudal law every enfeoffed *ministerialis* can pass judgment equally over fiefs of free noblemen and of *ministeriales*, though not over fiefs of princes',[75] although that is what the bishop of Liège asked them to do in 1227. In a more typical case the archbishop of Cologne in 1279 commissioned three of his *ministeriales*, the butler of Ahr, the burgrave of Lechenich, and the marshal of Westphalia, to settle the claims to Müllenark Castle, a Cologne fief, between two free-born nobles.[76]

If the *Landgerichte*, town-courts, and magnate households as feudal courts might meet regularly and frequently, *ministeriales* were also employed as commissioners, judges, and assessors in *ad hoc* courts of investigation or arbitration set up for some specific purpose. The arbitrations proved quite effective as an alternative to the inconvenience and destructiveness of feuds. Consisting of equal numbers of *ministeriales* representing the contending parties, the court usually had an impartial chairman, a churchman or a vassal from another retinue, and the place and date for delivery of judgement were laid down.[77] It was in this way that the *ministeriales* of the bishop of Eichstätt and the duke of Bavaria, under the chairmanship of Marshal Henry of Pappenheim, divided up Count Gebhard of Hirschberg's inheritance between them at Gaimersheim in 1305,[78] a complicated arrangement which awarded allodial possession to Eichstätt but the criminal jurisdiction to Bavaria, an agreement which lasted in nearly all its details until 1803.

The records of investigative commissions show up the variety of work undertaken by *ministeriales*, and the influence they exercised in local affairs. In the earlier twelfth century, when Bishop Otto of Bamberg instituted the rights of his proprietary monasteries at Osterhofen, Ering, and Asbach over their manors and serfs, he sent a commission of *ministeriales* to settle what the manorial revenues,

---

[74] UB Osnabrück ii, 144, pp. 105f., 1222 and 171, pp. 126f., 1223, and UB Mittelrhein iii, 609, p. 466, 1238-9.

[75] MGC ii, 279, ch. 1, p. 393, 1222.

[76] UB Niederrhein ii, 731, pp. 431 f., 1279.

[77] H. Krause, *Die geschichtliche Entwicklung des Schiedsgerichtswesens in Deutschland* (Berlin, 1930), pp. 2-39, and Mon. Boica xlix, 232, pp. 359-61, 1296 and 362, pp. 558-60, 1305.

[78] Wittmann, *Wittelsbach*, vol. ii, 222, pp. 134-41, 1305.

services, and jurisdictions were to be.[79] In 1157 Frederick Barbarossa instructed five Thuringian *ministeriales* to visit Pforta, to protect the monastic property from its oppressors and to survey its extent.[80] In 1188, when Count-Palatine Rudolf of Tübingen wished to acquire particular lands from the see of Speyer for the benefit of a new monastic foundation, the bishop sent ten of his *ministeriales* to see that the lands offered in exchange 'were better and more useful' than those to be surrendered by the bishop.[81] In 1191 Bishop Dietrich of Gurk sent a deputation of *ministeriales* to his father, Rudolf of Albeck, which successfully persuaded him to give up all the family possessions to the see, since his other heir had died on the Third Crusade. In exchange, the *ministeriales* assigned him a life-income from episcopal revenues, and the huge manor at Wolkenburg, which he was forbidden to pledge or to subinfeudate.[82] In 1239 a long dispute over woodlands between the abbots of Isny and Kempten was settled by a commission of *ministeriales* and free-born nobles under two judges, Conrad, butler of Winterstetten, and Ottoberthold, seneschal of Waldburg, *ministeriales* of the imperial household.[83] About 1260 the bishop of Passau instructed his *ministeriales* and the townsmen of Gallneukirchen to settle the laws of the town and to decide how often the magistrates should visit it,[84] and in 1276 the duke of Brunswick sent his marshal, Burchard of Asseburg, and his advocate, Godfrey of Vorsfelde, to adjudicate a dispute about property between an abbey and a knight.[85]

Sometimes these commissions were given a more than temporary status, such as those set up to supervise the peace-treaty between the count of Hirschberg and the duke of Bavaria in the 1290s.[86] In 1245 the bishops of Osnabrück and Münster drew up a treaty renewable every five years, between which epochs a committee of six

[79] Geier, *Asbach*, 8, pp. 94-7, 1170-7, where these *iura* were restored; A. Haverkamp, 'Das Bambergische Hofrecht für den niederbayerischen Hochstiftsbesitz', *ZBLG* xxx (1967), 423-506.

[80] MGD Frederick I, 178, p. 301, 1157. His grandson asked the *buticularius* of Nuremberg to do the same for Speinshart Abbey in 1235, Huillard-Bréholles, *Dipl. Friderici II.*, iv.2, pp. 783 f.

[81] UB Wirtemberg ii, 454 f., pp. 252-4, 1188.

[82] Mon. Carinthia i, 351, p. 262, 1191.

[83] UB Wirtemberg iii, 936 f., pp. 440-2, 1239.

[84] Keutgen, *Urkunden*, 161B, p. 200, *c.* 1260.

[85] UB Hildesheim iii, 455, pp. 213 f., 1276.

[86] Wittmann, *Wittelsbach*, vol. ii, 189, pp. 7-12, 1293.

ministeriales would endeavour to arbitrate in armed feuds.[87] In 1273, when Count Otto of Tecklenburg was appointed governor of the see of Münster during its vacancy, he was required to consult a council for diocesan affairs consisting of seven canons, one count, and five *ministeriales*.[88] In 1291 King Rudolf set up an arbitration court for cases involving the abbey and town of Weissenburg in Alsace. Fourteen townsmen would, when necessary, meet the abbot, convent, and seven of his *ministeriales*.[89]

Considerable knowledge of the law was expected of those *ministeriales* who regularly offered counsel as vassals to their lords and who possessed their own manorial jurisdictions, as well as functioning as magistrates of the empire, the towns, and the *Landgerichte*, and as advocates of the Church, as arbitrators, and as guardians of *Landfrieden*.[90] Another function was to witness charters, since worthy witnesses as well as seals conferred authenticity.[91] In a largely illiterate society, their memories might assist against future fraud; 'These are the witnesses who heard these things done according to Bavarian custom',[92] and in 1223, for example, more than two dozen of Margrave Henry of Istria's *ministeriales* watched his seal affixed to a charter of donation to Diessen Abbey.[93] *Ministeriales* also acted as sworn deputies when lands or serfs or other possessions were transferred between contracting parties, to see that the transaction was actually carried out once the written deed had been drawn up.[94] As experienced landowners they were entrusted with further tasks, such as assessing incomes and land-values, and acting as trustees in administering legacies.[95] In 1181

[87] U B Osnabrück ii, 464, pp. 367 f., 1245.

[88] U B Münster 936, pp. 485 f., 1273.

[89] M G C iii, 465, pp. 451 f., 1291.

[90] Kluckhohn, pp. 51-9, and Reimann, pp. 75-89.

[91] U B Niederrhein i, 328, pp. 218 f., 1138 has 'de familia beati petri legalibus et boni testimonii viris'.

[92] *Ex Libello Memoriali Pruveningensi*, M G S, XV.2, p. 1075, and almost the same phrase in Geier, *Asbach*, 6, pp. 91-3, 1171.

[93] Schlögl, *Dießen*, 11, pp. 117 f., 1223. When the Salzburg chancery issued the same charter twice by mistake, setting the monks of Formbach and Reichersberg about each others' ears, the Formbach version was quashed 'per eorum [the Salzburg clerks'] contradictiones et ministerialium nostrorum publicam reclamationem'; U B Salzburg ii, 248, pp. 357-9, *c.* 1146.

[94] Mon. Boica xlix, 11, pp. 29 f., 1158, 33, pp. 67 f., 1219, and Uhl, *Weihenstephan*, 282, pp. 228 f., 1166-72.

[95] Geier, *Asbach*, 3, pp. 85-7, 1163, Reg. Eichstätt 446, p. 141, 1169, and Mon. Boica xlix, 25, pp. 55-7, after 1195 and 326, pp. 501 f., 1303.

Archbishop Siegfried of Bremen commissioned one of his *minister-iales*, the advocate Alard, to supervise the sale of waste land for colonization;[96] in 1220 Frederick II instructed one of his Swabian officials, Bernard of Ravensburg, to survey woods for transfer to Weissenau Abbey;[97] and in 1243 Burgrave Gernand of Kaiser-swerth was asked to oversee the removal of Düssern Abbey to a new site.[98]

Ministeriales were regularly employed in the system of surety-ship, by which legal agreements of all kinds, as well as exchanges, pledges and purchases of real property, were guaranteed. The rules of suretyship might vary in different times and places in medieval Germany,[99] but it was accepted that one of the duties of knight-hood was to offer surety for lords in their more significant transac-tions.[100] *Ministeriales* also offered the service to their fellow-knights, should it be required. Generally the charter recording the transaction stated which knights had been appointed as *fideiussores* or sureties, as well as the time-limit by which they had sworn that their principals would fulfil the terms. Should the limit be exceeded, then they were held responsible, and were liable to confinement as oath-breakers until the terms were fulfilled by themselves or their principals. In effect they committed themselves as hostages for good faith, 'bound under peril of imprisonment according to the com-mon custom of the land' in order to 'make payment according to the custom of suretyship in the place stipulated'.[101] Since these

---

[96] Lappenberg, *Hamburg*, 249, pp. 226 f., 1181.

[97] Huillard-Bréholles, *Dipl. Friderici II.*, i.2, pp. 724-6, 1220.

[98] U B Niederrhein ii, 277, p. 144, 1243.

[99] F. Beyerle, 'Die Ursprung der Bürgschaft. Ein Deutungsversuch vom german-ischen Rechte her', *Z R G G A* xlvii (1927), 567-645, W. Ogris, 'Die persönlichen Sicherheiten im Spätmittelalter', *Z R G G A* lxxxii (1965), 140-89, and E. Kaufmann, 'Bürgschaft und Einlager im spätmittelalterlichen fränkischen Recht' in *Les Sûretés personnelles*, vol. ii Recueils de la Société Jean Bodin pour l'histoire comparative des institutions, XXIX (Brussels, 1971), pp. 653-72.

[100] e.g. in pledging their castles; *Chronicon Hildesheimense*, M G S, VII, pp. 857 f., 1187 for the counts of Hallermund to Hildesheim, U B Salzburg ii, 465, pp. 631-3, 1189 for the counts of Bogen to Salzburg.

[101] Mon. Boica xlix, 298, pp. 460 f., 1301 and 312, p. 484, 1302. The arrange-ments are explained in Latin, ibid. 109, pp. 163-5, 1280 about repaying debts, and in 312, pp. 481-5, 1302 about selling a castle, in Latin and German in 295 and 297 f., pp. 454-61, 1301 about selling another castle, and in German in 190, pp. 298-300, 1293, 232, pp. 359-61 and 235, pp. 365-8, 1296 about keeping the peace. In Reg. Eichstätt 1547 f., pp. 483 f., 1314 and 1564 f., p. 487, 1315 the sureties had to pay up for the bishop of Eichstätt, and in 1569, p. 488, 1315 a knight was recompensed for this.

commitments were most commonly made for financial transactions with terminal dates a few weeks or months ahead, the *ministeriales* were afforded some latitude for seeing that payment was made on time. They were also required to offer security in more serious circumstances. In 1236, when Bishop Liudolf of Münster negotiated peace between Count Otto of Tecklenburg and Bishop Conrad of Osnabrück, the former was obliged to hand over twenty *ministeriales* to the arbitrator as security for his future good behaviour.[102] They would be liable to imprisonment if he broke the terms of the treaty.

Counts, burgraves, and castellans

The comital title chiefly distinguished the territorial dynasties which had not secured the rank of duke, margrave, or landgrave, but the thirteenth-century regional magistracies were also quite often described as *comeciae* or counties because they were jurisdictions.[103] Of the *ministeriales* who presided over them, a few were called counts, though the title of *Landrichter* was more common in southern Germany. The *ministeriales* who were the archbishop of Mainz's magistrates over the Rheingau were always called counts, their hereditary fief the *iurisdictio seu comecia in Rinegowe* or 'the jurisdiction and county of the Rheingau'.[104]

In the later twelfth century the Saxon *ministerialis* Liudolf of Peine, who held the county of Peine from the bishops of Hildesheim, was also called count,[105] although the seneschals of Wolfenbüttel, who succeeded him, were not. Duke Henry the Lion's appointees to the Saxon counties of Stade, Lübeck, and the Leinegau were not ascribed the comital title,[106] nor were the chamberlains of Münzenberg for their county in the Wetterau, which was an

[102] U B Osnabrück ii, 350 f., pp. 270-3, 1236.
[103] For details of what they consisted in, see Wittmann, *Wittelsbach*, vol. ii, 204, pp. 72-6, 1295 and 208, pp. 88-92, 1296.
[104] Witte, pp. 25-39, U B Mainz i, 519, p. 425, 1124 and ii, 339, pp. 575 f., 1171, and C D Nassau 395, pp. 274 f., 1223.
[105] Jordan, *Urkunden Heinrichs des Löwen*, 45, p. 65, 1160, and *Annales Stederburgenses*, M G S, XVI, p. 213, 1176, and p. 218, 1187.
[106] Hildebrand, pp. 382-93, and Metz, *SG*, p. 138. Between 1095 and 1135 the margraves of Stade entrusted Stade county to an unfree dependent known as Frederick, *comes* of Stade; *Annalista Saxo*, M G S, VI, pp. 724, 729, and *Annales Stadenses*, M G S, XVI, pp. 319-23.

imperial fief.[107] In Westphalia the *ministeriales* placed over the regional magistracies were regularly called counts,[108] preserving the tradition that the comital title referred to judicial office long before it applied to the territorial possessions of the magnates.

In Bavaria too, *ministeriales* were enfeoffed with comital jurisdictions, without adopting the title of count in person.[109] In the most striking example, the ducal *ministerialis* Siegfried of Fraunberg inherited the county of Haag in 1246, and was confirmed in his authority by the emperor, without reference to the dukes, to hear cases about allods, inheritances, and fiefs, and to judge brigands arrested for breaking the *Landfriede*.[110] The Fraunbergs remained counsellors high in favour with the dukes of Bavaria, but their own county was a separate jurisdictional enclave.

The military defence of a large town was frequently entrusted to a count called a burgrave, latinized as *burcgravius, urbis praefectus,* or *comes civitatis*.[111] These urban counts were often drawn from the free-born aristocracy, men who already sported comital titles, such as the burgraves of Würzburg, who were counts of Henneberg, of Mainz, counts of Rieneck, and of Nuremberg, counts of

[107] Boehmer and Lau, *Frankfurt*, 44, pp. 21 f., 1216 and Kropat, pp. 95 f. The imperial *ministeriales* of Wolfskehlen similarly exercised the county of Haselberg, Metz, *SG*, pp. 67 f.

[108] Eight such counties were listed in 1225 in the diocese of Osnabrück, U B Osnabrück ii, 200, pp. 151 f., and see the varied terminology in 128, p. 95, 1220, 427, p. 335, 1243, iii, 107 f., pp. 80 f., 1254, 465, p. 318, 1272, and iv, 107, p. 74, 1283. On these jurisdictions, F. Philippi, 'Zur Gerichtsverfassung Sachsens im hohen Mittelalter', *MIöG* xxxv (1914), 250-9, A.K. Hömberg, *Grafschaft, Freigrafschaft, Gografschaft*, Schriften der Historischen Kommission für Westfalen, I (Münster, 1949), W. Metz, 'Studien zur Grafschaftsverfassung Althessens im Mittelalter', *Z R G G A* lxxi (1954), 167-208, H. Dannenbauer, 'Freigrafschaften und Freigerichte' in *Grundlagen*, pp. 309-28, and W. Schlesinger, 'Bemerkungen zum Problem der westfälischen Grafschaften und Freigrafschaften' in *Beiträge zur deutschen Verfassungsgeschichte des Mittelalters*, vol. ii (Göttingen, 1963), pp. 213-32.

[109] Spindler, *Anfänge*, pp. 122 f., for Dietrich of Schleibing by Duke Henry the Lion, Helbig and Weinrich, *Ostsiedlung*, vol. ii, 127, p. 480, 1230 for Arnold of Rodeneck by Count Albert of Tirol, and Wittmann, *Wittelsbach*, vol. i, 54, pp. 128-31, 1254 for four Salzburg *ministeriales* by Dukes Louis and Henry of Bavaria.

[110] Huillard-Bréholles, *Dipl. Friderici II.*, vi.1, pp. 417 f., 1246, and Spindler, *Anfänge*, p. 122 n. 1.

[111] U B Mainz ii, 50, pp. 96-8, 1144 and 250, p. 453, 1160, and Mon. Boica xxxvii, 76-158, pp. 37-156, 1115-99. On burgraves, S. Rietschel, *Das Burggrafenamt und die hohe Gerichtsbarkeit in den deutschen Bischofsstädten*, Untersuchungen zur Geschichte der deutschen Stadtverfassung, I (Leipzig, 1905), and K.A. Eckhardt, 'Präfekt und Burggraf', *Z R G G A* xlvi (1926), 163-205.

Zollern.[112] Sometimes the burgrave's powers were delegated to a *ministerialis*, called *subcomes* or sub-count at Cologne, *vicecomes* or viscount at Würzburg.[113] In other cases the burgraves were themselves *ministeriales*, as at Hersfeld,[114] Minden,[115] Nijmegen,[116] Strasburg,[117] Halberstadt,[118] Dortmund,[119] and elsewhere. In early twelfth-century Trier the archbishop's *ministerialis* Louis *de ponte* was described as 'burgrave, that is prefect of the city, belonging to the retinue of the church'. By degrees this able man had risen from chamberlain and *vicedominus* to burgrave, custodian of the archbishop's palace, and advocate of the cathedral church, but his power was broken by Archbishop Albero in the 1130s.[120] In somewhat similar circumstances the abbot of Corvey's seneschal Rabno usurped the office of burgrave of Corvey before 1150.[121] Not all town-commandants were designated burgrave. Small towns were quite often entrusted to *ministeriales* called magistrate or captain, with both military and juridical responsibilities.[122]

More often the *ministeriales* called burgraves were castellans assigned the command of a castle, not an entire town. In 1289, for example, the archbishop of Mainz mentioned that his *ministerialis*

[112] H. Parigger, 'Das Würzburger Burggrafenamt', *Mainfränkisches Jahrbuch für Geschichte und Kunst* xxxi (1979), 9-31, W. Spielberg, 'Die Herkunft der ältesten Burggrafen von Nürnberg', *MIöG* xliii (1929), 117-23, G. Pfeiffer, 'Comicia burcgravie in Nurenberg', *Jahrbuch für fränkische Landesforschung* xi-xii (1953), 45-52, and other free-born burgraves in P. Jaffé, *Monumenta Corbeiensia*, Bibliotheca Rerum Germanicarum, i (Berlin, 1864), 343, pp. 475-7, 1151, and Israël and Möllenberg, *Magdeburg*, 258, pp. 326f., 1145 and 298, pp. 371-3, 1159.
[113] UB Niederrhein i, 399, p. 276, 1159, Reimann, pp. 122, 216f., and Mon. Boica xxxvii, 113, p. 96, 1170.
[114] CD Saxony ii, 149, p. 107, 1141.
[115] CD Westphalia ii, 379, p. 132, 1176.
[116] Metz, *SG*, pp. 35, 38 and note 151; also at Andernach in UB Mittelrhein i, 466, p. 526, 1129.
[117] Reg. Straßburg i, 707, p. 375, 1199 and 726, p. 380, 1201.
[118] UB Halberstadt ii, 842, pp. 122f., 1251.
[119] UB Niederrhein ii, 559, p. 327, 1265.
[120] *Gesta Alberonis Archiepiscopis auctore Balderico*, MGS, VIII, pp. 243-60, and K. Schulz, *Ministerialität und Bürgertum in Trier. Untersuchungen zur rechtlichen und sozialen Gliederung der Trierer Bürgerschaft*, Rheinisches Archiv, LXVI (Bonn, 1968), pp. 29-32.
[121] MGD Conrad III, 221, pp. 390-4, 1150.
[122] These duties were mentioned in the letter-collection kept for the Austrian *ministerialis* Kadolt of Wehing when he was captain of Laa, 1262-4; Weltin, *Die Laaer Briefsammlung*, 33, p. 110 has '... civitatem suam Lâ nobis commiserit ad hoc, ut divitibus et pauperibus in ea manentibus iura sua debeamus generaliter conservare, specialius tamen nostris servitoribus alas tenemur expandere protectionis'.

Frederick of Rüdesheim had been installed *in burggravium et officia-tum castri nostri Scarpenstein*, or 'in the burgraviate and office of our castle at Scharfenstein'.[123] The archbishop of Cologne's prin-cipal castellans were called burgraves,[124] and so was the comman-dant of the strongest imperial fortress in the Rhineland, at Tri-fels.[125] Some of these *ministeriales* might be termed burgraves or castellans indifferently,[126] and another title for castellan was *mag-ister* or master,[127] possibly in imitation of the Teutonic Order's practice.

As castellans the *ministeriales* performed the fundamental task of holding together the scattered jurisdictions, communications, towns, villages, estates, forests, advocacies, and all the manorial possessions and incomes of their lords, the basis, in short, of the territorial principalities, some of which were to survive as indepen-dent authorities as late as 1918. It has been estimated that over twenty thousand castles were put up in medieval Germany,[128] an ambitious strategic enterprise representing a massive capital outlay accumulated from the manorial economy. In this undertaking the *ministeriales* were wholly involved since their inception as Ger-many's knighthood in the eleventh century. Without these castles garrisoned and commanded by *ministeriales*,[129] which gave the medieval empire its typical political landscape, Germany could hardly have been contrived into the congeries of dynastic and ecclesiastical dominions which achieved virtual state-sovereignty in 1648.

Were ministeriales *competent administrators?*

There are plentiful indications that, as officials, the *ministeriales* cheated their lords, abused their offices, and oppressed the people

[123] CD Nassau 1095, p. 648, 1289.   [124] Pötter, p. 114.
[125] Boos, *Worms*, 204, p. 143, 1242.
[126] UB Salzburg i, 317, p. 737, 1196-1214 and 457, 459, pp. 500f., 1199-1200.
[127] Mon. Boica xxxvii, 409, p. 473, 1277, Krühne, *Mansfeld*, 30, p. 350, 1292, and Reg. Eichstätt 1264, p. 391, 1303.
[128] C. Tillmann, *Lexikon der deutschen Burgen und Schlösser* (4 vols., Stuttgart, 1957-61), H. Ebner, 'Entwicklung und Rechtsverhältnisse der mittelalterlichen Burg', *Zeitschrift des Historischen Vereines für Steiermark* lxi (1970), 28, and H. Patze (ed.), *Die Burgen im deutschen Sprachraum. Ihre rechts- und verfassungsgeschichtliche Be-deutung*, VF, XIX.1-2 (Sigmaringen, 1976).
[129] On the connection of castles and territorial lordship, Klewitz, *Hildesheim*, pp. 29-40, J. Prinz, pp. 108-27, Reimann, pp. 129-34, and my thesis, pp. 201-19, 261-78.

committed to their charge. In 1062, when the huge imperial manor of Forchheim was taken away from Henry III's favoured *minister-ialis* Otnand of Eschenau and given to the cathedral church of Bamberg, the dean wrote to the bishop to tell him how the people were overjoyed, and likened the *ministerialis's* oppressions to 'an iron furnace in which that monster Otnand used to cook them'.[130] As we have seen, Balderic of Trier claimed that in the 1120s Burgrave Louis *de ponte*, having accumulated all the important secular offices in his hands, usurped the entire incomes of the archbishop, whose household was kept on short rations, and in a state of complete subjection in the palace.[131] Upon his accession Bishop Conrad of Hildesheim also discovered that his four household officers had overstepped their authority by appointing sub-officials of their own, and in arranging everything to do with the possessions of the see without any reference to the bishop.[132] A little later he decided to abolish the office of seneschal altogether, 'particularly because he had endured great losses in the matter of supplies from the seneschal'.[133] The office was repurchased from the incumbent in 1226, future bishops were enjoined to enfeoff no new seneschals, and the see made do with three household officers.[134]

If *ministeriales* as officials had opportunities to line their own pockets, there is also evidence that territorial princes were reasonably well served by them. The dukes of Bavaria might quarrel with them about their jurisdictions,[135] but as regional magistrates in the *Landgerichte* and as officials administering the ducal possessions, the new registers of lands and revenues compiled from the 1280s reveal a system which worked.[136] Bishops Reinboto and Conrad of Eichstätt (1279-1305) adopted similar ideas when they rebuilt their territorial administration, and the episcopal land-register drawn up about 1300 shows that the household officers who directed each portion of the see's possessions did fulfil the functions

---

[130] MGD Henry IV, 88, pp. 114f., and Erdmann and Fickermann, *Brief-sammlungen*, 5, pp. 196-8, 1062. The figure is from Deut. 4: 20.

[131] See p. 200, n. 120.

[132] MGC ii, 95f., pp. 118f., 1223.

[133] *Chronicon Hildesheimense*, MGS, VII, p. 860.

[134] UB Hildesheim ii, 160, pp. 69f., 1226 and iii, 515, p. 275, 1279. The last Hildesheim *dapifer* kept the title as an ornament; ii, 263, p. 116, 1228 and 290, pp. 131f., 1230.

[135] MGC iii, 278, ch. 6, p. 269, 1281 and Wittmann, *Wittelsbach*, vol. ii, 193, p. 30, 1293.

[136] Spindler, *Handbuch*, vol. ii, pp. 547-51.

delegated to them, and handed over the revenues to the bishops' treasury.[137] But such organization easily ran into difficulties. From 1305 the much enlarged Eichstätt territories were divided into nine portions or *officia*, each based upon its castle under one or more *ministeriales*. Seven of them functioned according to plan, but in two of them the shortcomings of landlord government were revealed when the nominees refused to cooperate with their lord. In one case the *vicedominus* in charge had to be removed by force,[138] and in the other the bishops' officials had long ago lost control to the neighbouring comital dynasty, which claimed to be the principal feoffee. Here too, coercion and compromise were necessary before the bishops could reappoint their own castellan and secure the revenues.[139]

Given the haphazard nature of territorial government in Germany and the belligerent tone of princely politics, it was hardly possible for any administration to be very just or efficient or protective. *Ministeriales* were military men, and their approach to the inferior orders of their society tended to be a crude one.[140] Nevertheless, they did preserve the knightly tradition of service, and could prove their worth as the most reliable officials available. We are told that Wolfhelm, the *scultetus* or magistrate of Hagenau whom Frederick II had appointed to supervise the extensive imperial fisc in Alsace, was not a *ministerialis* but a man of peasant origin.[141] For twenty years he oppressed the land, accumulating a huge private fortune of more than 16,000 marks. In 1237 he was arrested and imprisoned by the emperor, and died in confinement. To succeed him, Advocate William of Wimpfen, an experienced Swabian *ministerialis*, was transferred to Hagenau and was later given the burgraviate of Trifels as well.[142] During his long tenure of office in Alsace, no more was heard of harsh exactions on the previous scale.

[137] Bayerisches Staatsarchiv Nürnberg, Hochstift Eichstätt, Literalien 165.

[138] Reg. Eichstätt 1622, p. 502, 1317, and my thesis, pp. 262-6.

[139] See my thesis, pp. 293-99, 304-18, 323-5.

[140] Further complaints in Mon. Boica xxxvii, 169, pp. 169-71, 1206.

[141] *Richeri Gesta Senonensis Ecclesiae*, MGS, XXV, pp. 302f., and Bloch, *Annales Marbacenses*, pp. 98 f.

[142] Bosl, *RM*, pp. 400-3, and UB Wirtemberg v, 1269, p. 33, 1253.

Ministeriales *as townsmen*

The great majority of *ministeriales* lived in castles in the country, but knighthood in Germany was not exclusively a rural phenomenon. A proportion of *ministeriales* lived in towns without surrendering the advantages of vassalage under their lords, and some of them played a prominent part in urban affairs.[143] In some cases *ministeriales* were themselves engaged in commerce. In others, they had originally been installed by lords requiring administrative supervision of urban populations. Further, successful businessmen acquired the apparatus of knighthood to underline their prestige, and accepted the status of *ministerialis* as well as townsman.[144]

In the twelfth century the *ministeriales urbani*, as they were denoted in Augsburg in 1156,[145] identified themselves with the leading townsmen, called *cives* or *burgenses*, to make up dominant oligarchies or patriciates.[146] At Regensburg, for example, it can be shown that several families attached to the abbey of St Emmeram were labelled, over the generations, *ministeriales* as well as *concives* or fellow-citizens, and *milites urbis* or knights of the city.[147] At Mainz the more prom⋅ent of the inhabitants, some of whom were

[143] E. Maschke and J. Sydow (ed.), *Stadt und Ministerialität. Protokoll der IX. Arbeitstagung des Arbeitskreises für Südwestdeutsche Stadtgeschichtsforschung*, Veröffentlichungen der Kommission für geschichtliche Landeskunde in Baden-Württemberg, ser. B. Forschungen, LXXVI (Stuttgart, 1973), and the extensive literature cited there. In F.L. Wagner (ed.), *Ministerialität im Pfälzer Raum*, see E. Voltmer, 'Ministerialität und Oberschichten in den Städten Speyer und Worms', pp. 23-33, W. Metz, 'Ministerialität und Geldwirtschaft in mittelrheinischen Bischofsstädten des 11. und 12. Jahrhunderts', pp. 34-41, and L. Falck, 'Mainzer Ministerialität', pp. 44-59.

[144] F. Sengle, 'Die Patrizierdichtung "Der Gute Gerhard". Soziologische und dichtungsgeschichtliche Studien zur Frühzeit Rudolfs von Ems', *Deutsche Vierteljahrschrift für Literaturwissenschaft und Geistesgeschichte* xxiv (1950), 53-82.

[145] M G D Frederick I, 147, pp. 246-50, 1156.

[146] H.F. Friedrichs, 'Herkunft und ständische Zuordnung des Patriziats der wetterauischen Reichsstädte bis zum Ende des Staufertums', *Hessisches Jahrbuch für Landesgeschichte* ix (1959), 37-75, A. Dreher, *Das Patriziat der Reichsstadt Ravensburg von den Anfängen bis zum Beginn des 19. Jahrhunderts* (Stuttgart, 1966), pp. 40-138, H. Mosbacher, 'Kammerhandwerk, Ministerialität und Bürgertum in Straßburg', *Zeitschrift für die Geschichte des Oberrheins* cxix (1971), 33-173, and J. Fleckenstein, 'Ministerialität und Stadtherrschaft. Ein Beitrag zu ihrem Verhältnis am Beispiel von Hildesheim und Braunschweig' in K.-U. Jäschke and R. Wenskus (eds.), *Festschrift für Helmut Beumann* (Sigmaringen, 1977), pp. 349-64.

[147] Tr. Regensburg 792, p. 373, 1135, 911, pp. 449 f., 1177, 1026, p. 523, 1201-10 and 1046, p. 533, 1223; on this city, K. Bosl, *Die Sozialstruktur der mittelalterlichen Residenz- und Fernhandelsstadt Regensburg*, Bayerische Akademie der Wissenschaften, Abhandlungen der phil.-hist. Klasse, n.s., LXIII (Munich, 1966).

the archbishop's magistrates and fiscal officials with extensive property outside the city as well, were variously called *ministeriales*,
milites, *concives*, and *burgenses*,[148] as well as enjoying the less
specific epithet of 'big men', *principaliores* or *fortes viri*,[149] rather
like the *potentissimi civitatis* or 'most powerful burghers' at
Würzburg.[150] One of the rich Mainz *burgenses* who was regularly
called a *ministerialis* smoothly combined the attributes of knight
and townsman; '... a certain man of gentle family, burgher of the
city of Mainz'.[151] At Worms too, the ruling élite consisted of closely
connected townsmen and *ministeriales*,[152] so that the *civis* and
ministerialis descriptions were again interchangeable for the same
persons.[153]

The Rhineland sources do, nevertheless, continue well into the
thirteenth century to distinguish townsmen as such from *ministeriales* who inhabited towns, inferring legal or functional distinctions
which were hereditary. At Worms we are told that in former times
there were in the city 'forty consuls, that is, twenty-eight townsmen
and twelve knights, *ministeriales* of the church [i.e. of the bishops
of Worms], who themselves ruled the whole city without reference
to the bishop'.[154] This régime received imperial approval in 1220,
but was overthrown by the bishop in 1232 and then restored in
attenuated form under his own control.[155] Since the twelfth century the magistrates or consuls were being drawn from two distinct
urban groups in Worms, whose interests as city-councillors were,

[148] UB Mainz ii, 188, pp. 350f., 1143-53, 207, p. 376, 1155, 511, p. 841, 1189,
and 666, pp. 1086-8, 1196. L. Falck, *Mainz im frühen und hohen Mittelalter*, Geschichte der Stadt Mainz, II (Düsseldorf, 1972), pp. 135-54, and D. Demandt, *Stadtherrschaft und Stadtfreiheit im Spannungsfeld von Geistlichkeit und Bürgerschaft in
Mainz*, Geschichtliche Landeskunde, XV (Wiesbaden, 1977), pp. 31-46.
[149] UB Mainz ii, 66, p. 130, 1144 and 79, p. 157, 1145.
[150] Mon. Boica xxxvii, 78, p. 41, 1131 and Reimann, pp. 186-205, 211-34.
[151] UB Mainz ii, 218, pp. 394f., 1156. Not all the principal Mainz burghers were
knights; H.-J. Rieckenberg, 'Arnold Walpot, der Initiator des Rheinischen Bundes
von 1254', *DA* xvi (1960), 228-37.
[152] K. Schulz, 'Die Ministerialität als Problem der Stadtgeschichte. Einige allgemeine Bemerkungen, erläutert am Beispiel der Stadt Worms', *Rheinische Vierteljahrsblätter* xxxii (1968), 184-219, T. Zotz, 'Bischöfliche Herrschaft, Adel, Ministerialität
und Bürgertum in Stadt und Bistum Worms' in J. Fleckenstein (ed.), *Herrschaft und
Stand*, pp. 92-136, and H. Seider, 'Zur Wormser Ministerialität im Hochmittelalter'
in A. Gerlich (ed.), *Ministerialität in Mittelrheinraum*, pp. 1-19.
[153] Boos, *Worms*, 118, p. 92, 1213, 121, p. 94, 1218, and 129, p. 99, 1224.
[154] *Annales Wormatienses*, MGS, XVII, p. 40, 1232.
[155] Boos, *Worms*, 124, pp. 95-7, 1220, 154-60, pp. 116-21, 1232, 163f., pp. 122-
4, 1233 and 190, pp. 133f., 1238.

nevertheless, almost identical and divided them from 'the *minister-iales* of the lord of Worms living in the country beyond the city'.[156] The same identifications of interest have been shown for the other Rhineland cities, and elsewhere.[157]

The functions of *ministeriales* in the legal and fiscal administration of towns, and in their military defence, provided the impulse towards urban knighthood. If the military command of large towns was generally in the hands of aristocratic burgraves, a number of burgraves, as we have seen, were themselves *ministeriales*. The bishops of Brixen enfeoffed the corner-towers of their town-walls to four different families of *ministeriales*.[158] The history of Nuremberg also illustrates how *ministeriales* and townsmen acquired each other's knightly and commercial ways of existence. The Gross family, which rose to a great fortune founded upon trade in the fourteenth century, came to Nuremberg when their lord, Henry of Hilpoltstein, was appointed imperial butler there in 1258.[159] The burghers Frederick and Herdegen Holzschuher, on the other hand, acquired knightly status when they were appointed resident castellans of Kraftshof Castle by Burgrave Frederick in 1276, with half the manor, the tithes, and other rights.[160]

Unless they carried the place-names of rural castles, manors, or fiefs, it is often not possible to identify the origins of urban *ministeriales* or to determine which knightly families had risen by trade. At Worms, for example, two of the early thirteenth-century magistrates, called both *ministeriales* and burghers, were identified not by toponymics but by epithets, *de moro* or mulberry-tree, and *Mil-*

[156] Ibid. 91, p. 76, c. 1190.

[157] H. Planitz, 'Studien zur Rechtsgeschichte des städtischen Patriziats', *MIöG* lviii (1950), 317-35, O. Brunner, 'Zwei Studien zum Verhältnis von Bürgertum und Adel' in his *Neue Wege der Verfassungs- und Sozialgeschichte* (2nd edn., Göttingen, 1968), pp. 242-80, Schulz, *Ministerialität und Bürgertum in Trier*, and W. Petke, 'Pfalzstadt und Reichsministerialität', *Blätter für deutsche Landesgeschichte* cix (1973), 270-304.

[158] P. Feldauer, *Herren und Ritter*, Herrschaftsstruktur und Ständebildung, I (Vienna, 1973), pp. 208-13.

[159] H. Dannenbauer, *Die Entstehung des Territoriums der Reichsstadt Nürnberg*, Arbeiten zur deutschen Rechts- und Verfassungsgeschichte, VII (Stuttgart, 1928), pp. 92 f., UB Nürnberg 506A, p. 644, 1275, and my thesis, p. 165 and n. 2.

[160] von Stillfried and Maercker, *Mon. Zollerana*, vol. ii, 155, p. 87, 1276; on this patriciate, H.H. Hofmann, 'Nobiles Norimbergenses. Beobachtungen zur Struktur der reichsstädtischen Oberschicht' in T. Mayer (ed.), *Untersuchungen zur gesellschaftlichen Struktur der mittelalterlichen Städte in Europa*, VF, XI (Constance and Stuttgart, 1966), pp. 53-92.

itellus or Little Knight.[161] One may hazard that these families had
an urban origin, while Henry of Dirmstein, called 'secular person
of the town of Worms' and 'episcopal *ministerialis*' at the end of
the twelfth century,[162] was named from a rural castle. Clearly the
authority exercised by the council, and its struggles against the
bishops, drew such people together, so that later on a Burchard of
Krobsberg was called *miles*, and Eberhard of Krobsberg, whose
daughter married a Dirmstein, was called *civis* of Worms.[163]
Similarly in Regensburg the Grans family, who were in the provisions business, were none the less *ministeriales* who aspired to enter
members amongst the aristocratic ranks of St Emmeram's
monks.[164] The Granses doubtless rose through commerce, unlike
other urban *ministeriales* in Regensburg, who came in from
knightly families enfeoffed in the country.[165]

Urban *ministeriales* built, bought, inherited, or otherwise acquired castles in the country, such as the Mainz chamberlain
Dudo's adulterine fortification at Weisenau, after which he and his
descendants were called.[166] Town-life as such did not rob urban
knighthood of an active military existence. Their town-houses were
fortified dwellings, sometimes of great size, and formidable families
of *ministeriales* might derive their dynastic names from the quarter
of town which these urban castles must have dominated, such as
the bridge at Trier,[167] the square at Würzburg,[168] the gates at
Regensburg and Strasburg,[169] and both square and gates at Augsburg.[170] Especially in the Rhineland, Swabia, and Franconia,
where towns large and small were numerous, *ministeriales* appear
to have taken substantially to city-life.[171] There was some concern

[161] See p. 205, n. 153, and Boos, *Worms*, 132, pp. 100 f., 1224.
[162] Boos, *Worms*, 91, p. 76, *c.* 1190, and 96, p. 79, 1195.
[163] Ibid. 264, p. 176, 1255, and 399, pp. 255 f., 1283.
[164] Tr. Regensburg 1013, p. 517, 1197-1200.
[165] e.g. Arnold of Dünzling, ibid. 766, p. 356, *c.* 1120-6 and 792, p. 373, 1135.
[166] U B Mainz ii, 569, p. 939, 1192 and p. 878 n. 4 f.
[167] See p. 200, n. 120.
[168] Mon. Boica xxxvii, 128, p. 115, 1181 and 131, p. 119, 1182.
[169] Tr. Regensburg 979 and 982, pp. 497 f., *c.* 1185 and Reg. Straßburg i, 726,
p. 380, 1201.
[170] R. Hipper, *Die Urkunden des Reichsstiftes St. Ulrich und Afra in Augsburg*,
Schwäbische Forschungsgemeinschaft bei der Kommission für bayerische Landesgeschichte, ser. 2A. IV (Augsburg, 1956), 7, pp. 4 f., 1169.
[171] e.g. Boehmer and Lau, *Frankfurt*, 40, p. 19, 1215, 76, pp. 40 f., 1226, 90 f.,
pp. 46 f., 1230, 190, pp. 91 f., 1255 and 312 f., pp. 154 f., 1273 in the middle Rhine
and Wetterau towns.

expressed about the drift to the towns. Before 1178 the burghers of Freiburg im Breisgau insisted on giving their consent before the duke of Zähringen's vassals, *ministeriales*, and knights might take up residence there.[172] In other cases lords complained of losing sight of their *ministeriales* and their obligations. In 1226 King Henry forbade the archbishop of Mainz's *ministeriales* and other vassals from moving into Oppenheim, one of the imperial towns, and warned them not to confederate with townsmen against the archbishop's authority.[173] The bishop of Strasburg also complained that his *ministeriales* were living 'like townsmen', and asked for them back.[174] Without doubt their growing influence in cities such as Cologne,[175] Mainz, Worms, Strasburg, Würzburg, and elsewhere attracted *ministeriales* to towns, where they would still enjoy the privileges of their knightly rank. At Freiburg, for example, the Zähringen *ministeriales* in residence were exempt from tolls, and at Worms, *ministeriales'* houses were immune from the burgrave's jurisdiction.[176]

[172] Keutgen, *Urkunden*, 133.ii, ch. 13, p. 119, before 1178.

[173] MGC ii, 294, pp. 409 f., 1226.

[174] Reg. Straßburg ii, 868, p. 29, 1221.

[175] K. Schulz, 'Richerzeche, Meliorat und Ministerialität in Köln' in *Köln, das Reich und Europa*, Mitteilungen aus dem Stadtarchiv von Köln, LX (Cologne, 1971), pp. 149-72 and P. Strait, *Cologne in the Twelfth Century* (Gainesville, 1974), pp. 74-137.

[176] Keutgen, *Urkunden*, 133.iv, ch. 14, p. 124, and 130, p. 111, 1190.

CHAPTER 8

The Imperial Retinue of *Ministeriales* and its Part in German Politics

Were the imperial ministeriales *the agents of a reformed imperial government?*

A long tradition in German historiography credited the Salian and Hohenstaufen monarchs with a conscious scheme of reform in their German kingdom by means of regional administrations under their *ministeriales*.[1] This policy, already foundering upon Saxony's stubborn resistance to Henry IV and Henry V, was thought to have been jeopardized by the Hohenstaufen emperors' preoccupation with their Italian realms, and brought to nothing in the thirteenth century, when the princes, cities, and prelates had successfully established their regional autarky in Germany. This attractive theory gave a sense of political direction to an era of German imperial rule otherwise deficient in financial expertise, administrative innovation, or juridical reform, at least in comparison with the contemporary Angevin, Capetian, and Hauteville régimes in England, France, and Sicily.

That the imperial retinue of *ministeriales* figured prominently in Salian and Hohenstaufen politics and administration both in Germany and Italy is not in doubt.[2] In the eleventh century, several imperial treasurers, chamberlains, and seneschals were *ministeriales*, but almost nothing is known about their functions.[3] We do

---

[1] In G. Barraclough (ed.), *Medieval Germany 911–1250*, vol. ii, *Essays by German Historians* (Oxford, 1961), see the positive view of von Dungern, pp. 223–5, and Brackmann, pp. 291 f., and the doubts expressed by Mitteis, pp. 264 f. For the modern version of the idea, see Bosl, *RM*, pp. 140–90, 616–32, and *Frühformen*, pp. 326–56, but Metz, *SG*, pp. 134–52, is more cautious. See also Kirchner, 'Staatsplanung', and W. Schlesinger's review of Bosl in *ZRGGA* lxix (1952), 445–60.

[2] Von Gladiss, *Beiträge*, and Metz, *SG*.

[3] I. Latzke, 'Hofamt, Erzamt und Erbamt im mittelalterlichen Deutschen Reich' (Inaugural dissertation, Frankfurt, 1970), pp. 134–46.

know that after putting down the Saxons in 1075, Henry IV delivered some of their leaders into the custody of his *ministeriales*.[4]
In the 1090s the duke of Spoleto was an imperial *ministerialis* called
Wernher, perhaps the earliest of a long line of similar colonial
appointments to high office in Italy. It was he who endeavoured to
perpetuate the Wibertine schism by elevating Sylvester IV as anti-
pope in 1105.[5]

In a vain attempt to retrieve something of Salian authority over
the Saxons, Henry V appointed his most formidable *ministerialis*,
the captain Henry, as burgrave of Meissen in 1114.[6] He had already
achieved some notoriety in 1111 during the abortive negotiations
at Rome between Henry V and Paschal II to bring peace between
empire and papacy. When it was announced that the German episcopate was to surrender its temporalities to the crown, Archbishop
Conrad of Salzburg reproached the pope with betraying the
Church. In a fury, Captain Henry drew his sword upon the archbishop, to whose defence the king himself sprang forward with the
exclamation, 'No, no, Henry. Now is not the time!'[7] The new
burgrave's commission against the Saxons did not prosper. The
nobles proved too strong for him, and he was taken captive in
1116. Henry V valued him highly, so he was exchanged for two
Thuringian counts in imperial custody, and the last we hear of his
career in this part of Germany was that Duke Lothar of Saxony
besieged him in Lebus Castle in 1123.[8] Captain Henry was in all
likelihood the progenitor of the imperial marshals of Kalden and
Pappenheim.[9]

Another report from Henry V's time claims that the archbishop
of Cologne and other princes refused in 1114 to cooperate with the
emperor because one of his *ministeriales* had been exercising his
office very insolently in their region.[10] But the imperial *ministeriales*

---

[4] Lampert of Hersfeld, p. 274, and *Vita Wernheri Episcopi Merseburgensis*, MGS,
XII, p. 246.

[5] Meyer von Knonau v, pp. 273 f., Ekkehard of Aura, p. 274, and von Gladiss,
Beiträge, pp. 59–76.

[6] Meyer von Knonau vi, p. 277.

[7] Otto of Freising, p. 327, *Gesta Archiepiscoporum Salisburgensium*, MGS, XI,
p. 68, and Meyer von Knonau vi, p. 381.

[8] Meyer von Knonau vii, pp. 24 f., and Waitz, *Chronica Regia Coloniensis*, p. 62,
1123.

[9] Bosl, *RM*, pp. 103 f.

[10] Schmale and Schmale-Ott, *Anonymi Chronica Imperatorum*, AQ, XV, p. 264,
1114.

did not pose any real or long-lasting threat to the power of the territorial magnates. In 1164, when Frederick Barbarossa broke the authority of his troublesome half-brother Conrad, count-palatine of the Rhine, one annalist made the point that politically he had now fallen to the level of an imperial *ministerialis*.[11]

The rise of these *ministeriales* did not fundamentally alter the habits of the Salian court. Henry IV's monkish enemies accused him of improperly employing low-born persons in positions of trust,[12] but they also had to admit that he was surrounded and counselled, like his forebears, by dukes, counts, bishops, and knights of free birth, such as the seneschal Moricho and the constable Conrad, who distinguished himself on the First Crusade.[13] There are nevertheless several reliable reports about the uses which Henry IV did make of inferiors, that they gave him advice, carried out his instructions, and were rewarded with fiefs or salaries.[14] But this was what any lord would expect of his retinue of knights and *ministeriales*. Without actually naming them as *ministeriales*, Lampert and Bruno, both of whom hated the king, indicated that he installed Swabian garrisons in new or rebuilt castles in eastern Saxony and Thuringia. This was part of his campaign to resume the royal lands usurped during his minority. The Swabians were therefore unpopular with the Saxon nobles, but this did not prevent them from electing a Swabian as their king in 1077, and welcoming what Swabian support they could muster against Henry IV.

It is difficult to show that the Salians and Hohenstaufen were positive innovators in government because they recruited and employed enterprising *ministeriales*. Imperial authority in Germany rested upon the fisc with its manors, castles, and towns, the services owed by the cathedral and monastic churches, and the homages rendered by the secular aristocracy. The form, extent, and effectiveness of these elements might change greatly from the reign of

[11] *Annales Egmundani*, MGS, XVI, p. 463, 1164.

[12] Lampert of Hersfeld, pp. 147f. and 151, 1073, and Meyer von Knonau ii, pp. 857-73.

[13] Lampert of Hersfeld, p. 255 and Lohmann, *Brunos Buch*, p. 19. See the counsellors in MGD Henry IV, 265, p. 340, 1073, and on Constable Conrad, Meyer von Knonau v, pp. 136-41. Latzke, pp. 136-41, is not convincing in connecting him with the later marshals of Pappenheim. See also Bruno 'quidam vir potens, domni imperatoris miles, secretarius et mariscalchus' under Henry III, a free-born noble of the Bavarian Affecking family; Thiel, *Weltenburg*, 21, pp. 18-20,

[14] W. von Giesebrecht and L.B. von Oefele, *Annales Altahenses Maiores*, MG schol., IV (2nd edn, Hanover, 1891), p. 84, 1072.

Conrad II in the eleventh century to that of Frederick II in the thirteenth. But no monarch sought to override or replace them with a tax-based system of local government and jurisdictions under imperial *ministeriales*, who should somehow erode or eliminate the regional autonomy of territorial magnates. Instead, the crown underlined its prestige by other enterprises; crushing domestic rivals by armed force, the subjection of Italy, controversy with the papacy, and from 1147, crusades.

In these schemes the retinue of imperial *ministeriales* played a large part, and the career of a man such as Marshal Henry of Kalden-Pappenheim showed what reliance was placed upon their military and political diligence.[15] In its early stages he captained the imperial forces on the Third Crusade, and distinguished himself in the assault on Skribention.[16] He was imperial legate in Italy, and took part in Henry VI's subjection of the Sicilian kingdom.[17] During the conflict between Otto IV and Philip of Swabia, he attempted to reconcile the kings and arranged a conference outside Cologne in 1206.[18] With Otto's approval he avenged Philip's murder by tracking down the assassin, Count-Palatine Otto of Wittelsbach, to his hiding-place in a barn by the Danube, and decapitated him personally.[19] At the same time, he sought peace in Germany by reconciling himself with Otto IV, surrendering the imperial insignia and handing over the royal towns and castles which were under his command.[20] When Otto's cause began to crumble in 1212, the marshal returned to his Hohenstaufen allegiance, and died in 1214.

The Hohenstaufen ministeriales *in imperial service*

If the imperial *ministeriales* were not the personnel of a novel system of government in Germany, the emperors did, like all German

[15] K. Klohss, *Untersuchungen über Heinrich von Kalden, staufischen Marschall, und die ältesten Pappenheimer* (Berlin, 1901), K. Pfisterer, *Heinrich von Kalden. Reichsmarschall der Stauferzeit*, Quellen und Studien zur Geschichte und Kultur, VI (Heidelberg, 1937), Beckmann, pp. 56-62, and W. Kraft, 'Das Reichsmarschallamt in seiner geschichtlichen Entwicklung', *Jahrbuch des Historischen Vereins für Mittelfranken* lxxviii (1959), 1-36, lxxix (1960-1), 38-96.
[16] Chroust, *Kreuzzug Friedrichs I.*, pp. 45 and 141.
[17] MGC i, 333, p. 476, 1191.   [18] Waitz, *Chronica Regia Coloniensis*, p. 224.
[19] Burchard of Ursberg, pp. 90f., Otto of St Blasien, *Chronica*, pp. 82-4, and Conrad of Scheyern's *Annales*, MGS, XVII, pp. 631f.
[20] Holder-Egger, *Monumenta Erphesfurtensia*, p. 206.

landowners, rely upon their knights to administer their manors,[21] to garrison their towns and castles, and to serve on campaign, especially in Italy. The Hohenstaufen family had already enfeoffed numerous *ministeriales* in Swabia and Alsace, where their ancestral lands were situated.[22] As dukes of Swabia from 1079, they were close supporters of the Salians in southern Germany, and the second Hohenstaufen duke was, according to his half-brother Otto of Freising, a great builder of castles in the upper Rhineland, and had an extensive retinue of knights.[23] As eventual heirs of the Salians, the Hohenstaufen became well off for *ministeriales* on the middle and lower Rhine,[24] in Franconia, and in colonial territory to the east.[25] They also inherited the remnants of the imperial fisc in eastern Saxony and Thuringia, with *ministeriales* in a handful of towns and castles.[26]

Hohenstaufen *ministeriales* were not numerous in Lotharingia, Saxony, or Bavaria, but they were influential. Apart from the officials in charge of the imperial possessions on the lower Rhine, in Lotharingia their most notable *ministeriales* resided in Aachen; Conrad III's advocate Dietrich of Düren, Frederick I's chamberlain William of Aachen, and Hugo of Worms, whom one chronicler characterized as the imperial prefect of Lotharingia in Barbarossa's later years.[27] In Bavaria the principal *ministerialis* was the marshal of Pappenheim, enfeoffed with the advocacy of Neuburg and other imperial possessions since 1197, and there were other substantial knights in the Bavarian Nordgau and in the diocese of Passau.[28] It is thought that in 1236 and again in 1245 Frederick II was making some attempt to convert the Austrian and Styrian *ministe-*

---

[21] e.g. Gerhard of Sinzig's *procuratio* 'tam in hominibus quam in proventibus nostris' conferred by Frederick II in MGC ii, 55, p. 67, 1216.

[22] H. Heuermann, *Die Hausmachtpolitik der Staufer von Herzog Friedrich I. bis König Konrad III.* (Leipzig, 1939). They also inherited the Franconian allods listed in MGC i, 319, pp. 453 f., 1188.

[23] Otto and Rahewin, *Gesta Friderici*, p. 28.

[24] Bosl, *RM*, pp. 217-355, and Schalles-Fischer, pp. 373-432, 465-77.

[25] Bosl, *RM*, pp. 482-546, W. Schlesinger, 'Egerland, Vogtland, Pleißenland. Zur Geschichte des Reichsgutes im mitteldeutschen Osten' in *Mitteldeutsche Beiträge* (Göttingen, 1961), pp. 188-211.

[26] Bosl, *RM*, pp. 547-88.

[27] *Vita Alberti Episcopi Leodiensis*, MGS, XXV, ch. 18, p. 151, Gislebert of Mons, p. 231 and n. 4, and Bosl, *RM*, pp. 278-82.

[28] K. Bosl, 'Die Reichsministerialität als Träger staufischer Staatspolitik in Ostfranken und auf dem bayerischen Nordgau', *Jahresbericht des historischen Vereins für Mittelfranken* lxix (1941), 1-103 and his *RM*, pp. 468-82.

riales into imperial knights at a stroke, but without lasting success.[29]

More durable were several inheritances acquired by Frederick I and including the *ministeriales*, the most notable being the reversion of Duke Welf of Tuscany's Swabian possessions, arranged in the late 1170s. This enormous patrimony stretched from Lake Constance to the Danube, although most of it did not actually pass into Hohenstaufen hands until the duke's death in 1191. The Welf *ministeriales* who came with it provided the Hohenstaufen with some of their most efficient administrators, especially the knights of Tanne who acted as seneschals, butlers, and procurators of Swabia for Philip of Swabia and Frederick II, from their new castles at Waldburg and Winterstetten.[30] The Hohenstaufen also did well out of the Welf knights of Weida whom they recruited from Henry the Lion in 1180, and with Gunzelin, seneschal of Wolfenbüttel, who entered their service after Otto IV's death in 1218.

The imperial *ministeriales* inevitably made a great impression upon the Hohenstaufen style of monarchy. A small number of trusted individuals or dynasties appear again and again as household officers,[31] as feoffees on a great scale, and upon varied diplomatic and political business in Germany and abroad, notably in helping to negotiate or ratify treaties with the papacy, the Italian cities, and the French crown.[32] Reliance upon this inner circle was quite informal, and depended on individual talent and trust. Henry VI's most redoubtable *ministeriales* were Marshal Henry of Kalden-Pappenheim and Seneschal Markward of Annweiler, who ended his remarkable career as regent of Sicily for the infant Frederick II. But after their deaths early in the thirteenth century we hear nothing of their descendants' having any political importance at all, although they continued to enjoy their large fiefs and their honorific household titles. The same can be said for the descendants of the imperial seneschals Henry of Waldburg in Swabia and Gun-

---

[29] See p. 236, nn. 51-2.

[30] CD Salem 125, pp. 162f., 1222 for Eberhard *dapifer* of Waldburg and Conrad *pincerna* of Winterstetten 'qui eo temporis procuratores terre et regalium negotiorum extiterant'. On the Welf *ministeriales* transferred, Bosl, *RM*, pp. 412-48.

[31] J. Ficker, 'Die Reichshofbeamten der staufischen Periode', *Sitzungsberichte der phil.-hist. Classe der Kaiserlichen Akademie der Wissenschaften* xl.4 (Vienna, 1862), pp. 447-549, and P. Schubert, 'Die Reichshofämter und ihre Inhaber bis um die Wende des 12. Jahrhunderts', *MIöG* xxxiv (1913), 427-501.

[32] MGC i, 84, p. 138, 1111, 144f., pp. 201-3, 1153, 293, pp. 416f., 1183, 331, p. 470 and 340, p. 486, 1191, and ii, 1, p. 2, 1198.

zelin of Wolfenbüttel in Saxony, who fell into obscurity because the Hohenstaufen régime itself was collapsing in Germany after 1245. This did not happen to the same extent to the advocates of Weida and Gera, who held on to a handful of imperial offices in Eger, Altenburg, and elsewhere into the fourteenth century,[33] although their vast fiefs were diminished by rival territorial magnates. The seneschals of Falkenstein also survived the fall of the Hohenstaufen, succeeded to the title and fiefs of the chamberlains of Münzenberg in the 1250s,[34] and were confirmed in their offices by the succeeding régimes.

The other dynasties of household officers had already made political miscalculations in Frederick II's time which diminished their importance. The imperial butler Walter of Limburg, whose collateral forebears of Schüpf and Klingenberg had served at court since Conrad III's reign,[35] backed King Henry's rebellion in 1234. Although the butler was pardoned, he was obliged to surrender lands and castles, and later sought to regain favour by contributing funds to Conrad IV against the papalists.[36] For different reasons the marshals of Pappenheim were also greatly reduced in wealth and influence from the 1240s. They became involved in severe feuds with the duke of Bavaria, who had become the chief German supporter of the Hohenstaufen in 1246. Consequently there was little that Conrad IV could do to save the marshals. By the 1260s the Bavarian dukes had stripped them of their principal imperial fiefs, and when the marshals divided up what was left in 1279, the Pappenheim family sank into insignificance.[37]

The inner circle of *ministeriales* holding household offices was known personally to the monarchs, who entrusted them with important tasks. In 1211 Otto IV thought it good enough to send Seneschal Gunzelin of Wolfenbüttel to Landsberg to enfeoff Margrave Dietrich of Meissen with the march of Lusatia by proxy.[38] The most spectacular career of all was forged by Henry VI's seneschal Markward of Annweiler, whose sphere of action was Italy, not Germany at all.[39] He was responsible for coordinating the

[33] UB Weida 109-11, pp. 57f., 1257 and 253, p. 123, 1291.
[34] See p. 182, n. 117.   [35] Bosl, *RM*, pp. 376-83.
[36] UB Wirtemberg iv, 1211, p. 280, 1251.
[37] See p. 179.   [38] UB Asseburg i, 79, p. 57, 1211-12.
[39] T C. van Cleve, *Markward of Anweiler and the Sicilian Regency* (Princeton, 1937), Schubert, pp. 478-84, and Bosl, *RM*, pp. 590-8.

fleets which made possible Henry VI's conquest of his Sicilian kingdom in 1194, with the invasion of the island and the fall of Palermo. He was rewarded with the march of Ancona, the counties of the Abruzzi, and the duchy of Ravenna and Romagna; Burchard of Ursberg also reports that the emperor gave the new duke free status.[40] Upon Henry VI's death in 1197 the seneschal claimed the regency of Sicily against the wishes of the widowed empress and the pope, who was feudal overlord of Sicily. But Markward was accepted as imperial procurator of Sicily by Philip of Swabia,[41] and was able to occupy Palermo and take custody of the infant king Frederick II. These successes were quite unacceptable to Innocent III, which earned Markward the distinction of having a crusade proclaimed against him as an enemy of the Church.[42] His sudden death from dysentery delivered Sicily from German control in 1202. With an enthusiastic flourish, Peter of Eboli compared the resourceful Markward at war on land and sea to Mars and Neptune.[43]

Ministeriales *in the administration of the imperial fisc*

Portions of the fisc were entrusted to imperial *ministeriales*, notably the Neuburg crown-lands to the marshals of Pappenheim, the Wetterau to the chamberlains of Münzenberg, the Pleissenland to the advocates of Weida, the Bavarian Nordgau estates to the *buticularius* of Nuremberg, and the East Franconian possessions to the *magistri coquinae* of Rothenburg. This distribution of responsibilities was repeated regionally wherever the Hohenstaufen owned lands and rights, but it is hard to discern a system behind the nomenclature of the office-holders and feoffees. The crown appointed more than one family of *ministeriales* in each of the four

---

[40] Burchard of Ursberg, pp. 72 f., and his titles in Stumpf-Brentano, *Acta Imperii*, 198, p. 278, 1195 and MGC i, 378, p. 529, 1197.

[41] MGC i, 379, pp. 530 f., 1197 and ii, 3, pp. 3 f., 1199.

[42] E. Kennan, 'Innocent III and the First Political Crusade', *Traditio* xxvii (1971), 229-49.

[43] G.B. Siragusa, *Liber ad Honorem Augusti di Pietro da Eboli*, Fonti per la Storia d'Italia (Rome, 1906), p. 108. Shortly after this, Otto IV turned another German *ministerialis* into an Italian duke: Diepold of Schweinspeunt, from the retinue of the Bavarian counts of Graisbach and Lechsgemünd, was appointed count of Acerra and duke of Spoleto; E. Winkelmann, 'Über die Herkunft Dipolds des Grafen von Acerra und Herzogs von Spoleto', *Forschungen zur deutschen Geschichte* xvi (1876), 159-63.

household offices, and in some cases the local marshals, seneschals, and chamberlains appear to have exercised administrative and judicial functions over the fisc; these families included the seneschals of Boyneburg, the marshals of Hagenau and Kaiserslautern, and the chamberlains of Weinsberg, Wallhausen, Aachen, Mühlhausen, and Boppard.[44]

There were other offices and titles under which the imperial lands were administered; procurator and *provisor*, burgrave and advocate, *villicus* or bailiff, and *scultetus* or magistrate,[45] as well as the *magister coquinae* of Rothenburg and the *buticularius* of Nuremberg. The use of these names, and of the four household titles for parallel administrative functions, may well rest upon regional traditions going back to the eleventh century, possibly adopted by the crown when the lands in question were inherited or otherwise acquired for the fisc, and their *ministeriales* included in the imperial retinue. The administration of the fisc may perhaps have been contrived into an informal hierarchy embracing all the known titles and offices, but the details are lost to us. In what ways, during the time of Frederick II, were the Swabian bailiwicks, advocacies, royal towns, and all other imperial rights and possessions under *ministeriales* subjected in their turn to the procurators of the duchy, Butler Conrad of Winterstetten and Seneschal Eberhard of Waldburg?

The local distribution of offices and titles in the German fisc reflects its scattered geography, and probably the chronology of its acquisition, as well as the needs and convenience of the mobile royal and imperial courts. There could be little practical advantage in centralizing the fragments large and small, and it was never tried. However, the 1241 tax-list of the imperial towns in Franconia, the Rhineland, and Swabia[46] does look like a larger-scale review by a powerful officer, the butler of Winterstetten or the chamberlain of Münzenberg, who needed to put together a war-treasury for Conrad IV's campaigns against his new pro-papal enemies in Germany. Apart from a long catalogue of towns which we know had been entrusted to imperial *ministeriales*, the tax-list does include three of the smaller bailiwicks or *officia* run by

---

[44] Metz, *SG*, pp. 141 f. On the *buticularii* of Nuremberg, Dannenbauer, *Entstehung*, pp. 77–95, and the *magistri coquinae* of Rothenburg, Ficker, 'Reichshofbeamten', p. 483, and Bosl, *RM*, pp. 385–97.
[45] See pp. 190 f., nn. 54–8, p. 214, n. 30.
[46] See p. 188, n. 33.

knightly burgraves; Dortmund, Kaiserslautern, and Trifels. Further down the scale, imperial *ministeriales* in office employed officials and agents of their own; castellans, magistrates, advocates, bailiffs, provosts, notaries, and foresters.[47]

A further glance at records from the years 1240 to 1242 reveals something of how the imperial *ministeriales* did exploit the fisc for the service of the court. The emperor was in Italy, his son Conrad IV was his representative in Germany, and their concern was the new papalist coalition against their rule. We find that in 1240 the *buticularius* of Nuremberg, described as 'a power in the empire', sent to Italy an armed contingent 200 strong for the emperor's use.[48] The 1241 tax-list reflects to some extent the movements of Conrad IV and his retinue,[49] which had to be paid for, and it rescinded taxes where, in the current emergency, the towns were rebuilding their walls. Also revealing is the account which Gerhard of Sinzig, burgrave of Landskron and imperial bailiff in the Rhineland, presented to Conrad IV in May 1242.[50] The burgrave came to Rothenburg to complain of the great expenses he had borne against the king's enemies on the Rhine.[51] His ordinary revenues for the previous year had come to just over 120 marks, which he had managed almost to double by impositions or loot taken in the present campaigns. But his military expenses and losses had been very much greater. Over 190 marks had been spent on providing armed men, war-horses, and war-catapults with the shot, as well as paying for castle-guard. For sixteen weeks he had kept a further fifty armed men and their mounts at Conrad IV's service, and had received nothing for them. Sinzig Castle had been burned to the ground, with the destruction of all his stores and movables. Finally, he claimed to have lost over 400 marks' worth of ransoms when he freed his captives at the king's command. All that Conrad IV could do was to hold out hopes of recompense at some future date from the emperor and himself.[52]

[47] e.g. Metz, *SG*, pp. 52-76, Kraft, *Urbar*, pp. 89, 94, 118, 121, 128, 132-4, and my thesis, pp. 164 f.

[48] UB Nürnberg 293, p. 172, 1240.

[49] Metz, *SG*, pp. 102-4.

[50] See p. 188, n. 34.

[51] His military command is outlined in Huillard-Bréholles, *Dipl. Friderici II.*, vi.2, pp. 817 f., 1241.

[52] Later Gerhard received from the king further demands for cash, some compensation, and yet more thanks and promises, ibid. pp. 842, 871-3, 892 f., 1243-51.

The Sinzig account of 1242 tells more about the conduct of civil wars than the administration of the burgrave's bailiwick, but this is, of course, a sign of what German lords wanted of their *ministeriales*; military enthusiasm and prowess foremost, followed by administrative expertise largely in support of politics by violence. It also shows that cash was necessary for the prosecution of war, and that the imperial *ministeriales* enfeoffed with offices were expected to find it.

Proliferation of household titles under the Hohenstaufen

The four household titles were regarded as honours, which tended to their inflation within the imperial retinue. Apart from their enfeoffment to those who were entrusted with parts of the fisc, there were further reasons. First, the Hohenstaufen were also dukes of Swabia,[53] and the duchy was repeatedly handed out to junior members of the dynasty as their appanage. The duchy preserved its own rank of officers, such as the marshals of Hohenrechberg, the butlers of Staufen,[54] and the chamberlains of Siebeneich, Welf *ministeriales* in origin. Hartmann of Siebeneich accompanied Barbarossa on his Italian campaigns,[55] and according to one chronicler, saved the emperor's life by a stratagem in 1168. During the German army's return to the Alps, Barbarossa was warned of a plot to assassinate him at Susa. The chamberlain, who looked like the emperor, occupied his quarters while Barbarossa escaped from the town disguised as a servant. When Hartmann was uncovered, the conspiracy collapsed, and in the consternation the Germans left.[56] All the Swabian *ministeriales* were eclipsed by the rise of the Tanne brothers under Duke Philip, Barbarossa's fourth son, in the 1190s, and their sons were high in favour with Frederick II. When he left Germany in 1221 for the south, he entrusted the imperial insignia to Eberhard, seneschal of Tanne-Waldburg, and his young son King Henry to the care of Conrad, butler of Tanne-Winterstetten.[57]

[53] K. Schreiner, 'Die Staufer als Herzöge von Schwaben' in *Die Zeit der Staufer*, vol. iii, pp. 7–19.
[54] Ficker, 'Reichshofbeamten', p. 461, and Bosl, *RM*, pp. 357–60.
[55] MGC i, 205, p. 286, 211, p. 296 and 216, p. 308, 1162.
[56] Otto of St Blasien, *Chronica*, pp. 27 f.
[57] Burchard of Ursberg, pp. 114 f.

A second reason for the multiplication of titles was that successive monarchs desired to promote their own men, such as the Tannes, when they came to the throne themselves. This was the case with Markward of Annweiler, who was Henry V I's seneschal as king of the Romans before his accession to the empire in 1190.[58] Henry therefore compensated Barbarossa's seneschals of Rothenburg with the fifth household office, *magister coquinae* or kitchenmaster. A third reason was Frederick II's care to recruit support for his claim to the empire by honouring nearly all his predecessors' appointments. When he arrived in Germany in 1211, he commissioned Wernher of Bolanden as seneschal, Anselm of Justingen as marshal, and Diether of Ravensburg as chamberlain.[59] If Markward of Annweiler's son Dietrich of Hausen appears to have been passed over, he retained the title of seneschal and his fiefs. When Otto I V's officers came over to Frederick, the marshal of Pappenheim and the chamberlain of Münzenberg in 1212 and the seneschal of Wolfenbüttel in 1218, they as well as the Tanne family and the butlers of Limburg were confirmed in their titles.

A fourth reason was the habit among nearly all the male descendants of an imperial office-holder of distinguishing themselves by their ancestor's title as an honourable accoutrement. In this way the principal family of imperial marshals multiplied their title amongst branches named after Kalden, Biberbach, Donnsberg, and Pappenheim castles, and the Rhineland seneschals into the branches of Bolanden, Falkenstein, and Hohenfels. Titles might be further diffused by the marriages of cadets. In the 1240s Walter of Klingenberg, a junior member of the butlers of Schüpf and Limburg, married the heiress Elizabeth of Königstein and moved to her estates in the Bavarian Nordgau. Their sons also titled themselves butlers, but the dynastic toponymic they adopted was Reicheneck, one of their maternal grandfather's chief castles, since it was from him that nearly all their patrimony derived.[60]

The impact of the imperial retinue and its decline

The materials which survive about the administration of the imperial fisc, the chronicle-notices about crusades, civil conflicts, and

---

[58] U B Niederrhein i, 494, p. 348, 1185.
[59] Winkelmann, *Acta Imperii*, vol. ii, p. 328, 1211 and M G C ii, 57, p. 71, 1216.
[60] U B Nürnberg 319, p. 194, 1244, 332, p. 201, 1246 and 705.i, p. 414, 1286.

Italian campaigns, and the remnants of rural and urban fortifications in Germany bear witness to the tasks with which the *ministeriales* of the Roman Empire'[61] were entrusted by the Hohenstaufen monarchy. In the majority of cases we know nothing more
about them than the family toponymics which recur in the
witness-lists of charters, but the significance of these knights *en
masse* was appreciated at the time. Frederick Barbarossa recognized what they had done for him in Italy,[62] and Philip of Swabia
(1198–1208) was well aware of their importance to his cause against
Otto IV (1198–1214). In 1206 he wrote to the pope to try to
persuade him of his rightful title to the empire. He mentioned not
only his election by the princes and his possession of the imperial
insignia, but also that the extensive patrimony and inheritances of
his house, the lands, fortresses, manors, and towns, were manned
by an innumerable retinue of *ministeriales*, so many, he added with
pardonable rhetoric, 'that we can scarcely reckon their number
exactly'.[63] The 'officials and *ministeriales*' who met Philip at Hagenau Castle when he returned in 1197 from Italy were indeed
amongst the first to persuade him to try for the throne of Germany,
and a great number of *ministeriales imperii* were present at
Mühlhausen for his election by the princes in 1198.[64]

The imperial *ministeriales* proved not entirely trustworthy in a
civil war, or were, at the least, placed in a difficult position. In
some noteworthy passages Burchard of Ursberg imposed his own
interpretation upon events of his time, and made play with the
imperial *ministeriales'* loyalties. He claimed that Philip of Swabia
was obliged to hand out new fiefs on a ruinous scale to the barons
and *ministeriales* of Swabia to ensure their support, and that in the
year after his assassination, Otto IV married Philip's daughter
Beatrice to attract the Hohenstaufen *ministeriales* to his side.[65]
None of this is inherently improbable, for it was shown in the
1220s that Swabian *ministeriales* did have their hands on the rich
Pfullendorf lands acquired for the fisc by Frederick Barbarossa.[66]

[61] As in U B Wirtemberg iv, 1147, p. 213, 1250.
[62] M G C i, 302, pp. 426 f., 1185.
[63] M G C ii, 10, pp. 10–13, 1206.
[64] Burchard of Ursberg, p. 76 and M G C ii, 3, pp. 3 f., 1199.
[65] Burchard of Ursberg, pp. 91 f., 97.
[66] K. Schmid, *Graf Rudolf von Pfullendorf und Kaiser Friedrich I.*, Forschungen
zur oberrheinischen Landesgeschichte, I (Freiburg, 1954), p. 297, and Metz, *SG*,
pp. 94–7.

It is also known that Wernher of Bolanden and others joined Otto IV years before Philip was killed,[67] and the marshal of Kalden-Pappenheim and many more felt it right to do so once Otto was the sole king in Germany. To the pope Otto reported with satisfaction that the churchmen, castellans, and *ministeriales* of Swabia and the Rhineland, the old Hohenstaufen patrimony, had come round to accepting his rule.[68] This was not really surprising. In 1125 the majority of Henry V's *ministeriales* had gone over to his chief enemy, Duke Lothar of Saxony, once he was the legally elected king,[69] and this was not held against them by Conrad III after his own election in 1138, although he had considered himself the rightful heir of Henry V's lands, *ministeriales*, and royal titles, and had actually been anti-king in arms against Lothar III in the later 1120s.

The final papal campaign against the Hohenstaufen launched at the Council of Lyons in 1245 proved more serious to the coherence and survival of the imperial *ministeriales* as a loyal retinue. A number of them opted for the papal candidates to the German throne, such as Godfrey of Sulzbürg, who was enticed by promises of fresh fiefs.[70] He subverted his neighbour, Butler Walter of Klingenberg, by betrothing his son and heir Ulrich to the butler's daughter. In 1254 Godfrey had to secure a papal dispensation from this commitment, since Walter had returned to the Hohenstaufen cause.[71] Other royal *ministeriales* were placed in a dilemma when there was no longer a Hohenstaufen king in Germany itself after 1254. Without giving up the appellation '*ministerialis* of the imperial court', many sought, or were compelled to accept, new homages under the territorial princes who were powerful in their regions.[72] The dukes of Bavaria, for example, invited new allegiances from the imperial *ministeriales* of their northern borders,[73] and we have already seen how the seneschals of Wolfenbüttel were converted into marshals of the duchy of Brunswick.[74]

[67] *Gestorum Treverorum Continuatio IV*, M GS, XXIV, p. 391.
[68] M G C ii, 27, pp. 32 f., 1208.
[69] On these men, E. Wadle, *Reichsgut und Königsherrschaft unter Lothar III (1125-1137)* Schriften zur Verfassungsgeschichte, XII (Berlin, 1969), pp. 161-207.
[70] U B Nürnberg 335, p. 203, 1247, confirmed in Mon. Boica xxx.A, 797, p. 323, 1255.
[71] Reg. Eichstätt 773, pp. 240 f., 1254.
[72] Von Gladiss, *Beiträge*, pp. 89-162.
[73] See my thesis, pp. 157 f., 177-9.
[74] See p. 136, n. 200.

meER223

In another case, Burgrave Gernand of Kaiserswerth converted his castle, lands, and following into a fief of Cologne in 1271, and committed himself, in the current rivalries for the crown, to recognizing the archbishop's candidate as king.[75] Later, King Rudolf I had to accept that Kaiserswerth was a Cologne fief, but the burgrave himself was removed in 1276 and Kaiserswerth was no longer entrusted to *ministeriales*.[76] Amongst the last of all *ministeriales* to serve the Hohenstaufen dynasty was the Franconian knight Conrad Kropf of Flüglingen, who had been Conrad IV's burgrave at Trifels Castle and, as Conradin's marshal on the fatal adventure of 1268, died with him upon the scaffold at Naples. His sons did homage to the neighbouring magnates, the counts of Hirschberg, the burgraves of Nuremberg, and the bishops of Eichstätt, although Conradin's private heirs were the dukes of Bavaria.[77]

The dissolution of the Hohenstaufen retinue was inevitable once the dynasty withdrew to Italy in the final stages of its history. King Rudolf favoured the exclusion of imperial *ministeriales* from German affairs, although several were again appointed advocates of the last remnants of the fisc at the beginning of the fourteenth century.[78] The surviving household officers retained symbolic honours, which were formally incorporated into the electoral and coronation procedures of the empire in 1356. The marshal of Pappenheim, the chamberlain of Falkenstein, the *magister coquinae* of Nordenberg, and the butler of Limburg were to act as deputies of the four secular electors.[79]

If Frederick II's *ministeriales* can still be credited with political and administrative vigour, their descendants were not able to withstand the dispersal of the fisc into the hands of the territorial princes, the waning of the household offices into fitful ceremonials, and the collapse of automatic loyalty to the crown. In part this can be explained by incompetence, greed, or lack of essential resources on the part of certain individuals or dynasties of knights, but the

---

[75] U B Niederrhein ii, 617, pp. 364f., 1271.
[76] Ibid. 636, p. 373, 1273 and 687, pp. 401f., 1276.
[77] See my thesis, pp. 159-61.
[78] W. Küster, *Beiträge zur Finanzgeschichte des Deutschen Reiches*, vol. i, *Das Reichsgut in den Jahren 1273-1313* (Leipzig, 1883), pp. 73-85, Niese, pp. 267-322, M G C iii, 644, pp. 627-31, c.1300, and Dannenbauer, *Entstehung*, pp. 95-100.
[79] W. Fritz, *Die Goldene Bulle Kaiser Karls IV. vom Jahre 1356*, Fontes Iuris Germanici Antiqui ex M G, XI (Weimar, 1972), pp. 85f.

processes of disintegration after 1245 were beyond their control. Scattered across the empire as feoffees and garrison-commanders, their tradition as a militarily active knighthood was really no match for the territorial princes. The enterprising core of the imperial retinue as an instrument of the court was also not cast in a strategically unifying role. Diligent knights had been assigned individual tasks, such as Markward of Annweiler's in Italy, Henry of Kalden's on the Third Crusade, Gunzelin of Wolfenbüttel's in Saxony, or Gerhard of Sinzig's on the lower Rhine, but Frederick II was the last to count upon their services in any systematic way. The first Habsburg kings relied upon their own men, Swabian barons, *ministeriales*, and other vassals, and their successors imitated them.

The isolated commissions by which geographically widespread portions of the fisc were entrusted to imperial *ministeriales* in the twelfth and thirteenth centuries show that they were not pioneering or accumulating a realistic state-building or centralizing practice. Office-holding, garrisoning castles, and knightly local administrations did not add up to a unifying political awareness which was then thrown away after 1245. The Hohenstaufen *ministeriales* with their varied offices, great and small, were agents for patrimonial or manorial clusters of crown-estates within a given region, and many were successful in clinging to them, or parts of them, renewing their titles with the successive incumbents of the German throne, or simply perpetuating possession by use and descent. The rest remained what they had always been; a vassal-knighthood of hereditary landowners and feoffees with multiple allegiance amongst the territorial princes of their region who had always overshadowed them. Some reserved their residual loyalty to the crown by the appellation still in vogue about 1300, *imperialis aule ministerialis* or *'ministerialis* of the imperial court',[80] although this had quite lost its meaning.

[80] As in Mon. Boica xlix, 144, p. 236 and 147, p. 240, 1285, and 352, p. 542, 1305.

CHAPTER 9

Ministeriales and Violence

Violence as legitimate redress?

As a social order, the German *ministeriales* were imbued with the values of knightly vassalage,[1] but it was also true that the norms of loyalty and service often gave way to disorderly and self-interested abuses. They usurped offices, lands, and revenues, they pursued destructive feuds which could degenerate into extensive banditry over many years, and they might even engineer conspiracies ending in the expulsion or murder of their lords. They shared the contemporary aristocratic outlook which regarded feuds as a legitimate means of redress,[2] and since they possessed castles and looked for support amongst their kindred, fellow-knights, and armed followers, they could organize feuds on a scale to menace the whole of local society.

The monastic chroniclers quite often remarked upon the network to which an aggrieved *ministerialis* might turn for assistance. In 1191 we are told that Advocate Liudolf of Brunswick fell out with Henry the Lion over the custody or ransom of some captives taken in a recent campaign. With his sons and cousins the advocate fled to his castles at Dahlum and Wenden, and ravaged the country. He was supported by his nephew Liudolf of Peine, and by other Welf *ministeriales* whose precise relationship to the advocate is not given. But the ex-duke's son Count-Palatine Henry took all their castles in lightning sieges, resistance collapsed, and no serious reprisals were taken.[3] In another case, the cousins as well as 'his other friends, knights, and servants' were of more lasting help to Robert of Westerholte, who was 'in rebellion or opposition' to his lords, the counts of Oldenburg, throughout the 1260s. They built an adulterine fortification at Swippenbergen as their base, sought help from the counts' other enemies, and at one point actually seized

---

[1] See Ch. 4.

[2] Brunner, *Land und Herrschaft*, pp. 1-110, Kluckhohn, pp. 95-105, and my thesis, pp. 260 f., 283-5.

[3] *Annales Stederburgenses*, MGS, XVI, pp. 226 f., and Haendle, pp. 14-18.

Oldenburg itself. Eventually they were routed in a pitched battle, and the captured leaders were incarcerated in the towers of Oldenburg.[4]

Feuds of this nature might provide a cover for brigandage, but it is also clear that as a knightly order with recognized forms of service and land-holding, *ministeriales* did have legitimate interests which might be threatened by magnates much more powerful than themselves. This was the motive for murdering Count Sigehard of Burghausen in 1104 at Regensburg, who had, it was held, infringed their rights by delivering inequitable judgements against them.[5]

Conspiracies resulting in the assassination of lords

The German magnates were right to be concerned about conspiracies planned by their own or other lords' *ministeriales*, and the bishop of Bamberg had already warned in the eleventh century of their possible threats to his life, treasury, or fortifications.[6] Just at this time the new archbishop of Trier, a nephew whom Archbishop Anno of Cologne was trying to impose upon the neighbouring archdiocese, was caught and murdered at Uerzig Castle by the advocate of Trier and his men, in all likelihood *ministeriales*.[7] The possibility of assassination was always a lurking peril for a magnate whose strong-mindedness made him unpopular. Abbot Wibald of Corvey and Stablo-Malmedy, who fought vigorously against usurpations by his *ministeriales*, reported a mysterious nocturnal attempt to kidnap or kill him at Corvey late in 1148. He thought that the *ministeriales* responsible were supporters of his predecessor, who had been deposed in 1146.[8] In the 1150s a strong clique of *ministeriales*, townsmen, and clergy in Mainz conspired against Archbishop Arnold, who had been installed against their wishes in 1153. After numerous disturbances the archbishop managed to re-enter the city in 1160, only to be killed by the *ministeriales* when they sacked the Jakobsberg monastery, where he had fled for refuge.[9] Another prelate reported to have been assassinated by his

---

[4] *Historia Monasterii Rastedensis*, MGS, XXV, p. 509.

[5] Meyer von Knonau v, pp. 195-8 and n. 3.   [6] Jaffé, *MB*, p. 51.

[7] Schulz, *Ministerialität und Bürgertum in Trier*, pp. 28 f., believes they were *ministeriales*; Sigebert of Gembloux's *Chronica*, MGS, VI, p. 361 has *satellites*.

[8] Jaffé, *Monumenta Corbeiensia*, 149 f., pp. 230-56 and 174, pp. 295 f., 1149.

[9] Otto and Rahewin, *Gesta Friderici*, p. 347, Jaffé, *Monumenta Moguntina*, pp. 604-75, and Falck, *Mainz*, pp. 151-4.

ministeriales was Abbot Louis of Reichenau in 1135, at the insti-
gation of a powerful rival who succeeded him as abbot.[10]

Secular magnates might also go in peril of their lives. In 1152 the
obnoxious Saxon count Hermann of Winzenburg and his wife were
stabbed to death in their bed by a gang of disgruntled *ministeriales*,
his own and the bishop of Hildesheim's.[11] The Pegau annals claim
that a similar plot by the Meissen *ministeriales* against Margrave
Dietrich misfired in 1215. Tired of his unjust exactions upon their
manors, they tried and failed to gain access at night to his bedroom
in Isenburg Castle in order to murder him. However, they persuaded the town of Leipzig to join them in a rising, and a force of
ministeriales, said to have been 400 strong, ravaged the march for
two years before Frederick II mediated a settlement.[12]

In 1202 Bishop Conrad of Würzburg was killed by his *ministerialis*
Bodo of Rabensburg. This feud had originated in Bodo's murdering, for reasons unknown, the Würzburg official Eckhard in 1200,
whereupon Bodo's town-house in Würzburg was pulled down and
all his lands devastated. In revenge for this, Bodo and his men
managed to strike the bishop down in 1202. At the time, Philip of
Swabia was accused of complicity because Bishop Conrad had just
deserted him for Otto IV, but this smear did not stick.[13] Private
revenge also brought about Abbot Bertho of Fulda's violent end
in 1271. The abbots of Fulda had long been on bad terms with
their *ministeriales*, whom they were obliged to discipline by armed
force.[14] When the *ministerialis* Hermann of Ebersberg was captured and executed on Abbot Bertho's orders, nine knights, including three of the Ebersberg family, murdered the abbot at mass. The
Ebersbergs were arrested and subsequently put to death.[15]

The fear of sudden death at the hands of *ministeriales* might
generate unconfirmed rumours of assassination. A late source
claimed that a Styrian count Adalbero was killed at Leoben by his

[10] *Abbatum Augiensium Catalogus*, MGS, II, p. 38 and *Annales Magdeburgenses*,
MGS, XVI, p. 185.
[11] *Annales Palidenses*, MGS XVI, p. 86. In 1192 the *militares* who murdered
Count Christian of Oldenburg with the connivance of his brother were probably
ministeriales; *Historia Monasterii Rastedensis*, MGS, XXV, p. 505.
[12] *Annales Pegavienses*, MGS, XVI, pp. 268 f.
[13] Wendehorst, pp. 183-200.
[14] K. Lübeck, 'Die Ministerialen der Reichsabtei Fulda', *ZRG Kanonistische Abteilung*, lxvi (1948), 201 33.
[15] Heinemeyer, *Chronica Fuldensis*, pp. 129-33.

cousin the margrave's *ministeriales*, and in 1163 the Cologne chronicler thought that Archbishop Eberhard of Salzburg had been murdered by his *ministeriales*.[16] It is true that the Salzburg *ministeriales*
were often encouraged to make serious trouble for their archbishops, as we shall see, but Eberhard died in his bed at Admont
Abbey in 1164 mourned by all. Perhaps the chronicler was express-
ing the hopes of the imperialist Rhineland against the most
prominent Alexandrine prelate in Germany. More than one source
claimed that the last Przemyslid king of Bohemia was murdered by
his *ministeriales* in 1306, but who they were is not made clear.[17]

During the civil conflicts of Conrad IV's time, Abbot Hermann
of Niederaltaich recounted that the bishop of Regensburg's *ministeriales* almost succeeded in assassinating the king late in 1250.
Having ravaged the papalist see of Regensburg, Conrad entered
the city and put up at the abbey of St Emmeram. Bishop Albert's
spies found out that the king and four attendants slept in the same
room, whereupon Conrad of Hohenfels and other Regensburg *ministeriales* forced an entry, killed two persons, and carried off three
of the attendants. But the king was not one of the dead men after
all. That night there happened to be five attendants instead of four,
and in the darkness and confusion the quick-witted monarch had
escaped death by hiding under a bench. Upon this miscarriage the
bishop fled with his *ministeriales* from their rendezvous just outside
the city, and the unfortunate abbot, accused of negligence or
complicity, had his lands devastated too.[18]

Ministeriales *in opposition to ecclesiastical magnates*

In certain sees and abbacies the *ministeriales* claimed and exercised
participation in electing the candidates, and this gave them considerable political weight. But they were capable of abusing their
power, and were encouraged by their lords' political opponents in

[16] *Genealogia Marchionum de Stire*, MGS, XXIV, p. 72 and Waitz, *Chronica
Regia Coloniensis*, p. 114.

[17] John of Viktring, *Liber*, vol. i, p. 338, Holder-Egger, *Monumenta Erphesfurtensia*, p. 697, and Siegfried of Ballhausen's *Compendium Historiarum*, MGS, XXV, p.
717. Other magnates reported to have been killed by servants or vassals who may
have been *ministeriales* were a son of Margrave Dedo of the Saxon East March,
Frutolf of Michelsberg, pp. 78-80, 1070, Bishop Conrad of Utrecht, ibid. pp. 118
and Ekkehard of Aura, p. 158, 1099, and Count Louis of Mömpelgard, *Annales
Einsidlenses*, MGS, III, p. 146, 1102.

[18] *Hermanni Altahensis Annales*, MGS, XVII, p. 395.

MINISTERIALES AND VIOLENCE 229

conspiratorial traditions of trouble-making. This is plain to see in the archbishopric of Salzburg, which emerged as the principal bastion of papal allegiance within the German church under Archbishop Gebhard (1060-88). This motivated Henry IV, Henry V, and Frederick I in turn to demand support from the Salzburg *ministeriales* against the archbishops, which resulted in recurrent armed conflicts in the see. Archbishop Gebhard's biographer tells that the Salzburg *ministeriales* concurred in his election, subvented his plans for monastic reform, and assisted in his reinstatement after his exile by Henry IV.[19] But it is clear that the imperialist candidate Berthold of Moosburg (1085-1106) also enjoyed considerable support from the Salzburg *ministeriales* eventually expropriated for their pains by the new archbishop, Conrad I, in 1106. In revenge, they managed to expel him for a decade after 1112, which was also to the liking of the emperor.[20]

No election at Salzburg could be truly effective without support from the *ministeriales*. More than once Frederick Barbarossa summoned the principal *ministeriales* to instruct them to accept his nominees in the see.[21] These manœuvres brought about conflict between rival parties of *ministeriales*, in which Archbishop Conrad II's castellan Megingoz of Surberg was forward in defending him from the imperialists.[22] When peace between empire and papacy was patched up in 1177, it was followed in the archbishopric by a convention at Friesach in which the churchmen and *ministeriales* agreed upon recognizing the man now acceptable to both sides, Conrad of Wittelsbach.[23] Not surprisingly, Innocent III endeavoured to curb the excessive influence of the *ministeriales* by confining electoral rights to the Salzburg chapter, but this could not be turned into a political reality. Once again the see fell victim to schismatic elections during the wider struggle of papacy and empire which recommenced in 1245.

[19] *Vita Gebehardi et Successorum eius*, MGS, XI, pp. 35-9, and W. Steinböck, *Erzbischof Gebhard von Salzburg, 1060-1088*, Veröffentlichungen des Historischen Instituts der Universität Salzburg, IV (Vienna and Salzburg, 1972).
[20] *Vita Chunradi Archiepiscopi*, MGS, XI, pp. 65-70 and K. Zeillinger, *Erzbischof Konrad I. von Salzburg, 1106-1147*, Wiener Dissertationen aus dem Gebiete der Geschichte X (Vienna, 1968), pp. 19-25.
[21] MGD Frederick I, 488, p. 467, 1165 and *Chronicon Magni Presbiteri*, MGS, XVII, p. 498, 1174.
[22] *Annales Reicherspergenses*, MGS, XVII, p. 473, 1166.
[23] *Vita Gebehardi et Successorum eius*, MGS, IX, p. 49.

In 1246 the canons and *ministeriales* did unanimously choose Philip of Carinthia as their archbishop, an election which the papacy attempted, without success, to overturn in the following year. With greater circumspection a clique of *ministeriales* was recruited in 1256 to support Ulrich of Seckau, the new papalist rival to Archbishop Philip. The subsequent destructive feuds sustained for a decade by the *ministeriales* ended with the resignation of both archbishops in the mid 1260s and Philip's compensation with the patriarchate of Aquileia.[24] These conflicts were exacerbated by the unreliability of the Salzburg *ministeriales* themselves, who took advantage of rival lords to feather their own nests. In 1262, for example, when Duke Henry of Bavaria invaded the see on his own account, he was assisted by the *ministeriales* of Wiesbach, and in the following year, when the count of Görz was captured and entrusted by the chapter to Gebhard of Felb, he let him go for a large ransom which, the annalist noted, he turned to his own use.[25]

Ministeriales were also capable of exercising their leverage at election-time in a responsible fashion. When the abbacy of Corvey was vacant in 1146, the monks and *ministeriales* sent a deputation to Conrad III at Goslar to petition for Abbot Wibald of Stablo as their new lord, and were rewarded with success.[26] At Münster in 1203 the chapter and *ministeriales* successfully defended their candidate, Provost Otto of Bremen, against the abbot of Klarholz, who had been put up by the counts and free lords of the diocese.[27] In the archbishop of Salzburg's proprietary see of Gurk the *ministeriales* also enjoyed electoral influence, but in 1179 their nomination was thwarted. They and the clergy had chosen the archdeacon, Hermann of Ortenburg, but Archbishop Conrad imposed the provost, Dietrich of Albeck, and secured papal and imperial confirmations for him.[28] He was accepted, but in other cases the *ministeriales* were prepared to resort to schismatic candidacies and the subsequent feuds. The Einsiedeln *ministeriales* tried this in 1173,

[24] *Annales Sancti Rudberti Salisburgenses*, MGS, IX, pp. 789-98, 1246-69; on wrangling over the archdiocese, H. Dopsch, 'Die Wittelsbacher und das Erzstift Salzburg' and G. Hödl, 'Bayern, Österreich und die Steiermark in der Zeit der frühen Wittelsbacher' in Glaser (ed.), *Die Zeit der frühen Herzöge*, vol. i, pp. 268-84, 295-306.

[25] *Annales Sancti Rudberti Salisburgenses*, MGS, IX, p. 796.

[26] Jaffé, *Monumenta Corbeiensia*, pp. 49 f.

[27] Waitz, *Chronica Regia Coloniensis*, p. 202.

[28] Mon. Carinthia i, 309-14, pp. 233-8, 1179-80.

besieging the unwanted aspirant in the abbey. But the emperor upheld his election, and resistance collapsed.[29] In another scandalous case the cathedral advocate of Eichstätt, Count Gebhard of Hirschberg, instructed a commission of five canons and five *ministeriales* to elect his own candidate in 1223, but the man was removed in 1225 after a papal investigation, and a more suitable incumbent was installed.[30] The count did not give up. In the 1230s he encouraged the *ministeriales* and others to support a schismatic bishop of his choice, for which they were excommunicated.[31] So were the Regensburg *ministeriales* when they backed a schismatic candidate in the 1220s, and ravaged the episcopal lands.[32]

The schism at St Gallen in 1272 was more serious, since the rival abbots were supported by King Rudolf and the bishop of Constance respectively, and both were powerful men in Swabia. The *ministeriales* were divided, and both sides devastated the monastic estates in their attempts to coerce the other party. In the end the bishop's man was expelled from the abbey, and the king's candidate installed there by force.[33] In spite of such behaviour, the tradition that *ministeriales* who were vassals of the Church had a legitimate claim to be involved in choosing their new lords died hard. On the eve of his departure for Italy in 1157, Frederick Barbarossa warned both the Mainz clergy and the more powerful *ministeriales* there not to elect an archbishop without consulting him should the present incumbent, who was aged, die during his absence.[34] In the event he did die, murdered by those same *ministeriales*. When the see of Hildesheim fell vacant in 1221, the *ministeriales* sent two representatives to the royal court to petition that their long-standing right to participate in the Hildesheim episcopal elections should be recognized. Reproved by the imperial establishment as well as the pope, they were informed that such customs were contrary to church-law, and must be given up.[35]

Salzburg's misfortunes epitomized the wider rivalry of papal and imperial ideas about church-government as well as the narrow unreliability of *ministeriales*, as Gerhoh of Reichersberg, excoriating

[29] *Annales Einsidlenses*, MGS, III, pp. 147 f.
[30] Reg. Eichstätt 603 and 607 f., pp. 187-92, 1223-5.
[31] Holder-Egger, *Monumenta Erphesfurtensia*, p. 97, 1239.
[32] *Notae Sancti Emmerammi*, MGS, XVII, pp. 574 f.
[33] *Catalogi Abbatum Sancti Galli*, MGS, XIII, pp. 328-30.
[34] *Annales Sancti Disibodi*, MGS, XVII, p. 29.
[35] UB Hildesheim ii, 3-15, pp. 2-11, 1221.

the knights, realized at the time. In other dioceses the disorders created by *ministeriales* might also reflect the wider conflicts in the empire. In 1106, when Bishop Burchard of Münster went over to the young king Henry in his revolt against Henry IV, the *ministeriales* seized their lord and delivered him in chains to the emperor. From his deathbed later that year Henry IV, as a conciliatory gesture, sent the bishop to his son, who came to Münster and forcibly reinstated him.[36] As Westphalians the Münster *ministeriales* seem to have preferred Salian to Saxon domination, and in 1119 concurred in the expulsion of Bishop Dietrich for his hostility to Henry V. Once more they lost the game. In 1121 Duke Lothar of Saxony descended upon Münster, burned it to the ground, took captive a great number of nobles and *ministeriales*, and restored the bishop.[37]

In Lower Lotharingia the territorial magnates who were rivals of the bishops of Utrecht sought to subvert the loyalty of the episcopal *ministeriales*, and here too a dangerous tradition of opposition lasted a hundred years. In 1133 a group of Utrecht *ministeriales* received support from the count of Holland against the bishop, who excommunicated them.[38] In 1150 there was trouble because the *ministeriales* and the town supported one candidate to the see, the chapter another. The royal court backed the chapter's nominee, and the *ministeriales* had to accept him in 1152.[39] According to the Egmont annalist they revolted again in 1159 to defend their rights, and many transferred their allegiance to the count of Guelders. The bishop was besieged in Utrecht, but the archbishop of Cologne was able to arrange a peace before worse befel.[40]

At the beginning of the thirteenth century the *ministeriales*, in league with Holland and Guelders, continued to make trouble for their bishops,[41] but these incidents were quite eclipsed in the major rising of 1227. *The Deeds of the Bishops of Utrecht*, a source favourable to the bishops composed in 1232, admits that for a long time

[36] Waitz, *Chronica Regia Coloniensis*, pp. 44 f.

[37] Ibid. pp. 59 f.

[38] Jaffé, *MB*, 264, pp. 450-2, 1134 and *Annales Sanctae Mariae Ultraiectenses*, MGS, XV. 2, p. 1302, 1133.

[39] Otto and Rahewin, *Gesta Friderici*, pp. 95-8, 1150-2, *Annales Egmundani*, MGS, XVI, p. 456, 1150, and *Annales Sanctae Mariae Ultraiectenses*, MGS, XV. 2, p. 1303, 1151.

[40] *Annales Egmundani*, MGS, XVI, pp. 461 f., 1159.

[41] *Gesta Episcoporum Traiectensium*, MGS, XXIII, p. 408, 1202, p. 410, after 1215, and p. 412, 1225.

they had had difficulties with the knighthood and townsmen in the extensive episcopal territories beyond the River IJssel, where the castellans of Coevorden were the most formidable of the feoffees.[42] In 1227 Rudolf of Coevorden, who was in all probability a *ministerialis* himself,[43] organized a revolt on a large scale, in which the forces sent against him were wiped out and the bishop killed. As in earlier times, the Utrecht *ministeriales* were divided. In 1228 the *ministeriales* loyal to the new bishop moved into the revolted lands and forced Rudolf into exile. Within a year he was back in Coevorden and had once more taken command of the revolt. Although he was captured in 1230 and executed, the disaffection of these lands continued.[44] Some of the Utrecht *ministeriales* had motives for opposing the bishops,[45] and Rudolf of Coevorden's rebellion was unusual in combining knightly feuds with a general rising of the Frisian townsmen and peasantry against the domination of Utrecht.

In the Alpine bishopric of Brixen the counts of Tirol adopted tactics somewhat similar to those employed by the Netherlands princes against Utrecht, the seduction of *ministeriales'* loyalty from their bishop. This generated decades of conflict very destructive in such a poor diocese. In 1242, for example, the count practically destroyed Brixen itself and the bishop's castles with the assistance of the latter's *ministeriales*, who managed in 1258 to burn the town quite to the ground.[46] In another Alpine see, Bishop Ulrich of Gurk fell foul of his *ministeriales* in 1247. They seized his castles, ravaged his lands, imprisoned him in Strassburg Castle, and extorted a large ransom for his release. But the motives for these disturbances are not made clear.[47]

---

[42] Ibid. pp. 402-26 for the prelude, and events of 1227-32.

[43] Ibid. pp. 402 f., indicate free origins of the castellans, but Ganshof, *Étude*, pp. 221, 226 f., shows that Rudolf was called *ministerialis*.

[44] Warfare in the marshes and moors of Frisia was long-lasting and hazardous, as the Oldenburg *ministeriales* also found out: *Historia Monasterii Rastedensis*, MGS, XXV, pp. 507 f., 1238 and later.

[45] In another case, when the Stedinger peasants expelled the Bremen and Oldenburg *ministeriales* from their *terra* early in the 13th c., the knights of Kaihausen assisted them; ibid. p. 504, 1201-4.

[46] *Annales Sancti Rudberti Salisburgenses*, MGS, IX, p. 788, 1242 and p. 794, 1258.

[47] Mon. Carinthia ii, 587, pp. 46 f., 1249. In 1192 Bishop Conrad of Strasburg in Alsace was also, for obscure reasons, held captive by his *ministeriales*; *Annales Argentinenses*, MGS, XVII, p. 89, 1192.

In the prosperous Rhineland sees the bishops also encountered
opposition, notably at Cologne, Worms, and Trier, from city-based
ministeriales with close connections amongst the richest townsmen,
who desired to wrest greater control over urban affairs from the
clergy.[48] This was also the connection which brought about Archbishop Arnold of Mainz's violent downfall in 1160. As we have
seen at Trier, the leading *ministerialis*, Burgrave Louis *de ponte*, did
for a time gain entire control of the city from the archbishop in
the 1120s. Later the Trier *ministeriales* and townsmen again contrived, with some success, to gain ground against their archbishops
through sworn associations and political double-dealing.[49]

The Austrian and Styrian ministeriales in the thirteenth century

In the thirteenth century, a tradition of political opposition by
ministeriales seems to have achieved greater significance in the
duchies of Austria and Styria than anywhere else in the empire. This
had important consequences, chiefly in the installation of the Habsburg dynasty in these territories in the 1270s. In the twelfth century
the Babenberg dukes of Austria appear to have enjoyed cordial
support from their *ministeriales*, to whom the Styrians were added
by inheritance in 1192. For several reasons, none of them really
conclusive, this concord collapsed in the 1230s. With the backing
of the king of Bohemia, the most powerful Austrian *ministerialis*,
Henry of Kuenring, hatched a conspiracy against Duke Frederick,
and the Danube valley was badly devastated. The chronicles hint
that the *ministeriales* objected to the fiscal exactions of the previous duke, and when he died unexpectedly in 1230, the *ministeriales* apparently took an opportunity to show their disaffection.
Duke Frederick was able to settle with them in 1231, but this feud
illustrated some of the dangers threatening Austria in the next
decades.[50] Austria and Styria were involved in the rivalries of

[48] See pp. 204 f., nn. 143, 148, 154-5, p. 208, n. 175.
[49] Schulz, *Ministerialität und Bürgertum in Trier*, pp. 26-35.
[50] The principal Latin sources for events in and around Austria and Styria in the
13th c. make up a vigorous but not very distinguished chronicle tradition stemming
from the *Annales Mellicenses* composed at Melk Abbey, which were used and
continued in the other religious houses of Austria, in print in MGS, IX, pp. 479-
757. The Salzburg annals, ibid. pp. 757-818, and the Bavarian abbot Hermann of
Niederaltaich's account, in MGS, XVII, pp. 392-416, are also important. See K.
Lechner, *Die Babenberger. Markgrafen und Herzöge von Österreich 976-1246*,
Veröffentlichungen des Instituts für österreichische Geschichtsforschung, XXIII,

Bohemia, Hungary, Bavaria, Salzburg, and Carinthia, in which the parties sought to take advantage of each other through ephemeral military alliances and subsequent invasions. Geographically, Austria was unfavourably placed in this constellation, and suffered from perilous military insecurity, which called into question the effectiveness of ducal rule.

Institutionally the dukes were relatively strong in Austria, but the *ministeriales* were more prominent than in any other territory of the empire. Nearly all comital dynasties and families of free lords had died out in Austria and Styria by 1200, so that the important ducal vassals and feoffees were now *ministeriales*. Furthermore, the great ecclesiastical landowners who might have exercised a restraining influence were far away; the archbishops of Salzburg and the bishops of Passau, Bamberg, Freising, and Würzburg. By no means so numerous as the knighthoods of Swabia, Franconia, or Westphalia, the Austrian and Styrian *ministeriales* were enfeoffed on a much grander scale, and some of the families possessed numerous castles, manors, and armed retainers. As a result, the *ministeriales* were the most powerful political force in the duchies, where the only town of any significance was Vienna. If the dukes were strong, so were the *ministeriales*, and confrontations were bound to be dangerous.

The last of the Babenberg dukes appears to have been an unbalanced person with a tyrannical nature, who took a perverse pleasure in creating antagonism amongst his peers, vassals, and subjects. Fears about Duke Frederick's personality may have been a motive behind the rising of 1230-31, but it was his characteristic involvement in the abortive 1234 revolution against Emperor Frederick II which further undermined the loyalty of the Austrian *ministeriales*. In 1236 the emperor moved decisively against him, expelled him from Vienna, and attempted to settle Austria's future

(Vienna, Cologne, and Graz, 1976), pp. 275f., on the tradition of Frederick's evil character; on the Austrian *ministeriales*, H. Siegel, 'Die rechtliche Stellung der Dienstmannen in Oesterreich im zwölften und dreizehnten Jahrhundert', *Sitzungsberichte der phil.-hist. Classe der Akademie der Wissenschaften in Wien* cii (Vienna 1883), pp. 235-86, A. Dopsch, 'Die staatsrechtliche Stellung der Ministerialen in Österreich', *MIöG* xxxix (1923), 238-43, M. Mitterauer, 'Formen adeliger Herrschaftsbildung im hochmittelalterlichen Österreich. Zur Frage der "autogenen" Hoheitsrechte', *MIöG* lxxx (1972), 265-338, Feldbauer, *Herren und Ritter*, and Kusternig and Weltin (eds.), *Kuenringer-Forschungen*.

by concessions to the *ministeriales*.[51] It was held that Austrian *ministeriales* had been enfeoffed to the dukes by the empire, that the present duke had oppressed them, and that they were entitled to appeal to the imperial court against any future duke.[52] It is not clear what the emperor ultimately intended to do with the duchies, but the political reward to the *ministeriales* for their defection was to offer them something resembling condominium under the emperor as lord.

In the event Duke Frederick was able to regain Austria by 1240, and he made his peace with the emperor in 1245.[53] His cruelties against certain *ministeriales* contined with reports of incarceration, torture, and executions. In 1246 the duchies faced a new crisis when the childless duke was killed at the River Leitha during an attack by the Hungarians, and technically the duchies reverted to the empire as vacant fiefs. In effect the *ministeriales* took control, and Albero of Kuenring, butler of Austria, was installed as first captain.[54] It was even claimed that the unpopular duke had been killed in the rout by his *ministeriales*, and Butler Henry of Habsbach was named as the assassin.[55] This is an unlikely tale, but it does reflect that the duke was known to be on bad terms with his *ministeriales*.

Austria's isolation in the new German conflict of imperialists and papalists was redoubled by the external threats from Hungary and Bohemia. When it became apparent that the emperor, in spite of appointing captains of his own to the escheated duchies, could do nothing effective for them, Albero of Kuenring took the line of least resistance and surrendered them to the strongest claimant, Ottokar, heir to the Bohemian crown, in 1251.

[51] F. Hausmann, 'Kaiser Friedrich II. und Österreich' in J. Fleckenstein (ed.), *Probleme um Friedrich II.*, pp. 225-308.

[52] This concession appears in ch. 2 of the Austrian *Landrecht*, preserved in much later versions, but commentators date the original code to 1237 or earlier, basing ch. 2 upon ch. 7 of the 1236 edict for Austria in MGC ii, 201, p. 271; K.-H. Ganahl, 'Versuch einer Geschichte des österreichischen Landrechtes im 13. Jahrhundert', *MIöG* Ergänzungsband xiii (1935), 229-384, M. Uhlirz, *Handbuch der Geschichte Österreich-Ungarns*, vol. i (2nd edn., Graz, Vienna, and Cologne, 1963), pp. 357-60, and K. Brunner, 'Zum Prozeß gegen Herzog Friedrich II. von 1236', *MIöG* lxxviii (1970), 260-73.

[53] MGC ii, 260f., pp. 357-60, 1245.

[54] Fuchs, *Göttweig*, 124, pp. 131 f., 1246. His uncle Henry had been given custody of the duchy during Duke Liutpold's absence in 1227; C. Rodenberg, *Epistolae Saeculi XIII. e Regestis Pontificum Romanorum*, vol. i, MG (Berlin, 1883), 347, pp. 264 f.

[55] *Chronicon Magni Presbiteri Continuatio*, MGS, XVII, p. 529.

Duke Frederick's persecution of his *ministeriales* after the 1230–1 rising and later, the defection of 1236, the uncertainties of the late 1240s, and the failure of the *ministeriales* to keep out a Czech ruler, left a sour political legacy to the new duke and his vassals. If Ottokar, who became king of Bohemia in 1253, did not try to install Czech personnel in the duchies,[56] his rule deteriorated into a repetition of Duke Frederick's methods. *Ministeriales* were imprisoned, executed, exiled, or had castles razed and lands confiscated. King Ottokar was a powerful prince, and circumstances like those of 1236 did not offer themselves to the *ministeriales* until 1276, when they deserted him for the new German king, Rudolf of Habsburg, who reckoned on resuming Austria and Styria as imperial fiefs technically vacant since 1246. A conspiracy was hatched to support him,[57] and the Austrian *ministeriales* handed over the fortresses as he made his way down the Danube to Vienna. King Ottokar fled to Bohemia, his counter-invasion was foiled in 1278 at Dürnkrut, where he lost his life, and the duchies were secured by the Habsburgs. Some of the *ministeriales* who had suffered under Ottokar were rewarded with new titles and fiefs.

In 1282 King Rudolf enfeoffed the duchies to his sons, but it became evident that the tradition of opposition was ingrained in the Austrian and Styrian *ministeriales*' approach to politics. Conrad of Sumerau, who had betrayed Enns to King Rudolf in 1276, seems to have thought that his reward was inadequate. In 1284 Duke Albert was obliged to seize three castles from him, and in 1295 Conrad was instrumental in the plot which sought to repeat the events of 1276-8 by recruiting outside support to expel the duke. If the Habsburgs conciliated powerful families such as the Kuenrings, they could not avoid conspiratorial reactions to their rule. The chronicles cite the appointment of Swabian advisers, leading to a Styrian rebellion in 1292, and the much more extensive intrigue by both Austrian and Styrian *ministeriales* in 1295 to call upon the new German king, Adolf of Nassau, to invade Austria and evict the oppressor.[58] This plan came to nothing, and its prime mover,

[56] V. Novotný, 'Přemysl Otakar II. und der Adel von Steiermark', *MIöG* xxxi (1910), 291-301, and Fuchs, *Göttweig*, 148 f., pp. 146-9, 1264 for the Austrian *ministeriales* who were his counsellors, and M. Weltin and A. Kusternig (eds.), *Ottokar-Forschungen*, Jahrbuch für Landeskunde von Niederösterreich, n. s., XLIV-V (Vienna, 1978-9).

[57] MGC iii, 637, pp. 622 f., 1276.

[58] e.g. *Ellenhardi Chronicon*, MGS, XVII, p. 135.

Conrad of Sumerau, lost all his castles and fled into exile. According to the St Florian chronicle, it was King Adolf's involvement with the Austrian *ministeriales* rather than a concrete desire by Duke Albert to take the German throne which induced the duke to forestall the fate of his predecessors in 1236 and 1276 by marching to the Rhineland against the king in 1298.[59] This time it was the Austrian duke who destroyed the German monarch, and with him all hope the disaffected *ministeriales* may still have entertained about a further change of ducal dynasty. More Austrian *ministeriales* were punished in 1299, but King Albert took the trouble to reconcile essential men, notably Liutold of Kuenring, to his régime, and sixty years of conflict and conspiracy about the duchies came to an end. But the Habsburgs were unable to do anything essential against the entrenched political power of the *ministeriales* until early modern times. In the fourteenth and fifteenth centuries these families maintained their local independence, by military force when necessary, at the expense of a ducal dynasty seriously weakened by its internal divisions and signal external defeats.

Usurpation of offices and revenues, and the misuse of castles

Complaints were frequently levelled at *ministeriales* who usurped from the manorial economy revenues, services, and lands to which they were not entitled. Everywhere the military, fiscal, and legal functions delegated to *ministeriales* were open to abuse. In 1176 the monks of Corvey complained of the *ministeriales* who ran one of their manors: 'This sort of man is rarely content with what is due to him, but always tries to usurp more than has been committed to him.'[60] Another problem was that *ministeriales* tended to regard all administrative posts as hereditary fiefs, although many were granted for a term or a lifetime only.[61] This was Abbot Wibald of Stablo's principal charge against his *ministeriales*, and Conrad III forbade them to make any hereditary claims upon offices, which were to be held entirely at the abbot's discretion.[62] When the archbishop of Magdeburg's *ministerialis* Siegfried claimed the magis-

[59] *Continuatio Florianensis*, MGS, IX, p. 751.
[60] CD Westphalia ii, 380, pp. 132 f., 1176.
[61] UB Osnabrück i, 236, pp. 198 f., 1120 and UB Hildesheim iii, 681, pp. 353 f., 1284.
[62] MGD Conrad III, 40, pp. 64 ff., 1140.

tracy of the town as a hereditary fief, he was removed in 1159 with imperial backing. Siegfried received cash-compensation, and the archbishop recorded the imperial court's finding that 'from the law and custom of other towns, feudal title to this [office of *scultetus* or magistrate] is neither possible nor allowable'.[63]

Another irritation for landlords was that *ministeriales* usurped manors and offices to which they had not been appointed at all,[64] or took manorial renders, fines, and services to which they had no right,[65] or extorted payments in kind on grounds of custom which they themselves had invented.[66] Many times did the abbot of St Emmeram correct *ministeriales* who had wrongfully levied renders in cash and kind from the monastic manors and rural dependents. The oppressions of Dietrich of Hexenagger in this respect took an armed feud of many years' duration to settle.[67] Some *ministeriales* were little better than robbers, and apart from cattle and horses, they stole wine, hay, poultry, and even boats.[68] In 1152 Frederick Barbarossa required his *ministerialis* Henry of Thiel to return to the abbot of Floreffe the ship and its cargo which he had seized.[69] When the duke of Brunswick died in 1279, Advocate Bernard of Peine and his henchmen took the opportunity to descend upon Steterburg Abbey's manors and to carry off all the cattle and horses they could find. Eventually everything was restored apart from eleven cows, which had, no doubt, been surreptitiously sold or consumed.[70]

At the end of the 1180s Archbishop Conrad of Mainz drew up

---

[63] Israël and Möllenberg, *Magdeburg*, 298, pp. 371-3, 1159.

[64] *Casuum Sancti Galli Continuatio II*, MGS, II, p. 161.

[65] Mon. Boica xlix, 8, p. 26, 1144, UB Land ob der Enns ii, 400, p. 594, 1217, and UB St Stephan, 237, pp. 252f., 1225. Because of their remoteness, the Alpine lands pertaining to the bishops of Freising were peculiarly at risk from *ministeriales*, their own or other lords' knights; UB Krain ii, 149, pp. 115-17, 1248, 192, pp. 149-51, 1252, 200, pp. 158f., 1253, 299, pp. 236f., 1262, 320, pp. 251f., 1263, 353, pp. 275f., 1265, 384, pp. 295-7, 1268, and 399f., pp. 307-10, 1269.

[66] Augsburg and Hildesheim *ministeriales* were warned off such sharp practices in Hipper, *Augsburg*, 19A, pp. 15f., 1225 and 23A, pp. 17f., 1233, and in UB Hildesheim ii, 183, pp. 78f., 1226 and iii, 195, pp. 96f., 1268.

[67] Tr. Regensburg 778, pp. 362f., c.1126-9, 792, pp. 372f., 1135, 899, p. 440, 1169, 928, p. 460, 1179 and 933, pp. 464f., 1179.

[68] Jaffé, *MB*, 223, p. 395, 1111-25, CD Nassau 584, pp. 363f., and 615, pp. 379f., 1254, Mon. Boica xlix, 364, pp. 562f., 1305-6, and Reg. Eichstätt 1620, pp. 501f., before 1317.

[69] MGD Frederick I, 41, pp. 68f., 1152.

[70] *Gesta Praepositorum Stederburgensium Continuata*, MGS, XXV, p. 729.

an instructive record of the ways in which the property of his see had suffered during his exile between 1165 and 1183.[71] The principal *ministeriales* had taken over many manors, and had constructed adulterine fortifications. Chamberlain Dudo built a castle at Weisenau, for which he had prudently offered homage to the emperor, the *vicedominus* Conrad built Waldenburg Castle near Aschaffenburg, Wernher of Bolanden put up a tower in Bingen, and Cuno of Münzenberg another in Amöneburg. These fortifications could not now be removed, but the archbishop did insist that Dudo retrieve Weisenau from imperial overlordship and place it under his own. Wernher of Bolanden was not permitted to regard his tower as a hereditary fief, but he would continue to serve the archbishop as castellan in Bingen. They and other *ministeriales* had helped themselves to the see's property by force and fraud as well as enfeoffment and pledge. Wernher of Bolanden, Reinbodo of Bingen, and Chamberlain Dudo had seized manors in the Rhineland, the *vicedominus* of Rusteberg the forest around Fritzlar, and Henry of Weida the manor of Geismar. Nearly all these rich pickings were redeemed or otherwise recovered by Archbishop Conrad, who appears to have borne no grudge for the spoliation, and continued to employ these *ministeriales* as officials or advisers. What his instrument reveals is that *ministeriales* were rapacious, and unless a lord was able to govern his feoffees sternly, they would take advantage of their posts for their own interest, and run up the castles necessary to defend it.

The misuse of fortifications was a serious nuisance because the walls themselves inhibited effective discipline of *ministeriales* by their lords. In 1075 it was alleged that one of Archbishop Anno of Cologne's *ministri* had contumaciously refused service from behind the walls of the castle confided to him.[72] Once they had been entrusted with castles, *ministeriales* were reluctant to give them up again.[73] In the thirteenth century the Rhineland bishops were compelled to apply for assistance from the royal court to regain castles wrongfully detained by the Bolanden family,[74] amongst others. The related problem was the illicit construction of castles, especially

[71] UB Mainz ii, 531, pp. 876-85, 1189-90.
[72] *Vita Archiepiscopi Annonis Coloniensis*, MGS, XI, p. 487.
[73] e.g. in Mon. Carinthia i, 536, pp. 415f., 1232, where the bishop of Gurk regained Strassburg Castle, wrongfully retained by the *vicedominus* Hartwig.
[74] CD Nassau 374, pp. 263f., 1220-4 and Boos, *Worms*, 216, pp. 148-50, 1246.

in troubled times. As soon as their last landgrave, King Henry Raspe, had died in 1247, six prominent families of Thuringian *ministeriales* put up new strongholds, 'and many misfortunes were multiplied upon the country from these castles'.[75] In 1254 the bishop of Bamberg also lamented that the *ministeriales* built unlicensed castles in his territories.[76]

Whether their titles were recognized or not, *ministeriales* were tempted to use their castles as bases for extortions in the surrounding countryside. Some time before 1205 Archbishop Liudolf of Magdeburg seized Oschersleben Castle from a Halberstadt *ministerialis*, to put an end to his depredations. The castle was eventually restored to the bishop of Halberstadt, but not to the *ministerialis*.[77] In 1237, when the Würzburg *ministerialis* Louis of Stollberg was killed after a long feud, Bishop Hermann was able to seize his castle, convert it from allod into an episcopal fief, and oblige Louis's widow to accept there the castellan appointed by him.[78] In the 1240s the count-palatine of the Rhine's procurator and marshal Zorno, who had been subinfeudated with the archbishop of Trier's powerful castle of Thurant on the Mosel, oppressed the neighbourhood cruelly. The combined forces of Trier and Cologne took two years to reduce the castle, and the marshal's excesses everywhere in the Rhineland from Worms down to Coblenz eventually caused his own lord to incarcerate him in 1249.[79] In another case the bishop of Regensburg's *ministerialis* Alhard of Saulberg was arraigned for highway robbery and other misdemeanours in 1268, but he did have his castle restored to him. Twenty of his fellow knights stood surety for his future good behaviour, under pain of ultimately losing Saulberg Castle and his lands.[80]

Siege, confiscation, partial dismantling, or destruction of *ministeriales'* castles were so common a feature of regional politics that one more example may suffice. It was reported that Bishop Gerhard of Münster 'destroyed the castle in Lüdinghausen because of the

---

[75] Holder-Egger, *Monumenta Erphesfurtensia*, p. 765, and similar problems in *Chronicon Hildesheimense*, MGS, VII, p. 861, 1221–49.

[76] MGC ii, 461, pp. 633 f., 1254.

[77] *Gesta Episcoporum Halberstadensium*, MGS, XXIII, p. 121, 1205.

[78] Mon. Boica xxxvii, 248, pp. 271–3, 1237 and Reimann, pp. 170–5.

[79] *Gestorum Treverorum Continuatio V*, MGS, XXIV, pp. 408 f., Waitz, *Chronica Regia Coloniensis*, pp. 294, 298, and Wittmann, *Wittelsbach*, vol. i, 43, p. 103, 1249.

[80] Wittmann, *Wittelsbach*, vol. i, 95, pp. 228 f., 1268.

pillaging by its people',[81] but what actually happened was its partial dismantling. This happened elsewhere, for a razed stronghold was also useless to the victor. After a feud against Hermann and Bernard Wolf of Lüdinghausen, who were the bishop of Verden's *ministeriales*, the Münster forces besieged their castle in 1271 and obtained their surrender. Some of the fortifications were thrown down, but the castle was still defensible. The Wolf brothers were required to submit to the allegiance of Münster and to hold Lüdinghausen Castle open to Münster *ministeriales*.[82] Although this castle had to be reduced by force, many a magnate tried to safeguard himself by purchasing feudal lordship over *ministeriales'* castles with hard cash.[83]

Ministeriales' *feuds and the penalties*

Medieval German society paid a high price for the military mentality of the free nobility and of the *ministeriales* in the form of the extensive devastation arising from their feuds. Justified as a legal avenue of redress, these *guerrae* or feuds might deteriorate into large-scale knightly marauding. The prevalence of feuds launched by *ministeriales* was one of Frederick Barbarossa's preoccupations. On his return from the Second Crusade he hanged some of his Swabian *ministeriales* for their misbehaviour during his absence,[84] and one of his first acts after his election to the throne was to try to limit *ministeriales'* feuds,[85] but without effect. In a famous passage, Bishop Otto of Freising described Barbarossa's revival of ancient penalties for illicit feuding in 1155. On conviction, counts were required to shoulder a dog, *ministeriales* a saddle, and peasants a wheel, after which humiliations they were threatened with the death-penalty.[86] If such measures were ever taken in reality, the *ministeriales* were not fightened off. In 1185 the Pegau annalist laconically recorded that 'the royal *ministeriales* around the Elster River were in conflict, and inflicted mutual devastation

[81] *Menkonis Chronicon*, MGS, XXIII, p. 559.

[82] UB Münster 906, pp. 471 f., 1271.

[83] e.g. the bishop of Eichstätt's purchases in Mon. Boica xlix, 118 f., pp. 181-4, 1282 and 295, pp. 454-6, 1301, and Reg. Eichstätt 983, pp. 304 f., 1284.

[84] Otto and Rahewin, *Gesta Friderici*, p. 90, 1149.

[85] MGC i, 140, p. 198, ch. 19, 1152.

[86] Otto and Rahewin, *Gesta Friderici*, p. 154, 1155.

by fire'.[87] The next year the emperor attempted to outlaw arson during feuds.[88] Small wonder that even the quite substantial magnates were nervous of *ministeriales* and of what they might do. In 1166 the Bavarian Count Siboto of Falkenstein warned his vassals against the Austrian *ministeriales*, who he felt sure would try to seize many of the Falkenstein fiefs for themselves should he die before his sons came of age.[89]

If feuds against their own lords were not at all uncommon,[90] *ministeriales* also attacked their fellow-knights and frequently did violence to the Church. They were careless of the distinction between acts of self-defence, of seeking just redress by force, or of vengeances which were held to be permissible, and outright brigandage. In 1220, for example, a Franconian *ministerialis* robbed Reinhardsbrunn Abbey of a cartload of wine and its six horses. Landgrave Louis of Thuringia besieged him in his castle and forced restitution at swordpoint.[91] Other cases were more serious. Abbot Wibald of Stablo reported raids by the Liège *ministeriales* upon his lands, in which men were killed or wounded while cattle were carried off,[92] and more than once the Bamberg clergy lamented to the imperial court that the emperors' *ministeriales* had ravaged their lands.[93] In 1222 Bishop Gebhard of Passau complained to the court that a large consortium of free nobles and *ministeriales*, more than sixty of them operating from seven strong castles, had caused damages to his see assessed at the high sum of 6,000 marks. They were duly condemned to outlawry.[94] Feuds in Westphalia were incessant, so the bishops of Osnabrück and Münster in 1245 set up a permanent committee of arbitration manned by twelve *ministeriales*.[95]

Lords did not necessarily regard feuds launched against them by their own *ministeriales* as acts of unforgiveable disloyalty. They

[87] *Annales Pegavienses*, MGS, XVI, p. 265.
[88] MGC i, 318, pp. 449-52, 1186.
[89] Noichl, *Codex Falkensteinensis*, 2, pp. 4-7, 1166.
[90] e.g. CD Nassau 873, p. 510, 1275, 899, pp. 527-31, 1276 and 980, p. 582, 1281 where Rhinegrave Siegfried, Seneschal Siegfried of Rheinberg, and William of Rüdesheim were in arms against the archbishop of Mainz, who sought aid 'in presenti werra contra ministeriales, cives Maguntinos et coadiutores' in 895, pp. 524f., 1275.
[91] *Cronica Reinhardsbrunnensis*, MGS, XXX. 1, p. 595 and n. 1.
[92] Jaffé, *Monumenta Corbeiensia*, 109, p. 186, 1148.
[93] Jaffé, *MB*, 107, p. 193, 1084-1102 and 223, p. 395, 1111-25
[94] MGC ii, 278, pp. 391f., 1222.
[95] UB Osnabrück ii, 464, pp. 367f., 1245.

might confiscate fiefs, castles, and offices as the price of peace and renewed grace, or come to some other workable agreement. In 1248 the bishop of Passau required Henry of Morsbach to surrender his castles to episcopal custody, to commit his eldest son to marry at the bishop's discretion, and to assign half his fiefs and allods to the couple.[96] When the last count of Hirschberg died in 1305, his *ministerialis* Rüdiger of Erlingshofen refused to recognize the bishop of Eichstätt, who was the count's legal heir, as his new lord, and took to arms. In 1312 he submitted to the bishop, 'whose property I am', as he now admitted. His castle was partly dismantled, his new terms of service were laid down, and some of his possessions were surrendered to Eichstätt.[97]

Ministeriales also risked excommunication,[98] condemnation as outlaws, exile from their province, and the death-penalty itself. The archbishop of Cologne permitted excommunication of his *ministeriales* only when 'they unjustly seize or usurp for themselves the tithes or possessions of the church',[99] but few *ministeriales* were deterred by the inconveniences of this punishment. In 1288 the Hildesheim chapter complained that Conrad of Borsum had already been excommunicated for more than two years for keeping hold of one of their manors,[100] and it was armed force, not the perilous condition of his soul, which compelled the bishop of Münster's *ministerialis* Frederick of Warendorp to return the manor of Dakmar to its rightful owner, the abbot of Iburg.[101] Condemnation to outlawry, or proscription, by the imperial court was more serious, but not necessarily more effective. In 1296 Bishop Liudolf of Minden explained that one of his *ministeriales* had been proscribed for years, but had continued to pillage the land, to tax the bishop's dependents, to extort money from the bishop himself, and to refuse him entry to his castles, which he threatened to alienate to the dukes of Brunswick.[102] In this case one can discern the importance to a contumacious *ministerialis* of encouragement by

[96] UB Land ob der Enns iii, 144, pp. 144 f., 1248.

[97] Reg. Eichstätt 1514, pp. 473 f., 1312.

[98] UB Hildesheim ii, 67, p. 33, 1223, where the bishop of Hildesheim excommunicated Seneschal Gunzelin of Wolfenbüttel, his sons, and his accomplices for violating the peace.

[99] Weinrich, p. 274, c.1165.

[100] UB Hildesheim iii, 798, p. 408, 1288.

[101] UB Osnabrück ii, 380, pp. 298 f., 1238.

[102] MGC iii, 552 f., pp. 520 f., 1296.

the bishop's princely rivals. On the same subject the bishop of Regensburg and the duke of Bavaria agreed in 1213 not to shelter delinquent *ministeriales* belonging to the other party.[103]

Not uncommonly *ministeriales* killed each other in their quarrels. The homicide lost all his rights until his lord could arrange composition for him with the injured kindred. At Cologne in the twelfth century such arrangements were extremely elaborate, and if they failed, rendered the guilty knight liable to life-imprisonment. If compensation in cash was acceptable, then killers were restored to their standing amongst their fellow *ministeriales*.[104] On occasion the death-penalty was inflicted upon *ministeriales* whose violent behaviour was held to have broken the peace-legislation or *Landfrieden* enacted by the princes, the cities, and the empire itself. In 1242 the duke of Bavaria had two of the count of Bogen's *ministeriales*, Albert and Wernhard of Moos, decapitated in the market-place at Hengersberg for breaking the peace.[105] In a notorious affair in 1288, sixteen prominent Saxon *ministeriales*, whom one chronicler characterized as 'the cruellest of evil-doers and the greediest of robbers', were rounded up and executed at Helmstedt.[106]

The consequences of violence

At times the widescale feuds, killings, and brigandage perpetrated by *ministeriales* posed a serious menace to an entire region.[107] The regular response to this kind of disorder was the *Landfriede* or peace-keeping association, so often and ineffectually set up by the crown, princes, and Church.[108] In certain circumstances, acts of violence were acceptable to the noble orders in Germany, and their evil consequences to some extent mitigated by customs governing the conduct of feuds. The majority of feuds appear to have been

[103] Wittmann, *Wittelsbach*, vol. i, 5, pp. 14-19, 1213; Dukes Henry and Louis of Bavaria agreed the same in 86, p. 205, 1265.

[104] UB Niederrhein i, 196, p. 126, 1061, and UB Osnabrück ii, 216, pp. 164 f., 1226.

[105] Spindler, *Anfänge*, p. 109.

[106] Holder-Egger, *Monumenta Erphesfurtensia*, p. 292, *Cronica Reinhardsbrunnensis*, MGS, XXX. 1, p. 633, and MG Deutsche Chroniken, vol. II, pp. 587, 597.

[107] See the *werrae plurimae et graves* involving magnates and *ministeriales* in Waitz, *Chronica Regia Coloniensis*, p. 167, 1199.

[108] e.g. MGC ii, 425-46, pp. 566-616, 1200-69.

motivated by disputes over property rights, and to have had their
material cause in the social position of *ministeriales* as armed landowners with acquisitive tastes. The signs are that *ministeriales* in
arms on their own account were not always the mindless subverters
of repetitive peace-legislation. There were sudden acts of class-
redress, as in Regensburg in 1104, or long-term measures of political
opposition, often for obscure reasons, as in thirteenth-century Austria, Utrecht, or Salzburg.

Their use of violence was complicated and extended by the
medieval German nobleman's expectation of support in all such
actions from his relatives, friends, and armed following. Even when
the feud originated in the grievances of an individual, it became the
collective act of a kindred operating from more than one castle.

Violence was a double-edged instrument in knightly hands. Its
acceptable basis lay in custom permitting vengeance, redress, and
self-defence in noble society. Assassination of lords, on the other
hand, fundamentally defied both the wider code of knightly vassalage and the narrower obligations of familial dependence and
ascription of *ministeriales*. The custumals hint of or warn against
this peril, but lords were not very often murdered by their *ministeriales*. When it happened, it caused a sensation.[109]

More equivocal was the frequency of feuds, homicides, duels,
and other acts of violence amongst *ministeriales* who were members
of the same retinue, for they contradicted the solidarity and reliability of loyal service, and undermined lords' protective justice over
their followings. The custumals legislated against this kind of violence in the interests of familial discipline. Lords were not above
trying to manipulate such feuds for their own ends. In 1241 Diessen
Abbey compelled the Bavarian *ministerialis* Engelschalk of Heng-
nenberg to assist in feuds against the vassals of his own lord, the
duke of Bavaria,[110] who was the principal enemy of the abbey's
advocate, the duke of Merania.

When lords' lives and security were threatened, their retinues set
at loggerheads, or their peace-legislation flouted by robbery, arson,
and homicide, then violence by *ministeriales* was unacceptable.
Where the *ministeriales*' declared motives approximated to current
standards, never closely defined, about legitimate redress through

feuds, then the region also faced devastation, laying waste by fire, intimidation and extortion, violent deaths, and the seizure of cattle, treasure, movables, and captives. These sorrows were compounded by the ugly demoralization of the *ministeriales* through economic decline after 1300. The pretence of redress was thrown aside, and the increasingly redundant knightly order became characterized by its proneness to banditry as a mode of existence and survival.[111]

[111] Telling example in *Gesta Episcoporum Eichstetensium Continuata*, MGS, XXV, p. 605, 1408.

Conclusion

Undoubtedly the collective mentality of the German *ministeriales* favoured the stability of their rank and functions, underlined by legal rights, inherited traditions, and social sanctions. In reality they did not constitute a static social order. Their situation was continually modified by new opportunities, notably those based upon internal and external colonization and the elaboration of landlord government, and by political threats, such as the collapse of Hohenstaufen rule or the demise of ruling dynasties in the territorial principalities. *Ministeriales* in their economic standing were diverse, from the great feoffees and office-holders under the crown, Church, and territorial dynasts, to the poverty-stricken knights, inclined to banditry, who held no offices and lacked the material advantages provided by multiple allegiances.

The outward existence of the *ministeriales* as a knightly order was governed by the mutual relationship of lord and vassal. To maintain military retinues, land was sufficiently available to magnates for the economic basis of the *ministeriales* as a social order really to be secured by a massive endowment with hereditary fiefs in exchange for service-obligations. This endowment gained its momentum in the eleventh century, because it was an era of significant agrarian expansion, providing the German magnates with renewed resources. The enfeoffed retinues of *ministeriales* operated according to the rules of vassalage descended from the Carolingian model established in the eighth century, and becoming hereditary between the ninth and the eleventh centuries. This primary military purpose, sustained by the land held in fief, was supplemented by allodial possessions. The hereditary devolution of all their fiefs, offices, and allods gave the *ministeriales* inner cohesion as a social class, since they were, in any case, constrained by their lords to marry almost exclusively amongst themselves.

If the actual economic standing of *ministeriales* was varied, their legal rights and obligations were broadly similar everywhere in Germany. The surviving custumals, in revised or authentic redactions, together with other confections, forgeries, and legal frag-

ments, convey a reasonably precise catalogue of what these liabilities and privileges consisted.[1] The law or *ius* of *ministeriales*
comprised three interdependent parts: the rules of vassal-knighthood, which governed fiefs and services; the rules of personal servitude and ascription, which governed allods and marriages; and
the rules of the *familia* or household, which bound *ministeriales* to
their lords not by contracts, but by theoretically indissoluble affi-
liations heritable for ever in the female line. Like vassalage, the
strict familial nexus and the binding details of personal unfreedom
must have been founded upon Carolingian precedent, but the history of their institutional transmission into the German empire of
the eleventh century is, in all probability, too obscure to be deci-
phered. However, the laws for *ministeriales* actually reduced to
writing, and better twelfth-century evidence about their personal
servitude, are informative on how their integration with vassalage
worked in practice. We have seen that the earliest surviving custumal, the Bamberg list credited to Bishop Gunther (1057-65),[2] is
committed to granting heritable fiefs to *ministeriales* in exchange
for cavalry service. It reserves the best posts in the bishops' household to them, and also allows for mobility of service under other
lords.

The evidence for the emergence of the *ministeriales* in the eleventh century is dismayingly thin. Did the new order, its human
material, substantially move forward out of the free-born classes of
late Carolingian and Ottonian society, possibly from the *censuales*,
as the Saxon evidence has sometimes been taken to show?[3] Or was
the household and *familia* of the tenth and eleventh-century magnate, especially the bishop, who tended to promote the unfree men
who stood close to him,[4] the essentially creative institution? There
is positive but quite fragmentary evidence to show both that free
men became *ministeriales*, and that ecclesiastical magnates could
and did promote their unfree dependents into knights. If the social
origins of *ministeriales* as a new knighthood are perplexing,[5] the

[1] See Ch. 3.
[2] See p. 27, n. 17.
[3] See pp. 41 f., nn. 97-8, 100.
[4] See pp. 38-40, nn. 82-6, 88-94, p. 44, nn. 109-10.
[5] We also need wider understanding of problems about earlier military society
already tackled by Leyser (see p. 2, nn. 2-3, p. 7, n. 12), for it must be in 'development and change in the teeming womb of late Carolingian and Ottonian society
where the birth of a lesser nobility and the formation of new social frontiers must

vehicle, the enfeoffment of vassal-militias on a large scale in the eleventh century, is plain to see. So are the motives of the magnates, who needed great retinues to fight their feuds and to maintain their political standing in the empire. The mode of vassalage differed regionally in western Europe. In the German empire it embraced personal unfreedom for most knights, rendering the term *miles* ambiguous and leading, after confused experimentation, to the more laborious word *ministerialis* in the scribal Latin of the twelfth century.

If *ministeriales* can be characterized as unfree vassal-knights, other realities became apparent in their lives in the twelfth century. The legal attachment to their mothers' lords' retinues was eroded by multiple enfeoffment and allegiance, and by extrinsic marriage itself, for no retinue was an enclosed biological entity. The unfree status more precisely defined in the written custumals was not in itself a hindrance to the assumption of a noble rank and way of life, since residence in stone castles, the use of hereditary toponymics, and generosity to the Church, were the inevitable outcome of their knightly life and purpose.[6] To some extent the aristocratic spirit of Hohenstaufen knighthood is reflected in the fine vernacular poetry of that age. But the delineation is too capricious, theoretical, or indeterminate for any plausible or concrete deductions to be made from it about the real character or identity of the *ministeriales* as an actual social order.[7]

Their knightly way of life reflected the forces which had encouraged the enfeoffment of *ministeriales* in the first place, the prevalence of violence in the empire. Not only annals, chronicles, and letters, but also imperial edicts, peace-legislation, and charters of arbitration constitute a litany of turbulence in medieval Germany. Retinues of *ministeriales* were designed to partake in this, but one result was their adoption of belligerent or lawless means to gain their own ends. The grim evidence for their contumacy does not

---

somehow be traced'. See also Werner, 'Heeresorganisation und Kriegführung', and M G C i, 436, pp. 632 f., for the *loricati* of 981.

[6] See p. 70, nn. 104-7, pp. 151-9, nn. 67-123.

[7] See p. 36, n. 74, p. 70, n. 105, p. 73, n. 129, p. 99, n. 98. Bumke, *Ministerialität und Ritterdichtung*, has shown that though *ministeriales* did write poetry, the legal status of the poets has little or no significance for the composition, content, or sociological evaluation of that literature; see especially pp. 7-13, 66-9 and nn. 368A and 383.

quite outweigh the usefulness of their aggressive tendencies and expertise in the employ of their lords as an active knighthood.

Ministeriales were above all warriors, but the conduct of war increasingly depended upon ready cash, a commodity seldom at hand to the magnates or their *ministeriales* in any quantity. The *ministeriales* had always been provided with extra money for the imperial expeditions to Italy, and in the thirteenth century there are signs that they expected cash-subsidies in Germany as well.[8] Not enough money and credit were available to lords to be able to replace the customary armed services of enfeoffed vassals with more flexible hired hosts until the end of the middle ages. If the costs of war were rising, the continued use of *ministeriales* represented more antiquated techniques of mobilization than those of France or Italy.[9] As the science was elaborated, programmes of fortification also required larger cash outlays. We do not know how the erection of the small twelfth-century stone tower of refuge and *domus* was financed, but the much larger castles of the thirteenth and fourteenth centuries, some of them inhabited by several families of *ministeriales*, were enfeoffed by the magnates who had paid for building them.[10]

Much was demanded of the *ministeriales* as a knighthood, in warfare itself, in seigneurial administration, and in the political life of the empire. A great deal more could be shown of the way in which *ministeriales* belonging to individual ecclesiastical and secular princes contributed effectively to the political affairs of their region, on inner and more manageable lines of communication and strategic reality not available to the imperial retinue.[11] In spite of

[8] See p. 81, n. 23, p. 111, n. 52, p. 188, n. 34, p. 218, nn. 51-2.

[9] Shown e.g. in *Gesta Episcoporum Eichstetensium Continuata*, MGS, XXV, pp. 590-609, 1279-1445, borne out by Bayerisches Staatsarchiv Nürnberg, Hochstift Eichstätt, Lehenbücher I, ff. 74r-300r, 1365-1496.

[10] See p. 127, n. 148, and my thesis, pp. 263-9, 272-8. Compare the buildings still standing in the Eichstätt region, e.g. the simple ashlar *turres* of the 12th c. at Pappenheim and Wellheim with the multiple towers and curtain (1297-1305) at Nassenfels, where six *ministeriales* held garrison-offices.

[11] Von Guttenberg, *Territorienbildung*, pp. 299-358, Klewitz, *Entwicklung*, pp. 29-40, Prinz, *Osnabrück*, pp. 108-27, Patze, *Entstehung*, pp. 326-70, Reimann, pp. 1-266, J.M. van Winter, 'The Ministerial and Knightly Classes in Guelders and Zutphen', *Acta Historiae Neerlandica* i (1966), 171-86, W. Rösener, 'Ministerialität, Vasallität und niederadelige Ritterschaft im Herrschaftsbereich der Markgrafen von Baden vom 11. bis zum 14. Jahrhundert' in J. Fleckenstein (ed.), *Herrschaft und Stand*, pp. 40-91, Kusternig and Weltin (ed.), *Kuenringer-Forschungen*, and my thesis, pp. 88-90, 201-19, 261-78, 346-54.

the relatively open structure of retinues where extrinsic marriage and multiple allegiance had abridged the vigour of perpetual ascription, lords were compelled to rely upon their *ministeriales* to secure their regional jurisdictions and possessions. The long-term historical significance of the *ministeriales* lies in the construction out of these materials of the territorial principalities under their masters in the twelfth and thirteenth centuries. For these undertakings the *ministeriales*, rather than the clerical or bourgeois employees of a later age, were fitted by their knightly training in war and administration. The better *ministeriales* provided the princes with a rough-and-ready officialdom, and the mass of knights in their castles were committed to defending the land. In spite of wrangles about respective rights, the *ministeriales* had a future as the land-owning noble estate or *Landstand* offering counsel, consent, and service as vassals to their princes in peace and war.[12]

The retinue of *ministeriales* established by the twelfth century was projected genetically through to early modern times as the service-nobility of the selfsame princes' descendants, within the jurisdictionally more state-like territorial lordships. This had consequences for *ministeriales*' legal status.. As the outer territorial boundaries of princely and ecclesiastical possessions became more coherent after 1300, so maternal ascription and personal servitude of *ministeriales* lost their significance as mechanisms, at best unreliable, for keeping knights under political control. The more effective method was now geographical, to continue to tally the *ministeriales* as vassal-knights with their castles as fiefs, and to record them in new or revised books of fiefs.[13] Vassalage, of course, had always been of prime importance in the history of the *ministeriales*, and it wholly replaced personal unfreedom and maternal ascription by the fifteenth century.[14] Incorporated as an order or *Landstand*

---

[12] W. Volkert, 'Adel und Landstände' in Spindler, *Handbuch*, vol. ii, pp. 502-15; Bachmann, *Landstände*, E. Schubert, *Die Landstände des Hochstifts Würzburg*, Veröffentlichungen der Gesellschaft für fränkische Geschichte, ser. 9, XXIII (Würzburg, 1967), E. Klebel, 'Territorialstaat und Lehen' in *Studien zum mittelalterlichen Lehenswesen*, VF, V (Lindau and Constance, 1960), pp. 195-228, and G. Theuerkauf, *Land und Lehnswesen vom 14. bis zum 16. Jahrhundert. Ein Beitrag zur Verfassung des Hochstifts Münster*, Neue Münstersche Beiträge zur Geschichtsforschung, VII (Cologne and Graz, 1961).

[13] See p. 97, n. 90, p. 110, n. 50.

[14] Pötter, pp. 118-44, reckons that the Cologne *ministeriales* already enjoyed 'die landrechtliche Freiheit' by about 1230, emphasizing their vassalage, pp. 144-55;

under their princes' more formidable jurisdictions, the tradition of military and official service as vassals and fief-holders went on.

About 1300 the *ministeriales* were beginning, as a class, to face another challenge which broke them apart along the lines already indicated between rich and poor knights. This was the onset of contraction in the manorial economy, which struck at the basis of their existence as landowners. Already at the end of the thirteenth century whole retinues in impoverished parts of Germany were selling off their lands to the Church,[15] and the fourteenth century saw an upsurge of violence as knights took to brigandage in response to their disintegrating economic position. Perhaps the robber-knight was untypical, but impoverishment for the majority was not. A further consequence of the agrarian crisis was to identify the minority of richer *ministeriales* who could outride it with the remnants of the free nobility as one noble order.[16] This identification, eventually underlined by intermarriage, was another means by which servitude of persons and ascription by maternal descent were becoming outmoded,[17] turning the richer knights into a titled nobility of free status, the *Freiherren*. They carried over the *ministeriales'* tradition of military and administrative service into the princely territories and states of early modern and recent times.

As the old familial bonds of ascription and the assumptions advertised in the custumals gradually passed away, the rise of territorial lordship and the consolidation of princely authority emphasized the ingrained regional variation in the society of the medieval empire. It is not easy, therefore, to generalize about the

Ritter, pp. 110-15, thinks that the legal foundations of servile status were being abandoned by 1250, but this is much too early.

[15] See my thesis, pp. 198-201, 333-6.

[16] By 1422 some of them had achieved jurisdictional autonomy under the emperor, as the *Reichsritterschaft*; O. Eberbach, *Die deutsche Reichsritterschaft in ihrer staatsrechtlich-politischen Entwicklung von den Anfängen bis zum Jahre 1422* (Dresden, 1912).

[17] On the forces for change amongst the south German *ministeriales*, see Lieberich, *Landherren und Landleute*, H. Obenaus, *Recht und Verfassung der Gesellschaften mit St. Jörgenschild in Schwaben*, Veröffentlichungen des Max-Planck-Instituts für Geschichte, VII (Göttingen, 1961), G. Diepolder, 'Oberbayerische und niederbayerische Adelsherrschaften im wittelsbachischen Territorialstaat des 13.-15. Jahrhunderts', *ZBLG* xxv (1962), 33-70, P. Feldbauer, 'Rangprobleme und Konnubium österreichischer Landherrenfamilien. Zur sozialen Mobilität einer spätmittelalterlichen Führungsgruppe', ibid. xxxv (1972), 571-90, S. Krüger, 'Das Rittertum in den Schriften des Konrad von Megenberg' in Fleckenstein (ed.), *Herrschaft und Stand*, pp. 302-28, and pp. 110, n. 50, p. 119, n. 101 above.

ministeriales' future,[18] or their transformation into the lesser nobility of modern Germany, as the very name of *ministerialis* evaporated in the ebullition of political turmoil and economic stress
typical of the fourteenth and fifteenth centuries in Germany. These
medieval knights were nevertheless tenacious of a blunt sense of
military confidence, expressed in a political tract of 1338 by one of
their number, Conrad of Megenberg. Enlarging upon the high
worth of 'the German nation, summit of knighthood', he claimed
that 'eminent and victorious Germany, cradle of knighthood, is
guileless, prompt to arms, hardy and vigorous. "The outcome jus-
tifies the deed", and Germany furnishes the strength.'[19]

[18] J. Fleckenstein, 'Die Entstehung des niederen Adels und das Rittertum' in
Herrschaft und Stand, esp. pp. 35-9.
[19] H. Kusch, *Konrad von Megenberg. Klagelied der Kirche über Deutschland, Planctus Ecclesiae in Germaniam*, Leipziger Übersetzungen und Abhandlungen zum
Mittelalter, ser. A, I (Berlin, 1956), pp. 60-4.

Bibliography

I PRINTED SOURCES

Acht, P., *Die Traditionen des Klosters Tegernsee 1003-1242*, QE, IX. 1 (Munich, 1952).
——, *Mainzer Urkundenbuch. Die Urkunden seit dem Tode Erzbischof Adalberts I.* (*1137*) *bis zum Tode Erzbischof Konrads* (*1200*) Arbeiten der Hessischen Historischen Kommission (2 parts, Darmstadt, 1968 and 1971).
Bauer, A., and Rau, R., *Quellen zur Geschichte der sächsischen Kaiserzeit*, AQ, VIII (Darmstadt, 1977).
Bechstein, R., *Ulrichs von Liechtenstein Frauendienst*, Deutsche Dichtungen des Mittelalters, VI and VII (Leipzig, 1888).
Bendel, F.J., Heidingsfelder, F., and Kaufmann, M., *Urkundenbuch der Benediktiner-Abtei St. Stephan in Würzburg*, vol. i, Veröffentlichungen der Gesellschaft für fränkische Geschichte, ser. 3, Fränkische Urkundenbücher (Leipzig, 1912).
Beyer, H., Eltester, L., and Goerz, A., *Urkundenbuch zur Geschichte der Mittelrheinischen Territorien* (3 vols., Coblenz, 1860-74).
Bitterauf, T., *Die Traditionen des Hochstifts Freising 926-1283*, QE, V (Munich, 1909).
Bloch, H., *Annales Marbacenses qui dicuntur*, MG schol., IX (Hanover and Leipzig, 1907).
Bocholtz-Asseburg, J. Graf von, *Asseburger Urkundenbuch. Urkunden und Regesten zur Geschichte des Geschlechts Wolfenbüttel-Asseburg* (2 vols., Hanover, 1876-87).
Boehmer, J.F., and Lau, F., *Urkundenbuch der Reichsstadt Frankfurt*, I (new edn., Frankfurt, 1901).
Boos, H., *Urkundenbuch der Stadt Worms 627-1300*, Quellen zur Geschichte der Stadt Worms, I (Berlin, 1886).
Boretius, A., and Krause, V., *Capitularia Regum Francorum*, MG Legum sectio II (2 vols., Hanover, 1883-97).
Borman, C. de, *Chronique de l'abbaye de Saint-Trond*, (Publications de la Société des bibliophiles liégeois, X, XV (Liège, 1877).
Bresslau, H., *Die Werke Wipos*, MG schol., LXI (3rd edn., Hanover and Leipzig, 1915).
Busley, H.-J., *Die Traditionen, Urkunden und Urbare des Klosters Neustift bei Freising*, QE, XIX (Munich, 1961).

Chroust, A., *Quellen zur Geschichte des Kreuzzuges Kaiser Friedrichs I.*, MGS, n.s., V (Berlin, 1928).

Crecelius, W., *Traditiones Werdinenses*, part ii, Collectae ad augendam nominum propriorum Saxonicorum et Frisiorum scientiam spectantes, III.B (Berlin, 1870).

Dumrath, K., *Die Traditionsnotizen des Klosters Raitenhaslach*, QE, VII (Munich, 1938).

Eberhard, W., *Vita Heinrici IV. Imperatoris*, MG schol., LVIII (3rd edn., Hanover and Leipzig, 1899).

Eckhardt, K.A., *Sachsenspiegel Landrecht und Lehnrecht*, MG Fontes iuris Germanici antiqui, n.s., I. 1 and 2 (2nd edn., Göttingen, 1955-6).

——*Schwabenspiegel Kurzform*, vol. i, MG Fontes iuris Germanici antiqui, n.s. IV. 1 (Hanover, 1960).

——and Hübner, A., *Deutschenspiegel und Augsburger Sachsenspiegel*, MG Fontes iuris Germanici antiqui, n.s., III (Hanover, 1933).

Erdmann, C., *Die Briefe Heinrichs IV.*, MG Deutsches Mittelalter, I (Leipzig, 1937).

——and Fickermann, N., *Briefsammlungen der Zeit Heinrichs IV.*, MG Die Briefe der deutschen Kaiserzeit, V (Weimar, 1950).

Erhard, H.A., *Codex Diplomaticus Historiae Westfaliae* (2 vols., Münster, 1847-51).

Escher, J., and Schweizer, P., *Urkundenbuch der Stadt und Landschaft Zürich*, vol. i, (Zürich, 1888-90).

Finke, H., *Westfälisches Urkundenbuch*, vol. iv, *Die Urkunden des Bisthums Paderborn 3: 1251-1300* (Münster, 1889-94).

Franz, G., *Quellen zur Geschichte des deutschen Bauernstandes im Mittelalter*, AQ, XXXI (Darmstadt, 1967).

Frast, J. von, *Liber fundationum monasterii Zwetlensis*, Fontes Rerum Austriacarum, ser. 2, Diplomataria et Acta, III (Vienna, 1851).

Fritz, W., *Die Goldene Bulle Kaiser Karls IV. vom Jahre 1356*, Fontes iuris Germanici antiqui in usum scholarum ex MG, XI (Weimar, 1972).

Fuchs, A.F., *Urkunden und Regesten zur Geschichte des Benedictinerstiftes Göttweig*, vol. i, Fontes Rerum Austriacarum, ser. 2, Diplomataria et Acta, LI (Vienna, 1901).

Geier, J., *Die Traditionen, Urkunden und Urbare des Klosters Asbach*, QE XXIII (Munich, 1969).

Giesebrecht, W. von, and Oefele, L.B. von, *Annales Altahenses Maiores*, MG schol. IV (2nd edn., Hanover, 1891).

Glöckner, K., *Codex Laureshamensis*, 3 vols., Arbeiten der Historischen Kommission für den Volksstaat Hessen (Darmstadt, 1929-36).

Grünenwald, E., *Das Älteste Lehenbuch der Grafschaft Oettingen, 14. Jahrhundert bis 1477*, Schwäbische Forschungsgemeinschaft bei der Kommission für bayerische Landesgeschichte, ser. 5, Urbare, II (Augsburg, 1976).

Güterbock, F., *Das Geschichtswerk des Otto Morena und seiner Fortsetzer über die Taten Friedrichs I. in der Lombardei*, MGS, n.s., VII (Berlin, 1930).

Haefele, H. F., *Ekkehard IV. St. Galler Klostergeschichten*, AQ, X (Darmstadt, 1980).

Hauthaler, W. and Martin, F., *Salzburger Urkundenbuch*, 4 vols., including *Traditionscodices* (Salzburg, 1910–33).

Heidingsfelder, F., *Die Regesten der Bischöfe von Eichstätt*, Veröffentlichungen der Gesellschaft für fränkische Geschichte, ser. 6 (Innsbruck, Würzburg, and Erlangen, 1915–38).

Heinemann, O. von, *Codex Diplomaticus Anhaltinus*, part i (Dessau, 1867–73).

Heinemeyer, W., *Chronica Fuldensis. Die Darmstädter Fragmente der Fuldaer Chronik*, AD, Beiheft I (Cologne and Vienna, 1976).

Helbig, H. and Weinrich, L., *Urkunden und erzählende Quellen zur deutschen Ostsiedlung im Mittelalter*, vol. ii, AQ, XXVI.B (Darmstadt, 1970).

Hessel, A. and Krebs, M., *Regesten der Bischöfe von Straßburg*, vol. ii (Innsbruck, 1924).

Heuwieser, M., *Die Traditionen des Hochstifts Passau*, QE, vol. vi (Munich, 1930).

Hipper, R., *Die Urkunden des Reichsstiftes St Ulrich und Afra in Augsburg 1023–1440*, Schwäbische Forschungsgemeinschaft bei der Kommission für bayerische Landesgeschichte, ser. 2A, Urkunden und Regesten, IV (Augsburg, 1956).

Hirsch, P., and Lohmann, H.-E., *Die Sachsengeschichte des Widukind von Korvei*, MG schol. LX (5th edn., Hanover, 1935).

Hoffman, H., *Das älteste Lehenbuch des Hochstifts Würzburg 1303–1345*, Quellen und Forschungen zur Geschichte des Bistums und Hochstifts Würzburg, XXV (Würzburg, 1972).

Hofmeister, A., *Ottonis Episcopi Frisingensis Chronica sive Historia de Duabus Civitatibus*, MG schol. XLV (2nd edn., Hanover and Leipzig, 1912).

——*Ottonis de Sancto Blasio Chronica*, MG schol. XLVII (Hanover and Leipzig, 1912).

Holder-Egger, O., *Lamperti Monachi Hersfeldensis Opera*, MG schol. XXXVIII (Hanover and Leipzig, 1894).

——*Monumenta Erphesfurtensia saec. XII. XIII. XIV.*, MG schol. XLII (Hanover and Leipzig, 1899).

——and von Simson, B., *Die Chronik des Propstes Burchard von Ursberg*, MG schol. XVI (2nd edn., Hanover and Leipzig, 1916).

Hoogeweg, H., *Urkundenbuch des Hochstifts Hildesheim und seiner Bischöfe*, parts ii and iii, Quellen und Darstellungen zur Geschichte Niedersachsens, VI, XI (Hanover and Leipzig, 1901–3).

Huillard Bréholles, J.L.A., *Historia Diplomatica Friderici Secundi* (6 vols., Paris, 1852–61, 1963 reprint).

Hundt, F.H. Graf, *Das Cartular des Klosters Ebersberg*, Abhandlung der historischen Classe der königlich bayerischen Akademie der Wissenschaften, XIV. 3 (Munich, 1879), pp. 115-96.

Israël, F. and Möllenberg, W., *Urkundenbuch des Erzstifts Magdeburg*, vol. i, Geschichtsquellen der Provinz Sachsen und des Freistaates Anhalt, n.s. XVIII (Magdeburg, 1937).

Jaffé, P., *Monumenta Corbeiensia, Monumenta Moguntina,* and *Monumenta Bambergensia*, Bibliotheca Rerum Germanicarum, I, III, V (Berlin 1864-9).

Jaksch, A. von, *Monumenta Historica Ducatus Carinthiae* (4 vols., Klagenfurt, 1896-1906).

Janicke, K., *Urkundenbuch des Hochstifts Hildesheim und seiner Bischöfe*, part 1, Publicationen aus den königlich Preußischen Staatsarchiven, LXV (Leipzig, 1896).

Jordan, K., *Die Urkunden Heinrichs des Löwen Herzogs von Sachsen und Bayern*, MG Die deutschen Geschichtsquellen des Mittelalters, I. Urkundentexte (Stuttgart, 1957).

Kehr, P., *Urkundenbuch des Hochstifts Merseburg*, part i, Geschichtsquellen der Provinz Sachsen, XXXVI (Halle, 1899).

Kelleter, H., *Urkundenbuch des Stiftes Kaiserswerth*, Urkundenbücher der geistlichen Stiftungen des Niederrheins, I (Bonn, 1904).

Keutgen, F., *Urkunden zur städtischen Verfassungsgeschichte*, Ausgewählte Urkunden zur deutschen Verfassungs- und Wirtschaftsgeschichte, I (new edn., Aalen, 1965).

Kindlinger, N., *Geschichte der deutschen Hörigkeit insbesondere der sogenannten Leibeigenschaft* (Berlin, 1819).

König, E., *Historia Welforum*, Schwäbische Chroniken der Stauferzeit, I (Sigmaringen, 1978).

Krausen, E., *Die Urkunden des Klosters Raitenhaslach 1034-1350*, QE, XVII (Munich, 1959).

Krühne, M., *Urkundenbuch der Klöster der Grafschaft Mansfeld*, Geschichtsquellen der Provinz Sachsen, XX (Halle, 1888).

Kusch, H., *Konrad von Megenberg. Klagelied der Kirche über Deutschland, Planctus Ecclesiae in Germaniam*, Leipziger Übersetzungen und Abhandlungen zum Mittelalter, ser. A, I (Berlin, 1956).

Lacomblet, T.J., *Urkundenbuch für die Geschichte des Niederrheins* (4 vols., Düsseldorf, 1840-58).

Lappenberg, J.M., *Hamburgisches Urkundenbuch*, vol. i (2nd edn., Hamburg, 1907).

Lohmann, H.-E., *Brunos Buch vom Sachsenkrieg*, MG Deutsches Mittelalter, II (Leipzig, 1937).

Mai, H.-P., *Die Traditionen, die Urkunden und das älteste Urbarfragment des Stiftes Rohr 1133-1332*, QE, XXI (Munich, 1966).

Mayerhofer, J., 'Codex Augiensium' in Petz, H., Grauert, H., and Mayerhofer, J., *Drei bayerische Traditionsbücher aus dem XII. Jahrhundert.*

Festschrift zum 700jährigen Jubiläum der Wittelsbacher Thronbesteigung (Munich, 1880), pp. 87-152.

Menzel, K. and Sauer, W., *Codex Diplomaticus Nassoicus. Nassauisches Urkundenbuch*, vol. i (Wiesbaden, 1885-6).

Mierow, C.C. and Emery, R., *The Deeds of Frederick Barbarossa by Otto of Freising and his Continuator Rahewin*, Records of Civilization. Sources and Studies, XLIX (New York, 1953).

Mierow, C.C., *The Two Cities. A Chronicle of Universal History to the Year 1146 A.D. by Otto, Bishop of Freising*, Records of Civilization, Sources and Studies, IX (new edn., New York, 1966).

Mohr, C., *Die Traditionen des Klosters Oberalteich*, QE, XXX. 1 (Munich, 1979).

Mommsen, T.E. and Morrison, K.F., *Imperial Lives and Letters of the Eleventh Century*, Records of Civilization. Sources and Studies, LXVII (New York and London, 1962).

Monumenta Boica (60 vols., Munich, 1764-1954).

Monumenta Germaniae Historica, Scriptores in folio (30 vols., 1826-1926), Constitutiones et Acta Publica (4 vols., 1893-1906), and Diplomataria in folio (17 vols., 1872-1979).

Noichl, E., *Codex Falkensteinensis. Die Rechtsaufzeichnungen der Grafen von Falkenstein*, QE, XXIX (Munich, 1978).

Nürnberger Urkundenbuch, Quellen und Forschungen zur Geschichte der Stadt Nürnberg, I (Nuremberg, 1959).

Oefele, E. von, 'Traditionsnotizen des Klosters Kühbach', *Sitzungsberichte der phil.-hist. Classe der Akademie der Wissenschaften zu München 1894* (Munich, 1895), pp. 269-86.

Peeck, F., *Die Reinhardsbrunner Briefsammlung*, MG Epistolae selectae, V (Weimar, 1952).

Pfeiffer, F., *Berthold von Regensburg. Vollständige Ausgabe seiner Predigten*, Deutsche Neudrucke, Texte des Mittelalters (Berlin, 1965).

Philippi, F. and Bär, M., *Osnabrücker Urkundenbuch* (4 vols., Osnabrück, 1892-1902).

Piot, C., *Cartulaire de l'abbaye de Saint-Trond*, part i, Collection de chroniques belges inédites (Brussels, 1870).

Posse, O, and Ermisch, E., *Codex Diplomaticus Saxoniae Regiae*, part 1 *Urkunden der Markgrafen von Meißen und Landgrafen von Thüringen 1100 bis 1195*, vols. ii, iii (Leipzig, 1889-98).

Redlich, O., *Die Traditionsbücher des Hochstifts Brixen*, Acta Tirolensia. Urkundliche Quellen zur Geschichte Tirols, I (Innsbruck, 1886).

Reimer, H., *Hessisches Urkundenbuch ii. Urkundenbuch zur Geschichte der Herren von Hanau und der ehemaligen Provinz Hanau*, Publikationen aus den königlich Preußischen Staatsarchiven, XLVIII (Leipzig, 1891).

Rodenberg, C., *Epistolae Saeculi XIII. e Regestis Pontificum Romanorum*, vol. i, MG (Berlin, 1883).

Rosenfeld, F., *Urkundenbuch des Hochstifts Naumburg*, part i, Geschichtsquellen der Provinz Sachsen, n.s., I (Magdeburg, 1925).

Rothert, H., *Die mittelalterlichen Lehnbücher der Bischöfe von Osnabrück*, Osnabrücker Geschichtsquellen, V (Osnabrück, 1932).

Rüthning, G., *Oldenburgisches Urkundenbuch*, vols. ii–iv (Oldenburg, 1926-8).

Sackur, E., *Gerhohi Praepositi Reichersbergensis Libelli Selecti*, MG Libelli de lite, III (Hanover, 1897), pp. 131-525.

Schlögl, W., *Die Traditionen und Urkunden des Stiftes Dießen 1114-1362*, QE, XXII. 1 (Munich, 1967).

Schmale, F.-J. and Schmale-Ott, I., *Frutolfs und Ekkehards Chroniken und die Anonyme Kaiserchronik*, AQ, XV (Darmstadt, 1972).

Schmeidler, B., *Adam von Bremen. Hamburgische Kirchengeschichte*, MG schol. II (3rd edn., Hanover and Leipzig, 1917).

Schmidt, B., *Urkundenbuch der Vögte von Weida, Gera und Plauen*, vol. i, Thüringische Geschichtsquellen, n.s., II (Jena, 1885).

Schmidt, G., *Urkundenbuch des Hochstifts Halberstadt und seiner Bischöfe*, 2 parts, Publicationen aus den königlich Preußischen Staatsarchiven, XVII, XXI (Leipzig, 1883-4).

Schneider, F., *Iohannis Abbatis Victoriensis Liber Certarum Historiarum*, MG schol., XXXVI (2 vols., Hanover and Leipzig, 1909-10).

Schoepflin, J.D., *Alsatia Diplomatica*, vol. i (Mannheim, 1772).

Schumi, F., *Urkunden- und Regestenbuch des Herzogtums Krain*, (2 vols., Laibach [Ljubljana], 1882-7).

Seibertz, J.S., *Quellen der westfälischen Geschichte* (3 vols., Arnsberg, 1857-69).

Siragusa, G.B., *Liber ad Honorem Augusti di Pietro da Eboli*, Fonti per la Storia d'Italia (Rome, 1906).

Sloet, L.A.J.W., *Oorkondenboek der Graafschappen Gelre en Zutfen* (The Hague, 1872).

Stillfried, R. Freiherr von, and Maercker, T., *Monumenta Zollerana. Urkundenbuch zur Geschichte des Hauses Hohenzollern*, vol. ii (Berlin, 1856).

Stimming, M., *Mainzer Urkundenbuch. Die Urkunden bis zum Tode Erzbischof Adalberts I. (1137)*, Arbeiten der Historischen Kommission für den Volksstaat Hessen (Darmstadt, 1932).

Stoob, H., *Helmold von Bosau. Slawenchronik*, AQ, XIX (Darmstadt, 1973).

Stumpf-Brentano, K.F., *Die Reichskanzler vornehmlich des 10., 11. und 12. Jahrhunderts*, vol. iii, *Acta Imperii inde ab Heinrico I. ad Heinricum VI. usque adhuc inedita* (new edn., Aalen, 1964).

Sudendorf, H., *Urkundenbuch zur Geschichte der Herzöge von Braunschweig und Lüneburg und ihrer Lande*, vol. i (Hanover, 1859).

Tenckhoff, F., *Vita Meinwerci Episcopi Patherbrunnensis*, MG schol. LIX, (Hanover, 1921).

Thiel, M., *Die Traditionen, Urkunden und Urbare des Klosters Weltenburg*, QE, XIV (Munich, 1958).

Trillmich, W., *Thietmar von Merseburg. Chronik*, AQ, IX (Darmstadt, 1974).

Uhl, B., *Die Traditionen des Klosters Weihenstephan*, QE, XXVII.1 (Munich, 1972).

Urkundenbuch des Landes ob der Enns (3 vols., Vienna, 1852-62).

Vanderkindere, L., *La Chronique de Gislebert de Mons*, Commission royale d'histoire. Recueil de textes (Brussels, 1904).

Vock, W.E., *Die Urkunden des Hochstifts Augsburg 769-1420*, Schwäbische Forschungsgemeinschaft bei der Kommission für bayerische Landesgeschichte, ser. 2A, Urkunden und Regesten, VII (Augsburg, 1959).

Wailly, Delisle, and Jourdain, MM., *Recueil des historiens des Gaules et de la France*, vol. xxiii (Paris, 1894).

Waitz, G., *Annales Hildesheimenses*, MG schol. VIII (Hanover, 1878).

——*Chronica Regia Coloniensis. Annales Maximi Colonienses*, MG schol. XVIII (Hanover, 1880).

——and von Simson, B., *Ottonis et Rahewini Gesta Friderici I. Imperatoris*, MG schol. XLVI (Hanover and Leipzig, 1912).

Wartmann, H., *Urkundenbuch der Abtei Sanct Gallen*, part iii (St Gallen, 1875-82).

Weech, F. von, *Codex Diplomaticus Salemitanus. Urkundenbuch der Cisterzienserabtei Salem 1134-1266* (Karlsruhe, 1881-3).

Weinrich, L., *Quellen zur deutschen Verfassungs-, Wirtschafts-, und Sozialgeschichte bis 1250*, AQ, XXXII (Darmstadt, 1977).

Weissthanner, A., *Die Traditionen des Klosters Schäftlarn 760-1305*, QE, X. 1 (Munich, 1953).

Weller, K., *Hohenlohisches Urkundenbuch*, vol. i (Stuttgart, 1899).

Weltin, M., *Die 'Laaer Briefsammlung'. Eine Quelle zur inneren Geschichte Österreichs unter Ottokar II. Přemysl*, Veröffentlichungen des Instituts für österreichische Geschichtsforschung, XXI (Vienna, Cologne, and Graz, 1975).

Wenck, H.B., *Urkundenbuch zu dem dritten Bande von Wencks Hessischer Landesgeschichte* (Frankfurt am Main, 1803).

Wentzcke, P., *Regesten der Bischöfe von Straßburg bis zum Jahre 1202* (Innsbruck, 1908).

Widemann, J., *Die Traditionen des Hochstifts Regensburg und des Klosters S. Emmeram*, QE, VIII (Munich, 1943).

Wilmans, R., *Die Urkunden des Bisthums Münster 1201-1300* (Münster, 1859-71).

Winkelmann, E., *Acta Imperii Inedita Saeculi XIII. et XIV. Urkunden und Briefe zur Geschichte des Kaiserreiches und des Königreiches Sizilien* (2 vols., new edn., Aalen, 1964).

Wirtembergisches Urkundenbuch, vols. 1-5 (Stuttgart, 1849-89).

Wisplinghoff, E., *Urkunden und Quellen zur Geschichte von Stadt und Abtei Siegburg*, vol. i (Siegburg, 1964).

Wittmann, F.M., *Monumenta Wittelsbacensia*. *Urkundenbuch zur Geschichte des Hauses Wittelsbach*, QE, V, VI, (Munich, 1857-61).

Wittmann, P., *Monumenta Castellana*. *Urkundenbuch zur Geschichte des fränkischen Dynastengeschlechtes der Grafen und Herren zu Castell, 1057-1546* (Munich, 1890).

Zahn, J., *Codex Diplomaticus Austriaco-Frisingensis*, Fontes Rerum Austriacarum, ser. 2, Diplomataria et Acta, XXXI (Vienna, 1870).

——*Urkundenbuch des Herzogthums Steiermark* (3 vols., Graz, 1875-1903).

Zeumer, K., *Formulae Merowingici et Karolini Aevi*, MG Legum sectio V (Hanover, 1886).

2   SECONDARY WORKS

Acht, P., 'Unbekannte Fragmente Prüfeninger Traditionen des 12. Jahrhunderts. Eine Traditionsnotiz Kaiser Friedrichs I.', *MIöG* lxxviii (1970), 236-49.

Ahrens, J., *Die Ministerialität in Köln und am Niederrhein* (Leipzig, 1908).

Angermeier, H., 'Landfriedenspolitik und Landfriedensgesetzgebung unter den Staufern' in J. Fleckenstein (ed.), *Probleme um Friedrich II.*, pp. 167-86.

Appelt, H., 'Zur diplomatischen Kritik der Georgenberger Handfeste', *MIöG* lviii (1950), 97-112.

Arnold, B., '*Ministeriales* and the Development of Territorial Lordship in the Eichstätt Region, 1100-1350', (D. Phil thesis, Oxford, 1972).

Aubin, H., *Die Verwaltungsorganisation des Fürstentums Paderborn im Mittelalter* (Berlin and Leipzig, 1911).

——*Die Entstehung der Landeshoheit nach niederrheinischen Quellen* (2nd edn., Bonn, 1961).

Auer, L., 'Der Kriegsdienst des Klerus unter den sächsischen Kaisern', *MIöG* lxxix (1971), 316-407 and lxxx (1972), 48-70.

Bachmann, S., *Die Landstände des Hochstifts Bamberg. Ein Beitrag zur territorialen Verfassungsgeschichte* (Bamberg, 1962).

Bader, K.S., 'Volk, Stamm, Territorium', *HZ* clxxvi (1953), 449-77.

Bannasch, H., *Das Bistum Paderborn unter den Bischöfen Rethar und Meinwerk 983-1036*, Studien und Quellen zur westfälischen Geschichte, XII (Paderborn, 1972).

Barkhausen, W., 'Die Gesetzgebung Wichmanns von Magdeburg', *DA* iv (1940-1), 495-503.

Barraclough, G. (transl.), *Medieval Germany, 911-1250*, vol. ii, *Essays by German Historians* (Oxford, 1961).

Bast, J., *Die Ministerialität des Erzstifts Trier* (Trier, 1918).

Beckmann, G., 'Die Pappenheim und die Würzburg des 12. und 13. Jahrhunderts', *HJ* xlvii (1927), 1-62.

Bertau, K., 'Versuch über Wolfram', *Jahrbuch für fränkische Landesforschung* xxxvii (1977), 27-43.

Beyerle, F., 'Die Ursprung der Bürgschaft. Ein Deutungsversuch vom germanischen Rechte her', *ZRGGA* xlvii (1927), 567-645.

Bloch, M., 'Liberté et servitude personnelles au moyen âge' (1933) in id. *Mélanges historiques*, vol. i Bibliothèque générale de l'École pratique des hautes études (Paris, 1963), pp. 286-355.

Bog, I., 'Dorfgemeinde, Freiheit und Unfreiheit in Franken. Studien zur Geschichte der fränkischen Agrarverfassung', *Jahrbücher für Nationalökonomie und Statistik* clxviii (1956), 1-80.

Bonenfant, P. and Despy, G., 'La noblesse en Brabant aux XIIe et XIIIe siècles', *Le Moyen Âge* lxiv (1958), 27-66.

Borst, A. (ed.), *Das Rittertum im Mittelalter*, WF, CCCXLIX (Darmstadt, 1976).

Bosl, K., 'Die Reichsministerialität als Träger staufischer Staatspolitik in Ostfranken und auf dem bayerischen Nordgau', *Jahresbericht des Historischen Vereins für Mittelfranken* lxix (1941), 1-103.

——*Die Reichsministerialität der Salier und Staufer. Ein Beitrag zur Geschichte des hochmittelalterlichen deutschen Volkes, Staates und Reiches*, Schriften der MG, X (2 parts, Stuttgart, 1950-1).

——'Würzburg als Reichsbistum' in *Aus Verfassungs- und Landesgeschichte. Festschrift für Theodor Mayer* (Lindau and Constance, 1954) vol. i, pp. 161-81.

——*Frühformen der Gesellschaft im mittelalterlichen Europa* (Munich and Vienna, 1964).

——*Die Sozialstruktur der mittelalterlichen Residenz- und Fernhandelsstadt Regensburg*, Bayerische Akademie der Wissenschaften, phil.-hist. Klasse, Abhandlungen, n.s., LXIII (Munich, 1966).

——'Die Familia als Grundstruktur der mittelalterlichen Gesellschaft', *ZBLG* xxxviii (1975), 403-24.

Bradler, G., *Studien zur Geschichte der Ministerialität im Allgäu und in Oberschwaben*, Göppinger Akademische Beiträge, L (Göppingen, 1973).

Brühl, C., *Fodrum, Gistum, Servitium Regis. Studien zu den wirtschaftlichen Grundlagen des Königtums im Frankenreich und in den fränkischen Nachfolgestaaten Deutschland, Frankreich und Italien*, Kölner historische Abhandlungen, XIV (Cologne and Graz, 1968).

Brunner, K., 'Zum Prozess gegen Herzog Friedrich II. von 1236', *MIöG* lxxviii (1970), 260-73.

——'Die Herkunft der Kuenringer', *MIöG* lxxxvi (1978), 291-309.

Brunner, O., 'Zwei Studien zum Verhältnis von Bürgertum und Adel' in id., *Neue Wege der Verfassungsgeschichte* (2nd edn., Göttingen, 1968), pp. 242-80.

Brunner, O., *Land und Herrschaft. Grundfragen der territorialen Verfassungsgeschichte Österreichs im Mittelalter* (new edn., Darmstadt, 1973).

Budde, R., 'Die rechtliche Stellung des Klosters St Emmeram in Regensburg zu den öffentlichen und kirchlichen Gewalten vom 9. bis zum 14. Jahrhundert', *AU* v (1913), 153-238.

Bumke, J., *Studien zum Ritterbegriff im 12. und 13. Jahrhundert*, Beihefte zum Euphorion, I (Heidelberg, 1964), tr. W.T.H. and E. Jackson, *The Concept of Knighthood in the Middle Ages*, AMS Studies in the Middle Ages, II (New York, 1982).

——*Ministerialität und Ritterdichtung. Umrisse der Forschung* (Munich, 1976).

Caro, G., 'Zur Ministerialenfrage' in *Nova Turicensia. Beiträge zur schweizerischen und zürcherischen Geschichte* (Zürich, 1911), pp. 77-101.

Chew, H.M., *The English Ecclesiastical Tenants-in-Chief and Knight Service* (London, 1932).

Classen, P., *Gerhoch von Reichersberg. Eine Biographie* (Wiesbaden, 1960).

Claude, D., *Geschichte des Erzbistums Magdeburg bis in das 12. Jahrhundert*, Mitteldeutsche Forschungen, LXVII. 2 (Cologne and Vienna, 1975).

Cleve, T.C. van, *Markward of Anweiler and the Sicilian Regency* (Princeton, 1937).

Cohn, W., *Hermann von Salza*, Abhandlungen der Schlesischen Gesellschaft für vaterländische Cultur. Geisteswissenschaftliche Reihe, IV (Breslau, 1930).

Dannenbauer, H., *Die Entstehung des Territoriums der Reichsstadt Nürnberg*, Arbeiten zur deutschen Rechts- und Verfassungsgeschichte, VII (Stuttgart, 1928).

——*Grundlagen der mittelalterlichen Welt* (Stuttgart, 1958).

Decker-Hauff, H., 'Das Staufische Haus' in *Die Zeit der Staufer, Katalog der Ausstellung im Württembergischen Landesmuseum* (Stuttgart, 1977), vol. iii, pp. 339-74.

Demandt, D., *Stadtherrschaft und Stadtfreiheit im Spannungsfeld von Geistlichkeit und Bürgerschaft in Mainz, 11.-15. Jahrhundert*, Geschichtliche Landeskunde, XV (Wiesbaden, 1977).

Diepolder, G., 'Oberbayerische und niederbayerische Adelsherrschaften im Wittelsbachischen Territorialstaat des 13.-15. Jahrhunderts', *ZBLG* xxv (1962), 33-70.

Diestelkamp, B., *Das Lehnrecht der Grafschaft Katzenelnbogen, 13. Jahrhundert bis 1479*, Untersuchungen zur deutschen Staats- und Rechtsgeschichte, n.s., XI (Aalen, 1969).

Dollinger, P., *L'Évolution des classes rurales en Bavière depuis la fin de l'époque carolingienne jusqu'au milieu du XIIIe siècle*, Publications de la Faculté des lettres de l'Université de Strasbourg, CXII, (Paris, 1949).

Dollinger, R., 'Die Stauffer zu Ernfels', *ZBLG* xxxv (1972), 436-522.

Dopsch, A., 'Die Ebersheimer Urkundenfälschungen und ein bisher unbeachtetes Dienstrecht aus dem 12. Jahrhundert', *MIöG* xix (1898), 577–614.

——'Die staatsrechtliche Stellung der Ministerialen in Österreich', *MIöG* xxxix (1923), 238–43.

Dopsch, H., 'Ministerialität und Herrenstand in der Steiermark und in Salzburg', *Zeitschrift des Historischen Vereines für Steiermark*, lxii (1971), 3–31.

——'Probleme ständischer Wandlung beim Adel Österreichs, der Steiermark und Salzburgs vornehmlich im 13. Jahrhundert' in J. Fleckenstein (ed.), *Herrschaft und Stand*, pp. 219–44.

——'Die Wittelsbacher und das Erzstift Salzburg' in H. Glaser (ed.), *Die Zeit der frühen Herzöge*, vol. i, pp. 268–84.

Drabek, A.M., 'Die Waisen. Eine niederösterreichisch-mährische Adelsfamilie unter Babenbergern und Přemysliden', *MIöG* lxxiv (1966), 292–332.

Dreher, A., *Das Patriziat der Reichsstadt Ravensburg von den Anfängen bis zum Beginn des 19. Jahrhunderts* (Stuttgart, 1966).

Droege, G., *Landrecht und Lehnrecht im hohen Mittelalter* (Bonn, 1969).

Dubled, H., 'Allodium dans les textes latins du moyen âge', *Le Moyen Âge* lvii (1951), 241–6.

Duby, G., *La Société aux XIe et XIIe siècles dans la région mâconnaise*, Bibliothèque générale de l'École pratique des hautes études (Paris, 1953).

——*Les Trois Ordres ou l'imaginaire du féodalisme* (Paris, 1978); tr. A. Goldhammer, *The Three Orders. Feudal Society Imagined* (Chicago and London, 1980).

——*Hommes et structures du moyen âge*, Le Savoir historique I (Paris, 1973).

——*The Early Growth of the European Economy. Warriors and Peasants from the Seventh to the Twelfth Century* (London, 1974).

Dülmen, R. van, 'Zur Frühgeschichte Baumburgs', *ZBLG* xxxi (1968), 3–48.

Dungern, O. von, 'Comes, liber, nobilis in Urkunden des 11. bis 13. Jahrhunderts', *AU* xii (1932), 181–205.

——*Adelsherrschaft im Mittelalter*, Libelli, CXCVIII, (2nd edn., Darmstadt, 1972).

Eberbach, O., *Die deutsche Reichsritterschaft in ihrer staatsrechtlich-politischen Entwicklung von den Anfängen bis zum Jahre 1422* (Dresden, 1912).

Ebner, H., *Das Freie Eigen. Ein Beitrag zur Verfassungsgeschichte des Mittelalters*, Aus Forschung und Kunst, II, (Klagenfurt, 1969).

——'Entwicklung und Rechtsverhältnisse der mittelalterlichen Burg', *Zeitschrift des Historischen Vereines für Steiermark* lxi (1970), 27–50.

Eckhardt, A., 'Das älteste Bolander Lehnbuch. Versuch einer Neudatierung', *AD* xxii (1976), 317–44.

Eckhardt, K.A., 'Präfekt und Burggraf', *ZRGGA* xlvi (1926), 163–205.

——*Die Schenken zu Schweinsberg*, Germanenrechte. Deutschrechtliches Archiv, n.s., III (Göttingen, 1953).

Engels, O. 'Vorstufen der Staatwerdung im Hochmittelalter. Zum Kontext der Gottesfriedensbewegung', *HJ* xcvii–xcviii (1978), 71–86.

Erben, W., 'Beiträge zur Geschichte der Ministerialität im Erzstift Salzburg', *Mitteilungen der Gesellschaft für Salzburger Landeskunde* li (1911).

Fajkmajer, K., 'Die Ministerialen des Hochstiftes Brixen', *Zeitschrift des Ferdinandeums für Tirol und Vorarlberg*, ser. 3, lii (1908), 95–191.

Falck, L., *Mainz im frühen und hohen Mittelalter*, Geschichte der Stadt Mainz, II (Düsseldorf, 1972).

——'Mainzer Ministerialität' in F.L. Wagner (ed.), *Ministerialität im Pfälzer Raum*, pp. 44–59.

Faussner, H.C., 'Die Verfügungsgewalt des deutschen Königs über weltliches Reichsgut im Hochmittelalter', *DA* xxix (1973), 345–449.

Feldbauer, P., *Der Herrenstand in Oberösterreich. Ursprüngen, Anfänge, Frühformen*, Sozial- und wirtschaftshistorische Studien (Munich, 1972).

——'Rangprobleme und Konnubium österreichischer Landherrenfamilien. Zur sozialen Mobilität einer spätmittelalterlichen Führungsgruppe', *ZBLG* xxxv (1972), 571–90.

——*Herren und Ritter*, Herrschaftsstruktur und Ständebildung. Beiträge zur Typologie der österreichischen Länder aus ihren mittelalterlichen Grundlagen, I (Vienna, 1973).

Fenske, L., 'Ministerialität und Adel im Herrschaftsbereich der Bischöfe von Halberstadt während des 13. Jahrhunderts' in J. Fleckenstein (ed.), *Herrschaft und Stand*, pp. 157–206.

Fichtenau, H., 'Bamberg, Würzburg und die Stauferkanzlei', *MIöG* liii (1939), 241–85.

——*Von der Mark zum Herzogtum. Grundlagen und Sinn des 'Privilegium Minus' für Österreich*, Österreich-Archiv. Schriftenreihe des Arbeitskreises für österreichische Geschichte (2nd edn., Munich, 1965).

Ficker, J., 'Die Reichshofbeamten der staufischen Periode', *Sitzungsberichte der phil.-hist. Classe der Kaiserlichen Akademie der Wissenschaften*, vol. xl, part 4 (Vienna, 1862), pp. 447–549.

——'Ueber das Eigenthum des Reichs am Reichskirchengute', ibid., vol. lxxii (Vienna, 1872), pp. 55–146, 381–450.

Flach, D., *Untersuchungen zur Verfassung und Verwaltung des Aachener Reichsgutes von der Karlingerzeit bis zur Mitte des 14. Jahrhunderts*, Veröffentlichungen des Max-Planck-Instituts für Geschichte, XLVI (Göttingen, 1976).

Fleckenstein, J., *Die Hofkapelle der deutschen Könige*, Schriften der MG, XVI (2 parts, Stuttgart, 1959–66).

——'Ministerialität und Stadtherrschaft. Ein Beitrag zu ihrem Verhältnis am Beispiel von Hildesheim und Braunschweig' in K.-U. Jäschke, and R. Wenskus (eds.), *Festschrift für Helmut Beumann zum 65. Geburtstag* (Sigmaringen, 1977), pp. 349–64.

——'Friedrich Barbarossa und das Rittertum. Zur Bedeutung der großen Mainzer Hoftage von 1184 und 1188' in *Festschrift für Hermann Heimpel*, vol. ii, Veröffentlichungen des Max-Planck-Instituts für Geschichte, XXXVI.2 (Göttingen, 1972), pp. 1023-41.

——(ed.), *Probleme um Friedrich II*. VF, XVI (Sigmaringen, 1974).

——'Zum Problem der Abschließung des Ritterstandes' in H. Beumann (ed.), *Historische Forschungen für Walter Schlesinger* (Cologne and Vienna, 1974), pp. 252-71.

——'Zur Frage der Abgrenzung von Bauer und Ritter' in R. Wenskus, H. Jahnkuhn, and K. Grinda (eds.), *Wort und Begriff Bauer*, Abhandlungen der phil.-hist. Klasse der Wissenschaften in Göttingen, ser. 3, LXXXIX (Göttingen, 1975), pp. 246-53.

——(ed.), *Herrschaft und Stand. Untersuchungen zur Sozialgeschichte im 13. Jahrhundert*, Veröffentlichungen des Max-Planck-Instituts für Geschichte, LI (Göttingen, 1977), including id., 'Die Entstehung des niederen Adels und das Rittertum', pp. 17-39.

Flohrschütz, G., 'Die Freisinger Dienstmannen im 10. und 11. Jahrhundert', *Beiträge zur altbayerischen Kirchengeschichte* xxv (1967), 9-79.

——'Der Adel des Wartenburger Raumes im 12. Jahrhundert', *ZBLG* xxiv (1971), 85-164, 462-511.

——'Die Freisinger Dienstmannen im 12. Jahrhundert', *Oberbayerisches Archiv* xcvii (1973), 32-339.

——'Machtgrundlagen und Herrschaftspolitik der ersten Pfalzgrafen aus dem Haus Wittelsbach' in H. Glaser (ed.), *Die Zeit der frühen Herzöge*, vol. i, pp. 42-110.

Flori, J., 'Chevaliers et chevalerie au XIe siècle en France et dans l'Empire germanique', *Le Moyen Âge* lxxxii (1976), 125-36.

Folz, R., *The Concept of Empire in Western Europe from the Fifth to the Fourteenth Century*, tr. S.A. Ogilvie (London, 1969).

Freed, J.B., 'The Origins of the European Nobility: The Problem of the Ministerials', *Viator* vii (1976), 211-41.

——'The Formation of the Salzburg Ministerialage in the Tenth and Eleventh Centuries: An Example of Upward Social Mobility in the Early Middle Ages', *Viator* ix (1978), 67-102.

Fressel, R., *Das Ministerialenrecht der Grafen von Tecklenburg. Ein Beitrag zur Verfassungs- und Ständegeschichte des Mittelalters* (Münster, 1907).

Fried, P., 'Zur Herkunft der Grafen von Hirschberg', *ZBLG* xxviii (1965), 82-98.

Friedrichs, H.F., 'Herkunft und ständische Zuordnung des Patriziats der wetterauischen Reichsstädte bis zum Ende des Staufertums', *Hessisches Jahrbuch für Landesgeschichte* ix (1959), 37-75.

Ganahl, K.-H., *Studien zur Verfassungsgeschichte der Klosterherrschaft St. Gallen*, Forschungen zur Geschichte Vorarlbergs und Liechtensteins, VI (Innsbruck, 1931).

Ganahl, K.-H. 'Versuch einer Geschichte des österreichischen Landrechtes im 13. Jahrhundert', *MIöG*, Ergänzungsband xiii (1935), 229-384.

Ganshof, F.L., *Étude sur les ministériales en Flandre et en Lotharingie*, Mémoires de la classe des lettres de l'Académie royale de Belgique, XX. 1 (Brussels, 1926).

——*Feudalism* (London, 1952).

Geldner, F., 'Das Hochstift Bamberg in der Reichspolitik von Kaiser Heinrich II. bis Kaiser Friedrich Barbarossa', *HJ* lxxxiii (1964), 28-42.

Genicot, L., 'Le premier siècle de la "curia" de Hainaut, 1060 env.-1195', *Le Moyen Âge* liii (1947), 39-60.

——'La "noblesse" au xie siècle dans la région de Gembloux', *V S W G* xliv (1957), 97-104.

Gerlich, A. (ed.), *Geschichtliche Landeskunde. Ministerialitäten im Mittelrheinraum*, Veröffentlichungen des Instituts für geschichtliche Landeskunde an der Universität Mainz, XVII (Wiesbaden, 1978).

Gernhuber, J., *Die Landfriedensbewegung in Deutschland bis zum Mainzer Reichslandfrieden von 1235*, Bonner rechtswissenchaftliche Abhandlungen, XLIV (Bonn, 1952).

Gillingham, J.B., *The Kingdom of Germany in the High Middle Ages, 900-1200*, Historical Association Pamphlets, LXXVII (London, 1971).

Gladiss, D. von, *Beiträge zur Geschichte der staufischen Reichsministerialität*, Historische Studien, CCXLIX (Berlin, 1934).

——'Christentum und Hörigkeit in den Urkunden des fränkischen und deutschen Mittelalters', *V S W G* xxix (1936), 35-8.

——'Die Schenkungen der deutschen Könige zu privatem Eigen', *DA* i (1937), 80-137.

Glaser, H. (ed.), *Die Zeit der frühen Herzöge. Von Otto I. zu Ludwig dem Bayern*, Beiträge zur bayerischen Geschichte und Kunst 1180-1350, I. 1 (Munich and Zürich, 1980).

Glocke, F. von, 'Untersuchungen zur Rechts- und Sozialgeschichte der Ministerialitäten in Westfalen' in *Westfälische Forschungen* (Münster, 1939), vol. ii, pp. 214-32.

Goez, W., *Translatio Imperii. Ein Beitrag zur Geschichte des Geschichtsdenkens und der politischen Theorien im Mittelalter und in der frühen Neuzeit* (Tübingen, 1958).

Gründler, J., Wolfram, H., Brunner, K., and Stangler, G., *Die Kuenringer. Das Werden des Landes Niederösterreich*, Katalog des Niederösterreichischen Landesmuseums, n.s., CX (2nd edn., Vienna, 1981).

Grundmann, H., 'Rotten und Brabanzonen. Söldner-Heere im 12. Jahrhundert', *DA* v (1942), 419-92.

——'Freiheit als religiöses, politisches und persönliches Postulat im Mittelalter', *HZ* clxxxiii (1957), 23-53.

——*Der Cappenberger Barbarossakopf und die Anfänge des Stiftes Cappenberg*, Münstersche Forschungen, XII (Cologne and Graz, 1959).

——*Religiöse Bewegungen im Mittelalter. Untersuchungen über die geschichtlichen Zusammenhänge zwischen der Ketzerei, den Bettelorden und der
religiösen Frauenbewegungen* (3rd edn., Darmstadt, 1970).

Guttenberg, E. von, *Die Territorienbildung am Obermain*, Berichte des Historischen Vereins zu Bamberg, LXXIX (Bamberg, 1927).

Haendle, O., *Die Dienstmannen Heinrichs des Löwen. Ein Beitrag zur Frage
der Ministerialität*, Arbeiten zur deutschen Rechts- und Verfassungsgeschichte, VIII (Stuttgart, 1930).

Harding, A., 'Political Liberty in the Middle Ages', *Speculum* lv (1980),
423-43.

Harvey, S., 'The Knight and the Knight's Fee in England', *Past and
Present* xlix (1970), 3-43.

Hauck, A., *Die Entstehung der geistlichen Territorien*, Abhandlungen der
phil.-hist. Klasse der Sächsischen Gesellschaft, XXVII. 18 (Leipzig, 1909).

Hausmann, F., 'Kaiser Friedrich II. und Österreich' in J. Fleckenstein (ed.),
Probleme um Friedrich II., pp. 225-308.

Haverkamp, A., 'Das Bambergische Hofrecht für den niederbayerischen
Hochstiftsbesitz', *ZBLG* xxx (1967), 423-506.

Heck, P., 'Die Ursprung der sächsischen Dienstmannschaft', *VSWG* v
(1907), 116-72.

Heinemann, W., *Das Bistum Hildesheim im Kräftespiel der Reichs- und Territorialpolitik vornehmlich des 12. Jahrhunderts*, Quellen und Darstellungen zur Geschichte Niedersachsens, LXXII (Hildesheim, 1968).

Heinrichsen, A., 'Süddeutsche Adelsgeschlechter in Niedersachsen im 11.
und 12. Jahrhundert', *Niedersächsisches Jahrbuch für Landesgeschichte* xxvi
(1954), 24-116.

Helbig, H., 'Verfügungen über Reichsgut im Pleißenland' in H. Beumann
(ed.), *Festschrift für Walter Schlesinger*, vol. i, Mitteldeutsche Forschungen, LXXIV. 1, (Cologne and Vienna, 1973), pp. 273-85.

Hellmann, M., 'Bemerkungen zur sozialgeschichtlichen Erforschung des
Deutschen Ordens', *HJ* lxxx (1961), 126-42.

Henn, V., *Das ligische Lehnswesen im Westen und Nordwesten des mittelalterlichen deutschen Reiches* (Munich, 1970).

Hessel, A., 'Die Beziehungen der Straßburger Bischöfe zum Kaisertum und
zur Stadtgemeinde in der ersten Hälfte des 13. Jahrhunderts', *AU* vi
(1916-18), 266-75.

——*Jahrbücher des Deutschen Reiches unter König Albrecht I. von Habsburg*,
Jahrbücher der deutschen Geschichte, (Munich, 1931).

Heuermann, H., *Die Hausmachtpolitik der Staufer von Herzog Friedrich I.
bis König Konrad III., 1079-1152* (Leipzig, 1939).

Heusinger, B., 'Servitium regis in der deutschen Kaiserzeit', *AU* viii (1923),
26-159.

Heyen, F.-J., *Reichsgut im Rheinland. Die Geschichte des königlichen Fiskus
Boppard*, Rheinisches Archiv, XLVIII (Bonn, 1956).

Hildebrand, R., *Der sächsische 'Staat' Heinrichs des Löwen*, Historische Studien, CCCII (Berlin, 1937).

Hillebrand, W., *Besitz- und Standesverhältnisse des Osnabrücker Adels 800 bis 1300*, Studien und Vorarbeiten zum historischen Atlas Niedersachsens, XXIII (Göttingen, 1962).

Hirsch, H., *Die hohe Gerichtsbarkeit im deutschen Mittelalter* (2nd edn., Graz and Cologne, 1958).

His, R., *Geschichte des deutschen Strafrechts bis zur Karolina* (new edn., Darmstadt, 1967).

Hlawitschka, E., *Königswahl und Thronfolge in ottonisch-frühdeutscher Zeit*, WF, CLXXVIII (Darmstadt, 1971).

Hödl, G., 'Bayern, Österreich und die Steiermark in der Zeit der frühen Wittelsbacher' in H. Glaser (ed.), *Die Zeit der frühen Herzöge*, vol. i, pp. 295-306.

Hömberg, A.K., *Grafschaft, Freigrafschaft, Gografschaft*, Schriften der Historischen Kommission für Westfalen, I (Münster, 1949).

Hoffmann, H., *Gottesfriede und Treuga Dei*, Schriften der MG, XX (Stuttgart, 1964).

Hofmann, H.H., 'Nobiles Norimbergenses. Beobachtungen zur Struktur der reichsstädtischen Oberschicht' in T. Mayer (ed,), *Untersuchungen zur gesellschaftlichen Struktur der mittelalterlichen Städte in Europa*, VF, XI, (Constance and Stuttgart, 1966), pp. 53-92.

——'Sigena oder Was ist Freiheit?' in H. Beumann (ed.), *Historische Forschungen für Walter Schlesinger*, (Cologne and Vienna, 1974), pp. 194-214.

Holder-Egger, O., 'Studien zu thüringischen Geschichtsquellen, V', *Neues Archiv* xxi (1896), 685-735.

Imhof, O., *Die Ministerialitäten in den Stiftern Straßburg, Speier und Worms* (Tauberbischofsheim, 1912).

Janssen, W., 'Burg und Territorium am Niederrhein im späten Mittelalter' in H. Patze (ed.), *Die Burgen im deutschen Sprachraum*, part i, pp. 283-324.

Joetze, F., 'Die Ministerialität im Hochstifte Bamberg', *HJ* xxxvi (1915), 516-97, 748-98.

Johnson, E.N., *The Secular Activities of the German Episcopate 919-1024*, University of Nebraska Studies, XXX-XXXI (Lincoln, Neb., 1932).

Johrendt, J., 'Milites und Militia im 11. Jahrhundert in Deutschland' in A. Borst (ed.), *Das Rittertum im Mittelalter*, pp. 419-36.

Jordan, K., *Heinrich der Löwe. Eine Biographie* (Munich, 1979).

Kämpf, H. (ed.), *Die Entstehung des Deutschen Reiches. Deutschland um 900*, WF, I (3rd edn., Darmstadt, 1971).

——*Herrschaft und Staat im Mittelalter*, WF, II (Darmstadt, 1972).

Kaiser, G., 'Minnesang, Ritterideal, Ministerialität' in H. Wenzel, (ed.), *Adelsherrschaft und Literatur*, Beiträge zur älteren deutschen Literaturgeschichte, VI (Bonn and Frankfurt, 1980), pp. 181-208.

Kaminsky, H.H., *Studien zur Reichsabtei Corvey in der Salierzeit*, Abhandlungen zur Corveyer Geschichtsschreibung, IV (Cologne and Graz, 1972).

Kaufmann, E., 'Bürgschaft und Einlager im spätmittelalterlichen fränkischen Recht' in *Les sûretés personnelles*, vol. ii Recueils de la Société Jean Bodin pour l'histoire comparative des institutions, XXIX (Brussels, 1971), pp. 653-72.

Kennan, E., 'Innocent III and the First Political Crusade', *Traditio* xxvii (1971), 229-49.

Keutgen, F., 'Die Entstehung der deutschen Ministerialität', *VSWG* viii (1910), 1-16, 169-95, 481-547.

Kienast, W., *Der Herzogstitel in Frankreich und Deutschland, 9. bis 12. Jahrhundert* (Munich and Vienna, 1968).

Kirchner, G., 'Staatsplanung und Reichsministerialität. Kritische Bemerkungen zu Bosls Werk über die staufische Reichsministerialität', *DA* x (1953-4), 446-74.

Klafki, E., *Die kurpfälzischen Erbhofämter. Mit einem Überblick über die bayerischen Erbhofämter unter den wittelsbachischen Herzögen bis zur Trennung der Pfalz von Bayern 1329*, Veröffentlichungen der Kommission für geschichtliche Landeskunde in Baden-Württemberg, ser. B, Forschungen, XXXV (Stuttgart, 1966).

Klapeer, G., 'Zur Überlieferung der Constitutio de expeditione Romana', *MIöG* xxxv (1914), 725-32.

Klebel, E., 'Freies Eigen und Beutellehen in Ober- und Niederbayern', *ZBLG* xi (1938), 45-85.

——'Landeshoheit in und um Regensburg', *Verhandlungen des Historischen Vereins von Oberpfalz und Regensburg* xc (1940), 5-61.

——'Von Herzogtum zum Territorium' in *Aus Verfassungs- und Landesgeschichte. Festschrift für Theodor Mayer* (Lindau and Constance, 1954), vol. i, pp. 205-22.

——'Eichstätt zwischen Bayern und Franken' in *Probleme der bayerischen Verfassungsgeschichte*, Schriftenreihe zur bayerischen Landesgeschichte, LXII (Munich, 1957), pp. 341-4.

——'Territorialstaat und Lehen' in *Studien zum mittelalterlichen Lehenswesen*, VF, V (Lindau and Constance, 1960), pp. 195-228.

Klewitz, H.-W., *Studien zur territorialen Entwicklung des Bistums Hildesheim. Ein Beitrag zur historischen Geographie Niedersachsens*, Studien und Vorarbeiten zum Historischen Atlas Niedersachsens, XIII (Göttingen, 1932).

——'Königtum, Hofkapelle und Domkapitel im 10. und 11. Jahrhundert', *AU* xvi (1939), 102-56.

Klingelhöfer, E., *Die Reichsgesetze von 1220, 1231/32 und 1235. Ihr Werden und ihre Wirkung im deutschen Staat Friedrichs II.*, Quellen und Studien zur Verfassungsgeschichte des Deutschen Reiches in Mittelalter und Neuzeit, VIII. (Weimar, 1955).

Klohss, K., *Untersuchungen über Heinrich von Kalden, staufischen Marschall, und die ältesten Pappenheimer* (Berlin, 1901).

Kluckhohn, P., *Die Ministerialität in Südostdeutschland*, Quellen und Studien zur Verfassungsgeschichte des Deutschen Reiches in Mittelalter und Neuzeit, IV. 1 (Weimar, 1910).

——'Ministerialität und Ritterdichtung', *Zeitschrift für deutsches Altertum* lii (1910), 135-68.

Kötzschke, R., 'Staat und Bauertum im thüringisch-obersächsischen Raum' in T. Mayer, (ed.), *Adel und Bauern im deutschen Staat des Mittelalters* (new edn., Darmstadt, 1976), pp. 267-311.

Kraft, W., *Das Urbar der Reichsmarschälle von Pappenheim*, Schriftenreihe zur bayerischen Landesgeschichte, III (Munich, 1929).

——'Über Weißenburg und den Weißenburger Wald in ihren Beziehungen zu den Marschällen von Pappenheim', *Jahrbuch des Historischen Vereins für Mittelfranken* lxvi (1930), 145-74.

——'Das Reichsmarschallamt in seiner geschichtlichen Entwicklung', ibid. lxxviii (1959), 1-36, lxxix (1960-1), 38-96.

Krause, H., *Die Geschichtliche Entwicklung des Schiedsgerichtswesens in Deutschland* (Berlin, 1930).

Krieger, K.-F., 'Die königliche Lehnsgerichtsbarkeit im Zeitalter der Staufer', *DA* xxvi (1970), 400-33.

Kroeschell, K., *Haus und Herrschaft im frühen Deutschen Recht. Ein methodischer Versuch*, Göttinger rechtswissenschaftliche Studien, LXX (Göttingen, 1968).

——'Recht und Rechtsbegriff im 12. Jahrhundert' in *Probleme des 12. Jahrhunderts. Reichenau-Vorträge 1965-1967*, VF, XII (Constance and Stuttgart, 1968), pp. 309-35.

Kropat, W.-A., *Reich, Adel und Kirche in der Wetterau von der Karolinger- bis zur Stauferzeit*, Schriften des Hessischen Landesamts für geschichtliche Landeskunde, XXVIII (Marburg, 1965).

Krüger, S., 'Das Rittertum in den Schriften des Konrad von Megenberg' in J. Fleckenstein (ed.), *Herrschaft und Stand*, pp. 302-28.

Kühn, H., 'Die Grenzen der germanischen Gefolgschaft', *ZRGGA* lxxiii (1956), 1-83.

Küster, W., *Beiträge zur Finanzgeschichte des Deutschen Reiches nach dem Interregnum*, vol. i, *Das Reichsgut in den Jahren 1273-1313* (Leipzig, 1883).

Kusternig, A. and Weltin, M. (eds.), *Kuenringer-Forschungen*, Jahrbuch für Landeskunde von Niederösterreich, n.s., XLVI-XLVII (Vienna, 1981).

Lahusen, J., 'Zum Welser Brückenprivileg', *MIöG* xxxi (1910), 361-74.

Landwehr, G., *Die Verpfandung der deutschen Reichsstädte im Mittelalter*, Forschungen zur deutschen Rechtsgeschichte, vol. V (Cologne and Graz, 1967).

Latzke, I., 'Hofamt, Erzamt und Erbamt im mittelalterlichen Deutschen Reich' (Inaugural dissertation, Frankfurt am Main, 1970).

Lechner, K., *Die Babenberger. Markgrafen und Herzöge von Österreich 976-1246*, Veröffentlichungen des Instituts für österreichische Geschichtsforschung, XXIII (Vienna, Cologne, and Graz, 1976).

Leyser, K.J., 'The Battle of the Lech, 955. A Study in Tenth-century Warfare', *History* l (1965), 1-25.

——'The German Aristocracy from the Ninth to the Early Twelfth Century. A Historical and Cultural Sketch', *Past and Present* xli (1968), 25-53.

——'Henry I and the beginnings of the Saxon empire', *English Historical Review* lxxxiii (1968), 1-32.

——*Rule and Conflict in an Early Medieval Society. Ottonian Saxony* (London, 1979).

——'Ottonian Government', *English Historical Review* xcvi (1981), 721-53.

Lieberich, H., *Landherren und Landleute. Zur politischen Führungsschicht Baierns im Spätmittelalter*, Schriftenreihe zur bayerischen Landesgeschichte, LXIII (Munich, 1964).

Linck, E., *Sozialer Wandel in klösterlichen Grundherrschaften des 11. bis 13. Jahrhunderts. Studien zu den familiae von Gembloux, Stablo-Malmedy und St Trond*, Veröffentlichungen des Max-Planck-Instituts für Geschichte, LVII (Göttingen, 1979).

Loesch, H. von, 'Das kürzere Kölner Dienstmannenrecht', *Z R G G A* xliv (1924), 298-307.

Lübeck, K., 'Die Ministerialen der Reichsabtei Fulda', *Z R G Kanonistische Abteilung* lxvi (1948), 201-33.

——'Die Hofämter der Fuldaer Äbte', *Z R G G A* lxv (1947), 177-207.

Luyn, P. van, 'Les milites dans la France du xie siècle. Examen des sources narratives', *Le Moyen Âge* lxxvii (1971), 5-51, 193-238.

Manz, L., *Der Ordo-Gedanke. Ein Beitrag zur Frage des mittelalterlichen Ständegedankens*, Beihefte zur *V S W G*, XXXIII (Stuttgart and Berlin, 1937).

Martini, W., *Der Lehnshof der Mainzer Erzbischöfe im späten Mittelalter* (Düsseldorf, 1971).

Maschke, E. and Sydow, J., *Stadt und Ministerialität. Protokoll der IX. Arbeitstagung des Arbeitskreises für südwestdeutsche Stadtgeschichtsforschung Freiburg im Breisgau 13-15 November 1970*, Veröffentlichungen der Kommission für geschichtliche Landeskunde in Baden-Württemberg, ser. B, Forschungen, LXXVI (Stuttgart, 1973).

Maurer, H. *Der Herzog von Schwaben. Grundlagen, Wirkungen und Wesen seiner Herrschaft in ottonischer, salischer und staufischer Zeit* (Sigmaringen, 1978).

Mayer, T., 'Die älteren Urkunden des Klosters Klingenmünster', *MIöG* xlvii (1933), 137-85.

——'Die Entstehung des modernen Staates im Mittelalter und die freien Bauern', *Z R G G A* lvii (1937), 210-88.

Mayer, T., 'Analekten zum Problem der Entstehung der Landeshoheit, vornehmlich in Süddeutschland', *Blätter für deutsche Landesgeschichte* lxxxix (1952), 87-111.

——(ed.), *Das Problem der Freiheit in der deutschen und schweizerischen Geschichte*, V F, II (Lindau and Constance, 1955).

——'Königtum und Gemeinfreiheit im frühen Mittelalter' in id., *Mittelalterliche Studien*, pp. 139-63 (Lindau and Constance, 1959).

——Heilig, K., and Erdmann, C., *Kaisertum und Herzogsgewalt im Zeitalter Friedrichs I. Studien zur politischen und Verfassungsgeschichte des hohen Mittelalters*, Schriften des M G, IX (new edn., Stuttgart, 1952).

Mayhew, A., *Rural Settlement and Farming in Germany* (London, 1973).

Merzbacher, F., 'Die Bedeutung von Freiheit und Unfreiheit im weltlichen und kirchlichen Recht des deutschen Mittelalters', *H J* xc (1970), 257-83.

Metz, W., 'Studien zur Grafschaftsverfassung Althessens im Mittelalter. Ein Beitrag zur Frage der Freigrafschaften', *Z R G G A* lxxi (1954), 167-208.

——*Staufische Güterverzeichnisse. Untersuchungen zur Verfassungs- und Wirtschaftsgeschichte des 12. und 13. Jahrhunderts* (Berlin, 1964).

——'Tafelgut, Königsstraße und Servitium Regis in Deutschland vornehmlich im 10. und 11. Jahrhundert', *H J* xci (1971), 257-91.

——'Ministerialität und Geldwirtschaft in mittelrheinischen Bischofsstädten des 11. und 12. Jahrhunderts' in F.L. Wagner (ed.), *Ministerialität im Pfälzer Raum*, pp. 34-41.

——'Quellenstudien zum Servitium regis (900-1250)', *A D* xxii (1976), 187-271 and xxiv (1978), 203-91.

——*Das Servitium Regis. Zur Erforschung der wirtschaftlichen Grundlagen des hochmittelalterlichen deutschen Königtums*, Erträge der Forschung, LXXXIX (Darmstadt, 1978).

Meyer von Knonau, G., *Jahrbücher des Deutschen Reiches unter Heinrich IV. und Heinrich V.* (7 vols., Leipzig, 1890-1909).

Mitterauer, M., 'Formen adeliger Herrschaftsbildung im hochmittelalterlichen Österreich. Zur Frage der "autogenen Hoheitsrechte", *M I öG* lxxx (1972), 265-338.

Mohrmann, W.-D. (ed.), *Heinrich der Löwe*, Veröffentlichungen der Niedersächsischen Archivverwaltung, XXXIX (Göttingen, 1980).

Molitor, E., *Der Stand der Ministerialen vornehmlich auf Grund sächsischer, thüringischer und niederrheinischer Quellen*, Untersuchungen zur deutschen Staats- und Rechtsgeschichte, CXII (Breslau, 1912).

Mosbacher, H., 'Kammerhandwerk, Ministerialität und Bürgertum in Straßburg. Studien zur Zusammensetzung und Entwicklung des Patriziats im 13. Jahrhundert', *Zeitschrift für die Geschichte des Oberrheins* cxix (1971), 33-173.

Müller, E., 'Kuningstoph 1282 und koningesstope 1308 u.ff.', *A U* xi (1929-30), 423-34.

Niederkorn, J.P., 'Die Datierung des Tafelgüterverzeichnisses. Bemerkungen zu einer Neuerscheinung', *MIöG* lxxxvii (1979), 471-87.

Niermeyer, J.F., *Mediae Latinitatis Lexicon Minus* (Leiden, 1954-64).

Niese, H., *Die Verwaltung des Reichsgutes im 13. Jahrhundert* (Innsbruck, 1905).

Novotný, V., 'Přemysl Otakar II. und der Adel von Steiermark', *MIöG* xxxi (1910), 291-301.

Obenaus, H., *Recht und Verfassung der Gesellschaften mit St. Jörgenschild in Schwaben. Untersuchungen über Adel, Einung, Schiedsgericht und Fehde im fünfzehnten Jahrhundert*, Veröffentlichungen des Max-Planck-Instituts für Geschichte, VII (Göttingen, 1961).

Odegaard, C.E., *Vassi and Fideles in the Carolingian Empire*, Harvard Historical Monographs, XIX (2nd edn., Cambridge, Mass., 1972).

Ogris, W., 'Die persönlichen Sicherheiten im Spätmittelalter. Versuch eines Überblicks', *Z R G G A* lxxxii (1965), 140-89.

Otto, E.F., *Adel und Freiheit im deutschen Staat des frühen Mittelalters*, Neue deutsche Forschungen, CXXX (Berlin, 1937).

——'Von der Abschließung des Ritterstandes', *HZ* clxii (1940), 19-39.

Parigger, H., 'Das Würzburger Burggrafenamt', *Mainfränkisches Jahrbuch für Geschichte und Kunst* xxxi (1979), 9-31.

Patze, H., *Die Entstehung der Landesherrschaft in Thüringen*, Mitteldeutsche Forschungen, XXII (Cologne and Graz, 1962).

——(ed.), *Die Burgen im deutschen Sprachraum. Ihre rechts- und verfassungsgeschichtliche Bedeutung*, V F, XIX (2 parts, Sigmaringen, 1976).

Petke, W., 'Pfalzstadt und Reichsministerialität. Über einen neuen Beitrag zur Reichsgut- und Pfalzenforschung', *Blätter für deutsche Landesgeschichte* cix (1973), 270-304.

Pfeiffer, G., 'Comicia burcgravie in Nurenberg', *Jahrbuch für fränkische Landesforschung* xi-xii (1953), 42-52.

Pfisterer, K., *Heinrich von Kalden. Reichsmarschall der Stauferzeit*, Quellen und Studien zur Geschichte und Kultur des Altertums und des Mittelalters, VI (Heidelberg, 1937).

Philippi, F., 'Zur Gerichtsverfassung Sachsens im hohen Mittelalter', *MIöG* xxxv (1914), 209-59.

Planitz, H., 'Studien zur Rechtsgeschichte des städtischen Patriziats'. *MIöG* lviii (1950), 317-35.

Plassmann, J.O., *Princeps und Populus. Die Gefolgschaft im ottonischen Staatsaufbau nach den sächsischen Geschichtsschreibern des 10. Jahrhunderts*, Schriften der Forschungshilfe (Göttingen, 1954).

Pötter, W., *Die Ministerialität der Erzbischöfe von Köln vom Ende des 11. bis zum Ausgang des 13. Jahrhunderts*, Studien zur Kölner Kirchengeschichte, IX (Düsseldorf, 1967)

Posch, F., 'Siedlungsgeschichte der Oststeiermark', *MIöG* Ergänzungsband xiii (1941), 385-679.

Poth, K., *Die Ministerialität der Bischöfe von Münster* (Münster, 1912).

Prinz, F., *Klerus und Krieg im früheren Mittelalter. Untersuchungen zur Rolle der Kirche beim Aufbau der Königsherrschaft*, Monographien zur Geschichte des Mittelalters, II (Stuttgart, 1971).

Prinz, J., *Das Territorium des Bistums Osnabrück*, Studien und Vorarbeiten zum Historischen Atlas Niedersachsens, XV (Göttingen, 1934).

Puntschart, P., 'Das "Inwärts-Eigen" im österreichischen Dienstrecht des Mittelalters', *Z R G G A* xliii (1922), 66-102.

Reimann, J., 'Zur Besitz- und Familiengeschichte der Ministerialen des Hochstifts Würzburg', *Mainfränkisches Jahrbuch für Geschichte und Kunst* xv (1963), 1-117, and 'Die Ministerialen des Hochstifts Würzburg in sozial-, rechts- und verfassungsgeschichtlicher Sicht', ibid. xvi (1964), 1-266.

Reuter, H.G., *Die Lehre vom Ritterstand. Zum Ritterbegriff in Historiographie und Dichtung vom 11. bis zum 13. Jahrhundert*, Neue Wirtschaftsgeschichte, IV, (Cologne and Vienna, 1971).

Richey, M.F., *Studies of Wolfram von Eschenbach* (Edinburgh and London, 1957).

Rieckenberg, H.-J., 'Königsstraße und Königsgut in liudolfingischer und frühsalischer Zeit (919-1056)', *A U* xvii (1942), 32-154.

——'Arnold Walpot, der Initiator des Rheinischen Bundes von 1254', *D A* xvi (1960), 228-37.

——'Leben und Stand des Minnesängers Friedrich von Hausen', *Archiv für Kulturgeschichte* xliii (1961), 163-76.

Riedenauer, E., 'Kontinuität und Fluktuation im Mitgliederstand der fränkischen Reichsritterschaft. Eine Grundlegung zum Problem der Adelsstruktur in Franken' in *Gesellschaft und Herrschaft. Eine Festgabe für Karl Bosl zum 60. Geburtstag* (Munich, 1969), pp. 87-152.

Rietschel, S., *Das Burggrafenamt und die hohe Gerichtsbarkeit in den deutschen Bischofsstädten während des früheren Mittelalters*, Untersuchungen zur Geschichte der deutschen Stadtverfassung, I (Leipzig, 1905).

Ritter, J.-P., *Ministérialité et chevalerie. Dignité humaine et liberté dans le droit médiéval* (Lausanne, 1955).

Rödel, V., *Reichslehenswesen, Ministerialität, Burgmannschaft und Niederadel. Studien zur Rechts- und Sozialgeschichte des Adels in den Mittel- und Oberrheinlanden während des 13. und 14. Jahrhunderts*, Quellen und Forschungen zur hessischen Geschichte, XXXVIII (Damstadt and Marburg, 1979).

Rösener, W., 'Ministerialität, Vasallität und niederadelige Ritterschaft im Herrschaftsbereich der Markgrafen von Baden vom 11. bis zum 14. Jahrhunderts' in J. Fleckenstein (ed.), *Herrschaft und Stand*, pp. 40-91.

Rosenstock, E., 'Die Verdeutschung des Sachsenspiegels', *Z R G G A* xxxvii (1916), 498-504.

Rothert, H., *Die mittelalterlichen Lehnbücher der Bischöfe von Osnabrück*, Osnabrücker Geschichtsquellen, V (Osnabrück, 1932).

Sanders, I.J., *Feudal Military Service in England* (London, 1956).

Santifaller, L., *Zur Geschichte des ottonisch-salischen Reichskirchensystems*, Abhandlungen der phil.-hist. Klasse der österreichischen Akademie der Wissenschaften, Sitzungsberichte, CCXXIX (Vienna, 1954).

Schalles-Fischer, M., *Pfalz und Fiskus Frankfurt. Eine Untersuchung zur Verfassungsgeschichte des fränkisch-deutschen Königtums*, Veröffentlichungen des Max-Planck-Instituts für Geschichte, XX (Göttingen, 1969).

Scheffer-Boichorst, P., 'Zur Geschichte der Reichsabtei Erstein', *Zeitschrift für die Geschichte des Oberrheins* xliii (1889), 283-99.

Schieckel, H., *Herrschaftsbereich und Ministerialität der Markgrafen von Meißen im 12. und 13. Jahrhundert*, Mitteldeutsche Forschungen, VII (Cologne and Graz, 1956).

Schlesinger, W., *Die schönburgischen Lande bis zum Ausgang des Mittelalters*, Schriften für Heimatforschung, II (Dresden, 1935).

——*Die Landesherrschaft der Herren von Schönburg. Eine Studie zur Geschichte des Staates in Deutschland*, Quellen und Studien zur Verfassungsgeschichte des Deutschen Reiches in Mittelalter und Neuzeit, IX. 1 (Münster and Cologne, 1954).

——'Egerland, Vogtland, Pleißenland. Zur Geschichte des Reichsgutes im mitteldeutschen Osten' in id., *Mitteldeutsche Beiträge zur deutschen Verfassungsgeschichte des Mittelalters* (Göttingen, 1961), pp. 188-211.

——'Bemerkungen zum Problem der westfälischen Grafschaften und Freigrafschaften' in id., *Beiträge zur deutschen Verfassungsgeschichte des Mittelalters*, vol. ii, *Städte und Territorien* (Göttingen, 1963), pp. 213-32.

——*Die Entstehung der Landesherrschaft. Untersuchungen vorwiegend nach mitteldeutschen Quellen* (new edn., Darmstadt, 1973).

Schmid, K., *Graf Rudolf von Pfullendorf und Kaiser Friedrich I.*, Forschungen zur oberrheinischen Landesgeschichte, I (Freiburg im Breisgau, 1954).

Schmidt, R., *Königsumritt und Huldigung in ottonisch-salischer Zeit*, VF, VI (Constance and Stuttgart, 1961), pp. 97-223.

Schmitthenner, P., *Das freie Söldnertum im abendländischen Imperium des Mittelalters*, Münchener historische Abhandlungen, ser. 2, Kriegs- und Heeresgeschichte, IV (Munich, 1934).

Schön, T., 'Die Landvögte des Reiches in Ober- und Niederschwaben bis 1486', *MIöG* Ergänzungsband vi (1901), 280-92.

Schrader, E., 'Vom Werden und Wesen des würzburgischen Herzogtums Franken', *ZRGGA* lxxx (1963), 27-81.

Schramm, P.E., and Mütherich, F., *Denkmale der deutschen Könige und Kaiser. Ein Beitrag zur Herrschergeschichte von Karl dem Großen bis Friedrich II. 768-1250*, Veröffentlichungen des Zentralinstituts für Kunstgeschichte in Munchen, II (Munich, 1962).

Schreiner, K., 'Die Staufer als Herzöge von Schwaben' in *Die Zeit der*

Staufer, Katalog der Ausstellung im Württembergischen Landesmuseum, iii (Stuttgart, 1977), pp. 7-19.

Schubert, E., *Die Landstände des Hochstifts Würzburg,* Veröffentlichungen der Gesellschaft für fränkische Geschichte, ser. 9, XXIII (Würzburg, 1967).

Schubert, P., 'Die Reichshofämter und ihre Inhaber bis um die Wende des 12. Jahrhunderts', *MIöG* xxxiv (1913), 427-501.

Schulte, A., *Der Adel und die deutsche Kirche im Mittelalter,* Kirchenrechtliche Abhandlungen, LXIII-LXIV (Stuttgart, 1910).

Schulz, K., *Ministerialität und Bürgertum in Trier. Untersuchungen zur rechtlichen und sozialen Gliederung der Trierer Bürgerschaft vom ausgehenden 11. bis zum Ende des 14. Jahrhunderts,* Rheinisches Archiv, LXVI (Bonn, 1968).

——'Die Ministerialität als Problem der Stadtgeschichte. Einige allgemeine Bemerkungen, erläutert am Beispiel der Stadt Worms', *Rheinische Vierteljahrsblätter* xxxii (1968), 184-219.

——'Richerzeche, Meliorat und Ministerialität in Köln' in *Köln, das Reich und Europa,* Mitteilungen aus dem Stadtarchiv von Köln, LX (Cologne, 1971), pp. 149-72.

——'Zum Problem der Zensualität im Hochmittelalter' in id. (ed.), *Beiträge zur Wirtschafts- und Sozialgeschichte des Mittelalters. Festschrift für Herbert Helbig,* (Cologne and Vienna, 1976), pp. 86-127.

Schulze, H.K., *Adelsherrschaft und Landesherrschaft,* Mitteldeutsche Forschungen, XXIX (Cologne and Graz, 1963).

——'Rodungsfreiheit und Königsfreiheit. Zu Genesis und Kritik neuerer verfassungsgeschichtlicher Theorien', *HZ* ccxix (1974), 529-50.

Schwemmer, W., *Die ehemalige Herrschaft Breitenstein-Königstein,* Schriftenreihe der Altnürnberger Landschaft, XIII (Nuremberg, 1965).

Seider, H., 'Zur Wormser Ministerialität im Hochmittelalter' in A. Gerlich (ed.), *Geschichtliche Landeskunde,* pp. 1-19.

Semmler, J., *Die Klosterreform von Siegburg. Ihre Ausbreitung und ihr Reformprogramm im 11. und 12. Jahrhundert,* Rheinisches Archiv, LIII (Bonn, 1959).

Sengle, F., 'Die Patrizierdichtung "Der Gute Gerhard". Soziologische und dichtungsgeschichtliche Studien zur Frühzeit Rudolfs von Ems', *Deutsche Vierteljahrschrift für Literaturwissenschaft und Geistesgeschichte* xxiv (1950), 53-82.

Siegel, H., 'Die rechtliche Stellung der Dienstmannen in Oesterreich im zwölften und dreizehnten Jahrhundert' in *Sitzungsberichte der phil.-hist. Classe der Akademie der Wissenschaften,* vol. cii (Vienna, 1883), pp. 235-86.

Soenen, M. 'A propos de ministeriales brabançons propriétaires d'alleux aux xiie et xiiie siècles' in *Hommage au professeur Paul Bonenfant 1899-1965* (Brussels, 1965), pp. 139-49.

Spielberg, W., 'Die Herkunft der ältesten Burggrafen von Nürnberg', *MIöG* xliii (1929), 117-23.

Spiess, K.H., *Lehnsrecht, Lehnspolitik und Lehnsverwaltung der Pfalzgrafen bei Rhein im Spätmittelalter*, Geschichtliche Landeskunde, XVIII (Wiesbaden, 1978).

Spindler, M., *Die Anfänge des bayerischen Landesfürstentums*, Schriftenreihe zur bayerischen Landesgeschichte, XXVI (new edn., Aalen, 1973).

——(ed.), *Handbuch der bayerischen Geschichte*, vol. ii, *Das alte Bayern. Der Territorialstaat vom Ausgang des 12. Jahrhunderts bis zum Ausgang des 18. Jahrhunderts* (2nd edn., Munich, 1977).

Sprandel, R., 'Die Ritterschaft und das Hochstift Würzburg im Spätmittelalter', *Jahrbuch für fränkische Landesforschung* xxxvi (1976), 117-43.

Stahleder, H., 'Das Weltbild Bertholds von Regensburg', *ZBLG* xxxvii (1974), 728-98.

Steinbock, W., *Erzbischof Gebhard von Salzburg (1060-1088). Ein Beitrag zur Geschichte Salzburgs im Investiturstreit*, Veröffentlichungen des Historischen Instituts der Universität Salzburg, IV (Vienna and Salzburg, 1972).

Stengel, E.E., 'Über den Ursprung der Ministerialität' in *Papsttum und Kaisertum. Festschrift für Paul Kehr* (Munich, 1926), pp. 168-84.

Stimming, M., *Die Entstehung des weltlichen Territoriums des Erzbistums Mainz*, Quellen und Forschungen zur hessischen Geschichte, III (Darmstadt, 1915).

Stimming, *Das deutsche Königsgut im 11. und 12. Jahrhundert*, Historische Studien, CXLIX (Berlin, 1922).

Stingl, H., *Die Entstehung der deutschen Stammesherzogtümer am Anfang des 10. Jahrhunderts*, Untersuchungen zur deutschen Staats- und Rechtsgeschichte, n.s. XIX (Aalen, 1974).

Störmer, W., *Früher Adel. Studien zur politischen Führungsschicht im fränkisch-deutschen Reich vom 8. bis 11. Jahrhundert*, (Monographien zur Geschichte des Mittelalters, VI (2 parts, Stuttgart, 1973).

——'Adel und Ministerialität im Spiegel der bayerischen Namengebung bis zum 13. Jahrhundert. Ein Beitrag zum Selbstverständnis der Führungsschichten', *DA* xxxiii (1977), 84-152.

Strait, P., *Cologne in the Twelfth Century* (Gainesville, 1974).

Strauss, G. (ed.), *Pre-Reformation Germany* (London, 1972).

Stutz, U., 'Zum Ursprung und Wesen des niederen Adels', *Sitzungsberichte der phil.-hist. Klasse der Preußischen Akademie der Wissenschaften*, XXVII (Berlin, 1937), pp. 213-57.

Tellenbach, G., 'Servitus und libertas nach den Traditionen der Abtei Remiremont', *Saeculum* xxi (1970), 228-34.

Theuerkauf, G., *Land und Lehnswesen vom 14. bis zum 16. Jahrhundert. Ein Beitrag zur Verfassung des Hochstifts Münster und zum nordwest-*

deutschen Lehnrecht, Neue münstersche Beiträge zur Geschichtsforschung, VII, (Cologne and Graz, 1961).

Tillmann, C., *Lexikon der deutschen Burgen und Schlösser* (4 vols., Stuttgart, 1957-61).

Tits-Dieuaide, M.-J., 'Un exemple de passage de la ministérialité à la noblesse: la famille de Wesemael (1166-1250)', *Revue belge de philologie et d'histoire* xxxvi (1958), 335-55.

Uhlirz, M., *Handbuch der Geschichte Österreich-Ungarns*, vol. i (2nd edn., Graz, Vienna and Cologne, 1963).

Voit, G., *Die Wildensteiner*, Sonderheft der Mitteilungen der altnürnberger Landschaft (Nuremberg, 1964).

Vollrath, H., 'Herrschaft und Genossenschaft im Kontext frühmittelalterlicher Rechtsbeziehungen', *HJ* cii (1982), 33-71.

Voltelini, H. von, 'Der Gedanke der allgemeinen Freiheit in den deutschen Rechtsbüchern', *ZRGGA* lvii (1937), 182-209.

Voltmer, E., 'Ministerialität und Oberschichten in den Städten Speyer und Worms im 13. und 14. Jahrhundert' in F.L. Wagner (ed.), *Ministerialität im Pfälzer Raum*, pp. 23-33.

Waas, A., *Herrschaft und Staat im deutschen Frühmittelalter* (2nd edn., Darmstadt, 1965).

Wadle, E., *Reichsgut und Königsherrschaft unter Lothar III (1125-1137). Ein Beitrag zur Verfassungsgeschichte des 12. Jahrhunderts*, Schriften zur Verfassungsgeschichte, XII (Berlin, 1969).

——'Heinrich IV. und die deutsche Friedensbewegung', in J. Fleckenstein (ed.), *Investiturstreit und Reichsverfassung*, VF, XVII (Sigmaringen, 1973), pp. 141-73.

Wagner, F.L. (ed.), *Ministerialität im Pfälzer Raum*, Veröffentlichungen der Pfälzischen Gesellschaft zur Förderung der Wissenschaften, LXIV (Speyer, 1975).

Waitz, G. (ed. K. Zeumer), *Deutsche Verfassungsgeschichte*, vol. v (2nd edn., Berlin, 1893).

Weikmann, M., 'Königsdienst und Königsgastung in der Stauferzeit', *ZBLG* xxx (1967), 314-32.

Wellmer, M., 'Eine süddeutsche Proscriptionsliste im Staatsarchiv Wolfenbüttel' in *Aus Verfassungs- und Landesgeschichte. Festschrift für Theodor Mayer* (Lindau and Constance, 1955), vol. ii, pp. 105-24.

Weltin, M. and Kusternig, A. (eds.), *Ottokar-Forschungen*, Jahrbuch für Landeskunde von Niederösterreich, n.s. XLIV-XLV (Vienna, 1978-9).

Wendehorst, A., *Das Bistum Würzburg*, part i, *Die Bischofsreihe bis 1254*, Germania Sacra, n.s., Die Bistümer der Kirchenprovinz Mainz, I (Berlin, 1962).

Werle, H., 'Ministerialität und Heerschildordnung', in F.L. Wagner (ed.), *Ministerialität im Pfälzer Raum*, pp. 69-74.

Werner, K.-F., 'Heeresorganisation und Kriegführung im deutschen

Königreich des 10. und 11. Jahrhunderts' in *Ordinamenti militari in Occidente nell'alto Medioevo*, Settimane di Studio del Centro italiano di studi sull'alto medioevo, XV, (Spoleto, 1968), pp. 791-843.

Westrich, K.-P., 'Die Königspfalz Lautern im 12. und 13. Jahrhundert und ihre Bedeutung für die Ministerialität des pfälzischen Raumes' in F.L. Wagner (ed.), *Ministerialität im Pfälzer Raum*, pp. 75-83.

Winkelmann, E., 'Über die Herkunft Dipolds des Grafen von Acerra und Herzogs von Spoleto', *Forschungen zur deutschen Geschichte* xvi (1876), 159-63.

Winter, G., *Die Ministerialität in Brandenburg. Untersuchungen zur Geschichte der Ministerialität und zum Sachsenspiegel* (Munich and Berlin, 1922).

Winter, J.M. van, 'The Ministerial and Knightly Classes in Guelders and Zutphen', *Acta Historiae Neerlandica* i (1966), 171-86.

Wisplinghoff, E., 'Königsfreie und Scharmannen', *Rheinische Vierteljahrsblätter* xxviii (1963), 200-17.

——*Untersuchungen zur frühen Geschichte der Abtei S. Maximin bei Trier von den Anfängen bis etwa 1150*, Quellen und Abhandlungen zur mittelrheinischen Kirchengeschichte, XII (Mainz, 1970).

Witte, B., *Herrschaft und Land im Rheingau*, Mainzer Abhandlungen zur mittleren und neueren Geschichte, III (Meisenheim, 1959).

Wittich, W., 'Altfreiheit und Dienstbarkeit des Uradels in Niedersachsen', *VSWG* iv (1906), 1-127.

Wojtecki, D., *Studien zur Personengeschichte des Deutschen Ordens im 13. Jahrhundert*, Quellen und Studien zur Geschichte des östlichen Europa (Wiesbaden, 1971).

——'Der Deutsche Orden unter Friedrich II.' in J. Fleckenstein (ed.), *Probleme um Friedrich II.*, pp. 187-224.

Wretschko, A. von, *Das österreichische Marschallamt im Mittelalter. Ein Beitrag zur Geschichte der Verwaltung in den Territorien des Deutschen Reiches* (Vienna, 1897).

Wunder, G., *Die Schenken von Stauffenberg. Eine Familiengeschichte*, Schriften zur südwestdeutschen Landeskunde, XI (Stuttgart, 1972).

Zallinger, O. von, *Ministeriales und Milites* (Innsbruck, 1878).

Zeillinger, K., *Erzbischof Konrad I. von Salzburg 1106-1147*, Wiener Dissertationen aus dem Gebiete der Geschichte, X (Vienna, 1968).

Zimmermann, H. (ed.), *Otto der Große*, W F, CCCCL (Darmstadt, 1976).

Zinsmaier, P., 'Das gefälschte Diplom König Heinrichs VII. für Johann von Scharfeneck', *MIÖG* Ergänzungsband xiv (Festgabe Hans Hirsch, 1939), 289-302.

Zotz, T., 'Bischöfliche Herrschaft, Adel, Ministerialität und Bürgertum in Stadt und Bistum Worms' in J. Fleckenstein (ed.), *Herrschaft und Stand*, pp. 92-136.

Index

Würzburg—*cont.*
mm 51, 56, 66, 77, 91, 96; on fief and allod of their *mm* 114 n. 75, 115, 141 n. 3, 144 n. 17, 146 n. 29; on marriages of *mm* 164, 165 n. 17, 167, 168; their household offices 44, 186; their *buticularius* 189 n. 41; their *sculteti* 178, 186 n. 25, 189 n. 43; town and townsmen of 200, 205, 207, 208, 227; *see also* Conrad of Querfurt, Embricho, Godfrey, Henry, Hermann, Herold, Iring, bishops of; Henneberg, counts of; Poppo, count of (advocates and burgraves); St Stephen, abbey at

Wulfer, Paderborn *m* 132

Wunnenfels, castellan of, *m* 133

Xanten abbey 151

Zähringen, dynasty of 5, 208; *see also* Berthold, duke of; Berthold, duke of Carinthia; Clementia, Conrad of Zähringen

Zorno, procurator and marshal on the Rhine, *m* 241

Zülpich, monks of 160

Zürich 42, 43 n. 105; *see also fiscalini*

Zwettl, abbey 151 n. 69

Zwiefalten, abbey 67, 77, 88; *see also* Ortlieb of